William Wells

BROWN

NEGRO AMERICAN

BIOGRAPHIES AND

AUTOBIOGRAPHIES

John Hope Franklin / Series Editor

William Wells BROWN

AUTHOR & REFORMER

William Edward Farrison

The University of Chicago Press

CHICAGO AND LONDON

Library of Congress Catalog Card Number: 69-19275
The University of Chicago Press, Chicago 60637
The University of Chicago Press, Ltd., London W. C. 1

Published 1969
Printed in the United States of America

For Alice Marie

CONTENTS

EDITOR'S FOREWORD ix

PREFACE xi

I *An Awakening into Slavery* 3

II *An Education in the "Peculiar Institution"* 17

III *Hopes of Liberty* 35

IV *A Quest for Freedom* 51

V *The Making of an Antislavery Agent* 69

VI *"His Strong Manly Voice"* 81

VII *Between Proslavery Preachers and Political Abolitionists* 95

VIII *"This Eloquent Advocate of Liberty"* 109

IX *In the Strife of Truth with Falsehood* 127

X *Freedom on British Soil* 145
XI *Tours, Controversies, and Exhibitions* 163
XII *Exiles from Tyranny* 177
XIII *From Journalist to Author* 197
XIV *"Clotel; or, The President's Daughter"* 215
XV *Glory Exchanged for Hope* 233
XVI *America, but Not Yet the Beautiful* 247
XVII *With Eloquence, Wit, and Pathos* 261
XVIII *The Play's the Thing* 277
XIX *"The Escape; or, A Leap for Freedom"* 295
XX *Author and Bridegroom* 307
XXI *"Miralda"—but Little Time for Art* 323
XXII *An Odyssey without Splendor* 341
XXIII *Freedom for Victory* 357
XXIV *Years of Hopes and Fears* 379
XXV *A Doctor Almost in Spite of Himself* 399
XXVI *New Duties for New Occasions* 419
XXVII *Still to Shine in Use* 437
BIBLIOGRAPHY 457
INDEX 473

EDITOR'S FOREWORD

THE MID-NINETEENTH CENTURY WAS A TIME WHEN THE idealists of the United States were making a vigorous effort to create a perfect society in the New World's democratic showplace. Scarcely a social or economic or political defect escaped their scrutiny and their scorn. They inveighed against the exploitation of labor, the discrimination against women, the desecration of the sabbath, and the subjugation of the slaves. On the hustings, in the pulpit, and with the written word, they called on their fellows to join in their crusade for utopia. If they neglected some medium or some method, it was because they had neither the skill nor the talent to use it. If some of them remained far above the fray while others plunged into the midst of the battle, it was because some were mere theoreticians of the perfect society, while others were activists in the cause.

William Wells Brown was one of those remarkable figures of

the nineteenth century whose career clearly proved the compatibility of the intellectual and the activist. As fugitive slave, novelist, playwright, historian, essayist, lecturer, physician, and abolitionist, he used his ample talents to point up the injustices of society—particularly of slavery—and to suggest ways of eliminating them. He was as tireless in his search for truth and justice as he was in the quest for his own freedom and identity. On occasion he could be abstract and even abstruse. At other times he could be highly practical and quite concrete in his program for human betterment. He was a physician, but he preferred to lecture against slavery. He was a novelist, but he preferred to assist slaves in their bid for freedom.

Brown's interests and passions were boundless. He was the best known Negro historian of his time and a leading abolitionist on two continents. At home he was respected by Garrison and Phillips. Abroad he was honored by Hugo and Cobden. But freedom for the slaves was merely one of the passions of his life. He advocated prison reform, temperance, and equal rights for women.

Professor Farrison has devoted many years to the study of William Wells Brown and the era in which he lived. No phase of Brown's many-sided life, however insignificant, has escaped his attention. At the same time he has fully appreciated the larger significance of his subject and has given us a portrait that is at once full-bodied and vigorous. Full-length biographies of nineteenth-century Negroes are indeed rare. Biographies of such persons which place them in their setting and delineate their impact on the society of their times are still rarer. Students of the period will find Professor Farrison's life of Brown a valuable addition to the literature. The general public, in search for some greater meaning and significance of the turbulent times in which Brown lived and worked, will find in this biography an answer to many of the questions in their minds.

John Hope Franklin

PREFACE

AFTER SPENDING THE FIRST TWENTY YEARS OF HIS LIFE IN SLAVery and the next nine years in relative obscurity as a fugitive slave, William Wells Brown came into prominence in the 1840's as one of the band of reformers who led the crusade against American slavery. While that crusade continued and long afterwards, he also labored for the good not only of Negroes but of all his fellow Americans. Although he published more than a dozen books and pamphlets—including travel books, novels, at least one drama, histories, and lectures—he has been generally ignored by, if his works were known to, historians of American literature. Nor has he been accorded sufficient recognition in the history of American reform movements. This volume attempts to portray fully and objectively Brown and his activities against his time as a background, and thereby to show that his work as an author and reformer has merited for him an important place in the literary and the social history of America.

It is my pleasure to acknowledge my indebtedness to all who have helped in any way to make this book possible, and especially to the following persons: the late Dr. James Edward Shepard, founder and first president of North Carolina College at Durham, whose interest in my research was most encouraging; the late Daniel Eric Moore, Dean of the School of Library Science at the college, who kindly and promptly solved many reference problems for me; the staff of the James E. Shepard Memorial Library of the college for innumerable courtesies; Dr. John Hope Franklin, the editor of the series to which this volume belongs, for many suggestions which have proved stimulating as well as practical; and my wife, Alice Marie Farrison, who assiduously shared in my researches in many libraries, remained patient during my writing and rewriting, and proofread the final typescript of this work.

I am also grateful for permission from the Historical Society of Pennsylvania for the use of the photograph from which the frontispiece was developed; from the Ohio Historical Society for an adaptation of my article published in the *Ohio State Archaeological and Historical Quarterly* for July, 1952; and from the following periodicals for the use of passages somewhat revised from my articles as indicated: the *Journal of Negro History*, October, 1954; *Phylon: the Atlanta University Review of Race and Culture*, fourth quarter, 1954; and *CLA Journal*, December, 1958.

William Wells

BROWN

William Wells Brown
at the age of thirty-six

I

An Awakening Into Slavery

THE ANCESTRY OF WILLIAM WELLS BROWN, LIKE THAT OF the vast majority of others who were born into American slavery, has been almost lost to history. In the several editions of his *Narrative,* Brown said that his mother was a slave named Elizabeth, but he gave no information about her parentage.[1] William C. Nell, however, said that Brown's maternal grandfather was Simon Lee. According to Nell, Lee, who had been a slave in Virginia, served in the Continental Army in the American Revolution, apparently expecting to gain his freedom as a

1. *Narrative of William W. Brown, a Fugitive Slave, Written by Himself* (Boston, 1847), p. 13 (hereinafter cited as *Narrative*). This work, of which there were at least eight editions, is the principal source of information about the first twenty years of Brown's life. Where the subject matter is the same in the several editions, although the page numbers may be different, only the first edition is cited. References to later editions are always to the earliest ones in which the passages cited are found.

reward for his military service. After the war he was honorably discharged but was sent back to his master, on whose plantation he spent the remainder of his life in slavery.[2]

Neither the records of the Department of the Army, which are incomplete, nor the pension and bounty-land records in the National Archives list a Simon Lee of Virginia who was a soldier in the American Revolution. There is in the Virginia State Library in Richmond, however, a record of Simmons Lee of Prince George County, Virginia, who was drafted on September 17, 1777, and who served as a private in the Tenth and Fourteenth Continental Lines. After three years of service he was entitled to bounty land. The record does not indicate his race—a fact which leaves open the possibility that he might have been a mulatto who could easily pass for white.

Brown did not include the story of Simon Lee in any of his autobiographical sketches. In the autobiographical "Memoir of the Author" in his *The Black Man*, he said that his mother "was of mixed blood," that her father was said to have been "the noted Daniel Boone," and that her mother was "a negress."[3] This seems to be Brown's only recorded reference to his supposed relationship to Boone, and it is all the less convincing because it contains more of the inventive genius and more of the sensational than the story of Simon Lee contains. Moreover the story of Simon Lee is strongly supported by circumstantial evidence. Dr. John Young—Elizabeth's first known owner—his parents, and both his first and his second wife were natives of Virginia. When the Young family migrated to the vicinity of Lexington, Kentucky, where Brown was born, they doubtless carried with them some slaves from Virginia, and they might have acquired others from that state afterwards. That Elizabeth

2. William C. Nell, *The Colored Patriots of the American Revolution* (Boston, 1855), p. 223.

3. William Wells Brown, *The Black Man, His Antecedents, His Genius, and His Achievements* (New York and Boston, 1863), p. 11 (hereinafter cited as *Black Man*).

might have had a Virginia background, therefore, and might have been the daughter of Simon Lee, a slave who had been a soldier in the American Revolution, is at least a reasonable conjecture.

Whoever her parents were, Elizabeth herself was attractive not only to a male relative of her owner but also to other males, and she was possessed of such strength of body and mind as made her a most valuable servant. There was proof of her physical strength in the fact that she bore seven children, each for a different father, while she was a field hand; and there was evidence of her strength of mind in her motherly love and her abiding interest in her children even though slavery permitted her to do but little for them.[4]

"My father's name, as I learned from my mother," said Brown, "was George Higgins. He was a white man, a relative of my master, and connected with some of the first families in Kentucky." In a speech he made in Cincinnati, Ohio, on April 25, 1855, Brown referred to his mother's master, Dr. Young, as his uncle. According to Brown's daughter Josephine, who wrote a short biography of her father, George Higgins was Dr. Young's half brother.[5] Since Josephine wrote the biography under her father's tutelage, whatever she told about his ancestry and parentage was doubtless based on information she received from him. His information, however, was not a matter of record but of tradition; and time, alas, had wrought some confusion in it.

Dr. Young, Elizabeth's owner at the time of Brown's birth, was one of thirteen children of Leonard and Mary, or Molly (Higgins) Young. Near the end of the eighteenth century the Young family moved from Caroline County, Virginia, to the vicinity of Lexington in Fayette County, Kentucky, where Leonard and Mary Young spent the remainder of their lives.

4. *Narrative*, pp. 13, 15, 31–32.

5. *Ibid.*, p. 13; *Anti-Slavery Bugle*, May 5, 1855, p. 1; [Josephine Brown], *Biography of an American Bondman, by His Daughter* (Boston, 1856), p. 6.

Having studied medicine at the Philadelphia Medical College, Dr. Young became a physician and farmer near Lexington. He married Martha Fuqua, a Virginian, in 1805. After the death of his first wife, he married Sarah Scott, who was also a Virginian, in 1811. There were no children from either of his marriages.[6] Contrary to what Brown apparently told his daughter Josephine, Dr. Young and George Higgins probably were not half brothers but first cousins. Most probably the George Higgins who Brown said was his father was George W. Higgins, the son of William and Dinah (Tribble) Higgins of Fayette County. William Higgins was a brother of Dr. Young's mother.[7]

In three sketches of his life written in the 1850's, one of the first families of Kentucky to which Brown referred in his *Narrative* was identified by the name Wicklief or Wickliffe. In the third sketch another family was identified by the name Barber—probably Barbour. Speaking at a meeting of the American Anti-Slavery Society at Cooper Institute in New York on May 9, 1860, Brown referred half-seriously and half-humorously to three of the Wickliffes of Lexington as his cousins. These he identified as "my cousin Fanny," the wife of William Preston, who was then United States minister to Spain; Robert Wickliffe, who had recently died; and Charles A. Wickliffe, who was postmaster general under John Tyler.[8]

At the beginning of his *Narrative*, Brown said that he was born in Lexington; but since his mother was a field hand, most

6. William Smith Bryan and Robert Rose, *A History of the Pioneer Families of Missouri* (Saint Louis, 1876), pp. 225–26.

7. The last three statements are based on a letter of July 2, 1949, from a member of the Filson Club of Louisville, Kentucky, to me. The writer of the letter is a descendant of one of Dr. Young's sisters.

8. William Wells Brown, *Clotel; or, The President's Daughter: A Narrative of Slave Life in the United States* (London, 1853), p. 1 (hereinafter cited as *Clotel*); William Wells Brown, *The American Fugitive in Europe. Sketches of Places and People Abroad* (Boston, 1855), p. 9 (hereinafter cited as *Sketches*); *Memoir of William Wells Brown, an American Bondman, Written by Himself* (Boston, 1859), p. 3 (hereinafter cited as *Memoir*); *National Anti-Slavery Standard,* May 26, 1860, p. 4.

probably he was born not in the city but on Dr. Young's farm near it, as is said in both his daughter Josephine's *Biography of an American Bondman* and his *Memoir of William Wells Brown.* He also said that his master usually recorded the dates of birth of his slaves in a book that he kept for such data. Brown, however, seemed to have no idea of what was recorded about himself in the book. This fact is not surprising, because slaveholders often found it advantageous for one reason or another to keep slaves ignorant of their ages. As Brown found out during a year he spent in the service of James Walker, a notorious Missouri slave trader, persons who sold slaves frequently succeeded in selling old slaves for high prices by having their gray hairs dyed, plucked out, or shaved off and then falsifying their ages. If a slave did not know his age, the seller could conceal it without much fear of embarrassment, if not without a prick of conscience; whereas if a slave knew his age, he might—innocently or otherwise—embarrass the seller by telling the truth.

Furthermore there naturally comes with advancing age a sense of dignity as well as maturity of mind which is derived from experience. But from the point of view of the slaveholder, what need had a slave for dignity or maturity of mind? One of the best ways to keep him from acquiring either was to keep him ignorant of his age and, although he might be a man, to continue to call him "boy." Hence the point of view which Frederick Douglass said was held by his master was most probably far from exceptional. "I was not allowed," wrote Douglass in 1845, "to make any inquiries of my master concerning it [Douglass's age]. He deemed all such inquiries on the part of a slave improper and impertinent, and evidence of a restless spirit."[9]

Nowhere in his *Narrative* did Brown give any specific information about the date of his birth, probably because he was uncertain about it. The only reference he made in this book to his age is in the following sentence: "The slave is brought up to

9. *Narrative of the Life of Frederick Douglass, an American Slave, Written by Himself* (Boston, 1845), pp. 1–2.

look upon every white man as an enemy to him and his race; and twenty-one years in slavery had taught me that there were traitors, even among colored people."[10] Brown wrote this sentence in reference to the situation in which he found himself early in January, 1834, a few days after he had escaped from slavery. If his statement concerning the number of years he had spent in slavery was correct, he must have been born at least as early as 1813.

In 1852 Brown told William Farmer, a British journalist, that as far as he knew he was born in the autumn of 1814—" 'about corn-cutting time' of that year." What Brown told Farmer was corroborated two years later, probably unconsciously, by Enoch Price of Saint Louis, who was Brown's third and last owner. In the deed of emancipation which he wrote for Brown on April 24, 1854, Price said that Brown was then in his fortieth year.[11] At the beginning of her biography of her father, Josephine Brown, who was much more specific about dates in his life than he himself was in any of his autobiographical sketches, said that he was born on March 15, 1815. According to the Massachusetts state register of marriages, when Brown married the second time, as he did in Boston on April 12, 1860, he was forty-one years of age. According to the same state's register of deaths, when he died on November 6, 1884, he was sixty-eight years and seven months old.[12]

The date 1819 for Brown's birth, deducible from the registra-

10. *Narrative*, pp. 95–96.

11. William Farmer, "Memoir of William Wells Brown" in William Wells Brown, *Three Years in Europe; or Places I Have Seen and People I Have Met* (London, 1852), pp. ix–x (hereinafter cited as *Three Years in Europe*). Price's acknowledgment of the deed of emancipation was dated April 25, 1854. Circuit Court of the City of St. Louis, Permanent Record Book Number 24, p. 150.

12. Massachusetts, 19th Registration, 1860, Marriages, vol. 137, Suffolk–Worcester, p. 32, no. 574; 43rd Registration, 1884, Deaths, vol. 357, Suffolk–Worcester, p. 363, no. 396, State House, Boston, Massachusetts.

tion of Brown's second marriage, seems altogether wrong, because it is inconsistent not only with what Brown had told Farmer and what Price had recorded but also with facts of Brown's early life. Brown's age as recorded in this registration was doubtless based on his own statement, in which he might have erred unconsciously, since he did not know exactly how old he was anyway. The date 1816, deducible from the registration of his death, is close enough to the probable date to have resulted from a minor error on the part of whoever gave his age for this registration. Presumably this was his widow, who knew about his age only what she had learned from him and perhaps from his deed of emancipation. Since Brown himself as early as 1852 put the date of his birth in the autumn of 1814, and this date is corroborated by the only documentary source of information not derived from Brown himself, most probably the year of his birth was 1814.

Of the more than forty slaves Dr. Young owned during Brown's infancy, seven were Elizabeth's children. Of these—six boys and one girl—Brown was one of the youngest if not the youngest. The Christian names of these children were Solomon, Leander, Benjamin, Joseph, Milford, Elizabeth, and William. Neither Elizabeth nor any of her children had surnames. Among slaveholders such appendages were considered superfluous for slaves; and indeed if they had been bestowed from their customary sources, some of them would have been especially embarrassing. If Elizabeth's children had acquired surnames according to paternity, each would have had a different surname. Truly variety was not only the spice but also the very genius of life, and for Dr. Young it meant prosperity by means of increases in the number of his slaves. There seems to be no proof that he encouraged such promiscuity, as many slaveholders did—personally as well as otherwise—but there seems to be no reason for believing that he discouraged it. This kind of promiscuity was one of the evils inherent in American slavery, in which there could be no stable family life among slaves, since the members of families were frequently sold and separated from each other.

In 1816 Dr. Young moved from the vicinity of Lexington to the Missouri Territory, taking his slaves and other movable property with him. He settled on a tract of land on the northern bank of the Missouri River in what was then Saint Charles County. Near the river he laid out the town of Marthasville, naming it in memory of his first wife. During his residence in the Missouri Valley, in addition to practicing medicine, Dr. Young, as Brown remembered, "carried on milling, merchandizing and farming." It was on Dr. Young's farm that Brown discovered his station in life and became acquainted with plantation slavery.[13]

In 1820 Dr. Young became a member of the lower house of the first General Assembly of Missouri. Because his political activities kept him away from home for long periods, he left the management of his farm to an overseer whose name was Grove Cook. If slavery was the sum of all villainies, this man, with others in positions like his, was no inconsiderable addend to that total. In his *Narrative* Brown portrayed Cook as a brother in spirit of Messrs. Plummer, Severe, and Covey, overseers whom Frederick Douglass had already commemorated in his *Narrative* for their cruelty.

One of Brown's earliest recollections was of Cook's exercising one morning the heavy hand of discipline with a cowhide whip. It was scarcely daylight, but Elizabeth, Brown's mother, had been ten or fifteen minutes late for work in the field. Away in the plantation house, where he was already a servant, Brown heard and recognized his mother's voice in the cries and groans that followed the lashes from Cook's whip. At the time Brown was too small to think of trying to take his mother's part; but

13. Bryan and Rose, *Pioneer Families*, pp. 205, 226, 227; *Narrative*, p. 14.

even if he had been physically capable of defending her, according to the usages of slavery it would have been futile for her and almost suicidal for himself for him to intervene. To do so would have brought down the wrath of the slaveholders upon him for daring to raise his hands against a white man, even in opposition to inhuman punishment of his mother. Aside from saying that "The cold chills ran over me, and I wept aloud," he did not attempt to describe his feelings of that morning, perhaps because he found it impossible to do so.[14]

Brown was too young and too illiterate to know anything about Patrick Henry's query concerning the doubtful wisdom of purchasing life at the price of slavery. He was also too young to know anything about the legal monstrosity known as the slave code.[15] All he knew was that in his little world, which consisted of Dr. Young's plantation, there were two groups of people—a relatively large group called Negro slaves, among whom his mother and all of her children were included, and a small group called white people. The large group lived in the "slave quarters," which were at some distance behind the houses in which the small group lived. The slave quarters were cabins which were generally without windows or floors, and which were furnished with crude benches, chairs, and tables, and only hard, dirty bunks for beds. Most of those who were called Negro slaves worked in the fields from dawn until night, even in bad weather. They ate what was cooked for them by a slave woman who kept the quarters kitchen. Usually the food cooked in this kitchen did not smell, look, nor taste good enough to make anybody want much of it; but none of it was wasted, because seldom did everybody get enough to eat, and sometimes some got noth-

14. *Narrative*, pp. 15–16. It is said in *Clotel*, p. 2, that Brown was about ten years old when this incident occurred.

15. For a general account of the slave code of Missouri, see Harrison Anthony Trexler, *Slavery in Missouri, 1804–1865* (Baltimore, 1914), chaps. 2 and 7.

ing at all. The slaves' clothes were made of coarse cloth, and their shoes were rough and ill-fitting—when they had shoes. Worst of all, if slaves were late for work or slow at it or did not finish their tasks on time, they were beaten, as Elizabeth (and a giant slave named Randall) had been; or if they talked back to any of the white people or failed to obey any of their orders or even looked dissatisfied they were beaten.

On the contrary the small group lived in houses with many more rooms than such a few people seemed to need. They spent most of their time doing nothing. They did not even wait on themselves, for they had "house slaves" to wait on them. And seldom if ever did they work in the fields. Even the one who was called overseer did not do that; he only watched the slaves to make them work. Although this small group did little or no work, they had the best of everything: the best houses, the softest beds, the best food—more of it than they could eat—and the best clothes. Furthermore nobody ever tied them up and beat them with a cowhide whip no matter what they did or failed to do. Already it appeared to the little slave boy that the large group had but few of the things they needed, not to speak of the things they wanted, and that the small group had everything they wanted, far beyond their needs, including absolute power over the large group—power which was not only symbolized but also realized in the lashes of the cowhide whip which he had heard that morning falling on his mother's back.

To him the basis of the distinctions between the two groups was far from clear. Certainly it could not be simply a matter of complexion. True enough, all members of the small group were white, but so were many of the members of the large group, as his mother and he were. Why then were some white people considered white and other white people were classified as Negro slaves? This was a question whose answer he was to find only in the kinds of logic and law which were taught in the "peculiar institution" in which he was destined to spend twenty years as an involuntary enrollee. His experience of that memorable morning on which he heard his mother's groans was one of his first laboratory lessons in that institution, and he had many other and more difficult lessons to learn in it.

While Brown was still a child, Dr. and Mrs. Young, who had no children of their own, took into their home a nephew of the physician. At the time the nephew was only a few weeks old. In one place in his *Narrative*, Brown said that the name of this infant was William Moore, but in another place he said that the child was the son of Dr. Young's brother Benjamin.[16] In all probability this was Benjamin and Nancy (Moore) Young's son William, and it is also probable that Dr. and Mrs. Young had taken him because of the recent death of his mother.

As this infant grew into childhood, he must needs have a caretaker, companion, and servant. By what Elizabeth considered a stroke of good fortune, her son William, the same one who later acquired the surname Brown, and who was ten or twelve years older than the other William, was chosen to be the three in one.[17] But in this choice there was hardly less irony than good fortune. To have in one's household two legitimate relatives named William would have been confusing, to say the least; to have two therein with the same name when one of them was a slave was confounding, especially when the slave resembled his master as much as the legitimate relative did. Dr. and Mrs. Young found it easy to eliminate such confusion. They simply changed the name of William the slave to Sandford, thereby teaching him another lesson, namely that a slave had absolutely nothing —not even a name—which need be considered his if a white person had any use for it. As far as William the slave was concerned, Roger B. Taney's notorious pronouncement that a Negro had no rights which a white person was bound to respect was born into words thirty years too late; or at best, for him it was only a review lesson. From the time of the change mentioned

16. *Narrative*, pp. 38, 97. Benjamin Young was then living in Calloway County, Missouri. (Bryan and Rose, *Pioneer Families*, pp. 226, 335.)
17. *Black Man*, pp. 11–12.

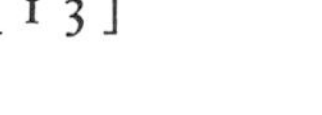

above until he escaped from slavery, William the slave was called Sandford.

To him now called Sandford, this robbing him of the only name he had was a wrong which even the logic of slavery did not justify. He had been denied at birth the individuality and the respect which a surname carries with it, and now he was deprived of the identity which his Christian name had previously afforded him—an identity that first names give even to domesticated animals. For a while he tried to ignore this injustice by continuing to call himself William, but for doing so he was severely whipped several times. Consequently it became clear to him that whatever might be in a name, it was not sufficient to compensate for horsewhippings. He decided, therefore, to season his determination with discretion, to bear in silence this injustice along with others, and to wait for the best that he hoped would be.[18]

Another injustice Brown suffered at this time was a veritable—almost diabolical—satire of circumstances. Because of his fair complexion and remarkable resemblance to his paternal relatives, sometimes visitors at the Youngs' home not only failed to recognize him as a slave but assumed that he was a legitimate member of the family. Whenever Mrs. Young discovered that visitors had confused matters thus, she became so embarrassed and vexed that she scolded and whipped the slave—as if he was the cause rather than an incidental effect of his father's licentiousness.[19] Mrs. Young, however, was not the only one who was inclined to visit the iniquity of the father upon the innocent son. Brown's fair complexion also incurred for him the scornful envy of some of his fellow slaves. Commenting some thirty years later upon the difficulties he had experienced in slavery because of his close resemblance to his white relatives, he observed that

> the nearer a slave approaches an Anglo-Saxon in complexion, the more he is abused by both owner and fellow-slaves. The

18. *Narrative*, pp. 97–98.

19. *Black Man*, pp. 18–19. See also Brown's *The Negro in the American Rebellion: His Heroism and His Fidelity* (Boston, 1867), pp. 363–64.

owner flogs him to keep him "in his place," and the slaves hate him on account of his being whiter than themselves. Thus the complexion of the slave becomes a crime, and he is made to curse his father for the Anglo-Saxon blood that courses through his veins.[20]

20. [Josephine Brown], *Biography*, pp. 10–11. See also Brown's *Memoir*, p. 7.

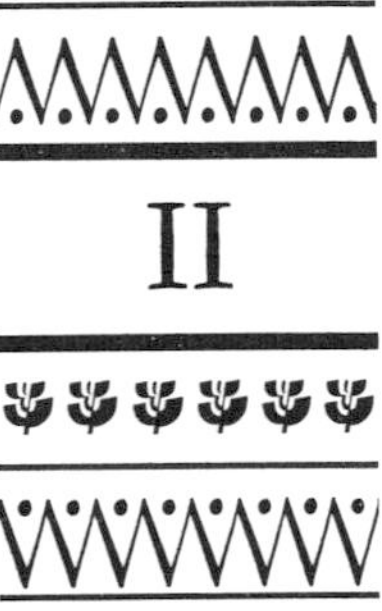

An Education in the "Peculiar Institution"

IN 1827 DR. YOUNG MOVED TO SAINT LOUIS AND BOUGHT A FARM of some three thousand acres four miles north of the city.[1] While he continued to practice medicine, he left his farm under the supervision of one Friend Haskel, a New Englander who had migrated to the Southwest and turned overseer. Among slaves there was the belief that Northerners who migrated to the South and became slaveholders or overseers generally became the worst slavedrivers. Haskel seems to have lived up to this belief. Brown and his mother were more fortunate—or at least less unfortunate—than their fellow slaves who found themselves under Haskel's domination. Instead of putting them on the farm, Dr. Young hired out both of them in Saint Louis.

1. William Smith Bryan and Robert Rose, *A History of the Pioneer Families of Missouri* (Saint Louis, 1876), p. 226. In his *My Southern Home: Or, The South and Its People* (Boston, 1880), p. 1, Brown incorrectly said that the farm was ten miles north of Saint Louis.

Chapter Two

During Brown's last six years in slavery, his principal place of residence, as far as a slave could be said to have such, was Saint Louis; and during this period he was subjected to what might well have been called an accelerated program of education in the "peculiar institution." Although he was never claimed as private property by more than three different slaveholders, he was worked during this period by at least ten different persons —seven in addition to his three owners. Indeed it would not have been surprising if he had sometimes found himself confused as to who, according to the usages of slavery, was entitled to his services. Withal, the frequent change of employers eventually proved advantageous to Brown in a remarkable way. It enabled him to get acquainted with many departments of the "peculiar institution," so that when he became an antislavery agent some years later, he could speak against slavery from a much broader background of experience than many other ex-slaves could.

One of the first persons to whom Brown was hired in Saint Louis was Major Freeland, the keeper of a tavern. Brown graphically characterized this man as "a horse-racer, cock-fighter, gambler, and withal an inveterate drunkard," with whom "when he was present, it was cut and slash—knock down and drag out."[2] If the major was tyrannical when he was sober, he was diabolical when he was drunk; and both he and his son, who was only a few years older than Brown, were frequently drunk. Brown's experience with Freeland contributed a great deal to his abhorrence of intoxicants—an abhorrence that eventually made him an ardent temperance reformer.

Brown was in Freeland's service only a short time before he found it necessary to report to his owner the bad treatment he was receiving, but his reports won him no sympathy as long as the owner received pay for the slave's work. After tolerating Freeland's cruelty for five or six months, Brown, who was then no more than fourteen or fifteen years of age, fled to a wood

2. *Narrative*, p. 21.

near Saint Louis. His flight, however, was both futile and brief. Within a few days he was captured by two slave catchers with the aid of bloodhounds owned by Major Benjamin O'Fallon and was returned to Freeland, who, of course, punished him for running away. With the assistance of his son, Freeland whipped Brown severely and then shut him in a smokehouse, had a fire made of tobacco stems near him, and left him to be smoked until he almost suffocated.

From the service of Freeland, Brown passed into employment in the steward's department of the steamboat *Missouri*, which plied between Saint Louis and Galena, Illinois. This employment was more or less pleasant, but it lasted only a few months. Brown was next hired as one of twenty servants at the Missouri Hotel in Saint Louis. The hotel-keeper to whom Brown was responsible was John Colburn, a Northerner. In Brown's opinion this man was one of the very worst Northerners who had become employers of slaves. Among the hired slaves he brutalized was Aaron, the property of John F. Darby. Aaron complained to Darby about Colburn's cruelty; but just as Brown's owner had proceeded with him in a similar situation, Darby ignored Aaron's complaints and sent him back to the hotel. Colburn then punished him for complaining by beating him so badly that he was unable to work for ten or twelve days.

Thanks to Freeland and Colburn, Brown had now learned that a slave must not even complain of bad treatment, not to speak of defending himself against it. Before his time with Colburn was ended, he learned something else—something about the intricacies of slavery and romance. One of the hired slaves at the Missouri Hotel was Patsey, who was in love with John, the property of Major William Christy, one of the prominent citizens of Saint Louis County. Because of his own amorous interest in Patsey, Colburn forbade her to bestow any attention upon John. Finding that she had disobeyed him by letting John walk home with her one evening, Colburn decided to whip John but could not catch him. Vengeance, nevertheless, must still be his; so he tied Patsey up "and whipped her until several of the boarders came out and begged him to desist."[3]

About the time of Brown's and his mother's removal to Saint Louis, two of his brothers died. Meanwhile his other three brothers and his sister Elizabeth were held to service on Dr. Young's farm. The disintegration of the family by the involuntary separation of its members had begun. While Brown was employed at the Missouri Hotel, his mother, his three surviving brothers, and his sister were sold—for a reason which often impelled planters to sell slaves. Dr. Young had to sell some of his slaves to relieve himself of financial difficulties. In his *Narrative* Brown said that his mother, sister, and two of his brothers were sold to Isaac Mansfield, a tinner who had "a large manufacturing establishment" in Saint Louis. He did not tell to whom his other brother was sold. In 1856, however, his daughter Josephine said that the three brothers were sold to a slave trader, who took them to the deep South and sold them to the owner of a plantation on the Yazoo River in Mississippi. Three years later Brown said that the last news he had heard of them was that they were still on that plantation, but he did not say when he had heard that news.[4]

After a hectic period with Colburn at the Missouri Hotel, Brown was relieved early in 1830 to find himself employed as a handy boy in the printing office of the Reverend Elijah P. Lovejoy, editor of the *Saint Louis Times.* This newspaper had been founded in June, 1829, and Lovejoy had become part owner as well as editor of it in 1830. He withdrew from it in February, 1831.[5] Brown found the future "Alton martyr" not only kind but also sympathetic. Writing from memory more than forty years later, he said that he was employed by Lovejoy "for a period of

3. *Ibid.*, pp. 23–25.

4. *Ibid.*, pp. 26, 32; [Josephine Brown], *Biography of an American Bondman* (Boston, 1856), p. 17; *Memoir*, p. 10.

5. John Thomas Scharf, *History of Saint Louis City and County*, 2 vols. (Philadelphia, 1883), 1:921.

six months." Meanwhile, in his *Narrative* he explained as follows how he lost his job in Lovejoy's office:

> While living with Mr. Lovejoy, I was often sent on errands to the office of the "Missouri Republican," published by Mr. Edward Charles. Once, while returning to the office with type, I was attacked by several large boys, sons of slave-holders, who pelted me with snow-balls. Having the heavy form of type in my hands, I could not make my escape by running; so I laid down the type and gave them battle. They gathered around me, pelting me with stones and sticks, until they overpowered me, and would have captured me, if I had not resorted to my heels. Upon my retreat, they took possession of the type; and what to do to regain it I could not devise. Knowing Mr. Lovejoy to be a very humane man, I went to the office, and laid the case before him. He told me to remain in the office. He took one of the apprentices with him, and went after the type, and soon returned with it; but on his return informed me that Samuel McKinney had told him that he would whip me, because I had hurt his boy. Soon after, McKinney was seen making his way to the office by one of the printers, who informed me of the fact, and I made my escape through the back door.
>
> McKinney not being able to find me on his arrival, left the office in a great rage, swearing that he would whip me to death. A few days after, as I was walking along Main Street, he seized me by the collar, and struck me over the head five or six times with a large cane, which caused the blood to gush from my nose and ears in such a manner that my clothes were completely saturated with blood. After beating me to his satisfaction, he let me go, and I returned to the office so weak from the loss of blood, that Mr. Lovejoy sent me home to my master. It was five weeks before I was able to walk again. During this time, it was necessary to have some one to supply my place at the office, and I lost the situation.[6]

6. William Wells Brown, *The Rising Son; or, The Antecedents and Advancement of the Colored Race* (Boston, 1874), p. 322 (hereinafter cited as *Rising Son*); *Narrative*, pp. 29–30.

Brown also said in his *Narrative* that "I am chiefly indebted to him [Lovejoy], and to my employment in the printing office, for what little learning I obtained while in slavery." When, however, the period of his employment by Lovejoy ended, he was still practically illiterate, and he never learned to read and write proficiently until after he escaped from slavery.

As soon as Brown was able to work again, he was hired to the steward's department of the steamboat *Enterprise*, which was engaged in the river trade from Saint Louis northward. Brown found his situation on this steamboat more or less pleasant, although not novel, until

> in passing from place to place, and seeing new faces every day, and knowing that they could go where they pleased, I soon became unhappy, and several times thought of leaving the boat at some landing place, and trying to make my escape to Canada, which I had heard much about as a place where the slave might live, be free, and be protected.[7]

In the meantime, perhaps while the *Enterprise* was at a wharf in Saint Louis, Brown heard Senator Thomas H. Benton deliver a Fourth of July oration in the city. In his speech Benton quoted approvingly the famous doctrine of the inalienable rights of man as it is set forth in the Declaration of Independence. Brown was less intrigued by Benton's oratory than confused by the gross inconsistencies between the professions and the practices of soi-disant American democrats. He knew that in spite of what Benton said about liberty, he still held slaves, as did most of the other prominent people in Saint Louis who professed a love for American democracy. But Brown was convinced that freedom must be more than a word, however eloquently the word might be uttered. Obviously either the theory of the rights of man or the practice of slaveholding must be wrong; and even at his age, because he was a rational human being, he found within himself that which told him taht the practice was wrong.

7. *Narrative,* p. 31.

The effect of Benton's speech, therefore, was to arouse in Brown a strong determination as well as a desire to free himself.[8] He might have realized his determination by deserting the *Enterprise* at some free port; but he could not make up his mind to do so while his mother, sister, and brothers were still in slavery in Saint Louis, whence presumably they might also escape. Especially did he find unbearable the thought of leaving his mother and his sister, even though he was aware that they might be separated still farther from him without previous knowledge on the part of any of them.

On one of its trips the *Enterprise* carried from Hannibal, Missouri, to Saint Louis a cargo of fifty or sixty slaves. James Walker, the slave trader, was en route with this group to the deep South to supply the slave markets there. During the trip Brown and Walker saw each other for the first time. Walker was impressed with Brown's efficiency as a waiter, barber, and general factotum on the steamboat; and Brown was impressed with Walker—not favorably but as the incarnation of the most revolting features of American slavery.[9]

Although Brown had lived long enough to learn that almost anything might happen to a slave, he could not then see that Walker, like a cloud, was threatening to darken his horizon; nor did he have any idea that Walker would turn his dreams of freedom into a series of nightmares, at least for a while. In the meantime, while the great gods—or rather demons—of slavery were trying to determine his future, they left him to the devices of two others of their agents—the slaveholder and his overseer.

When after a few months the captain of the *Enterprise* left it, Brown was sent to his master's plantation and put to work under Haskell, the overseer. Ignoring the fact that Brown was not accustomed to field work, Haskell demanded as much work from him as he did from the regular field hands and flogged him when he failed to do it. Happily a change in Brown's situation

8. [Josephine Brown], *Biography*, pp. 15–16.

9. *Narrative*, pp. 33–35.

soon occurred, putting him beyond Haskell's persecutions.

Having removed from Saint Louis to his plantation, Dr. Young again took Brown as a house servant. One of his reasons for choosing Brown was that he felt constrained to show some favor to the boy, whom he had privately acknowledged as a relative. Brown's situation as a house servant under Mrs. Young was by no means a bed of roses, but almost any situation in his master's house was better than being under Haskell. Still better, he was not always at Mrs. Young's command. When only eight years old he had served Dr. Young as an office boy.[10] Now he was made a part-time assistant to the physician, his principal duties being to prepare medicines, minister to ailing slaves, and run errands. From his own account it appears that his activities were sometimes exciting as well as interesting. As he remembered,

> Sometimes I committed sad mistakes, through my ignorance of the profession. On one occasion, being ordered by the doctor to extract a slave's tooth, I laid the patient flat on his back on the floor, got astraddle of his breast, put the rusty turn-keys on the wrong tooth, and pulled with all my strength. The result was, I took out a sound grinder, for which I came very near getting a flogging.[11]

However effective or ineffective, if not harmful, Brown's ministrations to his fellow slaves might have been, they had a stimulating effect upon him. His experience in Dr. Young's office aroused in him a lifelong interest in medicine. Many years later he used this experience as a basis for seriocomic incidents in his *Clotel* and *The Escape; or, A Leap for Freedom*—incidents which throw some light on the kind of medical care which was often provided for plantation slaves. What is more important, after more than half of his life had passed, he studied medicine and became a practicing physician.

While Brown was working on the *Enterprise*, Dr. Young got

10. [Josephine Brown], *Biography*, p. 7.
11. *Memoir*, pp. 8, 10.

religion. It was rather late in life for him to be converted, for he was in his fifties; and since 1811 he had been married to an aristocratic woman who had long taken pride in her belief that she was one of the Saviour's jewels. Perhaps it was better for Dr. Young himself to get religion late than never, but whether it was better for his slaves was at best a debatable question.

Like other owners of plantations, Dr. Young kept most of his slaves so busy working for him from dawn to night six days a week that they had time to do little or nothing for themselves. The only daytime they had free was on Sunday; and this day they generally spent gardening, hunting, or fishing to eke out their inadequate supply of food, washing and mending their clothes, or making brooms, baskets, etc. for sale. After Dr. Young got religion, he stopped all such activities on Sunday, without satisfying in any other way the needs they had satisfied, and compelled all of his slaves to attend Sabbath meetings. Going still further, he got other slaveholders to cooperate with him in hiring a preacher to preach to the slaves. He remembered the Sabbath Day, to keep it holy, although he ignored the Golden Rule; and fullness of spirit for the master resulted not infrequently in emptiness in the stomachs of his slaves.

Dr. Young even attempted to keep other days holy—at least in appearance—by having family worship both in the mornings and at night. But he required the majority of his slaves to attend only the night worship, for he wanted nothing to keep them from getting to work early in the mornings. He took literally for the nonce, one may suppose, the maxim *laborare est orare* and let his slaves pray in the mornings only by laboring, while he himself labored only by praying.

However good Dr. Young's religion might have been for his soul, it proved to be a hardship on Brown's body. One of Brown's duties was that of family coachman, and as such he had to drive the Youngs from their plantation to church in Saint Louis every Sunday. While the family went in to the service, although the weather might be fair or foul, Brown had to remain outside and take care of the carriage horses. Because of the exposure and the tedium he had to endure on such occasions, he came to dread the coming of the Sabbath.[12]

Brown was not very long—nor altogether wrong—in suspecting that the majority of slaveholders were much less interested in saving the souls of their slaves than in having religion bestowed upon them as a means of making them good slaves. The owners had been led by many of their preachers to believe what the Reverend Thomas Bacon (1700–1768) of Maryland had long ago said and the Reverend William Meade (1789–1862) of Virginia had repeated, namely, "that the *direct tendency* of the Gospel-doctrine is, *to make their negroes better servants, in proportion as they become better christians*." Consequently, as Brown observed, slaves were provided with a special kind of religious instruction. They were taught that God had made them to be slaves, and that they could serve their heavenly master best by being satisfied with their status and being subservient and faithful in all things to their earthly masters.[13]

Brown's casual observations as a slave gave him no reason to believe that other Christian slaveholders were any more Christ-like than Dr. Young. There was, for example, Daniel D. Page (1790–1869), who Brown incorrectly said was "a deacon in the Baptist church, in good and regular standing." As was proved some twenty years later, Page was not a member of a Baptist church but was the owner of a pew in the First Presbyterian Church in Saint Louis and was one of the most liberal supporters of that church.[14]

According to Brown, one Sunday while he was conveying the Youngs to church, he passed Page's house. Just then from his

12. *Narrative*, pp. 36–38.

13. [Thomas Bacon], *Sermons Addressed to Masters and Servants, and Published in the Year 1743* [1749], *Now Republished by the Rev. William Meade* (Winchester, Va. [1813]), p. 85; *Narrative*, pp. 83–84.

14. Artemas Bullard, "A Successful Impostor," *Congregationalist*, December 7, 1849; "Rev. Artemas Bullard, D. D. in Reply to Wm. Wells Brown," *Congregationalist*, August 8, 1851.

position on the box of the Youngs' carriage, he saw Page chasing and whipping a slave in his yard. Escaping from the yard the slave ran into the street. Seeing, however, that he was about to be caught, he stopped suddenly; whereupon Page stumbled over him, fell on the pavement, and fractured one of his own legs, thus crippling himself for the remainder of his life. A short time before this tragicomic incident, Brown continued, Page had tied up and whipped one of his female slaves almost to death, without losing the respect of his fellow churchmen for doing so. Brown said that the woman was named Delphia, that she belonged to the same church Page attended, and that he himself was well acquainted with her and saw her while she was recovering from the whipping.[15]

In his monograph on slavery in Missouri, Harrison Anthony Trexler referred to Brown's observations concerning the slaveholders' use of religious instruction to keep slaves contented, subservient, and faithful and then said that Brown "admits, however, that the owner really had a pious desire to give his negroes Christian training." In support of this statement, Trexler cited Brown's *Narrative.*[16] Because in other places in his monograph Trexler used Brown's *Narrative* so accurately, his statement just quoted is surprising. No one who carefully reads the book can find in it such an admission as Trexler attributes to Brown. The context of the first passage Trexler cited makes it clear that Brown was ridiculing the pretensions to religion of Dr. Young and other slaveholders. The context of the second passage makes it equally as clear that here Brown was not only ridiculing the religion of slaveholders but also condemning them for prostituting Christianity in order to promote their interest in slavery.

In another passage in his *Narrative,* to which Trexler did not refer, Brown spoke with unmistakable irony of "slavery with its Democratic whips—its Republican chains—its evangelical

15. *Narrative,* pp. 38–39.

16. Harrison Anthony Trexler, *Slavery in Missouri, 1804–1865* (Baltimore, 1914), p. 85.

blood-hounds, and its religious slave-holders." Indeed whenever he spoke of slaveholders and their Christianity, he spoke sarcastically if not contemptuously; for he himself was convinced—and he believed that the slaveholders themselves knew very well—that slaveholding and the Christian religion were incompatible. Moreover many of his fellow slaves seem to have shared his point of view. Writing almost thirty years after he escaped from slavery about religion in Dr. Young's household, he explained that "we [the slaves] regarded the religious profession of the whites around us as a farce, and our master and mistress, together with their guest [a traveling preacher], as mere hypocrites."[17]

Early in 1832 Dr. Young hired Brown to James Walker, the slave trader, for a year. The price Brown heard Dr. Young say that he received from Walker was $900. This was almost four times as much as the annual hiring price for slave men in Missouri in the 1830's. If Walker hired Brown for this price, either he was not a very shrewd businessman, or Brown, who was then seventeen or eighteen years old, must have been exceptional in many ways. Having seen Brown at work on the *Enterprise*, Walker thought that he would make a good custodian of slaves and had tried to purchase him. "Mr. Walker," said Brown, "had offered a high price for me, as I afterwards learned, but I suppose my master was restrained from selling me by the fact that I was a near relative of his."[18]

When Brown discovered that he had been hired to Walker, he was dismayed. Although he was assured by both Dr. Young and Walker that he had not been sold, he did not believe them for some time. Apparently he already knew enough about slave traders as well as about his master not to take seriously the word of either. He certainly knew enough about slavery to know

17. *Narrative*, p. 70; *Black Man*, p. 17.

18. *Narrative*, pp. 39–40, 64. According to Harrison Anthony Trexler, *Slavery in Missouri*, pp. 28–32, the annual rate of hire for a slave man was about 14 percent of his sale value.

that few thngs could be more depressing, if not disgusting, than working as a handyman for a slave trader. He was especially depressed by consciousness of the fact that as long as he was in Walker's service, he would have no chance to escape from slavery, for he would be under surveillance and in slave territory all of the time. Little did he realize that his employment by Walker, although by no means a blessing either in disguise or otherwise, had brought him a rare opportunity—even though it was one which he doubtless would have been glad to forego. It was an opportunity to do what might have been called advanced field work as an enrollee in the "peculiar institution."

A few days after Brown became his handy man, Walker set out from Saint Louis on a Mississippi River steamboat with him and a miscellaneous group of between fifty and seventy slaves for the markets in the Mississippi delta.[19] In the 1830's steamboats made the trip from Saint Louis to New Orleans in six or seven days; but Walker took much longer than this to make the trip because he stopped in Natchez, Mississippi, and sold some of his slaves there. Upon arriving in New Orleans, he sold some of his slaves at private sales, after which Isaac L. McCoy sold the remaining ones for him in the auction rooms of the Exchange Coffee House. At the time these auction rooms were one of the principal slave markets in the city, and McCoy was one of the best-known auctioneers there. The New Orleans *Bee* for 1832 and 1833 contains numerous advertisements of his.

Having disposed of his cargo, Walker returned to Saint Louis, carrying Brown with him. Because he had found his work with Walker exceedingly distasteful, Brown tried to get Dr. Young to withdraw him from Walker's service, but Dr. Young refused to do so. At once Walker began purchasing slaves for a second cargo, and after eight or nine weeks he set out again with his purchases for the Mississippi delta.

Brown was now somewhat familiar with Walker's business

19. *Narrative*, pp. 40–41; *Sketches*, p. 12; [Josephine Brown], *Biography*, p. 26; *Memoir*, p. 14.

as well as with the unhappy part he had to play in it, and he later recorded much more of what happened on his second trip to New Orleans than he did of what had happened on his first one. Said he,

> On our way down, and before we reached Rodney, the place where we made our first stop, I had to prepare the old slaves for market. I was ordered to have the old men's whiskers shaved off, and the gray hairs plucked out, where they were not too numerous, in which case he [Walker] had a preparation of blacking to color it, and with a blacking-brush we would put it on. This was new business to me, and was performed in a room where the passengers could not see us. These slaves were taught how old they were by Mr. Walker, and after going through the blacking process, they looked ten or fifteen years younger; and I am sure that some of those who purchased slaves of Mr. Walker, were dreadfully cheated, especially in the ages of the slaves which they bought.[20]

From experience and observation, notably from his experience with Samuel McKinney in Saint Louis, Brown had learned that any white man who got an impulse to cane or kick any slave seemed to have a right to do so. While he was with Walker in Natchez on the second trip, chance brought him a review of the lesson he had learned from McKinney. One day he went to see Lewis, a fellow slave whom he had known in Saint Louis, but who was now domiciled in Natchez. He found Lewis "hanging between the heavens and the earth"—in other words, tied by his wrists to a beam in a warehouse, with his toes barely touching the floor. Lewis's master, a Mr. Broadwell, had tied him there and whipped him for being caught away from home at night without permission. While Brown was talking with Lewis, Broadwell entered the warehouse and chased him out. In order to hurry him along, Broadwell struck him on the head with a cowhide whip, whose end cut a deep gash over Brown's

20. *Narrative*, p. 43.

right eye, causing a scar which he carried ever afterwards.[21]

The next day Walker, accompanied by Brown of course, proceeded with his unsold slaves to New Orleans. There, thanks to his handyman's efficiency and the current demand for slaves, he disposed of his group without difficulty. According to Brown,

> Before the slaves were exhibited for sale, they were dressed and driven out into the yard [the slave pen]. Some were set to dancing, some to jumping, some to singing, and some to playing cards. This was done to make them appear cheerful and happy. My business was to see that they were placed in those situations before the arrival of the purchasers, and I have often set them to dancing when their cheeks were wet with tears.[22]

Once again in Missouri, Walker began purchasing slaves for a third group to take down the Mississippi River. Evidently this business of buying and selling human beings—speculating, as it was called—was profitable. Because the Saint Louis market was too slow or too high, Walker did not tarry long in the city. Taking Brown with him, he went on a slave-buying expedition in the valley of the Missouri River as far as Jefferson City. On the farms and in the towns in the valley, he found and bought what he considered good bargains—more than twenty of them.

In one instance, however, Walker got what he came to consider an annoyance if not a bad bargain. With Brown on one horse, himself on another, and his coffle of slaves on foot, he set out from Saint Charles for his farm near Saint Louis. The distance was only twenty miles, but because of very bad roads the group took two days to make the trip. Among Walker's purchases was a woman with a baby four or five weeks old. En route the baby cried a great deal, in spite of its mother's efforts to keep it quiet and much to Walker's annoyance. Early in the morning of the second day, before Walker got his group

21. *Ibid.*, pp. 44–45.
22. *Ibid.*, pp. 45–46.

on their way, the baby began crying again; whereupon Walker said that he could tolerate the crying no longer, took the infant from its mother and made a present of it to the lady in whose home he had spent the night, and then continued homeward with his group.[23]

In the sketch of Brown's life in *Clotel*, the story of the crying baby is followed by an account of another more or less annoying experience Walker was said to have had while Brown was with him on a slave-buying expedition. When Walker bought a woman who had a little blind boy, so the story goes, the former owner of the woman gave him the boy, explaining that he wanted to keep the mother and her child together. Fearing that the boy would be troublesome, Walker did not want to take him. But in order to keep her son with her, the mother promised to carry him in her arms. She soon found it impossible, however, to carry him and keep up with the others; so after the first day's journey, Walker sold the boy to an innkeeper for a dollar and went on with his coffle. Not long afterwards a lady from a free state visited the inn where the boy had been left. Upon seeing him and hearing his sad story first from a slave and then from the innkeeper's wife, the lady wrote a poem about him, which was published in a newspaper a few days later. The story in *Clotel* ends with the poem, which is entitled "The Blind Slave Boy," but the newpaper in which it had been published is not identified.[24]

"The Blind Slave Boy" was included in George W. Clark's *The Liberty Minstrel* of 1844. In this songbook the poem is said to have been written by "Mrs. Dr. Bailey," and the tune indicated for it is "Sweet Afton." Brown included the poem, naming Mrs. Bailey as its author, in the second edition of his *Narrative*. He also included it in all three of the American editions of his songbook, *The Anti-Slavery Harp*, but therein he gave no information about its author. With the exception of

23. *Ibid.*, pp. 48–51.
24. *Clotel*, pp. 7–9.

minor differences in punctuation, the poem is the same in Brown's verisons as it is in Clark's songbook.[25]

Several weeks after his slave-buying expedition in the Missouri River Valley, Walker, still assisted by Brown, set out once more to sell his purchases in the Mississippi delta. His first stop was in Vicksburg. There he remained a week selling some of his slaves; and there Brown made him the unknowing antagonist in a tragicomedy of errors, Brown himself being the protagonist. One morning Walker sent Brown to the Vicksburg jail to be whipped for indirectly causing some of the slave trader's customers to spill wine on themselves. Brown maneuvered to get another Negro whipped in his stead and then bought from the latter a note which the jailer had written to Walker saying that he had whipped the "boy" as Walker had requested. The jailer had also remarked that he was "a very saucy boy, and tried to make me believe that he did not belong to you, and I put it on him for lying to me." Upon delivering the note to Walker, Brown sadly explained, apparently to the slave trader's satisfaction, that he had never had such a whipping in his life. Quite correctly Brown observed that "This incident shows how it is that slavery makes its victims lying and mean; for which vices it afterwards reproaches them, and uses them as arguments to prove that they deserve no better fate."[26]

Walker proceeded from Vicksburg to New Orleans, where he tarried long enough to sell the remaining number of his slaves; then, accompanied by Brown, he returned to Saint Louis. At last Brown had ended his year with the slave trader—"the longest year I ever lived," he said—and he returned to Dr. Young. The year had been both eventful and unhappy. What he had experienced and observed he was never to forget, although

25. George W. Clark, *The Liberty Minstrel* (New York and Boston, 1844), pp. 37–39; *Narrative*, 2d ed. (Boston, 1848), pp. 114–15; William W. Brown, Comp., *The Anti-Slavery Harp: A Collection of Songs for Anti-Slavery Meetings* (Boston, 1848, 1849, 1851, hereinafter cited as *Anti-Slavery Harp* [with a date]).

26. *Narrative*, pp. 53–57.

time might leave his memory hazy with regard to some details. The learning he had acquired while Walker was his "professor" in the "peculiar institution" he was destined to use in his efforts many years later to destroy his "alma mater."

Brown accounted in his *Narrative* for only three trips with Walker to the Mississippi delta, but late in the 1850's he said that he had made not fewer than four.[27] This discrepancy most probably resulted from confusion in his memory. While he was in slavery he made a fourth trip to New Orleans, not with Walker, but with Enoch Price; and in his *Narrative* he mislocated in time an incident which he said he had witnessed on that trip. The account of his fourth trip belongs to the record of his servitude to Price during the last three months of 1833.

In *Clotel,* Brown told of a steamboat race and explosion on the Mississippi River and of gambling on the steamboat. Here, as in other places in his novel, he wrote from memory of what he had observed while he was in Walker's service; and six years after the publication of *Clotel,* he identified as his own observations what he had related about gambling. Still later he said that soon after his year with Walker ended, he was hired "as an under steward on the steamer Patriot, running to New Orleans," and that a few weeks after he was hired, he witnessed the race, the explosion, and the gambling about which he had told in his novel.[28]

While Brown was with Walker, he doubtless witnessed some steamboat racing and a great deal of gambling on steamers on the Mississippi River, for the former was frequent and the latter was common between 1830 and 1860.[29] Nevertheless his statement that he was employed on the *Patriot* soon after his year with Walker ended is inconsistent with details recorded in his *Narrative,* as will become evident further on in this work.

27. [Josephine Brown], *Biography,* p. 26; *Memoir,* pp. 14–15.

28. *Clotel,* pp. 66–70; *Memoir,* pp. 17–19; *Black Man,* pp. 20–23.

29. Charles Augustus Murray, *Travels in North America During the Years 1834, 1835, & 1836,* 2 vols. (New York, 1839), 2:67; Richard Edwards and M. Hopewell, *Edwards's Great West and Her Metropolis* (Saint Louis, 1860), pp. 354–55.

III

Hopes of Liberty

When Brown was released from Walker's service, probably early in the spring of 1833, and returned to Dr. Young, he found a twice unhappy situation facing him. First, he found that being in need of money, Dr. Young had decided to sell him. For the nonce, however, Dr. Young was almost liberal—or seemed to be. He would agree to no arrangement Brown proposed by which to buy his freedom, but he gave Brown a week to find himself a purchaser in Saint Louis. Second, Brown found out that his only sister had been sold again and was in the Saint Louis jail awaiting an unspeakable fate. She was about to be taken by her new owner to his house in Natchez, Mississippi. After trying several times to see her, Brown succeeded in doing so. Both he and she realized that he had no power to help her; but during his visit with her, he gave her a ring as a memento and forthworth resolved by all means to rescue their mother and himself from slavery.

Chapter Three

Although Elizabeth, Brown's mother, was at first unwilling to try to escape with him, she urged him to run away. But now that she had no relatives in Saint Louis except him, he could not think of leaving her there alone. Instead he persisted until he persuaded her to join him in an attempt to escape to Canada. Leaving Saint Louis about nine o'clock one night, they appropriated a boat near the northern end of the city and rowed across the Mississippi River to Illinois. They set out immediately on the road to Alton and were north of that town by dawn of the next day. Fearing that Isaac Mansfield, who still owned Elizabeth, and Dr. Young would discover their escape and send slave catchers in pursuit of them, they decided to hide in the woods by day and to travel by night with the North Star as their guide. They proceeded thus for ten days, enduring bad weather and hunger but urged on by thoughts of the evils from which they were fleeing and nourished by the hope of freedom ahead of them. At last they arrived in central Illinois. Uninformed as they were, they assumed that they were now far enough from Saint Louis to travel safely by day, and unfortunately their assumption was supported by a rural family at whose home they stopped for food and with whom they spent a night.

The next morning they set out again and traveled until late in the afternoon—until their hopes of liberty were suddenly blasted. Here follows Brown's account of the appalling turn of events they experienced:

> I had just been telling mother how I should try to get employment as soon as we reached Canada, and how I intended to purchase us a little farm, and how I would earn money enough to buy sister and brothers, and how happy we would be in our own FREE HOME,—when three men came up on horseback, and ordered us to stop.
>
> I turned to the one who appeared to be the principal man, and asked him what he wanted. He said he had a warrant to take us up. The three immediately dismounted, and one took from his pocket a handbill, advertising us as runaways, and

> offering a reward of two hundred dollars for our apprehension, and delivery in the city of St. Louis. The advertisement had been put out by Isaac Mansfield and John Young.
>
> While they were reading the advertisement, mother looked me in the face, and burst into tears. A cold chill ran over me, and such a sensation I never experienced before, and I hope never to again.[1]

It had taken Brown and his mother eleven days to travel on foot about 150 miles on the road to freedom; it took only four days by wagon to get them back into slavery in Saint Louis. They had committed an unpardonable sin against the gods of slavery —they had attempted to flee to freedom in Canada—and they must straightway be punished for their sin. They knew what the customary punishment for it was, namely, immediate sale and transportation to the deep South. For a while they were lodged in the Saint Louis jail, where they were leered at by speculators.

After about a week Brown was taken to Dr. Young's plantation. As he had heard, Dr. Young had been ill but was then convalescing, in spite of the slave's fervent prayers for him—prayers which had not been for his recovery. For all Brown could tell, his polyphemian prayers had received only the consideration such prayers merited. He did not know that Dr. Young had less than a year to live.

Just now, however, Rhadamanthus must sit in judgment. Dr. Young had Brown brought before him. The scene was not without its moments of levity. Indeed seldom are powerful judges and great trials wholly devoid of such. Dr. Young asked Brown where he had been. Brown responded by begging the question, but as usual Rhadamanthus was equal to the occasion. "I told [him] I had acted according to his orders. He had told me to look for a master, and I had been to look for one. He answered that he did not tell me to go to Canada to look for a master." Brown bravely attempted to shift from the role of a

1. *Narrative*, pp. 71–72.

defendant to that of a plaintiff: "I told him that as I had served him faithfully, and had been the means of putting a number of hundreds of dollars into his pocket, I thought I had a right to my liberty." Rhadamanthus ignored the would-be plaintiff's argument.[2]

Fortunately for Brown, Dr. Young had promised the slave's father that he would never sell this slave "to supply the New Orleans market." Even so he had not promised not to punish the slave for committing what slaveholders considered a heinous crime. While he took the slave's case under advisement, he sent the slave to work in the fields. The overseer knew very well what to do with the recaptured runaway. He worked him hard, whipped him severely upon the first provocation, watched him closely by day, and locked him up at night. Thus the overseer used him for two or three weeks. Then one day Dr. Young went to Saint Louis. When he returned home he had news for Brown. He had sold Brown to Samuel Willi, a merchant tailor in the city, for $500. After being thus disposed of, Brown had no further contact with his relative and first owner.

If Brown went into Willi's service without high hopes, he also left Dr. Young's without regrets. Dr. Young having hired him to Willi for "three or four months some years before," probably some time in 1831, he was already acquainted with his new owner. Evidently Willi considered Brown an investment, for he sought at once to hire Brown out. Knowing that he had had experience as a servant on steamboats, Willi gave him the privilege of finding himself a job on a steamer. Willi must not have known that Brown had recently attempted to escape from slavery. Otherwise he doubtless would not have permitted Brown to work on a steamboat, for such employment frequently offered temptations as well as opportunities to slaves to flee to freedom. Brown readily found a job on a steamer which was being reconditioned, and he had to wait until it was ready for use. The prospect of this job was brighter than any he had had for a long

2. *Ibid.*, p. 75.

time. Before he went to work, however, he had to suffer another terribly depressing experience. He had to bid his beloved mother farewell for the last time.

Since her and Brown's return to Saint Louis, Elizabeth had been kept in jail. Brown had tried several times to see her but had not been permitted to do so. Nevertheless he was informed by some means that she had been sold and was soon to be taken to New Orleans. He managed to find out on which steamboat she was to be carried away and when it was to leave Saint Louis. About ten o'clock in the morning of the day on which the steamboat was to depart, he went on board "and found her there in company with fifty of sixty other slaves." He was agonized by remorse. She had attempted to escape from slavery because he had persuaded her to try to do so; and because she had tried and failed, she had been sold and was about to be transported to the deep South, whence escape would be next to impossible. Falling upon his knees, he begged her to forgive him for bringing so much misfortune upon her. Calmly and lovingly she told him that he was not to blame for her being where she was. " '*You have done nothing more nor less than your duty*,' " she assured him.

Their conversation was interrupted by Isaac Mansfield. Coming into their presence, he railed at Brown for persuading Elizabeth to run away and thus causing him to spend a hundred dollars " 'to get this wench back,' " He ordered Brown to leave the steamboat at once, and he emphasized his command by means of a kick with a heavy boot. Again—the boys in the street, Samuel McKinney, Broadwell, and now Mansfield—Oh, yes, he remembered—any white person who got an impulse to cane him or kick him seemed to have a right to do so.

But at the moment he had no time to think of himself. He must needs think of his mother.

> As I left her, she gave one shriek, saying, "God be with you!" It was the last time that I saw her, and the last word I heard her utter. I walked on shore. The bell was tolling. The

> boat was about to start. I stood with a heavy heart, waiting to see her leave the wharf.[3]

He stood on the wharf and watched the steamboat until it was too far down the river for him to discern it; then he returned to Willi's home. The steamboat had carried his mother away from him forever, but nothing could carry her out of his memory. Sixteen years later he published his "Lament of the Fugitive Slave," an elegy in which he paid her a noble tribute for her "Roman-mother spirit."[4]

A few days after Brown's mother was carried away, the steamboat on which he had got a job began its runs. It was the *Otto*, which plied the Mississippi and Missouri Rivers between Saint Louis and Independence. On its second trip southward it carried James Walker with a group of "between one and two hundred slaves" to Saint Louis. Apparently Walker had been on another slave-buying expedition in central Missouri, had found business very good, and was now on his way with his purchases to the Mississippi delta. Brown would have been glad to forget this man, if not all others whose business was the same as his. Yet here he was reviving Brown's memory of a most unhappy year he had been compelled to spend attending to this man's slaves, almost half of the time on steamboats.[5]

For a day or two it must have seemed to Brown that he was still in Walker's service. The same man and the same kinds of scenes were before him, as they had been almost all of the time a year earlier. Although this was really a different situation, it doubtless became by association a continuation of his life with Walker and was thus recorded in his memory. When late in the

3. *Ibid.*, pp. 77–79.

4. *Narrative*, 4th ed. (Boston, 1849), p. 132; *Anti-Slavery Harp*, 2d ed., pp. 30–31.

5. *Narrative*, pp. 76, 80–81. Brown said in his *Memoir*, p. 17, that the steamboat on which he worked after Willi bought him plied between Saint Louis and New Orleans. I have followed the account in his *Narrative*, because its proximity in time to the event renders it more probable than the later account.

1850's he reviewed his early life for his daughter Josephine and still later wrote other sketches of it himself, it was probably the trip on the *Otto* that he erroneously remembered as his fourth trip with Walker down the Mississippi River. In his experience, Walker the slave trader, life on the Mississippi, and New Orleans had been closely associated; and he had indeed made a fourth trip to New Orleans toward the end of 1833, a few months after his trip with Walker on the *Otto*. When, therefore, he wrote in *The Black Man* about his employment on the *Patriot*, he probably had in mind—albeit not very clearly—his employment on the *Otto*.

Brown's job on the *Otto* ended with "the close of navigation," and Brown went back to Willi's home. There he fared better than he had fared with Dr. Young, but comparatively good treatment for a slave did not satisfy him. If it influenced him at all, it made him more unhappy; for he could not forget that he was still a slave and was subject to all of the vagaries and outrages of slave life. He had learned enough about slavery and freedom to know that they were opposites with no middle ground between them. He knew that the former was bad at its best and that the latter was good even at its worst. He had seen too many white people around him enjoying freedom and had heard too much good about it to believe that it was not infinitely better than slavery.

Although at times Brown almost lost hope of ever getting his freedom, he still desired it above everything else. "I would think," he said long afterwards, "of the northern cities that I had heard so much about;—of Canada, where so many of my acquaintances had found refuge. I would dream at night that I was in Canada, a freeman, and on waking in the morning, weep to find myself so sadly mistaken." And all the time there echoed in his memory the advice his mother had given to him just before they were separated forever. A moment before Isaac Mansfield drove him away from her, she had whispered in his ear, "'*You have ever said that you would not die a slave; that you would be a freeman. Now try to get your liberty!'"* Just now however, he could only keep on dreaming, hoping, and planning.

Just now he must also look for another job by which he could earn some money for Willi, so as to relieve his own situation of at least some of its uncertainty. He had no trade at which he could work regularly. He was only a handyman, or at best only a seasonal worker. Perhaps he began to appear to Willi as a bad investment. He had been in Willi's possession only about six months—by no means long enough, to be sure, for the income from his labor to equal the amount of money he had cost—but just the same he doubted that Willi would risk losing money on him very long; and in fact Willi did not.[6]

On October 2, 1833, Willi sold Brown to Enoch Price, a Saint Louis commission merchant and steamboat owner. According to Brown, Price paid Willi $700 for him; but in a letter he wrote to Edmund Quincy on January 10, 1848, Price said that he had paid $650 for the slave.[7] No matter which of these prices was correct, Willi sold Brown at a profit. Once more it was good business for the slave seller; but it was the last time Brown was to be sold at a profit to anybody—unless it was at a profit to himself. It was the last time anybody needed to pay a tuition fee for his education in the "peculiar institution," but as will be noted in the proper place, twenty-one years later a sort of graduation fee had to be paid for him.

Until he became Price's property, Brown knew little or nothing about Price. Had he known more about his new purchaser, he probably would have been fearful about his own future. Both

6. In her *Biography of an American Bondman, by His Daughter* (Boston, 1856), p. 36, Josephine Brown said that Brown was Willi's property "more than a year." In Brown's *Narrative,* however, the sequence of events from his and his mother's attempt to escape from slavery to the date on which he was sold to Enoch Price shows that he was Willi's property considerably less than a year.

7. *Narrative,* p. 85. Brown published Price's letter in his *Narrative,* 3d. ed. (Boston, 1848), pp. vii–viii.

Price and his wife were originally Northerners, and Brown knew well the tradition concerning the harshness of Northerners who became slaveholders.

Price bought Brown for use as a coachman. To Mrs. Price at least, the acquisition of a new coachman was a good reason for acquiring a new carriage; and with Brown as the driver, neatly dressed, as all of the Prices' servants were, the family made a good appearance. Withal Mrs. Price was not interested merely in appearances, at least not where her new coachman was concerned. She was eager for him to live blissfully as well as look satisfied and well cared for. Her eagerness was based not on altruistic but on egoistic reasons. As she knew, a slave without local parental, filial, or marital attachments—without a semblance of family life—was much less contented and much more likely to try to escape from slavery than was one who had such attachments. Obviously it was more difficult for a slave to flee with a wife and children than it was for him to flee alone, and a slave with a family would naturally think twice before leaving his wife and children in slavery. After considering all of these facts, Mrs. Price decided not simply to encourage but to urge Brown to take a wife.

One of the Prices' other three slaves was Maria, a likely girl about Brown's age. In Mrs. Price's opinion, Maria was all that Brown's heart could possibly wish, but there seemed to be a difference of opinion between her and Brown even after she explained how advantageous a match between servants belonging to the same family would be. Unlike some of her fellow slaveholders, to whom Brown referred in his *Narrative*, she was too tactful to compel the slave to marry against his will. But half-correctly she surmised that if Brown could not fall in love with Maria, it must be because he was already in love with another girl. Upon discovering that the other girl was Eliza, the property of a Dr. Mills, Mrs. Price bought her to facilitate Brown's marrying her. To keep Mrs. Price from becoming suspicious or losing her patience, and to keep Eliza from feeling spurned, Brown promised to marry Eliza but said that he was not then ready to do so.

Brown knew as well as Mrs. Price knew, although it might not have occurred to her that he did, that there was really no such thing as marriage among slaves. He knew from experience that no matter how devoted to each other the members of a slave family might be, and he knew from observation that no matter how seriously slave couples might regard their union, husbands, wives, parents, and children were all subject to sudden and permanent separation at the discretion or whims of their owners. He could not forget what had happened to his own mother and her seven children. Nor could he forget the husband Colonel John O'Fallon of Saint Louis had sold to James Walker more than a year earlier, nor Solomon, the husband and preacher, whom Dr. Young's brother Aaron had sold to Walker, and whom he had seen in the slave trader's group on the *Otto* during the preceding summer. The sales, he remembered, had separated both of these husbands from their wives and children beyond any hope of reunion.[8] Clearly any slave who tried to bring up a family was merely storing up future heartaches for himself.

Furthermore the aplomb with which slaveholders compelled involuntarily separated spouses to take other mates left nobody in doubt about their real interest in slave marriages. Brown did not need to search for proof of this fact. He knew what had recently happened to Sally, a slave of Dr. Bernard Gaines Farrar, one of the most prominent physicians in Saint Louis. Dr. Farrar lived across the street from the Prices. A few days after he sold Sally's husband, he compelled her to marry another of his slaves, as she herself admitted to Brown.[9] Knowing all of these things, Brown was determined not to marry until he got out of slavery. And he was now planning as well as hoping to get out of it very soon.

8. *Narrative*, pp. 42 and 81.

9. *Ibid.*, p. 89. See also John Thomas Scharf, *History of Saint Louis City and County*, 2 vols. (Philadelphia, 1883), 2:1518–19.

In spite of his best efforts, events had too often proved to be contrary to his hopes, as they had been when he attempted to rescue his mother and himself from slavery. Might they not prove to be so again? Who could tell? Perhaps nobody could, but there could be no harm in investigating all possible available sources of information—even those which had no probable value to recommend them. About ten o'clock one night in November, he went to see Frank, an old slave fortune-teller in the city.

Brown was half-amused by Frank, who was "very distinguished" as a soothsayer among white people as well as Negro slaves. As soon as he entered Frank's cabin, which had no light save that which came from the fireplace, he was nonplussed to find that upon lighting a lamp and looking into his face, Frank seemed to know that he wanted his fortune told. Apparently it did not occur to Brown that Frank had doubtless begun with him as he usually began with lonely individuals who called on him at night. Frank had no crystal ball, but he did have a gourd full of water—which probably answered his purpose just as well. After collecting his fee of twenty-five cents, he looked into the gourd and predicted, in Delphic language, that Brown would eventually be free—whether in this world or the next he did not specify—but he warned the young slave that in trying to get his freedom, he would experience many difficulties. Upon hearing Frank's prophecy, Brown told himself that "any fool could tell me that!"

Fourteen years later Brown remarked somewhat cynically in his *Narrative* that whether Frank was really a prophet or not, "he had the *name*, and that is about half of what one needs in this gullible age." Although he was no believer in soothsaying, he avowed, Brown admitted that he was still "sometimes at a loss to know how Uncle Frank could tell so accurately what would occur in the future."[10] Frank had told Brown mainly what he probably thought Brown wanted to hear, as Brown

10. *Narrative*, pp. 91–93.

himself realized; but by thus stimulating Brown's will to freedom, he may be said to have earned his fee. Anyway, when so many otherwise intelligent people believed in clairvoyance and magic, as many still do, it should not be surprising that one who had been a slave much longer than he had been a freeman would have taken such things even half-seriously.

About seven weeks after he bought Brown, Price took his family on his steamer, the *Chester*, with himself as captain, on a trip to New Orleans. Along with his family he took Eliza and Brown, the latter as a steward because of his experience as such on steamboats. Although Brown liked to work on steamers, he was not enthusiastic about going to New Orleans at this time, for he feared that the trip would further delay his escape from slavery.

Brown's statement in his *Narrative* that the *Chester* left Saint Louis in December and arrived in New Orleans "about the middle of the month" is questionable, to say the least.[11] According to a report on the second page of the *New Orleans Bee* for November 30, the *Chester* with Price as captain arrived in New Orleans from Saint Louis on Friday, November 29. Since the trip from Saint Louis to New Orleans by steamboat early in the 1830's took six or seven days, the *Chester* must have left Saint Louis not later than November 23. The *Bee* contains no announcement of the arrival of the *Chester* in New Orelans at any time in December. Moreover, if Price spent even a day in New Orleans after his arrival there on November 29, he hardly had time to go back to Saint Louis and return to New Orleans by the middle of December.

In his *Narrative* Brown told of a horrible incident which he said he had witnessed in New Orleans while he was on his third trip there with Walker. He said that while he was on shore between seven and eight o'clock one evening, a mob chased a Negro slave into the Mississippi River and harassed him until he was chilled by the water and was drowned. They then hauled

11. *Ibid.*, p. 90.

his body upon a deck of the steamer *Trenton;* and after ascertaining that he was not " '*playing possum*' " but was dead, they all started away from the scene. Just then Captain Hart, the master of the *Trenton,* called them back and insisted that they remove the corpse from the steamer; whereupon some of them threw it upon the shore. The next morning, Brown concluded, while he was again on shore, he saw the corpse thrown with trash into a cart and carried away.[12]

This was the incident that Brown mislocated in time. As he noted in his *Narrative,* Theodore Dwight Weld had previously included a version of it in his *American Slavery as It Is.* As Weld himself had noted, this version had been published in 1834 by the Reverend James A. Thome, the son of a former slaveholder of Augusta, Kentucky. Thome said that he had witnessed the incident one dark and rainy night in December, 1833, soon after he arrived by steamer at New Orleans. If Thome's dating of the incident is correct, Brown must have witnessed it during his fourth visit to New Orleans, the visit he made not with Walker but with Price. Thome's version is more detailed than Brown's, and in it the Negro is portrayed as a hero dying but fighting back. It does not identify, however, either the steamer or its captain by name, and it ends with Thome's account of the removal of the corpse from the steamer to the shore.[13]

While the *Chester* was in New Orleans, Brown discovered, very much to his satisfaction, that Price had decided to take the steamer with his family and servants to Cincinnati. Price, however, had some misgivings about taking to a free state a slave so reflective and noncommunicative as Brown was. In order to allay his fear that Brown might run away, he questioned the slave directly. Had he ever been in a free state? "Oh, yes," Brown replied, thinking of his flight into Illinois and telling nothing but the truth, although not the whole truth. Then telling much

12. *Ibid.,* pp. 59–61.
13. [Theodore Dwight Weld], *American Slavery as It Is: Testimony of a Thousand Witnesses* (New York, 1839), pp. 158–59.

more than the truth, he explained that his master had taken him to Ohio once, but that he never liked a free state.

Price was satisfied, but Mrs. Price's fear remained to be dispelled. With much more tact and ingenuity than her husband had exercised, Mrs. Price questioned Brown only indirectly as far as his desire to escape from slavery was concerned. Rather, still believing in the power of marital attachments to keep slaves from running away, she asked Brown whether he loved Eliza as much as ever. He immediately assured her that Eliza was "very dear" to him, that "nothing but death" should part them, and that indeed it was the same as if they were already married. Mrs. Price was now satisfied—with no better reason for being so than her husband had.[14]

The Prices' fears with regard to taking Brown to a free state were very easily allayed, it appears. In his letter to Edmund Quincy, Price said that he had been offered $2,000 for Brown in New Orleans and $1,500 for him in Louisville. Price also said in the same letter that he had been warned on the day before Brown ran away that the slave was planning to do so, but that he did not heed the warning because he had "so much confidence" in Brown. So much easiness of mind where such a valuable piece of property was involved must have been extraordinary.

Meanwhile, Brown had decided that he would gladly ride to Cincinnati with the Prices and Eliza, but not back to Saint Louis with them. He made a cotton-cloth bag in which to carry his belongings and counted over and over the small amount of money he had accumulated from time to time. The *Chester* proceeded northward from New Orleans and stopped for a few hours one day at Cairo, Illinois, which Brown knew was in a free state. Then he remembered—even central Illinois was too close to Saint Louis. The steamer stopped overnight at Louisville. It was needless for him to think of disembarking there, in a state in which some of his relatives probably still held some of his and their relatives in slavery.

14. *Narrative*, pp. 90–91.

At last the *Chester* arrived in Cincinnati on Tuesday night, December 31, too late for either baggage or freight to be unloaded. Everything must wait until the next morning—everything. It would have been good for the slave to go to sleep and rest through the night, but he could not sleep. The last day of the dying year would end, he hoped, a most unhappy period of his life. Still he could not choose but remember much of that past, in which his mother, sister, and brothers were all lost to him except in his memory. As he watched for the beginning of a new day and a new year, he could not avoid mingling hopes and fears for his future.[15] Alas, sleepless nights are long nights.

15. *Ibid.*, pp. 93–94.

A Quest for Freedom

It was January 1, 1834. It was already a Happy New Year for many of those around him. Would it become that for him? It would indeed if he could only make good his escape. For a moment he stood beside the trunk he had brought to the landing to give himself a reason for coming ashore at that time. Then casually he made his way through the dispersing crowd on the landing and into the neighboring street. Turning at the first corner he reached, he began to walk a little faster, but not fast enough to give any casual observer the impression that he was hurrying away from anything. Within a few mintues he was on the outskirts of the city; and what was more, not far in the distance he saw a wood. Thither he hurried and soon found himself in "a marshy woodland," a swamp so uninviting that nobody was likely to look for him there, because no one would have expected to find anybody there, especially on a cold day.[1] He was sure that even on this cold day, there were more security and peace for him in that swamp than among the people of the city through which he had just passed. For there were many in that city who would gladly return him to slavery for a fee. He remembered all too well what had happened to a man who belonged to General Ashley of Saint Louis. While en route with his owner to Washington, D. C., the man had run away near Cincinnati but had been recaptured and carried back into bondage.

Brown also remembered how he and his mother had been recaptured in central Illinois when they had attempted to flee to Canada in the spring of the preceding year. Perhaps a similar fate now awaited him. Lest he might be overtaken by it, he must not permit himself to be seen by anybody. In order to avoid contact with either travelers or others who might be curious, he decided to hide in the woods by day and travel by night, when he would have the roads to himself. He waited in the woods, therefore, for night and the appearance of what was to be his guide to freedom—the North Star.

At last night came bringing with it clouds that hid the North Star. Nevertheless the fugitive was eager to be on his way. Emerging from his hiding place, he found a main road but did not know which way on it led to freedom, if either way did. There was nothing he could do, it seemed, but pray and wait for the North Star to appear. The night was much colder than the day had been, and he was not dressed for winter weather in Ohio. Both his suit and his shoes were old, and he had no overcoat. He had no clothes save those he was wearing nor any other belongings except a tinderbox and a small bag of "provisions." To keep himself warm he walked to and fro in the road. After what seemed like hours, the North Star appeared, and at once the fugitive was on his way to freedom—in Canada, he then

1. "Letter from W. W. Brown," *National Anti-Slavery Standard*, April 21, 1855, p. 3.

hoped.[2] "Freedom" was a beautiful word, he thought, but surely it must be more than a word. Eventually he would see what it really was.

When Brown escaped from slavery, the Underground Railroad in Ohio had not yet been very well organized, and few if any of its routes had been established. Without the assistance of conductors or any appreciable knowledge of the geography of the state, he traveled about half of the way from Cincinnati to Cleveland. In none of the editions of his *Narrative* did he give specific information about the route he followed across the state, perhaps because he could not give very much, or possibly because he did not wish to disclose to slaveholders any secrets about the ways by which fugitive slaves might get to freedom. He did not revisit southwestern Ohio for twenty-one years or central Ohio for ten years after his flight; and the changes which had taken place in those sections during those periods had made it difficult, if not impossible, for him to identify accurately the route along which he had fled. With regard to the time it took him to get across the state, he was more specific; and the record his *Narrative* gives of his progress northward, principally in terms of time, indicates generally the route he probably followed from Cincinnati to Cleveland.

When on the night of January 1 the North Star appeared, it was, according to Brown's reckoning, almost twelve o'clock. Having started at last in the right direction, Brown must have walked very fast, for before dawn the next day he had gone, he estimated, "twenty or twenty-five miles." The testimony of the Reverend William M. Mitchell renders this distance remarkable if not questionable. Mitchell was a conductor of the Underground Railroad in Ross County and elsewhere in Ohio from 1843 to 1855, after the activities of this railroad had been well organized. Speaking of his work as a conductor, he said, "I have taken them [fugitive slaves] 20 miles in a night, but that is not a usual distance, 6 to 12 miles is more commonly the length of

2. *Narrative*, pp. 95–97.

each journey."[3] Apparently Brown traveled much faster without a guide than fugitive slaves usually traveled with guides.

On the fourth day of his flight, while Brown was still in southwestern Ohio, his provisions gave out. To suffering from exposure was now added the threat of starvation. There were three ways by which he could obtain food: he could buy it, beg for it, or forage for it. He decided against both buying and begging, for either would have necessitated direct contact with strangers, and he was still afraid to be seen by anyone. Although he knew that he could get no feast by foraging, he resorted to that method, because the small risk of discovery which it involved made it comparatively safe, and just now safety from recapture was as important as food.

During the first night after his food was gone, Brown took ten or twelve ears of corn from a roadside barn. These he roasted and ate in a wood the next day, "thanking God that I was so well provided for." During another night, while in quest of corn he found what he thought was "a hill of potatoes." Upon digging into the mound with a sharp piece of wood, he found that it contained turnips. He took about a half-dozen of these and continued his journey.[4]

On the fifth or sixth day Brown was caught in a freezing rain. He traveled on at night until he became "so chilled and benumbed" that he had to take shelter in a barn, where he had to walk about to keep from freezing. "Nothing but the providence of God," he remembered, "and that old barn, saved me from freezing to death." Even so he caught a severe cold, which he said settled upon his lungs; and because his feet had been frostbitten from time to time, he could now walk only with difficulty.[5]

3. [William M. Mitchell], *The Under-Ground Railroad* (London, 1860), pp. 5, 17.

4. *Narrative*, p. 97; [Josephine Brown], *Biography of an American Bondman, by His Daughter* (Boston, 1856), p. 39.

5. *Narrative*, p. 99.

As unhappy as his plight was, he preferred it or even death to being reenslaved; so with more strength of will than of body, he walked on for two more nights. After that time he must get help from somebody or die. But how could he get help from anybody without the risk of being recaptured? He was uncertain, but necessity made him hopeful. Concealing himself one morning "behind some logs and brush" beside a road, he waited for someone to come along on whom he might call for aid.

> The first person that passed [the fugitive observed] was a man in a buggy-wagon. He looked too genteel for me to hail him. Very soon, another passed by on horseback. I attempted speaking to him, but fear made my voice fail me. As he passed, I left my hiding-place, and was approaching the road, when I observed an old man walking towards me, leading a white horse. He had on a broad-brimmed hat and a very long coat, and was evidently walking for exercise. As soon as I saw him, and observed his dress, I thought to myself, "You are the man that I have been looking for!" Nor was I mistaken. He was the very man!

By the same providence of God which had kept him from freezing in the barn two or three nights earlier, Brown recognized the man who was to be his Good Samaritan. When the old man got close enough to speak to Brown, he asked whether Brown was a fugitive slave. Without answering his question, Brown explained that he was ill and asked whether the old man knew anyone who would help him.

> He answered that he would; but again asked, if I was not a slave. I told him I was. He then said that I was in a very pro-slavery neighborhood, and if I would wait until he went home, he would get a covered wagon for me. I promised to remain. He mounted his horse, and was soon out of sight.
>
> After he was gone, I meditated whether to wait or not; being apprehensive that he had gone for some one to arrest me. But I finally concluded to remain until he should return; removing some few rods to watch his movements. After a sus-

pense of an hour and a half or more, he returned with a two horse covered-wagon, such as are usually seen under the shed of a Quaker meeting-house on Sundays and Thursdays; for the old man proved to be a Quaker of the George Fox stamp.[6]

Upon arriving at the Friend's home with him, Brown hesitated to enter it until the housewife herself urged him to do so. "I thought I saw something in the old lady's cap that told me I was not only safe, but welcome, in her house." Although he had not had a decent meal for more than a week, at first he could not eat, partly because he was not at ease and partly because he was ill from exposure. Taking notice of his physical condition, the good housewife soon improved it with one of her home remedies—a cupful or two of "composition," or "number six."

By both words and deeds the Friend and his wife made it clear to Brown that he need not hurry away from their home—that certainly he must not leave them while he was ill. In spite of their kindness, however, he was uncomfortable with them for at least a day or two. Slavery had left its scars upon his mind no less than upon his body. In the "peculiar institution" he had been effectively taught that a slave was, at the very best, an inferior human being who could never expect to associate on equal terms with white people of any class. And as he had observed, the fact that he looked as much like a white person as any of his owners was of no importance whatever. It was as much a matter of legal and social status as of racial identity. On the contrary, here were two white people whom he had known only a day or two and who had not only taken him into their home but were also treating him as if he was a member of their family. It was an experience such as he had never had, even with the white man who had admitted that he was a relative.

This transition from the unnatural status of human property to the natural status of a human being equal to any other human

6. *Ibid.*, pp. 101–02.

being was too sudden to be easily made by one who had been proscribed all of his life by the adroit and grotesque logic of American slavery. Brown could not help feeling amazed at his situation. But fortunately slavery had only wounded, because it could not kill, the freedom-loving human spirit which belonged as much to him as to the rest of mankind; and ere long, in the home of his new friends, he began to feel like a normal person among other normal persons.

The name of Brown's Good Samaritan was Wells Brown, and his home was "about fifty or sixty miles from Dayton, in the State of Ohio, and between one and two hundred miles from Cleaveland [*sic.*]." Brown did not give the name of Wells Brown's wife, and his reference to the location of his benefactors' home is so indefinite that one may wonder whether he did not know where it was or was vague about it on purpose. Because Wells Brown had helped many fugitive slaves, perhaps Brown thought that if he had told specifically where his benefactors' home was, he would have disclosed information that might have proved valuable to slave catchers. At the time Wells Brown "was very old, and not in the enjoyment of good health." Apparently Brown never saw him nor heard from him afterwards. Nevertheless, thirteen years later he dedicated the first edition of his *Narrative* to him.[7]

According to Brown's reference to its location, the Wells Browns' home might have been anywhere in the rectangular area bounded by Washington Court House, Marysville, Delaware, and Circleville. One circumstance, however, makes it probable that their home was somewhere in the northern half of this area. The more direct and doubtless the more frequently traveled of the two Cincinnati-Cleveland roads which existed in 1834 ran northeastward across the northern half of this area.[8] It is

7. *Ibid.*, pp. iii–iv, 104.

8. William F. Gephart, *Transportation and Industrial Development in the Middle West* (New York, 1909), map facing p. 139.

accordingly presumable that this was the route Brown followed northward; and if it was, the Wells Browns' home must have been near it.

Apparently the only extant references to Wells Brown are those made by William Wells Brown and those based on the latter's references to him. His name seems not to have been recorded in the registers of either deeds or wills in any of the counties comprising the area in which he probably lived, nor is it listed in the printed records of the Ohio Anti-Slavery Society or in William Wade Hinshaw's *Encyclopedia of American Quaker Genealogy*. He was, it appears, one of those who helped their unfortunate fellowmen whenever they could do so, but with no thought of making places for themselves in history—like the original Good Samaritan who, in addition to doing all he could for the victim of the thieves, paid the innkeeper to care further for him but did not bother to identify himself by name. Indeed if providence or chance had not brought to Wells Brown for aid a fugitive slave who eventually became a prominent abolitionist and author, his name might have been lost from the records of the antislavery movement in America.

Brown remained in his benefactors' home "twelve or fifteen days." And now having fully recovered from the cold he had caught, he was eager to continue his journey northward. In addition to helping him to revive his body, before letting him depart Wells Brown also helped him to revive his spirit by individualizing him with a complete name. After Brown had been on the road to freedom only a few days, he had resolved to abandon the name "Sandford" and to resume the name "William"; and by this name he had identified himself to the Browns. Wells Brown asked the fugitive what name he had in addition to William. When the fugitive replied that as a slave he had had no surname, the Friend remarked that since the fugitive had got out of slavery and had become a man, he must have an additional name, because all freemen had at least two names. In appreciation for Wells Brown's fatherly kindness, Brown gave the Friend the privilege of naming him; whereupon the Friend offered his own name. But finding that the fugitive was unwilling to give up the name "William" the Friend settled matters by calling him William Wells Brown.[9]

With some new clothes, new shoes, a small amount of money, a parcel of food, and the name of a freeman—all of which he had received from his Quaker benefactors—Brown set out again for Canada. Within four days he traveled half of the distance from central Ohio to Cleveland, but by the end of this time his supply of food and money was exhausted, and he was beginning to suffer again from exposure. The need for comfort became so urgent that he stopped one day to warm himself in "a public house." While he was there he heard some customers at the bar talking about some fugitive slaves who, it seemed, had just passed that way. He was immediately chilled with fear lest he might be recognized as a fugitive slave and recaptured. As soon as he could summon enough courage to withdraw from the public house, he did so and hastened into a wood, where he waited until night to continue his journey.

The next day, having existed without food for almost two days, Brown was impelled to beg for some at a farmhouse he was about to pass. In response to his knock, a man came to the door and asked him several questions, refused to satisfy his plea for food, and advised him to go and work for something to eat. Brown found the man's lecture no more nourishing spiritually than physically and was about to withdraw when the man's wife came to the door to find out what was happening. When her husband hesitated to explain the situation, she questioned Brown directly. Said he in his *Narrative*,

> I told her that I had asked for something to eat. After a few other questions, she told me to come in, and that she would give me something to eat.
>
> I walked up to the door, but the husband remained in the passage, as if unwilling to let me enter.

9. *Narrative*, pp. 105–06.

> She asked him two or three times to get out of the way, and let me in. But as he did not move, she pushed him on one side, bidding me walk in! I was never before so glad to see a woman push a man aside! Ever since that act, I have been in favor of "woman's rights!"
>
> After giving me as much food as I could eat, she presented me with ten cents, all the money then at her disposal, accompanied with a note to a friend, a few miles further on the road. Thanking this angel of mercy from an overflowing heart, I pushed on my way, and in three days arrived at Cleaveland [*sic*], Ohio.[10]

Probably this housewife had recognized Brown as a fugitive slave but had refrained from asking him too many questions for fear of frightening him unnecessarily. The dime and the note she gave him suggest that she might have been one of the pioneer stationmistresses on the Underground Railroad in Ohio. It is regrettable that Brown gave no more information about her than he did.

Arriving in Cleveland at the end of January, Brown was dismayed to find that there was ice on Lake Erie and that no steamboats were running. To get to Canada he must go by land through Buffalo or Detroit. Either way would have necessitated a long trip on foot, for he had no money for stagecoach fares; and still worse, he would have had to travel in such midwinter weather as he had never experienced before. He was a stranger in Cleveland; but believing that he would be secure in that city for a while, he decided to remain there at least until the winter ended and navigation on the lake was resumed.

Although Brown rejoiced in his new freedom, for a few days he found life in Cleveland precarious. He had nowhere to stay, the getting of food was uncertain, and because of the amount of walking and sleeping out-of-doors he had done since leaving Wells Brown's home, his shoes and clothes were again woebegone. Being in dire need he accepted a job as choreman for a

10. *Ibid.*, pp. 107–08.

family, his remuneration being room and board, but no wages. In his spare time, however, he did odd jobs for others who paid him in cash. From the choreman's job he went to one as a waiter in the Mansion House, of which E. M. Segur was the owner. At first he received no cash wages on this job, but he doubtless found it more congenial than the one he had left; and soon he began to receive a salary of twelve dollars a month—a fact which seems to indicate that Segur was well pleased with his work. He remained on this job until the spring, when he found employment on the Lake Erie steamer *Detroit.* Meanwhile, having acquired only some rudiments of learning while he was in slavery, he now began to educate himself by purchasing books and newspapers and reading them when he was at leisure.[11]

Long afterwards, with more interest in autobiographical anecdote than in the literal truth, Brown told two stories concerning his first efforts to achieve literacy. In August, 1849, he related to an audience in Dublin, Ireland, a fanciful story of how he learned to read. He said that while he was still in slavery, he bought a Webster's spelling book and managed to get his master's two young sons to teach him out of it by paying them with sticks of sugar candy. This story is rendered questionable by the fact that Brown never had a master who had two sons. Four years later the story of the spelling book, the boys, and the candy was repeated in the sketch of Brown's life in *Clotel;* but here the event was said to have occurred in Cleveland soon after Brown arrived there, and the boys were said to have been members of the family he served as a choreman. It was also said in the sketch in *Clotel,* although by no means convincingly, that Brown learned to write by practicing writing with chalk on fences and wheedling corrections of his writing from white boys who happened to come along.[12] In none of the editions

11. *Ibid.*, pp. 108–10; *Clotel,* p. 25; [Josephine Brown], *Biography,* p. 45.

12. *National Anti-Slavery Standard,* September 13, 1849, p. 62; *Clotel,* pp. 25–29.

of his *Narrative* did Brown refer to either of these stories.

There were good reasons why Brown went to work on a Lake Erie steamer. While in slavery he had become familiar with the life on steamboats and had learned to like it. Because he was a fugitive slave, he was doubtless cognizant that it was safer to move about than to remain daily in the same locality; and he knew that working on a lake steamer would bring him opportunities to learn about other free places on the United States side of the lake as well as those on the Canadian side. It was also true, although Brown probably did not then understand why, that because of the westward expansion in the 1830's, commerce and travel on the Great Lakes were rapidly increasing and were bringing profits to steamboat owners and comparatively good wages to their employees.[13] That Brown found working on the lake steamers profitable is indicated by the fact that he continued to do it for about nine seasons. During most of this time he was in what his daughter Josephine referred to as "a lucrative situation on one of the lake steamboats." This was probably Josephine's fine phrase for "steward," a stewardship being the highest position a Negro could then get on a steamboat.[14]

Life for Brown, withal, was not all labor and study; there was also love in it. In the summer of 1834 in Cleveland he met and fell in love with Elizabeth Schooner, whom he later called, more or less affectionately, Betsey. Theirs must have been a whirlwind, if not cyclonic, courtship; for they were married by the end of the summer, before Brown became acquainted with the members of Elizabeth's family, to say nothing of becoming informed about its history. It proved to be a case of marriage in haste and repentence at leisure, but there were some happy years before the repentence began.[15]

13. James Cooke Mills, *Our Inland Seas, Their Shipping & Commerce for Three Centuries* (Chicago, 1910), chap. 9.

14. [Josephine Brown], *Biography*, p. 50; *Rising Son*, p. 541.

15. William Wells Brown, "To the Public," *Liberator*, July 12, 1850, p. 111.

In due time, probably late in the spring of 1835, the Browns became the parents of a daughter. The joy which the birth of this firstborn brought to her parents was suddenly terminated by their grief over her death, which occurred when she was only a few months old. The Browns' loss of their first child was followed not long afterwards by Brown's loss of his summer's earnings, but the sequel to the latter loss was not without a comic interlude. Many years later, after he had acquired considerable skill as a writer, he told of this sequel in the manner of the raconteur he had become. Said he,

> In the autumn of 1835, having been cheated out of the previous summer's earnings, by the captain of the steamer in which I had been employed running away with the money, I was, like the rest of the men, left without any means of support during the winter, and therefore had to seek employment in the neighbouring towns. I went to the town of Monroe, in the state of Michigan, and while going through the principal streets looking for work, I passed the door of the only barber in the town, whose shop appeared to be filled with persons waiting to be shaved. As there was but one man at work, and as I had, while employed in the steamer, occasionally shaved a gentleman who could not perform that office himself, it occurred to me that I might get employment here as a journeyman barber. I therefore made immediate application for work, but the barber told me he did not need a hand. But I was not to be put off so easily, and after making several offers to work cheap, I frankly told him, that if he would not employ me I would get a room near to him, and set up an opposition establishment. This threat, however, made no impression on the barber; and as I was leaving, one of the men who were waiting to be shaved said, "If you want a room in which to commence business, I have one on the opposite side of the street." This man followed me out; we went over, and I looked at the room. He strongly urged me to set up, at the same time promising to give me his influence. I took the room, purchased an old table, two chairs, got a pole

with a red stripe painted around it, and the next day opened, with a sign over the door, "Fashionable Hair-dresser from New York, Emperor of the West." I need not add that my enterprise was very annoying to the "shop over the way"—especially my sign, which happened to be the most expensive part of the concern. Of course, I had to tell all who came in that my neighbour on the opposite side did not keep clean towels, that his razors were dull, and, above all, he had never been to New York to see the fashions. Neither had I. In a few weeks I had the entire business of the town, to the great discomfiture of the other barber.

At this time, money matters in the Western States were in a sad condition. Any person who could raise a small amount of money was permitted to establish a bank, and allowed to issue notes for four times the sum raised. This being the case, many persons borrowed monely merely long enough to exhibit to the bank inspectors, and the borrowed money was returned, and the bank left without a dollar in its vaults, if, indeed, it had a vault about its premises. The result was, that banks were started all over the Western States, and the country flooded with worthless paper. These were known as the "Wild Cat Banks." Silver coin being very scarce, and the banks not being allowed to issue notes for a smaller amount than one dollar, several persons put out notes from 6 to 75 cents in value; these were called "Shinplasters." The Shinplaster was in the shape of a promissory note, made payable on demand. I have often seen persons with large rolls of these bills, the whole not amounting to more than five dollars. Some weeks after I had commenced business on my "own hook," I was one evening very much crowded with customers; and while they were talking over the events of the day, one of them said to me, "Emperor, you seem to be doing a thriving business. You should do as other business men, issue your Shinplasters." This, of course, as it was intended, created a laugh; but with me it was no laughing matter, for from that moment I began to think seriously of becoming a banker. I accordingly went a few days after to a printer, and he, wishing to get the job of printing, urged me to put out my notes, and showed me some specimens of engravings that he had just received from Detroit. My head being already filled with the idea of a bank, I needed but little persuasion to set the thing finally afloat. Before I left the printer the notes were partly in type, and I studying how I should keep the public from counterfeiting them. The next day my Shinplasters were handed to me, the whole amount being twenty dollars, and after being duly signed were ready for circulation. At first my notes did not take well; they were too new, and viewed with a suspicious eye. But through the assistance of my customers, and a good deal of exertion on my own part, my bills were soon in circulation; and nearly all the money received in return for my notes was spent in fitting up and decorating my shop.

Few bankers get through this world without their difficulties, and I was not to be an exception. A short time after my money had been out, a party of young men, either wishing to pull down my vanity, or to try the soundness of my bank, determined to give it "a run." After collecting together a number of my bills, they came one at a time to demand other money for them, and I, not being aware of what was going on, was taken by surprise. One day as I was sitting at my table, strapping some new razors I had just got with the avails of my "Shinplasters," one of the men entered and said, "Emperor, you will oblige me if you will give me some other money for these notes of yours." I immediately cashed the notes with the most worthless of the Wild Cat money that I had on hand, but which was a lawful tender. The young man had scarcely left when a second appeared with a similar amount, and demanded payment. These were cashed, and soon a third came with his roll of notes. I paid these with an air of triumph, although I had but half a dollar left. I began now to think seriously what I should do, or how to act, provided another demand should be made. While I was thus engaged in thought, I saw the fourth man crossing the street, with a handful of notes, evidently my "Shinplasters." I instantaneously shut the door, and looking out of the window, said "I have

> closed business for the day: come to-morrow and I will see you. In looking across the street, I saw my rival standing in his shop-door, grinning and clapping his hands at my apparent downfall. I was completely "done *Brown*" for the day. However, I was not to be "used up" in this way; so I escaped by the back door, and went in search of my friend who had first suggested to me the idea of issuing notes. I found him, told him of the difficulty I was in, and wished him to point out a way by which I might extricate myself. He laughed heartily, and then said, "You must act as all bankers do in this part of the country." I inquired how they did, and he said, "When your notes are brought to you, you must redeem them, and then send them out and get other money for them; and, with the latter, you can keep cashing your own Shinplasters." This was indeed a new job to me. I immediately commenced putting in circulation the notes which I had just redeemed, and my efforts were crowned with so much success, that before I slept that night my "Shinplasters" were again in circulation, and my bank once more on a sound basis.[16]

When the next navigation season began, Brown went back to work on a lake steamer. Meanwhile the hope that springs with a new life came into his home in Cleveland. In the spring of 1836 the second daughter was born to the Browns and was named Clarissa. This daughter is not mentioned by name in Brown's *Narrative* nor in any of his autobiographical sketches nor in Josephine Brown's *Biography of an American Bondman.* When, however, the United States census for 1850 was taken, she and her sister Josephine were living in the home of Nathan Johnson (incorrectly listed in the census as Johnston) in New Bedford, Massachusetts, where they were attending school. The original schedules of the census of 1850 for New Bedford listed Clarissa and Josephine as the only two girls with the surname "Brown" in Johnson's household. They gave Clarissa's birthplace as Ohio and her age as fourteen years. All of these details are consistent

16. *Three Years in Europe*, pp. 97–104.

with what is otherwise known about her, so that her identity can hardly be questioned.[17]

Soon after he began working on the lake steamers, Brown began to carry fugitive slaves—fugitives from injustice, as they came to be called—to Canada by way of both Detroit and Buffalo; and he often found it adventurous to do so. By the summer of 1836 he had become a practicing abolitionist who could take just pride in the fact that he was losing none of his cases. Having saved himself from the region of horrors, he was now busy helping others to save themselves from it.

17. U.S., Bureau of the Census, United States Census, 1850, Massachusetts, vol. 5, New Bedford, p. 353.

Brown's family, which was living in Buffalo in 1840, and which then consisted of himself, his wife, and two daughters under five years of age, seems not to have been listed in the United States census for that year. The only Negro family headed by a William Brown which was listed in Buffalo in that census consisted of one man who was at least thirty-six years old and two women both of whom were at least twenty-four. (U.S., Bureau of the Census, Sixth Census, 1840, Population, New York, vol. 10, Erie County, p. 666.)

The Making of an Antislavery Agent

At the end of the summer of 1836, Brown moved his family to Buffalo for several reasons. Because that city was a terminus of the lake steamboat lines, it was more convenient for a steamboat worker to reside there than in Cleveland. In addition to being then three times as large as Cleveland, it had a much larger Negro population—a fact which seemed to indicate that opportunities for employment for Negroes were more numerous there.[1] Brown was interested in such opportunities, of course, for after every navigation season he would need to find other work, as he had had to do during the two preceding winters. Another fact which Brown could not have overlooked was that it was comparatively easy to move very quickly from Buffalo

1. In 1835, according to a state census, the population of Buffalo was 15,661. (H. Perry Smith, ed., *History of the City of Buffalo and Erie County*, 2 vols. [Syracuse, N.Y., 1884], 1:211, 2:149.)

to Canada—whither he knew not now soon he might find it expedient to move to avoid being carried back into slavery.

When Brown moved to Buffalo, presumably he found a house somewhere in the area east of Michigan Avenue between Exchange Street and Broadway, for that was where the majority of the Negroes in the city were living when he settled there. The directories of Buffalo for 1837–40 listed no Negro resident named Brown. In the directories for 1841 and 1842, "William Brown, cook," was listed as a householder on North Division Street, and in the diretcory for 1844, "William W. Brown, lecturer," was listed as a householder at 13 Pine Street.[2] Both of these addresses were in the area designated above. The first two listings might or might not have referred to Brown. Inasmuch as the name "William Brown" was common then, as it still is, and Negro cooks were relatively numerous, as they still are, there might have been in Buffalo in 1841 and 1842 another Negro who had this name and who was a cook—which William Wells Brown is not known to have been. The third listing undoubtedly referred to Brown, for before 1844 he had become a lecturer for the Western New York Anti-Slavery Society, and lecturing of any kind was not a common occupation among Negroes.

No Buffalo directory for 1843 or 1845 seems to have been published. Early in the summer of the latter year, Brown moved his home to Farmington, Ontario County, and there was no reason for his name to be included in later directories of Buffalo.

Within a few weeks after his removal to Buffalo, Brown participated in what might have been called the clearing of a wreck on the Underground Railroad. About this time Bacon Tate, a slave trader of Nashville, Tennessee, went to Buffalo for the purpose of recapturing slaves who had escaped from Nashville and had settled in the Niagara area. Among these was a family whose surname was Stanford, and who had established

2. *Crary's Directory for the City of Buffalo* (Buffalo, 1841), p. 17 [193]; *Walker's Buffalo City Directory* (Buffalo, 1842), p. 94; (1844), p. 65.

a home in Saint Catharines, Ontario. The family consisted of a man and his wife and their child about six weeks old. With the assistance of "a profligate colored woman" who was a servant in the Eagle Tavern in Buffalo, Tate located the Stanfords, and late one Saturday night he had them kidnapped. Early the next morning, with their captives bound and gagged in a carriage, the kidnappers crossed the Black Rock Ferry on the Niagara River. After stopping for a few minutes in Buffalo, they continued southward to an inn in Hamburg, where they stopped again.

Meanwhile, news of the kidnapping having reached Buffalo before noon, a group of Negroes from that city, including Brown, went in pursuit of the kidnappers and their captives and overtook them at the inn in Hamburg. Encouraged by the innkeeper, they quickly rescued the Stanfords and took them northward again, followed by the kidnappers. When Tate, who was still in Buffalo, was informed about the turn of affairs, he appealed to the sheriff of Erie County for aid. Late in the afternoon a group of about fifty persons, most of whom were Negroes, armed with pistols, knives, and clubs took the Stanfords to the Black Rock Ferry to send them back to Saint Catharines. They were intercepted near the ferry by a sheriff's posse of "some sixty or seventy men," and a free-for-all fight between the two groups ensued. Amid the confusion thus created, the Stanfords were put in a boat and rowed across the Niagara River to Canada, while the rescuers and their sympathizers cheered.

Now that their aim had been accomplished, about forty of the rescuers submitted to arrest by the sheriff's posse and were taken to Buffalo and imprisoned for the night. On the following morning they were arraigned before a justice named Grosvenor and charged with breaking the peace of the Sabbath and apparently with unlawful assembly. Twenty-five of them were eventually found guilty by a higher court and fined from five to fifty dollars. No one had been killed in the melee at the ferry; but one man, who was an actor, had been so badly wounded that he died about three months later. "Thus ended," said Brown, "one of the most fearful fights for human freedom that I have ever witnessed." Freedom, he had found, was indeed more than a word. It involved fighting not only for one's own security but also for the security of others; and paradoxically enough, it might mean imprisonment or even death for its defenders.[3]

Brown also did antislavery work in Buffalo in less dramatic but nonetheless effective ways. He welcomed antislavery agents and lecturers into his home. He made his home a station on the Underground Railroad; and because many fugitive slaves passed through Buffalo en route to Canada, he frequently had stopover passengers to accommodate. Moreover,

> As Niagara Falls were [*sic*] only twenty miles from Buffalo, slaveholders not unfrequently passed through the latter place attended by one or more slave servants. Mr. Brown was always on the look-out for such, to inform them that they were free by the laws of New York, and to give them necessary aid.[4]

Among the Negroes in Buffalo, Brown discovered many who, like himself, had freed themselves from chattel slavery; but among them he also found many who were being victimized by servitude to intoxicating drinks. In order to abolish this kind of slavery, Brown organized a temperance society—one of the first to be organized in western New York—and served as its president for three terms. The society became popular and grew rapidly. Brown said in his earliest published account of it that within three years its membership numbered more than 500 out of the total Negro population of 700 which Buffalo then had. In 1843, however, after Brown had retired from the presidency

3. *Narrative*, 4th ed. (Boston, 1849), pp. 109–24. In his *A Description of William Wells Brown's Original Panoramic Views* (London, [1850]), pp. 35–38, Brown added some minor details to this story. Here he said that the news of the kidnapping had been carried to Buffalo by Leander, a fugitive slave he had saved from capture in Cleveland and had helped to get to Canada in the fall of 1835.

4. [Josephine Brown], *Biography of an American Bondman, by His Daughter* (Boston, 1856), pp. 52–53.

of the society, it was said to have "upwards of 300 members."[5] Whether the number Brown had given was too large, the more recently given number was too small, or many members had back-slidden ere long is unknown.

While this society flourished, it met periodically to discuss and promote temperance, but its meetings also served other good purposes. They became forums in which members were afforded opportunities to learn the funadmentals of parliamentary procedure and public speaking. In these meetings Brown learned much about both and thereby further prepared himself for the work he was to begin doing as an antislavery lecturer within the next few years. He did not then know, of course, exactly what work he was to do during the next twenty-five years—that temperance reform was not to be his primary interest for that period, nor that he would devote much time to it during the last twenty years of his life. Without losing interest in the cause of temperance, he became increasingly interested in the organized abolition movement and sought to translate his interest into action more extensive than his work as a conductor on the Underground Railroad. In the meantime other things besides temperance and antislavery work claimed some of his attention. Important among these was the study of English grammar, mathematics, history, and literature—study by which he prepared himself still further for the future.

In the summer of 1839 the third daughter was born to the Browns and was named Josephine. This was the child who within twenty years was to make her father proud of her for many reasons. But now while she was an infant, he was worried about her and her sister Clarissa's future. Because of the proslavery power in the South and the anti-Negro sentiment in the North, he could hardly expect his children to realize in America

5. *Narrative*, 2d ed. (Boston, 1848), p. 108; *Three Years in Europe*, p. xix; *Minutes of the National Convention of Colored Citizens: Held at Buffalo on the 15th, 16th, 17th, 18th and 19th of August, 1843* (New York, 1843), pp. 36, 37.

the kind of future he wanted to be theirs. Could they realize it anywhere else? he wondered. Why not travel a little, he asked himself, and try to find out?

In 1840 Brown visited Haiti and Cuba and possibly other islands in the West Indies. If the purpose of his visit was what has been conjectured above, Haiti was probably his principal objective. He had doubtless heard of the successful revolution of the Haitian Negroes and was interested in the possibilities of life unhampered by race prejudice in the Negro republic. On the contrary, knowing that slavery still existed in Cuba and that it had been only recently abolished from the British West Indies, he could scarcely have expected to find better prospects in the former than in the United States or as good opportunities in the latter as in Canada.

Brown said nothing about his trip in any of the editions of his *Narrative*, nor is it mentioned in the sketches of his life in any of his other works, nor by his daughter Josephine in her biography of her father. But in a letter which he wrote from London on October 12, 1849, to William Lloyd Garrison for the *Liberator*, he referred to "the bitter cold night in the winter of 1840, when I was compelled to walk the deck of the steamer Swallow on the Hudson river, on account of my complexion." Most probably he had the experience mentioned here en route from Buffalo to New York to embark for the West Indies or on his way home from the islands. In a lecture in Poughkeepsie, New York, on November 6, 1861, he gave "a history of his tour of Hayti." The newspaper report of his lecture gave no information, however, about the time or any events of the tour. About thirteen years later Brown said casually that he had visited Havana in 1840 and Haiti about the same time.[6]

After visiting the West Indies, Brown returned to his work on one of the lake steamers and therewith to his conductorship on the Underground Railroad. Between the first of May and the first

6. *Liberator*, November 2, 1849, p. 175; *Pine and Palm, Supplement* [Boston], January 2, 1862; *Rising Son*, pp. 80, 140.

of December, 1842, he carried sixty-nine fugitive slaves to Canada. In 1843, on a trip to southern Ontario, he renewed acquaintances with many Negroes whom he had helped to get there.[7]

During nine years of freedom, as a result of his observations in Cleveland, Buffalo, and elsewhere, Brown had developed a profound interest in the welfare and the future of Negroes in America; but he had not learned much about what Negroes beyond the communities with which he was familiar were doing as a group to improve their condition, nor did he become acquainted with the Negroes who might have been correctly considered leaders beyond their respective communities. Before the end of the summer of 1843, he learned a great deal about what Negroes as a group were trying to do for themselves, and he also came to know many of the Negroes who had achieved some prominence and whose names he had occasionally seen in antislavery newspapers.

Early in August, with the Reverend George Bradburn of Massachusetts, Frederick Douglass arrived in Buffalo to hold antislavery meetings. These meetings had been scheduled as a part of the second series of the "One Hundred Anti-Slavery Conventions" which were to be held during the last six months of 1843 "chiefly in New-York, Pennsylvania, Ohio, and Indiana."[8] Being displeased with the place provided for the meetings and also with the first audience, which seemed to him to consist of "ragamuffins," Bradburn withdrew and took the next steamboat to Cleveland, where his brother Charles resided. The meetings were held at first in an old building at the intersection of Washington and Seneca Streets, because it was the best place available to the local abolitionists who had arranged for them. There Douglass spoke daily for almost a week "to audiences constantly increasing in numbers and respectability," until a Baptist church

7. *Narrative*, pp. 109–10.

8. The notice concerning these conventions in the *National Anti-Slavery Standard*, July 20, 1843, p. 27, said that meetings were to be held in Buffalo August 7–9.

"was thrown open" to him. When the church became overcrowded he "went on Sunday into the open Park and addressed an assembly of four or five thousand persons."[9] If Brown attended these meetings, as presumably he did, they were most probably the first occasions on which he saw Douglass and heard him speak; and as will be noted, he credited Douglass with doing remarkable good for abolitionism in Buffalo.

Meanwhile, late in July, Brown had doubtless read in the *National Anti-Slavery Standard* and in the *Liberator* announcements saying that "a national convention of colored citizens of the United States" would be held in Buffalo on the third Tuesday in August. The convention began "agreeably to call" on Tuesday, August 15, and continued for five days.[10] The "large public hall" in which the first session was held was the same building in which Douglass had recently lectured against slavery. Among about forty persons who were present for this session were the Reverend Amos G. Beman of New Haven, Frederick Douglass, the Reverend Henry Highland Garnet then of Troy, New York, J. P. Morris of Rochester, Charles B. Ray of New York City, Charles Lenox Remond of Salem, Massachusetts, and A. M. Sumner of Cincinnati. Four of the six representatives from Buffalo were Brown, Samuel H. Davis, Abner H. Francis, and Henry Thomas, one of the temporary secretaries. Beman was chosen president of the convention and was supported by seven vice-presidents, one of whom was Douglass.

Brown served on the committee on the roll of delegates, the committee on rules, and the committee on finance. A. H. Francis and J. P. Morris were the other two members of the committee on rules. The fifteen rules drawn up by this committee evinced a clear understanding on its part of the fundamentals of parlia-

9. *Life and Times of Frederick Douglass, Written by Himself*, new rev. ed. (Boston, 1895), p. 284.

10. *National Anti-Slavery Standard*, July 20, 1843, p. 27; *Liberator*, July 21, 1843, p. 115; *Minutes of the National Convention of Colored Citizens. Held at Buffalo . . . . . August, 1843*, New York, 1843.

mentary procedure. Brown spoke at several of the sessions but did not attract special attention as a speaker. Nothing he said and only extracts from other speeches were recorded in the minutes of the convention. On its third page the *Buffalo Daily Gazette* for August 18 more or less favorably reported the convention and especially commended Douglas and Garnet as speakers, but it did not mention the activities of Brown or any other representative from Buffalo.

At one of the sessions Garnet read his *Address to the Slaves of the United States of America,* advising the bondmen to choose "Liberty or Death" and urging them to resort to violence if necessary to free themselves. The address provoked a considerable amount of discussion. Sumner of Cincinnati argued that adoption of it by the convention "would be fatal to the safety of the free people of color of the slave States, but especially so to those who lived on the borders of the free states." Others who spoke against adoption were Brown, Beman, Douglass, and Remond. A motion for adoption of the address was considered at two sessions and was lost both times.

At the session Thursday afternoon, a resolution proclaiming it "the duty of every lover of liberty to vote the Liberty [party] ticket so long as they are consistent with their principles" was passed with seven dissenting votes. Brown, Douglass, and Remond were among the dissenters. At the session Friday afternoon, a resolution was offered proposing that the convention "hail with pleasure the organization of the Freeman's Party, based upon the great principles contained in the Declaration of Independence." Brown, Douglass, and Remond opposed this resolution, because they took it for granted that the Freeman's party was the same as the Liberty party, and they "neither believed in the party, nor in the leading men of the party, and as a matter of course could not and would not enroll themselves under its broad banner, nor encourage others to do so." As Garrisonian abolitionists, who advocated immediate emancipation but did not expect it to be achieved directly by means of partisan politics,

Douglass at that time and Remond were naturally unsympathetic towards the Liberty party. There is no telling whether Brown's vote was determined by their influence or by his knowledge of the brief history of the party. In spite of opposition the resolution was adopted; but for Garnet, who had supported both resolutions, and for Brown this was not the end of the matter.

On August 30–31, less than two weeks after the adjournment of the National Convention of Colored Citizens, the Liberty party held a national convention in Buffalo. The twenty-one resolutions adopted at that convention were a curious blending of generalizations and ambiguities which could have been expected only to displease radicals without pleasing conservatives.[11] The adoption of these resolutions proved that Brown, Douglass, Remond, and others had been wise in refusing to promise beforehand to support the party's ticket.

Brown was not among the 148 delegates to the convention of the Liberty party, but he was present at one of its sessions at which Garnet spoke. The latter's remarks on that occasion gave impulse to what seems to have been Brown's first writing to appear in print, namely, the following letter which was published not long afterwards in the *National Anti-Slavery Standard:*

> MR. EDITOR—Permit me through the columns of the Standard, to correct a statement made by Mr. Garnet, at the late liberty convention in the city of Buffalo. Mr. Garnet used the following language: "We, the colored people, have held a national convention, and in that convention we adopted the views of the liberty party [*sic*]; and the resolution was adopted, with but two opposing votes; and I am sorry to say that those two were from Massachusetts. I need not tell you who they were," meaning Remond and Douglas[*sic*]. Now, I ask, where in the name of heaven did Mr. Garnet learn that there were but two opposing votes to that resolution? I am

11. The resolutions are quoted in Edward Stanwood's *A History of the Presidency from 1788 to 1897*, rev. by Charles Knowles Bolton (Boston and New York, 1928), pp. 216–20.

sure he did not learn it in the convention. Mr. Garnet knew, as did every member of that convention, that there were more than two that voted against the resolution adopting the views of the liberty party; yet Mr. Garnet singled out Remond and Douglas as the only ones that voted against the resolution. Why did he single them out? If he wished to single out two, why did he not single out some other two? I am sure he might have done it with propriety. Knowing that six or seven voted against the resolution, he comes out in [the] presence of one or two thousand people, and says that there were but two opposing votes, and that those two were from Massachusetts. Did Mr. Garnet say so because Remond and Douglas were the agents of the American Anti-Slavery Society? or did he wish to carry the impression that Remond and Douglas were not the friends of the slave? I ask, what could have been this motive in making that statement? Are not Remond and Douglas the friends of the slave? Who was it that came to Buffalo, and by their eloquence and enthusiasm in behalf of bleeding humanity, called thousands to hear them, and greet them with thunders of applause? Who was it that tore the veil of prejudice from the eyes of the whites of this city? Who was it that came here when the doors of the churches were barred, and with their mighty voices caused them to open to the friends of the slave? Who [*sic*] are we mainly indebted to for the great change in public sentiment in this city? The unanimous voice of Buffalo will answer, Abby Kelley, George Bradburn, C. Lenox Remond, and Frederic[*sic*] Douglas. It was they that came here and prepared the citizens of the city to receive friend Garnet, and the rest of those talented men that have visited Buffalo within the past summer; yet according to Mr. Garnet, everybody was liberty party men in the national colored convention, but C. Lenox Remond and Frederic Douglas. When I see such quibbling, by such men as Henry Highland Garnet, it makes me tremble for the fate of the slave at the hands of political parties. I am willing that Mr. Garnet should receive all the praise that he can from his political friends; but as a member of the convention, I am not willing that he should misrepresent the convention.

Now, I shall challenge Mr. Garnet to repeat, that there were but two that opposed the passage of the resolution adopting the views of the third party.

I am, with respect, the public's obedient servant,

WILLIAM W. BROWN

Buffalo, N. Y. Sept. 26, 1843.[12]

Aside from directness and simplicity, this letter has none of the qualities by which Brown's writing at its best was eventually characterized. Ineffective repetition, a labored effort towards clarity, and a want of good humor, which is always desirable in objective argument, all indicate that Brown still had a great deal to learn about writing. Considering, however, what he had taught himself in nine years while he was working to support a growing family, he had good reasons for hoping to learn to express himself effectively in the none too distant future.

From the official minutes of the National Convention of Colored Citizens, it appears that Garnet's account of the vote on the resolution pertaining to the Liberty party was erroneous, as Brown said it was. If Garnet ever publicly acknowledged his error, he did not do so in the *National Anti-Slavery Standard*, the journal in which he would have been expected to reply to a letter published therein about him.

12. *National Anti-Slavery Standard*, October 5, 1843, p. 70.

VI

"His Strong Manly Voice"

LATE IN THE FALL OF 1843, PROBABLY NOT UNTIL AFTER THE navigation season on Lake Erie had ended for the year, Brown became a lecturing agent for the Western New York Anti-Slavery Society. The details of the new agent's agreement with the society seem to have remained unrecorded. It is exceedingly probable, however, that he began working for no specified salary, but received a part of whatever collections were taken after his lectures, as he was still doing as late as the spring of 1846. At that time Joseph C. Hathaway of Farmington, N. Y., who was then president of the society, explained to the public that as a lecturer and general agent for the society, Brown was "dependent for his sustenance on the aid of the philanthropist." Accordingly Hathaway appealed to the friends of freedom to contribute "to the support of those who are laboring in the cause of our suffering brethren in the South, and to ask your friends and neighbors to do the same, however small the sum may be."[1]

At first Brown limited his lecture trips to towns and villages in Erie County or near it, for he was restricted not only by his want of experience as a lecturer but also by the inconveniences which traveling in cold weather entailed, especially for Negroes. But wherever he went, he found many who needed to be divested of race prejudice and converted to abolitionism. One of the first towns to which he went to lecture was Attica, about thirty-five miles east of Buffalo. After his meeting, which he held in a church in the evening, he found that no tavern in the town would lodge him for the night. As a last resort he went back to the church and spent the night there. Because it was extremely cold, he had to walk around in the building most of the night to keep from freezing.[2]

If Brown was surprised by the indifference to abolitionism which he found in some places, he had good reasons to be astonished by the antagonism towards it which he found in others, as in Aurora in Erie County, for example. Early in the winter of 1844, probably in January, he went to that town to lecture and almost missed getting a hearing because of the antiabolition spirit that prevailed there. His account of his experience in Aurora on that occasion was later corroborated by Alonzo D. Moore, a native of the town. At the time of Brown's visit, Moore was a boy, but his father was Brown's host and introduced him to the assembly in the church in which he was to speak. Thirty years later Moore wrote a "Memoir of the Author'" for Brown's *Rising Son*, and in it he recounted some of the incidents which occurred during Brown's visit to Aurora.[3]

Upon arriving at the church early in the evening, Moore's father and Brown found it already crowded—with what kind

1. *Narrative*, 2d ed. (Boston, 1848), p. 108; *National Anti-Slavery Standard*, May 7, 1846, p. 195.

2. [Josephine Brown], *Biography of an American Bondman, by His Daughter* (Boston, 1856), p. 55.

3. *Black Man*, pp. 26–27; *Rising Son*, pp. 9, 33–35.

of audience they were not long discovering. As soon as Brown began his speech, a mob consisting of the majority of the men present began coughing, whistling, and stamping their feet. During the barrage of noise thus created, "unsalable eggs, peas, and other missiles were liberally thrown at the speaker." One of the eggs hit him in the face and spattered the bosom of his shirt, making him look somewhat ridiculous for a few moments. If this was his first time to be so unceremoniously received by an audience, it was certainly not to be his last. From the experiences of other antislavery agents, he already knew that he must either learn to master situations like this one or give up as an antislavery lecturer. After half an hour of excitement, he descended from the pulpit; and standing in front of the altar, he told the rabble that he would not address them even if they wanted him to do so, and that if any of them had been held in slavery as he had been, they would not have had the courage to escape; for their actions of the last half-hour had shown them to be cowards. Then he told of his life as a slave and how he had escaped from slavery, and concluded with an appeal for the abolition of both slavery and race prejudice. In his speech of an hour and a half, he not only won the support of an erstwhile antagonistic audience but also learned something about how to deal with hostile assemblies.

Before the meeting, some members of the mob had taken a bag of flour to the belfry over the main entrance to the church. They had intended to empty the flour on Brown when he went out, and one of them had been designated to decoy him into position for the flouring and to signal his cohorts in the belfry at the opportune time for it. But this man had been so favorably impressed by Brown's speech that instead of leading Brown into the trap, he warned him concerning it, even telling him what the signal for the pouring of the flour was to be. Taking the scheme for a hoax, Brown maneuvered to get the flour poured on others, who proved to be some of the best citizens of the town, and thereby he caused the perpetrators of the prank to be arrested.

On February 3, while he was in Rochester, Brown wrote a letter to Mrs. Maria Weston Chapman, who was one of the most prominent abolitionists in Boston, and who was then manager of the Massachusetts Anti-Slavery Fair as well as editor of the *Liberty Bell*, an antislavery annual. In his letter Brown asked what disposition should be made of a parcel of books which Mrs. Chapman had shipped about six months earlier to James Monroe in care of Charles Lenox Remond in Buffalo, and which having remained unclaimed by the addressees, was now at Brown's home. For the safety of the parcel he had paid certain charges which had been assessed upon it and had taken possession of it. In his letter Brown also gave a few details about his current activities as an antislavery lecturer. Mrs. Chapman noted on the back of the letter that she had answered it but said nothing about what she had told Brown to do with the books.

Remond, it may be remembered, had attended the National Convention of Colored Citizens in Buffalo in August of the preceding year. The parcel of books had probably arrived there, however, after he had gone to join Monroe in Ohio, where they had continued the work of the One Hundred Anti-Slavery Conventions. Long before the end of 1843, Remond had returned to Boston; and upon seeing Mrs. Chapman, he had doubtless told her of his and Monroe's failure to receive the parcel.

Brown's letter fills a page eight by twelve inches, with the superscription on its back. It is important less because of its contents than because it is apparently the earliest extant manuscript of Brown's; and as such it shows what progress its author had made in self-education within ten years after his escape from slavery. It is not a model of excellent composition—but worse letters have been written by present-day college students with handbooks of composition and dictionaries at their elbows. The principal errors in the letter consist of four misspellings, one instance of lack of agreement between a subject and its verb, and the incorrect use of several capitals.[4]

4. Brown to Mrs. Chapman, February 3, 1844, Anti-Slavery—Weston Papers.

The American Anti-Slavery Society held its tenth anniversary meeting in New York from Tuesday through Friday, May 7–10, 1844. This was the first interstate convention of abolitionists that Brown attended. But what was more important, it was the meeting at which the society officially condemned the Constitution as a proslavery document and resolved to advocate the peaceful separation of the free states from the slave states, adopting as its slogan "No Union with Slaveholders."

Although these acts of the society perturbed many, even among the abolitionists, the idea that the Constitution was a proslavery document did not originate, it should be remembered, with the abolitionists. Beginning with its adoption, proslavery statesmen, not without good reasons, had considered it such. There was a fugitive-slave law embedded in its Article 4, Section 2. From this document the federal government derived no authority to interfere with slavery in the several states, and whether it gave the federal government authority to exclude slavery from new territory had long been a question for heated arguments both in and out of Congress.

As to the doctrine of disunion, credit, however doubtful it might have been, was also due to proslavery statesmen for originating it by implication if not otherwise. For the logical end of nullification, which some of them advocated in the 1820's, certainly would have been disunion, as they were doubtless aware. If a state had the right to nullify any federal regulations, it had the right to nullify all of them; and simply by exercising this right, it could free itself from all responsibilities to the federal government, and thus it could separate itself from that government in fact as well as in theory. Moreover, within recent years proslavery leaders had been advocating disunion not indirectly but as an alternative to the annexation of Texas and the extension of slave territory.

Now if proslavery leaders considered disunion justifiable when it seemed to them to be necessary for the preservation of the "peculiar institution" of the slave states, it should not have been surprising for the abolitionists to consider disunion justifiable when such seemed to them to be necessary for the preservation of freedom in the free states. That the existence of slavery in half of the United States was more than an imaginary threat to freedom in the other half had been evidenced by the violent antiabolition outbursts against freedom of assembly and freedom of speech in many of the free states and also by the kidnapping of free Negroes and the legalized slave hunting in these states. Typical events of these kinds were the riots against abolitionists in Boston, Montpelier, and Utica in October, 1835, in Cincinnati in August, 1836, and September, 1841, and in Alton, Illinois, in November, 1837; the burning of Pennsylvania Hall in Philadelphia in May, 1838; the kidnapping of Solomon Northup in Washington in 1841; and the case of George Latimer in Boston in the fall of 1842.

To return to the anniversary meeting of the American Anti-Slavery Society in May, 1844—at the session Thursday morning, May 9, Garrison presented an address, "To the Friends of Freedom in the United States." In this address he proposed that "until slavery be abolished, the watchword, the rallying-cry, the motto on the banner of the American Anti-Slavery Society shall be, 'NO UNION WITH SLAVEHOLDERS!' " The address, with resolutions in harmony with it offered by Wendell Phillips, became the subject of a long discussion. Among those who favored its adoption were Brown, Stephen S. Foster, Joseph C. Hathaway, Phillips, and Edmund Quincy, along with others who were opposed to the moribund Liberty party and were mistrustful of political abolitionism of any kind. Among those who opposed its adoption were Charles C. Burleigh, David Lee Child, Ellis Gray Loring, James Miller McKim, and James McCune Smith, a Negro physician of New York.

At the session Thursday afternoon, Brown not only supported Garrison's address and Phillips's resolutions but also voiced his own opinion that the Constitution—certainly as the South interpreted it—was a bulwark of slavery. Eschewing the theoretical aspects of the matter, he informed the audience that he had seen his mother, sister, and brothers chained as slaves, and that as far as he knew, they were still held in slavery where the Constitution was recognized, nevertheless, as the supreme law of the land. "I would have the Constitution torn to shreds, and scattered to the four winds of heaven," he concluded.

This being Brown's first speech at a national antislavery convention and in the presence of a large number of talented thinkers and orators, it probably did not lift the audience to great heights. The *National Anti-Slavery Standard* reported his words very briefly; the *Liberator* did not report them at all. By virtue of his experience, however, he had been able to bring to the discussion of the nature of the Constitution with regard to slavery a point of view which could have been brought only by an ex-slave. To him, whether the Constitution was antislavery or proslavery in theory, slavery itself had been and still was indisputably constitutional in fact; and just now the removal of the fact was vastly more urgent than proving or disproving a theory. Garrison's address with Phillips's resolutions was finally adopted by a vote of 59–21.[5]

At the meeting in New York, Brown saw and heard for the first time Garrison, Phillips, and many of the other leading abolitionists. The views concerning the Constitution and disunion which he expressed in the meeting were mainly the products of his experience and private study, but they had been influenced, no doubt, by what he had read in the *Liberator* and the *National Anti-Slavery Standard* and also by what he had heard said by these leaders during the long discussion of these subjects. He returned home with his convictions strengthened by the arguments he had heard and by the official action the American Anti-Slavery Society had taken. Having become a confirmed disciple of Garrison, he resumed his lecturing in western New

5. *National Anti-Slavery Standard*, May 16, 1844, pp. 198–99; *Liberator*, May 17, 1844, p. 79, May 24, 1844, pp. 82, 84; Oliver Johnson, *William Lloyd Garrison and His Times*, new rev. and enl. ed. (Boston, 1881), pp. 337–38.

York; and in addition to delineating the iniquities of slavery, he discussed more and more frequently its influence upon the church, politics, economics, and American life in general.

Late in July, Brown went to lecture in Albion in Orleans County. Because of the "mobocratic spirit" with which the village was reputed to be possessed, he expected everything except a welcome, but he was surprised to meet with no opposition save what was offered by clergymen. None of them would permit him to hold meetings in their churches. Fortunately "The friends of the cause obtained the Court-house, and long before the time for the meeting to commence, the house was crowded to *a jam,* and that, too, with some of the first citizens of this place." They all listened attentively while he "sounded the tocsin of Disunion;" and when the meeting ended, he was requested to hold another one the next night in the same place. He told all of this in a letter he wrote from Albion the day after the first meeting to Sidney Howard Gay, one of the editors of the *National Anti-Slavery Standard.*[6]

In accordance with his plans to which he had referred in his letter to Gay, Brown went to Ohio about the middle of August to lecture and also to obtain subscriptions for the *National Anti-Slavery Standard.*[7] He remained in Ohio at least until the end of September, spending the time in the northern and eastern sections of the state.

One day on a train on the Mad River and Lake Erie Railroad en route from Sandusky to Republic, Brown was ejected from one of the coaches, he said, because Negroes were not permitted to ride in the coaches with white people. There being no other accommodations on the train, he had to either postpone his trip or ride in an open freight car. He chose to do the latter, because he had an engagement in Republic a few hours later. As the

6. *National Anti-Slavery Standard,* August 29, 1844, p. 50.

7. See the notice under "Agents" in the *National Anti-Slavery Standard* for August 22, 1844, p. 43.

train neared Republic, while Brown was seated on a flour barrel reading Alexander Pope's *Essay on Man,* the conductor who had excluded him from the coaches came and asked for his fare—$1.25, as those in the coaches had paid. Brown refused to pay this amount. Instead he asked how much was the charge for the transportation of freight per hundred pounds. The conductor replied that it was 25¢; whereupon Brown nonplussed him by paying him only 37½¢, Brown's weight being about 150 pounds.

Brown first related this incident, in which he meticulously followed the dialectics of racial segregation to its logical conclusion, in his *Clotel.* Therein he made it an experience of William, a fugitive slave from Vicksburg, Mississippi. The incident was first recorded as an experience of Brown's by his daughter Josephine. Brown himself later retold it autobiographically and essentially as it had already been told.[8]

In Warren during the last week in August, Brown delivered in the county courthouse what the *Liberty Herald*, a local newspaper, called "two powerful lectures." A Methodist deacon voluntarily opened one of Brown's meetings with a prayer. The deacon complained to the Almighty about the "hard things" some of the abolitionists were saying about Henry Clay, who was then the Whig candidate for President of the United States. He prayed that Clay might be elected in spite of the opposition of the abolitionists. He petitioned the Lord to let the speaker for the occasion present nothing but the truth and not to let him say anything about politics. Apparently the Almighty paid no more attention to the last petition than he did to the one beseeching the election of Clay in the following November. Challenged by the deacon's prayer, Brown took for his text Henry Clay " 'the Farmer of Ashland' " and dwelt at length on "the merits and demerits of the two great political parties"—the Whigs and

8. *Clotel,* pp. 172–74; [Josephine Brown], *Biography,* pp. 56–59; William Wells Brown, *The Negro in the American Rebellion: His Heroism and His Fidelity* (Boston, 1867), pp. 370–73.

the Democrats. At the end of the meeting he requested the deacon to pray again, but the deacon courteously refused to do so.[9]

On September 9 and 10 Brown lectured in New Lisbon in Columbiana County. Said a report in a local newspaper,

> On the first evening, he had a considerable house full to address—the second evening, the Seceder church was about as full as it could hold. On both occasions, he did lash slavery, slaveholders, and their apologists, severely—no quarter was given for such fugitives from righteousness by this fugitive from Sodom. He exposed pro-slavery hypocrisy and shallowness most essentially. The audience was frequently in roars of laughter, and anon everything was as quiet as the tomb, save his strong manly voice. His views of the Constitution, and his advocacy for dissolution were new things to some here—a few were cross about it and said he ought to be apprehended for treason, lynched, &c. He remained here until this afternoon, unmolested, when he started for New-Garden. If 9 o'clock had not come so soon last evening, he would have given the whigs a dose on annexation that even Mr. Giddings could not cure them of.[10]

Brown spent the last week in September in the vicinity of Cadiz and Mount Pleasant, the last-named village being not far from the Ohio River. On the eastern side of the river was slave territory in Virginia, now the panhandle of West Virginia. Alas it was much easier for slave catchers and kidnappers to get from the western side of the river to Virginia than it was for fugitive slaves to get from the eastern side to Ohio, as Brown discovered on his first visit to Mount Pleasant and its vicinity.

About ten o'clock at night on September 26, five or six white men broke into the home of John Wilkinson, a Negro who

9. *Liberty Herald* [Warren, Ohio], September 4, 1844; "Letter from Wm. W. Brown," *National Anti-Slavery Standard*, September 26, 1844, p. 66.

10. *New Lisbon* [Ohio], *Aurora*, September 11, 1844.

lived in Georgetown near Mount Pleasant, severely beat him and his wife, and absconded with their fourteen-year-old son. Brown arrived in the village early the next morning while its inhabitants were still excited about the kidnapping. Upon hearing about what had happened, he visited the Wilkinsons' home. While he was there Wilkinson returned with the news that the kidnappers had eluded the group which had pursued them and had escaped with the boy across the Ohio River to Virginia. A Negro had recognized one of the kidnappers; but because it was illegal for a Negro to testify against a white person in the courts of Ohio, it would have been futile to attempt to prosecute the man. "What have [*sic*] the North to do with Slavery?" Brown asked pointedly in a letter he wrote from Mount Pleasant to Gay the day after the kidnapping, telling him about it.[11]

Again in western New York, Brown had a half-dozen lecture engagements in Rochester and the area immediately east of it for November 25–30.[12] Sometime in December, after one of his lecture tours, he returned to his home in Buffalo—but did not receive a cordial welcome from his spouse. He had been away from home most of the time since the middle of the preceding summer; and now that he was at home for a while, "I was treated with anything but kindness by Mrs. Brown," he wrote almost six years later—"a change of which I tried in vain to find out the cause." The Fates did not keep him long in suspense, for they had decreed that he must now begin his period of leisurely repentence for his hasty marriage—a period destined to last several years. Within the next few months he became convinced that it was the old story of a love triangle with himself at one angle, his beloved Betsey at another, and his quasi friend James Garrett at the third.

All of this and much more about the affair are related in an article entitled "To the Public," which Brown wrote from

11. *National Anti-Slavery Standard*, November 7, 1844, p. 90.

12. *Ibid.*, October 31, 1844, p. 87, November 7, 1844, p. 91, November 14, 1844, p. 95, November 21, 1844, p. 99.

London on June 1, 1850, for the *Liberator*.[13] Only Brown's version of the affair seems to have been preserved. Ingenuous and convincing as that seems, it can hardly be considered all of the truth from all of the relevant points of view, and a lengthy retelling of anything less than that would perhaps be not only uncharitable but also unfair to Mrs. Brown.

Domestic unhappiness notwithstanding, Brown kept busy with his antislavery work. The Western New York Anti-Slavery Society held its second annual meeting in Talman Hall in Rochester on February 5–7, 1845. Again the principal subjects for discussion were the Constitution and disunion, as they had been at a convention in Farmington early in January. In addition to participating in the discussions, at one of the evening sessions Brown surprised the audience, pleasantly, one hopes, by singing a song. Finally, on the last day of the meeting, "the great Dissolution resolution was passed with scarcely an opposing vote."[14]

Before the news of the annual meeting was very widely circulated, E. W. Capron, general agent of the society, announced that Brown and other lecturers would hold four two-day conventions in Syracuse and towns in the vicinity of Cayuga Lake between February 25 and March 20.[15] If Brown participated in all of these conventions, he returned home immediately after the last one; for before the end of March, he went from Buffalo to Genesee County on a lecture trip which he expected to last ten days. After six days, however, illness made it necessary for him to return home, where he arrived at an embarrassing moment; for it was eleven o'clock at night, and James Garrett was there. Because his "infatuated attachment" to his wife possessed him with a will to believe only the best about her, Brown let this incident involving Garrett pass without receiving a convincing explanation from anybody, but with the

13. *Liberator*, July 12, 1850, p. 111.

14. *National Anti-Slavery Standard*, January 30, 1845, p. 138, March 6, 1845, p. 158.

15. *Ibid.*, February 20, 1845, p. 151.

understanding that Garrett would visit the Browns' home no more.

A few weeks later, perhaps not altogether innocent of an inclination to make a virtue of understandable jealousy, Brown returned home one night from another trip and entered his house through the back door. Again he found Garrett there, "and under circumstances of a still more revolting character than on a former occasion." He was now convinced "beyond the shadow of a doubt, that my worst apprehensions were too true."

At first Brown thought somewhat impulsively of exposing the whole affair. He refrained from doing so, however, because of his concern for his two little daughters and because of his love not only for them but also for Mrs. Brown. Instead he reverted to a decision he had previously made and abandoned. Sometime during the preceding winter he had decided to move to Farmington and had arranged to occupy a house there; but having found that Mrs. Brown was strongly opposed to moving, he had given up the idea of doing so. Now, on the contrary, Mrs. Brown was in favor of their moving. Accordingly, early in the summer, after some confusion resulting from the crossing of purposes by the husband and the wife, the Browns moved to Farmington.[16]

Brown's original reason for wanting to move to Farmington was that it was then the center of the antislavery activities in western and central New York—a reason which probably did not matter very much to Mrs. Brown. The reason on which he and she now agreed was that removal as far from Buffalo as Farmington—Brown said that it was more than a hundred miles —would get them a considerable distance from an environment that had become embarrassing to them. There was still another reason why Brown was pleased to move to Farmington. In Buffalo "colored children were not permitted to be educated with the whites;" and Brown would not send his children to the Jim

16. William Wells Brown, "To the Public," *Liberator*, July 12, 1850, p. 111.

Crow school, because to do so, he thought, "would have been, to some extent, giving sanction to the proscriptive prejudice."[17] But in Farmington there were no racially segregated schools. As Brown saw matters, therefore, educational opportunities for his children were better in that village than they were in the separate and unequal schools then provided for Negroes in Buffalo.

17. Josephine Brown to Samuel May, Jr., April 27, 1854, reprinted in *Liberator*, May 26, 1854, p. 82.

VII

Between Proslavery Preachers and Political Abolitionists

SETTLING HIS FAMILY IN A NEW HOME IN A NEW ENVIRONMENT doubtless brought Brown some new problems, but none serious enough to interfere very long with his antislavery work. In the middle of the summer he went on a lecture tour in Livingston County. Because of what he described as the proslavery influence of the clergy in Livonia Centre, in the northeastern section of the county, abolitionists had been unable to get a hearing in that town; nor did he himself fare any better there than his predecessors had fared. One of the preachers there even refused to read in his church announcements of antislavery meetings. While Brown was lecturing in a village "a short distance from Livonia Centre," a mob made him a target for eggs, sticks, and stones, "one of which did me considerable injury," he said in a letter which he wrote soon afterwards to the *National Anti-Slavery Standard* telling about his tour.[1]

1. *National Anti-Slavery Standard,* September 18, 1845, p. 62.

Brown's experience in Livingston County reconfirmed his belief that one of the strongest proslavery influences in the North was that of the clergy—a belief which he shared with many other Garrisonian abolitionists. In the letter just referred to, he said that many clergymen were opposed to free discussion because they were afraid of it, and that instead of accepting the abolitionists' invitations to open debates, they contented themselves with assailing the abolitionists behind their backs. There were in western New York, he observed, preachers who not only opposed abolitionists but also preached avowedly proslavery sermons. Typical of these was, in his opinion, the Reverend Dr. Thomas Lounsbury, who "preached seven sermons, within the past year, against abolitionism, and endeavored to prove American Slavery to be right, and sanctioned by the Bible. . . . These pro-slavery clergy," Brown summarized, "do nothing but build up a public sentiment against the oppressed."

By the summer of 1845 Brown was generally known as a leader among Negroes in western New York. As such he became a member of a committee which planned a free suffrage convention of Negroes to be held in Geneva on October 8. The purpose of the convention was "to adopt measures to secure for them [Negroes] the elective franchise." At the time a Negro could not vote in New York unless, in addition to possessing all of the qualifications required of white citizens, he owned property worth at least $250. On behalf of the committee, Brown wrote on September 12 to the Honorable William H. Seward, inviting him to attend and address the convention, because Seward's liberal views and actions, Brown assured him, "have secured for you a home in the heart of every colored American."

In his reply Seward explained that because of "absorbing professional engagements" he could not "promise myself the pleasure of accepting your invitation." He repeated, nevertheless, his opinion that Negroes in the North should have the right to vote on equal terms with other citizens. Then following the lead which less trustworthy "friends of Negroes" had taken before his time and which some had subsequently followed, he tried to soften his declination of the invitation by complimenting Negroes in general for their loyalty—in this instance for their loyalty to the North. More specifically he expressed his hope "for the restoration of your right of suffrage" and for the universal abolition of slavery.

The convention was held as planned, but it did not achieve the removal of the restriction which applied exclusively to potential Negro voters.[2] Presumably it did not occur to Brown that there was anything anomalous about his participating in a suffrage convention when, because of his Garrisonian convictions, he could not take an oath to support the Constitution and consequently could not have qualified as a voter even if he had satisfied all other requirements.

On December 30–31 the Western New York Anti-Slavery Society held its third anniversary meeting in Monroe Hall in Rochester. Since there were no questions like those involving the Constitution and disunion, the meeting was relatively uneventful and brief. Brown's friend Joseph C. Hathaway was elected president, and Brown himself was elected general agent and corresponding secretary.[3]

Late in the spring of 1846 the New York State Liberty party held a two-day convention in Farmington. According to Brown, who was present as an interested observer, the convention was well attended. He recognized among the speakers five preachers whom he knew personally. He took their presence at and participation in the proceedings as evidence of an unholy alliance between the clergy and the exponents of political abolitionism, in which he had no faith. At one of the sessions the Reverend Mr. Peck of Rochester argued against the doctrine of natural, inalienable rights. He called the doctrine "a humbug," although he was cognizant that Thomas Jefferson had set it forth in the

2. *Ibid.*, October 30, 1845, pp. 85–86. This brief report of the convention includes the correspondence between Brown and Seward.

3. *Ibid.*, January 22, 1846, p. 134.

Declaration of Independence.[4] Brown was not favorably impressed by Peck's argument, but he remembered it; and when in 1853 he wrote *Clotel,* he portrayed Peck under his actual name as a prototype of the proslavery preacher and so-called Christian slaveholder.

In the summer of 1846 Gerrit Smith decided to give tracts of land of from forty to sixty acres each to three thousand Negroes in the state of New York. He was motivated not only by an interest in the economic welfare of Negroes but also by a desire to enable them to satisfy the property qualification for voting. Forthwith he appointed several committees to select three thousand eligible grantees, stipulating that no drunkard should be among them. The members of the committee for the western half of the state were the Reverend Samuel Ringgold Ward, the Reverend Jermain W. Loguen of Syracuse, and Gerrit Smith Duffin of Geneva.[5] All three of these men were active abolitionists and acquaintances of Brown's.

Among the lists of grantees in Smith's *Register of Distribution of Land Among Colored Men,* is one naming residents of Ontario County—the county in which Farmington is located—to whom grants were made. The Reverend William Thompson of Geneva, Austin Steward of Canandaigua, and Brown are listed near the bottom of page 73. On September 1, 1846, Smith deeded to Thompson Lot 57, Subdivision Number 4, northeast quarter, 32 acres. On November 1, 1847, he deeded to Steward Lot 24, southwest quarter, 40 acres in the Old Military Ward, Township Number 12. The grant to Brown was Lot 57, Subdivision Number 4, southeast quarter, 32 acres. Instead of a date, however, there is a notation opposite Brown's name saying that a duplicate deed had been given to him.

4. William Wells Brown to S. H. Gay, *National Anti-Slavery Standard,* June 25, 1846, p. 14.

5. Gerrit Smith, *Letter Book, 1843–1855,* Gerrit Smith Miller Collection; Octavius Brooks Frothingham, *Gerrit Smith: A Biography* (New York, 1878), pp. 102–07; Ralph Volney Harlow, *Gerrit Smith: Philanthropist and Reformer* (New York: Henry Holt and Co., 1939), pp. 242–46.

Since Brown's grant was, it appears, contiguous with Thompson's, one might have supposed that his original deed and Thompson's bore the same date; and in truth they did. The land which Smith gave to Thompson and Brown is in Florence Township in Oneida County, and in the register of deeds of that county there are recorded two deeds by which Smith conveyed land to Brown. Both of these deeds were dated at Peterboro, Madison County, New York, September 1, 1846, and both refer to the parcel of land specified after Brown's name in Smith's *Register.* One of these deeds was recorded on July 20, 1847, and the other on April 3, 1858. Presumably the latter was the duplicate referred to in Smith's *Register.*[6]

For Brown, Smith's generosity was not effective either economically or politically. Being busy with his antislavery work and having no time, therefore, for farming, Brown never actually took possession of the land. Moreover, within a year after the land was given to him, he left the state never to reestablish residence in it.

In July, 1846, Brown and E. D. Hudson went on a lecture tour of the western end of New York and remained there until September. While they were in Erie County, they saw in the *Albany Patriot* for August 19 an open letter from the Reverend C. C. Foote accusing them of acting inconsistently. They opposed political abolitionism in general and the Liberty party in particular, said Foote, yet they accepted the help of Liberty party men in arranging for meetings and also accepted the hospitality of such men while touring western New York.

In a reply in the *National Anti-Slavery Standard* for September 10, Brown denied that there was any inconsistency in his and Hudson's actions, inasmuch as both he and Hudson were known among Liberty party men, as among others, to be critics of the Constitution and advocates of "No Union with Slave-

6. Gerrit Smith, *Register of Distribution of Land Among Colored Men,* pp. 73–74, Gerrit Smith Miller Collection; Oneida County Register of Deeds, Utica, New York, Book 133, p. 5, and Book 209, p. 92.

holders." Assuming the offensive, he accused Foote of aiming not so much to warn Liberty party men against him and Hudson because of their alleged inconsistency as to prevent them from getting a hearing in western New York. He was glad to say, nevertheless, that if such was Foote's aim, it had been crowned only with failure. Meanwhile he turned the tables on Foote by reading and commenting on the letter in the *Albany Patriot* at the beginning of several meetings, thus using it as a sort of introduction and recommendation. He also bantered the preacher with the remark that "recommendations from clergymen were generally considered good." Finally and seriously, he took Foote's criticism as another instance of antiabolitionism on the part of a clergyman.[7]

Brown and Hudson filled about eight engagements in Orleans and Monroe Counties between September 14 and 21. Afterwards, between the first of October and the end of the year, Brown went alone on tours of Wyoming, Livingston, Wayne, Cayuga, Oswego, and Monroe Counties—tours on which he had engagements for about fifty meetings. He lectured in Warsaw, the county seat of Wyoming County, on Wednesday evening, October 21; and although the county court was in session that evening, he had what he considered "a good audience." On the following Friday evening, upon the invitation of Judge Skinner, who recessed court for the occasion, he lectured "to a very large audience" in the county courthouse. To Brown, the recessing of a county court in western New York so that a Negro abolitionist might address an assembly was evidence of the remarkable progress the antislavery cause was making in the area.[8]

Brown had engagements in Oswego County for almost every

7. *National Anti-Slavery Standard,* July 30, 1846, p. 35, August 6, 1846, pp. 37–38, August 13, 1846, p. 43, September 10, 1846, pp. 57–58, 59.

8. *Ibid.,* October 8, 1846, p. 75, October 26, 1846, p. 83; W. W. Brown to S. H. Gay, October 24, 1846, *ibid.,* November 12, 1846, p. 94; *ibid.,* December 3, 1846, p. 107.

evening from November 19 through December 7. Bad weather, however, and the consequent inconveniences of travel, plus the difficulties of getting places in which to hold meetings, brought many changes in his plans. The rumor that he advocated "no Government, no Church, no Sabbath, no politics, &c." had been so widely spread in the county, by Liberty party men, he thought, that at first he could get permission to lecture in only a few buildings of any kind. But thanks to Morris Kingsbury, a Garrisonian abolitionist who lived near Fulton in the southwestern part of the county, two or three churches in different villages were opened to him. After the people heard him once or twice, opposition to his holding meetings waned.[9]

On Saturday evening, November 21, having been granted and refused soon afterwards the use of the Methodist Episcopal church in Fulton, Brown held a meeting in "the session room" of the Baptist church there. He was sufficiently encouraged by this meeting to lecture in Fulton again on the following Sunday, Monday, and Wednesday evenings. By Monday the wardens of the Methodist Episcopal church must have had a change of heart, for the meeting of that evening was held in that church. According to Henry C. Hibbard, at that meeting, when several Liberty party men attempted to question the lecturer, "Mr. Brown did discharge at them a volley of wit, and sarcasm, and buffoonery, of a coarse kind, and they hid their heads, rabbit-like, being disgusted with the speaker." From Brown's own account of the meeting, it does not appear that all of those who were present "sat quietly until eleven o'clock, p. m.," as Kingsbury said they did. Brown said that because of his attack on the Constitution and his advocacy of disunion, the Liberty party men "came down upon me like an avalanche;" and that his lecture

9. *National Anti-Slavery Standard,* November 12, 1846, p. 95; Morris Kingsbury, "Letter from Western New York," *ibid.,* December 10, 1846, p. 110: William W. Brown to S. H. Gay, March 1, 1847, *ibid.,* March 4, 1847, p. 157.

was interrupted by Ira Bristol, a local leader of the Liberty party, "with loud talk, and crying out at the top of his voice, 'false, false, false.' "[10]

Soon after Brown began his tour of Oswego County, Martin Mitchel, general agent of the New York State Anti-Slavery Society, came to lecture there. The society which Mitchel represented had never officially accepted Garrison's doctrine of disunion, nor was it opposed to political abolitionism. It was, therefore, acceptable to Liberty party men, as the Western New York Anti-Slavery Society was not. After Mitchel had been in the county only a short time, it was alleged by those who were pro-Brown, or at least anti–Liberty party, that local leaders of this party had brought Mitchel into the county to follow Brown and try to counteract his influence. Liberty party men straightway denied the allegation. In Brown's opinion, however, they could not deny that they had brought to their rescue a more powerful opponent for him in the person of Asa S. Wing, a shrewd lawyer who was well known in the area.

Brown lectured on Sunday evening, November 29, in a schoolhouse in Colosse, about fifteen miles northeast of Fulton. In spite of bad roads and stormy weather, the schoolhouse was full. Again he argued against the Constitution and in favor of disunion. He was answered by Wing and Levi Downing, a local lawyer, but he succeeded in safeguarding his argument, as he did the next evening in a speech in Mexicoville, about five miles northwest of Colosse.

The next day Brown and Wing debated from two o'clock in the afternoon "until about nine o'clock in the evening" concerning the nature of the Constitution. In the opinion of a local

10. Henry C. Hibbard, letter, December 19, 1846, *National Anti-Slavery Standard*, December 31, 1846, p. 122: William W. Brown to S. H. Gay, March 1, 1847, *National Anti-Slavery Standard*, March 4, 1847, p. 157. For favorable comments on Brown's visit to Fulton in addition to those in Kingsbury's previously cited letter, see "Letter from Oswego County," by "A Subscriber," *ibid.*, January 7, 1847, p. 126. For unfavorable comments in addition to those by Hibbard, see *ibid.*, February 18, 1847, pp. 149.

correspondent for the *National Anti-Slavery Standard*, the discussion "was very ably and politely handled by both parties. It was admitted by all that Brown did himself great credit, and, I thought, had altogether the best of the argument." A "rough man" who had heard the discussion remarked that there was no wonder that Brown had defeated Wing in the argument, "for he had the most talented blood in his veins that Kentucky could produce."[11]

The annual meeting of the Western New York Anti-Slavery Society was held in the courthouse in Rochester on December 28–31. At the session of the second evening, Brown thrust himself in the limelight by offering a resolution urging Negroes "to assert their right to suffrage" and advising them to fight against the United States if they were called upon for military service of any kind. The latter half of the resolution was doubtless inspired by the fact that the Mexican War was then going on, and the United States needed soldiers to fight in it. Because of its belligerency the resolution was generally opposed, and Brown finally withdrew it.

It was said in the report of the executive committee that Brown had been officially employed as a lecturing agent for the society for eight months of the year then closing, and that during that time he had held 167 meetings "usually with good, and often large and interested audiences." His salary, it was also explained in the report, had been paid out of contributions and donations collected by himself and others and supplemented out of the proceeds from the Ladies' Anti-Slavery Fair which had been recently held in Rochester.[12]

About the middle of January, 1847, Brown went to Steuben County where he spent about a week holding meetings in Bath, Corning, and other towns. Returning northward he went to Penn Yan in Yates County, where he held meetings on January

11. Letter dated at Colosse, "December 3" and signed "A. W.," *National Anti-Slavery Standard*, December 17, 1846, p. 114.

12. *National Anti-Slavery Standard*, January 14, 1847, p. 130.

23 and 24. This town and especially its Congregational church had an antislavery reputation which Brown's experience there led him to believe that neither deserved. Having refused to allow Brown to hold an antislavery meeting in the church, the minister announced after one of the services on Sunday, the twenty-fourth, that on the following Monday evening the church would hold its "monthly concert to pray for the slave!" Henry Bradley, who had recently been the Liberty party's candidate for governor of New York, and who was to be the leading abolitionist in the town, was, Brown said, a member of this church. Brown had met Bradley at a convention in Farmington a year earlier and had extended some courtesies to him. "But when I met him in his own village, and in his own church," Brown observed, "he passed me like the priest and Levite of old."[13]

On February 3 Brown and Charles Lenox Remond lectured in Cazenovia, about twenty miles southeast of Syracuse. In his speech Brown asserted that "some of our Liberty Party friends" were actively supporting the Mexican War and were thereby fighting "the battles of Slavery." He also asserted that some Liberty party newspapers were "advocating the impious doctrine, 'My country right or wrong.' " Next, with Hathaway and Remond he went to Westfield in Herkimer County to participate in an antislavery fair on February 10 and 11. This was his first trip so far east to lecture.

En route westward again Brown attended an antislavery convention in Cazenovia on February 16–18. At a session on the first day he read a statement which A. B. Murch, a local citizen, had published in the *Liberty Press* of Utica for February 11. Murch's statement demanded that Brown "corroborate, by facts" his assertions of February 3 concerning Liberty party members and newspapers, or be branded "a calumniator of the slave's friends—an unmitigated liar." In proof of his assertions, Brown

13. *Ibid.*, December 31, 1846, p. 123, January 21, 1847, p. 135; William W. Brown to S. H. Gay, February 1, 1847, *ibid.*, February 11, 1847, p. 146.

not only cited a statement which William Goodell, one of the founders of the Liberty party, had made six months earlier but also quoted passages from six Liberty party newspapers showing their prowar attitude. He also said that Colonel Cilley, a senator from New Hampshire whom he identified as a member of the Liberty party, was known to be in favor of the war. Murch, who was present, as he had been on February 3, now "came forward in great confusion of face, and said he was ignorant of the position of such papers, and the conduct of certain Liberty Party men." Upon a motion by Hudson a resolution concluding that Brown had proved his assertions "was adopted almost unanimously."[14]

Soon afterwards, with a desire to be fair, Murch wrote a retraction of his statement concerning Brown and sent it to the *Liberty Press.* The editor of the newspaper acknowledged receipt of Murch's retraction but refused to publish it. Instead he explained in a comment in the newspaper that "our columns are not open to the dissemination of the slanders of the Garrisonian lecturers, and the waste of paper for their refutation. Some lies," he continued, "are so foolish and the iniquity of the motives for relating them so obvious, that we do not deem an attempted refutation worth the ink and paper." The editor did not make clear, withal, just whom he considered the liar or whose refutation he deemed worthless. In a letter dated March 24, Murch reprehended the editor for refusing to publish his retraction and for thus acting more in the interest of party than of truth.[15] The editor did not take the trouble to explain whether he deemed Murch's criticism of him beneath or above refutation. He simply ignored it.

14. *National Anti-Slavery Standard,* March 4, 1847, p. 158, March 11, 1847, p. 161. Joseph Cilley, a Democrat, represented New Hampshire in the United States Senate from June 13, 1846, to March 3, 1847. (*Biographical Directory of the American Congress, 1774–1961* [Washington, 1961], p. 693.)

15. *National Anti-Slavery Standard,* March 11, 1847, p. 163, and April 8, 1847, p. 178.

Brown attended an antislavery fair in Waterloo in Seneca County on February 25 and 26. This proved to be the last meeting for him in western New York for seven years. Early in March he went eastward again, and from the middle of that month until the first week in May, he and Hudson lectured in eastern New York under the auspices of the American Anti-Slavery Society. The success of the lecturers during this period, especially in Columbia and Dutchess Counties, was not uniformly remarkable. As Brown remembered twelve years later, on many occasions he and Hudson "had to speak to empty benches, and felt ourselves fortunate if we were allowed to do this unmolested."[16]

The American Anti-Slavery Society held its thirteenth annual meeting in New York City on May 11–13, a few days after Brown and Hudson's lecture tour of eastern New York was scheduled to end. Brown attended this meeting—probably the first one he attended since the meeting of May, 1844, at which Garrison's doctrine of disunion had been officially approved. At the session of the first afternoon, he was appointed a member of the business committee, whose function was to determine the agenda for the remainder of the meeting. Among the other ten members of this committee were Wendell Phillips, J. Elizabeth Jones (one of the editors of the *Anti-Slavery Bugle*), Charles Lenox Remond, Oliver Johnson, Samuel May, Jr., Edmund Quincy, and Robert Purvis.[17] Most of these persons were much more widely known in antislavery circles than Brown was; consequently he must have felt honored to be appointed with them to membership on such an important committee. It was an indication that he had achieved some prominence as an abolitionist. From this time on, whenever he was present at an antislavery convention, he was usually made a member of the business committee or the committee on finance.

16. *Ibid.*, February 18, 1847, p. 151, March 25, 1847, pp. 169–70, April 22, 1847, p. 187; William W. Brown, to William Lloyd Garrison, September 10, 1859, *Liberator*, September 23, 1859, p. 151.

17. *National Anti-Slavery Standard*, May 20, 1847, p. 202.

It was most probably at this meeting that arrangements were completed for Brown, Hathaway, and Remond to go to New England within the next three weeks to lecture for a while under the auspices of the Massachusetts Anti-Slavery Society.[18] It might also have been that Brown was prompted by these arrangements to consider moving to Boston, the capital of abolitionism. Whether this conjecture is correct or not, he was not long without a good reason for leaving western New York.

If Brown had not already learned by either study or personal experience that it is impossible to run away from trouble, especially trouble resulting from moral conflicts, he should have learned this fact soon after he moved his family to Farmington. According to his account of his marital difficulties—an account which is none too clear at this point—after their removal to Farmington, Mrs. Brown could keep neither her mind nor her body out of Buffalo very long, even though one of her trips there had proved most embarrassing to her as well as to him. He gave no information about what caused their embarrassment, perhaps because he would have found it exceedingly embarrassing to do so.

From Mrs. Brown's point of view, of course, there were other things to be considered. With her husband away from home most of the time, and with the constant care of two little daughters, she doubtless found life in Farmington uneventful if not dull. Brown left home early in March on his trip to the eastern part of the state, and it was then May. During the unvaried days and long nights, she had had time to think as well as to be lonely, and at last she had made a decision. While Brown was at the meeting of the American Anti-Slavery Society in New York City, he received a letter from Mrs. Brown telling him that if he did not come and get their two children, she would leave them with some neighbors; for she was going away. Brown hurried to Farmington.

18. Massachusetts Anti-Slavery Society, *Sixteenth Annual Report* (Boston, 1848), p. 45.

Chapter Seven

After several conversations in their home, the Browns mutually agreed to separate, with Brown's taking the custody of the children. Mrs. Brown forthwith went back to Buffalo. What now was Brown to do? For him life had become almost as embarrassing in Farmington as it had become in Buffalo two years earlier.

The 1840's were still a time, it should be noted, when the voluntary separation of husbands and wives was not taken as casually as chain marriages and divorces are taken nowadays. Brown probably would have found it difficult, therefore, to remain at ease in Farmington even if he had been able to make satisfactory arrangements there for the care of his children. Furthermore, the conflicting stories which were sure to be circulated about his domestic trouble would have had a derogatory effect upon his work as an antislavery agent in western New York, for those stories would have been seized upon by anti-abolitionists as a means of damning the cause the man represented by damning the man himself. Clearly it was wise for him to go somewhere else while he had an opportunity to do so—where his domestic trouble would not be a common subject for gossip. There was no need to indulge in long deliberation, which, as he doubtless knew, often results in unnecessary delay. Within four days after the separation, Brown set out with his two little daughters for Boston. With the exception of a residence of five years in Great Britain, he was destined to make his home in that city or its environs for the rest of his life.

"This Eloquent Advocate of Liberty"

UPON HIS ARRIVAL IN BOSTON, BROWN PROBABLY MADE HIS home somewhere in the West End, the section northwest of Beacon Hill, for that was where the vast majority of Negroes in Boston were then living. As late as the first half of 1849, he was living at 106 Cedar Street in that section.[1]

Brown was first heard as a speaker in Boston at the New England Anti-Slavery Convention which was held in Marlborough Chapel from Tuesday through Thursday, May 25–27. During this three-days meeting he spoke at length four times, and his speeches were reported in some detail by Thomas Gill for the *Boston Morning Post*.[2] At the opening session Tuesday morning, Brown admitted that he was a fugitive slave and implied that slavery was a national institution, inasmuch as he

1. *The Boston Directory for 1849–1850*, p. 85.
2. Quoted in *Liberator*, June 4, 1847, p. 91.

could be legally seized as a fugitive slave in Massachusetts or any other free state as well as in any of the slave states.

At the session Wednesday morning, Brown argued, with impeccable logic, that the people of Great Britain and continental Europe had as much right to organize societies to promote the abolition of slavery in the United States as the people of the United States had to organize societies for the promotion of democracy in Greece, Poland, and Ireland, as some Americans were then doing. He enlivened his argument with some satirical comments on Boston's being called the cradle of liberty and on "President Polk's war" and ended with "a string of puns upon the name of the President." At the evening session of the same day, he indicated that he was a confirmed Garrisonian by denouncing the Constitution and proslavery churches and by advocating disunion. He brought forth "a shower of hisses" with the remark that no Northerner could travel safely in the South unless he fawned upon slaveholders, as he said Daniel Webster, who was then in South Carolina, was doing. By an opportune reference to the Boston Tea Party, he immediately recaptivated his audience "and came off with a round of applause."

Speaking Thursday afternoon on slavery as a general subject, Brown referred to its bad influence on the free states. He attributed to the existence of slavery in Kentucky, for example, the law in Ohio that prohibited Negroes from testifying in lawsuits involving white people. From the slaveholder's point of view, he asserted, equal rights for Negroes in the free states would have had an undesirable effect upon the slave states. Brown thus introduced himself to Boston as a lecturer, mingling wry humor, taunts, logic, and flippancy with a remarkable insight into the public questions of the time. The introduction was reasonably indicative of the kind of man he was.

With Joseph C. Hathaway and Parker Pillsbury, Brown attended the fourteenth annual meeting of the New Hampshire Anti-Slavery Society in Concord on June 3 and 4. The House of Representatives permitted the abolitionists to hold their first evening session in its chamber, Pillsbury informed Garrison in a letter of June 6, and "a large number of the most distinguished of the members" were present. On June 12 and 13 the Bristol County Anti-Slavery Society held its quarterly meeting in Liberty Hall in New Bedford. The several sessions were addressed by Brown, Hathaway, Remond, and Frederick Douglass. After a residence of two years in Great Britain, Douglass had been back in America not quite two months. Two days after the meeting, Deborah Weston, who was present, gave her impressions of some of the speakers. "Remond," she said, "was of course rather sulky at times but no more than he always is. Douglass spoke finely & appeared well. . . . Brown acquitted himself admirably, we are very much pleased with him. If he does as well everywhere as he did here, he is a great gain to the cause."[3]

Within the next three days the four speakers held a meeting in Fall River; and Brown, Hathaway, and Remond held one in Abington. After the latter meeting Brown was surprised to find himself involved in some confusion with Remond about the collection which had been taken, and which amounted to twenty-four dollars. The sponsors of the meeting decided to divide this money equally among the three lecturers. Remond thought it outrageous that any of the collection should be given to Brown, because the Massachusetts Anti-Slavery Society was paying him as an agent. Brown explained that he would merely receive the money as an agent of the society and would account for it to the society. Still displeased, "Remond then told Brown that if he touched that money he did it *at the price of his friendship.* And he refused to take his $8 if they persisted in giving any to Brown. They told him that he might take it, or leave it alone." By way of compromise Brown suggested that the sponsors of the meeting send the money apportioned to him directly to the treasurer of the Massachusetts Anti-Slavery Society.[4]

3. *Liberator,* June 11, 1847, p. 95, July 2, 1847, p. 105; Deborah Weston to Lucia Weston, June 15, 1847, Anti-Slavery—Weston Papers.

4. *Fall River Weekly News,* June 17, 1847, quoted in *Liberator,* June 25, 1847, p. 101; Edmund Quincy to Caroline Weston, July 2, 1847, Anti-Slavery—Weston Papers.

On June 17 and 18, Brown, Hathaway, and Remond shared the same platform at the annual meeting of the Essex County Anti-Slavery Society in Lyceum Hall in Salem, Remond's home town. An unknown friend and correspondent of the *Liberator* was especially impressed by Hathaway's "manly, open and expressive face" as well as by "his earnest and convincing manner of speaking." Said the same correspondent,

> W. W. Brown spoke with his usual power and effect. . . . There is an expression of fine and true humanity in the face of friend Brown, that is most pleasant to behold, and which will commend him to the love of all good men, wherever he may go.[5]

By the middle of June, Brown had completed and submitted to Edmund Quincy for criticism the manuscript of his *Narrative of William W. Brown, a Fugitive Slave*. Having repeated the story of his life many times in his lectures, he had probably conceived the idea of writing his autobiography before he left western New York. He might have been stimulated to do so by the publication of the *Narrative of the Life of Frederick Douglass, an American Slave* in May, 1845; and most probably he had begun writing before his removal to Boston. During the month he had been in New England before he submitted his manuscript to Quincy, his traveling and lecturing had left him but little time for writing—hardly more than enough for him to rewrite parts of his manuscript, as he seems to have done "seated here in sight of Bunker Hill Monument."[6] He was doubtless encouraged to complete his manuscript by the fact that it was much easier for him to get it published in Boston than it would have been for him to get it published in western New York.

After keeping Brown's manuscript unnoticed for "a fortnight," as he confessed in his letter of July 2 to Caroline Weston, Quincy began reading it on the morning of July 1. "I thought

5. *Liberator,* June 25, 1847, p. 107 [103].
6. *Narrative,* p. 105.

I would glance over a few pages," he explained, "to see what it was like. But it was so good that I could not lay it down until dinner-time." Quincy pronounced the *Narrative* "a terrible picture of Slavery, told with great simplicity." Observing that Brown had had much more extensive experience in slavery than Douglass had had, he compared Brown's *Narrative* with Douglass's and found it "a much more striking story than Douglass's & as well told." Quincy also noted, quite correctly, that in Brown's *Narrative* there was "no attempt at fine writing, but only a minute account of scenes & things he saw & suffered, told with a good deal of skill & great propriety & delicacy."

Quincy had scarcely finished reading the manuscript when Brown called to talk with him about it. He was as favorably impressed with the author himself as he had been with the author's work, as was evidenced by the following passage from his letter referred to above:

> He [Brown] is an extraordinary fellow. I do not know that his intellectual power is equal to that of Douglass, but he is of a much higher cast of character. There seems to be no meanness, no littleness, no envy or suspiciousness about him. His mind seems to be singularly healthy & he never seems [to] (& he says he never does) think uncomfortably about his being a black man. He understands everything about the Cause . . . & has no twaddle about him. He is the most valuable man we have got since Douglass—& in many respects he is more valuable than he.

With regard to a title for the work, said Quincy in the same letter, Brown "wished to have something different from Douglass's, & yet to be simple & without affectation." The title finally selected seems to have been Quincy's choice as much as Brown's. Meanwhile, Quincy suggested "one or two alterations" in the text itself and corrected "a few errors, which appeared to be merely clerical ones, committed in the hurry of composition, under unfavorable circumstances." Brown wrote the dedication to Wells Brown of Ohio, Quincy wrote a complimentary letter to the author, in which he said that some of Brown's descriptions of scenes were "not unworthy of De Foe himself," and Hathaway wrote the preface. With Quincy's few corrections and these additions, the text was sent to press just as Brown had written it.

Late in July the *Narrative* was published in a thin duodecimo volume of 110 pages, with the imprint of the Boston Anti-Slavery Office. Its only illustration is the frontispiece, which, said a notice in the *Liberator*, "is an engraved likeness of the author, which is very accurate." This likeness, which was made from a daguerreotype, is the earliest known picture of Brown.[7]

Brown's *Narrative* immediately became a best-seller in antislavery literature. Three thousand copies of it were sold "in less than six months from the time of its publication," and a second edition was demanded.[8] The work became popular enough to go through four editions totaling ten thousand copies in two years. It was widely read, no doubt, because it was a good example of what Brown intended it to be, namely, a forceful argument by means of narration. It was the same kind of argument that his first antislavery speeches had been, but it presented many more details than he could have given in any one speech, even in an age when two-hour speeches were not unusual; and there was indeed the possibility that it might convince as well as reach many who could not be reached from the antislavery platform. It presented the facts so that any reader might ponder them at leisure and unemotionally—even verify some of them—and be led by his intelligence and his conscience to work for the immediate abolition of slavery. In recounting his varied experiences

7. *Liberator*, July 30, 1847, p. 122. Favorable comments on the volume appeared in the following newspapers: *New Bedford Bulletin*, quoted in *Liberator*, September 3, 1847, p. 141; *Anti-Slavery Bugle*, September 17, 1847, p. 3; *Christian Citizen*, *Christian World*, and *Herkimer Freeman*, quoted in *Liberator*, October 1, 1847, p. 158; *Boston Daily Whig*, quoted in *Liberator*, November 26, 1847, p. 189.

8. *Narrative*, 2d ed. (Boston, 1848), p. iv; *Liberator*, February 11, 1848, p. 22.

as a slave, Brown graphically portrayed slavery in ever so many of its phases, showing all of them to be ugly and incidentally destroying all doubts that he was a fugitive slave.

After filling engagements in Worcester County, Brown lectured in Waltham on July 5. The next day a "highly intelligent and estimable lady" of West Newton, who was "far advanced in the journey of life," and who had seen him only twice and had never spoken to him, was impelled to write to him to "give vent to the overwhelming tide of thought and feeling" that swelled within her when she heard him speak. On the same day Mrs. F. H. Drake of Leominster wrote similarly about him to Garrison. She had "repeatedly heard him in public, and seen him in private circles" and had found him "always the same—calm, gentle, and convincing. From all that I can learn of him abroad," she continued, "he sustains a high moral character, wherever he is known; and wherever he speaks, he gains the love and respect of his hearers. I can say with my whole heart, thank God for so noble a specimen of humanity."[9]

Brown had never had recorded the deed by which Gerrit Smith had given him a parcel of land in Oneida County, New York, almost a year earlier. For some reason he now became sufficiently concerned to make a trip to Utica to attend to this legal detail. There on July 20 he had his deed recorded in the office of the clerk of Oneida County.[10]

Within the next few days, Brown returned to Massachusetts to continue his lecturing. On August 30 he held a meeting in Upton in Worcester County. Because this was his first visit to this village and he was "so little known in this section,'" and because it was early in the week, it was surprising to a correspondent for the *Liberator* who signed himself "A Hearer" that the hall in which he spoke "was filled at an early hour with

9. *Liberator,* June 11, 1847, p. 94; unknown woman to Brown, July 6, 1847, *ibid.*, July 30, 1847, p. 122; *ibid.*, July 16, 1847, p. 115.

10. Oneida County Register of Deeds, Utica, New York, Book 133, p. 5.

a quiet, attentive audience." In the opinion of this correspondent, the lecture by "this eloquent advocate of liberty" was "a thrilling performance," with which "he held the large audience in almost breathless silence for nearly two hours."[11]

Brown interrupted his lecturing long enough to attend a national convention of colored people which was held in Troy, New York, on October 6–9. In addition to serving on committees, he participated frequently in the discussions to which the several sessions of the convention were devoted. At one of these sessions it was recommended that a national Negro press be established. With Douglass and others, Brown opposed the recommendation. A national press established by Negroes should be supported by Negroes, he argued, and he feared that Negroes could not support it. After much discussion, which was continued in the next two sessions, the recommendation was approved by a vote of 27–9. At another session it was recommended that "Colored Colleges" be established. Henry Highland Garnet favored the establishment of "Colored Academies" but not "Colored Colleges," because there already existed colleges which admitted Negroes. The report of the committee on education, apparently including the proposal concerning the establishment of "Colored Colleges," was adopted by a vote of 26–17. Brown, Douglass, and William C. Nell were among those who voted "nay."

During a still later session, the report of the committee on abolition precipitated a brief exchange of opinions between Garnet and Brown. Garnet contended that political action as well as moral suasion was necessary for the termination of American slavery—a point of view which was eventually substantiated. Without diametrically opposing Garnet's argument, as a Garrisonian might have been expected to do, Brown replied

11. *Liberator,* August 6, 1847, p. 127, August 20, 1847, p. 135, August 27, 1847, p. 139; William W. Brown to Samuel May, Jr., August 9, 1847, *ibid.,* September 3, 1847, p. 143; Letter signed "A Hearer," September 4, 1847, *ibid.,* September 17, 1847, p. 151; *ibid.,* October 8, 1847, p. 162

that "Moral Suasion was needed in order to convince and convert the white people here in favor of abolishing Slavery." In spite of the comparatively large votes favoring the establishment of a national Negro press and "Colored Colleges," the convention was adjourned with no prospects of translating either of these ideas into realities.[12]

En route from Troy back to eastern Massachusetts, Brown stopped and lectured in Springfield and also in several villages in the center of the state. On October 19, while in West Brookfield, he attended the annual meeting of the Brookfield Association of Orthodox Ministers. After one Reverend Mr. Butler made a speech stressing the need of the American Bible Society for funds, Brown asked the chairman of the meeting whether the society had ever tried to send Bibles to the slaves in the South. The chairman referred Brown's question to Mr. Butler, who, Brown thought, did not answer it because of either ignorance of the society or moral cowardice. Brown was aware, of course, that it would have been a travesty on Christianity to distribute Bibles among the slaves, the vast majority of whom could not read, and leave them in slavery; for he considered the Bible "peculiarly the companion of liberty," as Douglass later said it was. The aim of Brown's question, therefore, was to emphasize the fact that the American Bible Society could not honestly propagate Christianity unless it also advocated the abolition of slavery. And this it had refused, or at least had failed, to do.[13]

Beginning on October 17, the Female Anti-Slavery Society of Salem sponsored a series of six Sunday-evening lectures in Lyceum Hall in their city. The three most widely-known persons the ladies invited to lecture were Quincy, Brown, and Gar-

12. *Proceedings of the National Convention of Colored People, and Their Friends, Held in Troy, N. Y., on the 6th, 7th, 8th, and 9th of October, 1847* (Troy, New York, 1847).

13. *Liberator*, November 5, 1847, p. 179; "Letter from W. W. Brown," October 20, 1847, *ibid.*, November 12, 1847, p. 182; Frederick Douglass, "Bibles for the Slaves," in *The Liberty Bell* (by "The Friends of Freedom"), 15 vols. (Boston, 1848), p. 125.

rison. Brown delivered his lecture, the fifth in the series, on November 14. Using notes rather than a manuscript, he spoke for about an hour. In his speech he avoided the rhetorical flourishes that so frequently characterized contemporary oratory; on the contrary he achieved a simple, dignified, and challenging style which showed the influence of Garrison and Phillips.

Brown's subject for the occasion was "Slavery as it is, and its influence upon the morals and the character of the American people." Most of what he said on this subject had been said before by himself as well as by others, but it was important enough to justify his effective repetition of it. He characterized slavery as the "murder of the soul" of the enslaved. He endeavored to illustrate its evil effects upon slaveholders by citing instances of what he considered a general decadence of morality and religion in the South. With grim humor he ridiculed the American Tract Society, a Northern organization, for publishing a prize tract "against the sin of dancing" and deliberately ignoring the three million slaves "dancing every day at the end of the master's cowhide." He was appalled, he admitted, by the ease of conscience with which Northern businessmen profited from slavery and yet denied that the North had anything to do with it. He observed that the inconsistency between Americans' "profession of liberty, and their practice in opposition to their profession" made the American people a nation of hypocrites both in the light of their own history and in the sight of the Old World. In spite of discouragements, however, he was convinced, he said, that the antislavery crusade started by Garrison would eventually abolish slavery; and he appealed to all who were present to join in that crusade.

The lecture was "phonographically" reported by Henry M. Parkhurst of Boston and was published in that city in December in a small pamphlet of twenty-two pages with the imprint of the Massachusetts Anti-Slavery Society. The pamphlet is entitled *A Lecture Delivered Before the Female Anti-Slavery Society of*

Salem, at Lyceum Hall, Nov. 14, 1847. This seems to have been the first of Brown's speeches to be published in full.[14]

Although Brown was being generally acclaimed as an antislavery lecturer, some of his speeches evoked conflicting opinions, as did two he delivered in Lawrence on December 11 and 12. Not convinced beyond all doubt that he was a fugitive slave, the *Lawrence Messenger* admitted that he had shown himself to be "a man of undoubted ability and talent," and that he had succeeded "right well in riveting the attention of a large audience" for almost three hours with his speech of the twelfth. To this newspaper it seemed doubtful, nevertheless, that "such tirades against all mankind in general, and the church in particular, as he indulged in" would help the antislavery cause very much. On the contrary, the *Lawrence Courier* said that although the remarks of "this talented American slave" might have been "rather spicy for the tender ears of those who despise a man on account of the color of his skin," they had not been as severe "as ought to have been expected from one who has himself *felt* the scourge of involuntary servitude."[15]

Sometime before the end of the year, Brown wrote a brief essay entitled "The American Slave-Trade," noting especially its enormity and cruelties. He based his essay on his own experience and observations as a slave and on his subsequent reading of newspapers and antislavery tracts, but he did not treat its subject either extensively or thoroughly. Nevertheless the essay impressed Mrs. Maria Weston Chapman, the editor of *The Liberty Bell,* favorably enough for her to include it in the volume of that annual for 1848.

Brown's routine of antislavery meetings was briefly varied by his participation in a meeting of colored citizens in the Belk-

14. *Liberator,* October 22, 1847, p. 171, December 31, 1847, p. 211.

15. *Newburyport Christian Herald,* quoted in *National Anti-Slavery Standard,* December 9, 1847, p. 109. A correspondent's favorable comment on a recent lecture of Brown's in Lexington and the comments of the two Lawrence newspapers were quoted in *Liberator,* December 31, 1847, p. 211.

nap Street Church in Boston on the evening of January 24, 1848. The purpose of the meeting was to consider "the necessity of forming a political or any kind of association among us, for the purpose of acting with or against any of the anti-slavery bodies or societies now in existence." After some discussion, in which the opposition was led by Brown and Robert Morris, a lawyer, the assembly decided against forming any organization of the kind proposed.[16]

Two days later, on Wednesday morning, the twenty-sixth, the Massachusetts Anti-Slavery Society began its sixteenth annual meeting in the Melodeon in Boston and continued it through the next day. At the session Wednesday afternoon, Brown came forward by request, he said, to comment on a letter which Quincy had recently received from Enoch Price. In this letter, which was dated at Saint Louis, January 10, Price acknowledged receipt of a copy of Brown's *Narrative;* and without being specific, he asserted that some of what the book said was false but admitted that some of it was true. Saying also that he no longer wanted Brown for a slave, he offered to sell the fugitive either to himself or to the Massachusetts Anti-Slavery Society for $325—exactly half of what, according to his letter, he had paid for Brown. Finally he said that if his offer was satisfactory to Brown or the society, he would be glad to negotiate the sale through his agent in Boston—an agent whom he did not identify.

Brown said that he had now for the first time seen Price's letter. He admitted that he had long felt that in going around in Massachusetts as he had been doing, he was in danger of being seized and carried back into slavery. He was especially sensible of this danger, he said, now that he knew that an unknown agent in Boston might have a specific interest in having him recaptured. "Mr. Brown spoke with evident agitation," but he

16. *Liberator*, January 28, 1848, p. 15; William C. Nell, *The Colored Patriots of the American Revolution* (Boston, 1855), p. 365.

was immediately assured by many of those present that they "would stand forth in his defence in any time of danger."[17]

When Brown spoke during the following evening session, which was held in Faneuil Hall, he no longer appeared to be agitated. To convince those who still doubted that he had ever been a slave, he exhibited Price's letter. With regard to the offer of some of the citizens of Boston to defend him against seizure, he explained with seeming bluntness that what he wanted "chiefly" was not protection from recapture, but the repeal of the laws that made slaves of himself and millions of others—something which he must have known before he mentioned it that most of his audience as well as he himself wanted.[18]

Early in February the second edition of Brown's *Narrative* was published by the Boston Anti-Slavery Office.[19] This is a reprint of the first edition with minor changes and enough additions to enlarge the work to 144 pages. Immediately after the narrative itself, Brown's "The American Slave-Trade" was reprinted from *The Liberty Bell*, and this is followed by "The Blind Slave Boy." The last addition is an Appendix consisting of an essay against slavery, more than twenty excerpts from Southern newspapers exemplifying the villainies of the "peculiar institution," and numerous extracts from the slave codes of the Southern states.

If Brown thought that there was danger in his going around freely in Massachusetts, he was not deterred by it. As the year advanced, he increased his activities as a lecturer, and where he was to be from time to time was generally announced in the *Liberator*. From the last week in January to the last week in July, announcements of at least sixty engagements for him were

17. *Boston Evening Herald,* quoted in *Liberator,* February 11, 1848, p. 21; Massachusetts Anti-Slavery Society, *Sixteenth Annual Report* (Boston, 1848), p. 88.

18. *Liberator,* February 4, 1848, p. 19.

19. *Ibid.,* February 11, 1848, p. 22.

published, some of them repeatedly in successive numbers of that newspaper and others; and reports of his lectures were multiplied in them.[20]

The annual New England Anti-Slavery Convention began in Boston on May 30 and continued for three days. In a speech during an evening session in Faneuil Hall, Brown endeavored to win the sympathies of the laboring classes for abolition. Referring to "the degraded condition of the laboring population in the Southern States, whether black or white," he said that slaveholders were opposed to the best interests of the working classes everywhere and were inclined to look down on them. The logical conclusion was, therefore, that free labor could not thrive where it had to compete with slave labor.[21] Although Brown probably was not enough of a political economist to make the most of this argument, it is interesting to note that he presented it to a Boston audience nine years before Hinton R. Helper published his *The Impending Crisis* exposing the unavoidable economic conflict between slavery and free labor.

Ever since the beginning of his career as an antislavery lecturer, Brown had given on various occasions evidence of his interest in and genius—whether great or small—for singing. He was especially interested in songs for antislavery meetings, believing that such songs contributed to the progress of abolitionism. By the middle of June he had finished compiling a collection of antislavery songs. The collection was published in Boston during the first week in July in a booklet of forty-eight pages with the title *The Anti-Slavery Harp: A Collection of Songs for Anti-Slavery Meetings*. Its publisher was Bela Marsh,

20. Typical reports of Brown's activities from February to May are found in the following: *Liberator*, January 28, 1848, p. 15, March 31, 1848, p. 51, April 7, 1848, p. 55, May 5, 1848, pp. 69, 71, June 2, 1848, p. 87; *North Star*, February 25, 1848, p. 3; *National Anti-Slavery Standard*, May 18, 1848, p. 202.

21. *Liberator*, June 9, 1848, p. 90; Massachusetts Anti-Slavery Society, *Seventeenth Annual Report* (Boston, 1849), p. 55.

whose office was only a few doors from the Boston Anti-Slavery Office.[22]

In his preface, Brown acknowledged his indebtedness to two older antislavery songbooks: Jairus Lincoln's *Anti-Slavery Melodies* and George W. Clark's *The Liberty Minstrel*.[23] Both of these works contain music as well as words. Brown's booklet contains no music, but in most instances it indicates by titles tunes, or "airs," for the several songs. Brown erred, however, in saying that "the larger portion of the songs" had not been previously published. Only seventeen of the forty-eight songs in his collection had not been included in either Lincoln's or Clark's songbook, and many of these Brown had found in anti-slavery newspapers.

One of the songs included by Lincoln and Brown but not by Clark is "I Am an Abolitionist." This is the same as "Song of the Abolitionist," which Garrison had composed to the tune of "Auld Lang Syne" early in November, 1841, and which had been published a few weeks later in *The Liberty Bell* for 1842. Because of the popularity of this song among the Garrisonians, Brown's familiarity with it was probably independent of his knowledge of Lincoln's songbook. Neither Lincoln's compilation nor Brown's contains more than the first four of the five stanzas of the song which are found in *The Liberty Bell.*

One of the songs Brown found, not in Lincoln's, but in Clark's collection is John Greenleaf Whittier's high-spirited "The Yankee Girl," for which Clark had composed the music. Besides Whittier the only famous American poet represented in Brown's collection is James Russell Lowell, and the one poem by this author which Brown included is his "Stanzas on Freedom." Following Clark, however, Brown entitled the poem "Are Ye

22. *Liberator,* July 7, 1848, p. 106; *National Anti-Slavery Standard,* July 13, 1848, p. 25.

23. These songbooks had been published respectively in Hingham, Mass., 1843, and in New York and Boston, 1844.

Truly Free?" and indicated for it the tune "Martyn." Few people probably knew the tune by this name, but almost everyone knows it as the tune to which Charles Wesley's "Jesus, Lover of My Soul" is usually sung.

Two of the songs which Brown, like Clark, included in his collection are endued with much more of the spirit of the blood-shedding revolutionist than of the Garrisonian pacifist which he was then supposed to be. These are Mrs. J. G. Carter's "Ye Sons of Freemen," whose tune is that of Rouget de Lisle's "La Marseillaise," and Mrs. Sarah Towne Martyn's "On to Victory," whose meter is the same as that of Robert Burns's "Scots wha ha'e wi' Wallace bled."

However inconsistent with Garrisonian pacifism the sentiments expressed in these songs might have been, the common-sense point of view concerning the possibility of a violent termination of American slavery was unmistakable to the abolitionists. All abolitionists hoped that slavery would be peacefully abolished from the United States, as it had been from the British West Indies, and none of them wanted to be instrumental in starting a war to abolish the institution. It was obvious to all of them, nevertheless, that if a war of some kind proved feasible or necessary as a means of effecting the immediate abolition of slavery, even that would have been a lesser evil than the continuation of slavery itself. Brown certainly shared this point of view, as he said in substance in a speech in Lynn on August 1, less than a month after the publication of his songbook. The occasion was the celebration of the anniversary of emancipation in the British West Indies; and he was reported to have said in his speech that "he wished not for scenes of blood and carnage,—but if a favorable opening should occur to the slave population of this country, he could hardly subdue himself to counsel non-resistance, or to act upon its principles himself."[24]

Six of the seventeen songs that Brown found in neither Lincoln's nor Clark's collection deserve special notice for vari-

24. *Liberator,* August 25, 1848, p. 133.

ous reasons. D. B. Harris's "Freedom's Star" and Elias Smith's "Flight of the Bondman" had been dedicated by their authors to Brown, and the second of these songs had become a part of the repertory of the Hutchinson Singers, a popular group of anti-slavery songsters.[25] One of the six, which is entitled "Fling out the Anti-Slavery Flag," was composed by Brown himself to the tune of "Auld Lang Syne." It consists of four stanzas of eight lines each, the first line of each stanza being the same as the title. As verse the song is studiedly correct, but it is devoid of the fervor which is essential to the best lyric poetry. Perhaps the most remarkable fact about this song is that it is apparently Brown's earliest published attempt to write verse.

The sensational piece in Brown's collection, which seems to have been included in no other antislavery songbook, is "Jefferson's Daughter." This poem had been published nine years earlier in *Tait's Edinburgh Magazine*, July, 1839. In that periodical it was prefaced by the following statement quoted from the *London Morning Chronicle:* "It is asserted, on the authority of an American newspaper, that the daughter of Thomas Jefferson, late President of the United States, was sold at New Orleans *for 1000 dollars.*" The American newspaper referred to might have been either William Goodell's *Friend of Man*, published weekly in Utica, New York, or the *Liberator*. Upon Goodell's request, Dr. Levi Gaylord of Sodus, New York, had retold in a letter in the *Friend of Man*, August 22, 1838, what he had heard about the alleged sale. According to Gaylord, his informant was Otis Reynolds, "a gentleman from *St. Louis, Missouri*, himself a practical, as well as theoretical supporter of slavery," who said that he had witnessed the sale.[26]

Brown referred to *Tait's Edinburgh Magazine* as the source of the poem and included the prefatory statement quoted above.

25. *Narrative*, 4th ed. (Boston, 1849), pp. 130–31.

26. *Tait's Edinburgh Magazine*, 6 (July, 1839): 452; *Friend of Man*, August 22, 1838, p. 246. Gaylord's letter was reprinted in *Liberator*, September 21, 1838, p. 152.

His immediate source, however, was most probably the *Liberator*, May 26, 1848, where the poem together with the prefatory statement had been reprinted from the periodical. The punctuation in Brown's version is practically identical with that of the version in the *Liberator*, which is noticeably different from that of the version in the periodical.

"Jefferson's Daughter" is a satire in seven quatrains of anapestic tetrameters with alternate rhymes. Taking as its point of departure the story of the alleged sale of Jefferson's daughter, the poem castigated the descendants of the American Revolutionists for grandly extolling freedom while they unblushingly practiced despotism by maintaining chattel slavery.

"The Colonization Song" and John Pierpont's "Slaveholder's Address to the North Star" are noteworthy because of their use of the comic, which is generally absent from the songs. The former, which was addressed "To the Free Colored People" and suited to the tune of "The Spider and the Fly," ironically presented arguments from a slaveholder's point of view in favor of colonization. The latter combined a mock complaint against the "abolition star" for guiding slaves to freedom and a threat to hale it before Judge Lynch and have it "fixed" with a coat of tar and feathers for shining south of the Mason-Dixon line.[27] Of the fourteen stanzas in the original, Brown gave only the first two and the last two, making minor changes in their wording. He suggested no tune for this poem, nor for "Jefferson's Daughter," perhaps because he considered both of them more suitable for recitation than for singing.

27. [John Pierpont], *The Anti-Slavery Poems of John Pierpont* (Boston, 1843), pp. 34–38.

IX

In the Strife of Truth with Falsehood

SINCE HIS SEPARATION FROM MRS. BROWN MORE THAN A YEAR earlier, Brown had neither seen nor heard much about her—until the middle of July, 1848, when she appeared in Boston carrying a little child with her. With what Brown considered evil intentions, she spent a few days at the home of the Garrisons and, said he, tried "to poison the minds of the best of friends against me." On the day after her arrival in Boston, Brown went to the Garrisons' home to see her. After some hesitation she received him but neither let him see the child nor even referred to it. Before their interview ended, however, she let him know that she needed money and that she wanted to see their daughters, Clarissa and Josephine, who were then in school in New Bedford. Brown had sent them to New Bedford because the schools there were not segregated as they were in Boston. With money Brown gave her, Mrs. Brown went to New Bedford, and Brown continued with his anti-slavery work.

Before Mrs. Brown ended her visit with their daughters, she needed or at least wanted more money. Accordingly she wrote to Brown asking for additional funds and explaining that she wished to use them to return to Buffalo. Before the end of July, instead of sending her money, Brown carried it to her, and she set out, he thought, for Buffalo. Assuming that his marital affairs were thus settled, Brown returned to Boston.[1]

On August 7 Brown left Boston for his first visit to Philadelphia and arrived in "the city of Brotherly Love," as he called it somewhat ironically, in the afternoon of the next day. During the following evening he attended a meeting of the Philadelphia Vigilance Committee, an organization consisting principally of Negroes and devoted to the aid of fugitive slaves. At this meeting he was officially welcomed by Robert Purvis, whom he had previously met at antislavery conventions. He also became acquainted with William Still, the future historian of the Underground Railroad, who was then a clerk in the office of the Pennsylvania Society for the Abolition of Slavery.

Brown spent the next three days in Norristown at the eleventh annual meeting of the Anti-Slavery Society of Eastern Pennsylvania, New Jersey, and Delaware. Thereafter he spent a week lecturing in Philadelphia and its vicinity. Contrary to its name, Brown found Philadelphia neither very brotherly nor very lovely towards a visiting antislavery lecturer. He found not only the white churches unavailable for lectures but also all of the Negro churches except two—"the Big and Little Wesley churches." En route back to Boston he stopped in New York, whence he wrote a letter to Samuel May, Jr. on August 17, telling about his activities of the preceding ten days.[2]

1. William Wells Brown, "To the Public," *Liberator,* July 12, 1850, p. 111.

2. *Liberator,* September 1, 1848, pp. 137–38; W. W. Brown, "My First Visit to Philadelphia," *ibid.*, p. 137.

During the next three weeks, Brown figured prominently in meetings in eastern Massachusetts in which the abolitionists' blunt criticism of contemporary affairs was said to have provoked "a mobocratic spirit." This spirit became flesh in the form of a riot at a convention which was held at Harwich on Cape Cod from Friday to Sunday, August 25–27. The cape had been, in Pillsbury's phrase, "the grand nursery of navigators," and it was still home to many sea captains who engaged in commerce along the Atlantic seaboard from New England to the Gulf of Mexico. Some of these seamen were staunch abolitionists, but a considerable number of them were indifferent toward slavery if not in favor of it, and their attitudes were shared by many others who lived on the cape. Because of this fact it became the aim of the Massachusetts Anti-Slavery Society not merely to win the seamen to the antislavery cause but to invest all of the cape with abolitionism by means of mammoth conventions. The first of these was the one just mentioned. The antislavery press was subsequently filled with reports and comments concerning what happened at this convention.[3]

Since they could not get permission to use any church, schoolhouse, or hall in Harwich, the abolitionists held their convention in a grove near the town. Therein they had a platform constructed for the speakers and seats of rough planks for the audience. The convention proceeded, not without threats of disturbances by antiabolitionists, until late Sunday afternoon, when about 2,500 people were present. Among the speakers for the day were Brown, Pillsbury, and Stephen S. Foster. Sometime during the morning a Cape Cod resident named Sears, who was captain of a coastwise steamer, admitted to Pillsbury that he had recently accepted $100 from a Norfolk, Virginia, slave to carry him and a fellow slave to a Northern port, but that he had instead had the slave arrested as a fugitive and had received a

3. *National Anti-Slavery Standard,* September 7, 1848, p. 59; *Liberator,* September 8, 1848, p. 142, September 15, 1848, pp. 145, 146–47, September 22, 1848, p. 151, October 6, 1848, p. 160, October 20, 1848, p. 168.

part of the slave's money as a reward. "At a convenient time in the afternoon," Pillsbury publicly recounted what Sears had admitted to him but did not identify the captain by name. A few minutes later Sears came forward, identified himself, and verified what Pillsbury had told about him. In answer to a question from Foster, Sears, who was now seated on the platform, said that he was a member of the Baptist church and in good standing in it. "Foster then took the case in hand" and declared, among other things, Pillsbury remembered, that the American church was indeed "the bulwark of American slavery," as James G. Birney had said it was. "Who would defend such a church?" Foster queried.

Captain Stillman Snow, who was a member of the Harwich Congregational church, and who was said to have come directly from church service to the grove, rushed to the platform saying that he would defend the church, accused Foster of telling "a damned lie," and "made a leap" at him. Snow's leap was apparently a signal to his cohorts to begin a riot, and in a few minutes there was a reign of terror in the grove.

Lucy Stone, who was on the platform, was rushed away by Foster without being harmed; but both Foster and Pillsbury were mauled and kicked, and their clothes were badly torn. Worse still, Brown was picked up and thrown over the back of the platform "down six or eight feet" and was then "trampled on by the throng gathered there." He escaped being killed only when the attention of his assailants was distracted by threats of torture which were being made against Foster and Pillsbury. In the commotion Brown lost "quite a number" of copies of his songbook, said the report of Charles Stearns and Lucy Stone, the secretaries of the convention. Meanwhile Foster and Pillsbury were saved partly by their own courage and partly by their friends, and the rioters satiated their fury by demolishing the platform.

In the opinion of a correspondent for the *Boston Daily Republican*, whose report was reprinted in the *Liberator* for

September 8, Pillsbury and Foster, "by the extreme plainness of their speaking," and Brown, "by his complexion and the familiar manner with which he strode the platform," had aroused some people to indignation. But in the opinion of the abolitionists themselves and some of their sympathizers, the riot had been instigated by certain Boston merchants, prominent people on Cape Cod, and by the *Barnstable Patriot*, an all too influential newspaper. Whatever its causes might have been, far from resulting only in evil, the riot seemed to the abolitionists to have produced remarkable good. According to the secretaries' report, in less than three weeks afterwards, interest in the cause of human freedom was greatly intensified on the cape, and contributions from that area for the promotion of that cause had almost doubled themselves. In the strife of truth with falsehood at Harwich, truth, the antislavery leaders felt assured, had won a victory.

Soon after Brown returned from Philadelphia, he was astonished to find that Mrs. Brown had not left Massachusetts. On the contrary she had been in Springfield and Worcester and again in New Bedford, "spreading injurious reports against me" and "using up the time in going among influential abolitionists, to prejudice them against me."

Some of those who heard Mrs. Brown's reports concerning her husband took them seriously enough to question the wisdom of the Massachusetts Anti-Slavery Society in keeping as one of its agents a man whose wife was openly complaining against him. To clarify matters pertaining to the Browns, the officials of the society appointed a committee to hold a conference with the Browns in Boston sometime during the week of September 4. Two members of the committee were Francis Jackson, president of the society, and Samuel May, Jr., its general agent. Returning to Boston upon Brown's request that she attend the conference and finding that her estranged husband "intended to bring up the cause" of their separation, Mrs. Brown refused to meet with the committee until May "prevailed upon her" to do so. Even then the conference proved futile until Brown threatened to write to Buffalo "to procure some evidence against her."

After the conference, in a private conversation with Brown, Mrs. Brown agreed to join him in a petition for a divorce, provided that he would give her "a certain sum of money." The two of them further agreed to meet on September 25 for another conversation. All of these details concerning the conference and the conversations were related by Brown in a letter he wrote from Newburyport to Garrison on September 15.[4] Garrison was then convalescing at David Ruggles's water cure near Northampton, having been there since early in August.

Although the Browns had more conversations, apparently they never got beyond the conversational stage with their plans for a divorce. In one of their conversations Mrs. Brown told her estranged spouse that she wanted to return to Buffalo; whereupon he gave her money for traveling expenses thither. This time she went back to Buffalo, and they never saw each other again. Whether they corresponded with each other during the few years Mrs. Brown had yet to live is not known, but later they did some more writing about each other.

The committee of the Massachusetts Anti-Slavery Society wisely refrained from passing judgment on all of the difficulties between the Browns, for it was aware that all of the facts involved were known only to the couple themselves. But in addition to conferring with the Browns, it made some inquiries among their former neighbors. As a result of its investigations, the committee exonerated Brown, and the society, of course, retained him as an agent; but it published no official report concerning the matter until almost two years later.

Brown was one of the principal speakers at a three-day convention which was begun in Newburyport on September 13. In the letter he wrote from Newburyport to Garrison on Sep-

4. Brown to Garrison, September 15, 1848, Anti-Slavery Letters Written to W. L. Garrison and Others.

tember 15, he related some of the incidents which occurred at that convention.

> Our meeting [he said] was held the first evening at Market Hall; but we were turned out of it very uncerimoniously [*sic*] by the Select men of the Town. There being a Democrat present who owned a hall in the place, [he] very generously came forward and offered it to us, as long as we wished to remain in the place. We accepted the offer, and last evening we had another meeting. In the course of my remarks, I said that Newburyport, had done nothing for the anti-slavery cause, and that I supposed that she would be behind every other place in the commonwealth.

The next speaker was the Reverend Thomas Wentworth Higginson, who was then pastor of a local Unitarian church. He could not agree with Brown, he said, that Newburyport had done nothing for the antislavery cause. In his opinion it had done more than any other town in New England. At this point Higginson was interrupted by applause from the proslavery members of the audience; but when he was allowed to continue, he reminded those present that Newburyport had given Garrison to the cause. "I wished at the time," Brown informed Garrison, "that you had been there, to hear with what applause it [Higginson's reference to Garrison] was received. . . . You have many friends in your native place; many who when they hear your name mentioned in meetings find themselves applauding, before they know what they are about." Thus a meeting which had started inauspiciously became something of a testimonial for Garrison in absentia.[5]

Long before September, 1848, the second edition of Brown's *Narrative*, consisting of two thousand copies, had been sold. In

5. Reports of Brown's engagements for lectures and of his participation in conventions, principally in eastern Massachusetts, from the middle of September to November are found in the following numbers of *Liberator:* September 29, 1848, p. 155; October 6, 1848, p. 159, October 20, 1848, pp. 165, 167, October 27, 1848, p. 171, November 10, 1848, p. 179.

order that the continuing demand for the book might be met, the third edition was published early in October.[6] In this edition Hathaway's preface was replaced with one written by Brown himself. This consists principally of Enoch Price's letter to Quincy, which was now published for the first time, and Brown's comment on it. Otherwise this edition is the same as the second.

Early in November, Brown paid his second visit to Philadelphia with the expectation of staying in its vicinity about six weeks. He remained in eastern Pennsylvania, however, through the first week of the new year, lecturing and attending during the week before Christmas a convention of the Eastern Pennsylvania Anti-Slavery Society, which was held in Philadelphia.[7]

On January 4, 1849, Brown was in Pineville, a village in Bucks County, about thirty miles north of Philadelphia. He was there on special business for the Underground Railroad. The business pertained to William and Ellen Craft, who had arrived in Philadelphia on Christmas Day on their flight from slavery in Macon, Georgia. Brown dispatched a letter from Pineville on January 4 to Garrison, giving some details about the Crafts' escape as he had heard them from the fugitives themselves. He explained that for their safety the Crafts were then "hid away within 25 miles of Philadelphia" but were to leave with him for New England on January 6. Already cognizant of the value of the Crafts to the antislavery crusade, Brown requested Garrison to announce in the *Liberator* that he would lecture "in connexion with them" in cities in Connecticut and Massachusetts between January 18 and 28, and that they would also attend the next annual meeting of the Massachusetts Anti-Slavery Society in Boston "in the latter part of this month." With the publication of his letter in the *Liberator* for January 12, Brown became the first person to put into print the story of what is still remembered

6. *Liberator*, October 20, 1848, p. 166.

7. *Ibid.*, November 3, 1848, p. 175; *National Anti-Slavery Standard*, December 28, 1848, p. 123.

as the most famous, if not the most ingenious, escape from American slavery.[8]

Brown did not mention the name of the family with which the Crafts were hidden when he wrote his letter from Pineville, for to do so would have been to increase the danger that the fugitives might be recaptured. Eleven years later, however, in his *Running a Thousand Miles for Freedom,* which he wrote with the assistance of his wife Ellen, Craft said that their hosts were a family of Friends which consisted of "Barkley Ivens," his wife, and their three daughters and a son. The family he had in mind was that of Barclay and Mary (Thompson) Ivins, who lived in the Henry Drinker House in Penn's Manor, less than twenty miles from Pineville.[9]

Craft also said that he and Ellen spent three weeks with the Ivinses—a statement which is inconsistent with Brown's explanation in his letter from Pineville that he would set out with them for New England on January 6. Since the Crafts could not have arrived at the Ivinses' home until late on Christmas Day at the earliest, three weeks would have prolonged their stay until after January 12, the date of publication of the number of the *Liberator* containing Brown's letter. Now it is extremely doubtful that the friends of the Crafts would have risked keeping them near Philadelphia after the publication of Brown's letter.

8. "Singular Escape," *Liberator,* January 12, 1849, p. 7; [William Craft], *Running a Thousand Miles for Freedom; or, The Escape of William and Ellen Craft from Slavery* (London, 1860), pp. 68, 79–80, 82–86. Other newspaper reports of the Crafts' escape which appeared soon after Brown's were as follows: *New York Herald,* January 17, 1849; "An Incident at the South," *Newark Daily Mercury,* January 19, 1849, reprinted in *National Anti-Slavery Standard,* February 8, 1849, p. 146, and in *Liberator,* February 9, 1849, p. 23 (where it was incorrectly ascribed to the *Newark Advertiser*).

9. This statement is based on information sent to me in December, 1952, by Mrs. Eva Wallen Lovett of Yardley, Pennsylvania, a great-granddaughter of Barclay and Mary Ivins, and also on William Wade Hinshaw's *Encyclopedia of American Quaker Genealogy,* Ann Arbor, Michigan, 1936–50, 2:802, 1005.

If, therefore, Brown did not carry them away on January 6, it is most probable that he did so before the twelfth. Incidentally, while the Ivinses had the Crafts in their care, Brown not only visited them but also did some sight-seeing in the surrounding country. He took the trouble one day, for example, to walk over what had once been William Penn's farm not far away on the right bank of the Delaware River.[10]

Brown was in Boston with the Crafts by January 24. On that day the first evening session of the seventeenth annual meeting of the Massachusetts Anti-Slavery Society was held in Faneuil Hall. At that session Brown gave a brief account of the escape of the Crafts from slavery and introduced them to the audience. He then finished his part on the program with "an Anti-Slavery song, which was much applauded." Two evenings later, at the final session of the meeting, he again introduced the Crafts and retold the story of their escape.[11]

During the next four months, Brown and the Crafts went on lecture tours which carried them over all of Massachusetts except Cape Cod and the western end of the state. Within the period just mentioned, they had more than sixty meetings scheduled. Apparently many of their engagements were made without much regard for geography, so that the trio often had to travel the same road several times within a few days to get from one meeting to another.[12]

Brown and the Crafts followed a simple routine for their meetings. First, with appropriate remarks—which were seldom brief—Brown introduced Craft, who recounted his and his wife's lives as slaves and their escape from slavery. As Craft became

10. *Three Years in Europe*, p. 95.

11. Massachusetts Anti-Slavery Society, *Seventeenth Annual Report* (Boston, 1849), pp. 82, 87.

12. Announcements and reports concerning their activities are found in *Liberator* as follows: February 9, 1849, p. 23, February 23, 1849, p. 31, March 2, 1849, p. 35, March 9, 1849, p. 39, April 6, 1849, pp. 54, 55, April 27, 1849, p. 67, May 18, 1849, p. 79, June 8, 1849, p. 89. There was also a report in *National Anti-Slavery Standard*, June 7, 1849, pp. 5–7.

more accustomed to facing audiences, he lengthened his story until he usually took about an hour to tell it. Next Brown delivered a speech whose purpose was critical and persuasive, and which lasted about an hour. After this he introduced Mrs. Craft, who sometimes added a few words to what her husband had said. Occasionally Brown sang a song or two. Finally a collection for the antislavery cause was taken, abolition publications were offered for sale, and the meeting was adjourned.

Sometimes the meetings were varied by sudden turns of humor, as was the one in the town hall of Northboro on the evening of February 16. A member of the audience who either doubted that the Crafts had been slaves or merely wanted to be troublesome asked Craft who was the governor of Georgia seven years earlier. When Craft failed to answer the question, another member of the audience nonplussed the questioner by asking him the same question with regard to Massachusetts—a question which the questioner could not answer.

The Brown and Crafts' tours were interrupted when Brown went to the fifteenth annual meeting of the American Anti-Slavery Society, which was held in New York May 8–10. In addition to being made a member of the committee on finance, as he frequently was at such meetings, Brown was made a member of the "Committee of Conference on the state and prospects of the cause"—a committee whose membership consisted of many, if not most, of the acknowledged leaders of the antislavery movement. Among its twenty-nine members besides Brown, were Phillips, Foster, Pillsbury, Douglass, Mrs. Lucretia Mott, Lucy Stone, Sidney Howard Gay, Garrison, Quincy, and Samuel May, Jr. Brown was also chosen to preside at the first evening session, which was, of course, open to the public, and at which two of the speakers were Phillips and Miss Stone.[13]

While Brown was traveling and holding joint meetings with the Crafts, he found time to prepare new editions of both his

13. *National Anti-Slavery Standard,* May 17, 1849, pp. 201–03; *Liberator,* May 18, 1849, pp. 78–79.

autobiography and his songbook. Late in May the fourth edition of his *Narrative* was published, not by the Boston Anti-Slavery Office, as the first three editions had been, but by Bela Marsh, the publisher of the *Anti-Slavery Harp*.[14] The first 108 pages of this edition are the same as they are in the third edition. Pages 109–24 comprise the twelfth and last chapter in the work. This chapter tells of the kidnapping and rescue of the Stanfords of Saint Catharines, Ontario. Chapter 12 is followed by "The American Slave-Trade," and this is followed by three poems, the last of which is Brown's "Lament of the Fugitive Slave." This poem, which is an elegy on the author's mother, has remained his best effort in verse. The last two of its six stanzas are as follows:

> Yet blessings on thy Roman-mother spirit;
> Could I forget it, then,
> The parting scene, and struggle not to inherit
> A freeman's birth-right once again?
> O noble words! O holy love, which gave
> Thee strength to utter them, a poor, heart-broken slave!
>
> Be near me, mother, be thy spirit near me,
> Wherever thou may'st be;
> In hours like this bend near that I may hear thee,
> And know that thou art free;
> Summoned at length from bondage, toil and pain,
> To God's free world, a world without a chain!

The appendix, which fills the last 30 of the 162 pages in the volume, contains additional newspaper excerpts and advertisements portraying the manifold evils of slavery, extracts from slave codes, and examples of slave states' laws which restricted free Negroes in various ways. This was the last edition of Brown's *Narrative* to be published in the United States.

The second edition of the *Anti-Slavery Harp* was published about the same time that the fourth edition of the *Narrative*

14. *Liberator*, June 1, 1849, p. 87.

was, and by the same publisher.[15] This edition is the same in format as the first one, but it contains only forty-six songs. Eight of the selections in the first edition had been omitted, and only six new ones had been added. Two of the selections eliminated were "The Colonization Song" and Pierpont's "Slaveholder's Address to the North Star." These were the only two satires in the collection, and replacing them with nothing of the kind was a loss to the songbook—unless satire is not to be considered a legitimate and effective means of reform. The best of the six replacements are Brown's "Lament of the Fugitive Slave" and "The Slave's a Man, For A' That," a poem in imitation of Burns's familiar "For A' That and A' That."

About June 10 Brown went to Maine to spend ten or twelve days lecturing in Portland, Bath, Bangor, and other towns near the coast. Although he was now far away from slave territory, he was still close enough to it, he discovered, to be victimized by race prejudice, which he considered a product of slavery. He was "excluded from the saloon of the steamer Huntress, on the passage from Portland to Bath . . . by which exclusion I was compelled to fast twelve hours."[16]

A notice in the *Liberator* for June 15, which announced that Brown would speak at a meeting in Abington on June 24, also said that that would be "one of the last of a series of meetings" which he would attend before his departure for England. Writing on June 20 to Elizabeth Pease, an abolitionist of Darlington, England, Garrison said that Brown expected to visit that country "this summer."[17] Also, during an antislavery celebration of July 4 in Abington, Garrison remarked after a long speech by Brown that the speaker had been elected a delegate to the Peace Congress

15. *Ibid.*, June 15, 1849, p. 95.

16. Brown to Garrison, October 12, 1849, *Liberator*, November 2, 1849, p. 175. See also *ibid.*, June 8, 1849, p. 91, June 15, 1849, p. 95, June 22, 1849, p. 99, July 13, 1849, pp. 110–11, for reports concerning Brown's lecture engagements for the last week in June and the first week in July.

17. Garrison to Elizabeth Pease, June 20, 1849, Anti-Slavery Letters Written by W. L. Garrison.

which was to be held in Paris later in the summer. In the introductory note to his *Narrative of William W. Brown, an American Slave*, published in London soon after he arrived in England, Brown gave two reasons for going to Europe. First, as Garrison had said, he went to attend the Peace Congress. Second, "I wished to follow up the work of my friends and fellow-labourers, Charles Lenox Remond and Frederick Douglas [*sic*], and to lay before the people of Great Britain and Ireland the wrongs that are still committed upon the slaves and the free coloured people of America."

On July 6 Brown wrote to John M. Clayton, United States Secretary of State, explaining that he expected to sail on July 18 for France by way of Liverpool and London, and requesting a passport to France. He also explained that "I am a native of the State of Kentucky, and I am a colored man." His letter was received in Clayton's office on July 9, as a notation on it shows. He never received a reply from Clayton, but he soon found from that official's reply to a similar request what kind of answer he would have received if he had received one. On June 9 Clayton had written to Edward Hurst of Philadelphia refusing to grant "a passport or protection" which Hurst had solicited for Henry Hambleton, a colored man. The reason for his refusal, Clayton had explained, was that passports were not granted by his office to "persons of color," and that "protections" were given to them only when they were "in the service of diplomatic agents, &c. of the United States, going abroad."[18]

With the aid of Phillips, Brown obtained from William B. Calhoun, secretary of the commonwealth of Massachusetts, a certificate that permitted him to go to Great Britain. Upon his arrival in London he found that he did not need a passport to go on to Paris, because through the courtesy of the French govern-

18. Clayton to Hurst, June 9, 1849, *New York Evening Post*, August 2, 1849, and *North Star*, August 24, 1849, p. 1, quoted in W. Wells Brown to the Reverend William Allen, September 2, 1849, *Liberator*, October 12, 1849, p. 161.

ment, delegates to the Peace Congress were permitted to enter France without passports. On October 31, however, preparatory to going again from England to the continent, Brown succeeded in getting a passport from the American embassy in London.[19]

A group of Boston citizens, most of whom were Negroes, made Brown's going away the occasion for a presentation and farewell meeting. The committee of twelve persons which had the responsibility of arranging for the occasion advertised it not only in the *Liberator* but also by means of broadsides 16½ in. by 20 in. The meeting was held in the Washingtonian Hall on Bromfield Street on Monday evening, July 16. John T. Hilton, who presided, stated the three purposes of the meeting, namely, to present to Garrison, the champion of immediate emancipation, a silver pitcher from the Negroes of Boston, to give "the hand of farewell" to Brown, and "to put our veto anew upon that nefarious combination, the American Colonization Society, which seeks the expatriation of the free colored population of this country to the shores of Africa." The presentation speech was made by William C. Nell. It was indeed a learned, if not scholarly, speech, replete with classical allusions and Shakespearean quotations, and it was withal a grand tribute to Garrison. In his speech of acceptance Garrison was appropriately modest and brief.

The Reverend Thomas Paul Smith next "tendered the farewell of the meeting" to Brown. Like Garrison, Brown responded with appropriate modesty in a speech longer than Garrison's but shorter than Smith's. He accepted the honor bestowed upon him by the group, he said, not as something he had merited but as their homage to the antislavery cause, which he believed they all loved, and to which he himself was deeply indebted. "All that I am now," he averred somewhat sentimentally, "or expect to

19. William W. Brown to Wendell Phillips, November 22, 1849, *Liberator*, November 30, 1849, p. 191. See also *ibid.*, November 10, 1854, p. 178; William C. Nell, *The Colored Patriots of the American Revolution* (Boston, 1855), pp. 323–26.

be in this world, I owe to the anti-slavery cause." He expressed great hopes for both the Peace Congress and the antislavery cause, for which he expected to work in Europe as he had worked in America, "for the two reforms," he observed, "blend harmoniously in promoting 'peace on earth and good will to men.' "

Proceeding to the third purpose of the meeting, Robert Morris read several excerpts from Garrison's *Thoughts on African Colonization* (Boston, 1832). After some discussion, resolutions were unanimously adopted bidding Brown "God speed on his mission to Europe," forwarding abroad by him "our renewed protest against the American Colonization Society," and reconfirming Garrison's views concerning that organization. Upon request, Phillips, who had arrived a few minutes late, spoke briefly, paying eloquent tributes to Garrison and Brown.[20]

Although Brown went as a delegate from the American Peace Society to the Peace Congress in Paris, that society paid none of the expenses of his trip. Nor did friends help to defray his expenses, as friends of Douglass had done when he went to England in 1845. In a letter he wrote from Buffalo to *Frederick Douglass' Paper* on September 27, 1859, Brown said, "I went to Europe entirely at my own expense," and there seems to be no reason to doubt his statement.[21]

Brown carried abroad with him several introductory and complimentary letters. One of these was dated at Boston, July 17, and signed by Garrison, Robert F. Wallcut, and Samuel May, Jr. for the board of managers of the Massachusetts Anti-Slavery Society. This letter commended Brown "to the confidence, respect, esteem, and hospitality" of the abolitionists of Europe. Another letter, dated at Boston, July 18, addressed to Brown and signed by Garrison as president of the American

20. *Liberator*, July 13, 1849, p. 110, July 20, 1849, p. 114, July 27, 1849, pp. 118–19.

21. Benjamin Quarles, *Frederick Douglass* (Washington, 1948), p. 36. Brown to *Frederick Douglass' Paper*, quoted in *Weekly Anglo-African*, October 22, 1859, p. 3.

Anti-Slavery Society, advised that Brown "Challenge all that is free, all that is humane, all that is pious, across the Atlantic, to raise a united testimony against American slaveholders and their abettors, as the enemies of God and the human race!"[22]

Especially noteworthy among these letters was one from Garrison dated at Boston, July 17, and addressed to Elizabeth Pease of Darlington. In this letter Garrison explained that

> Mr. Brown does not go out officially from any anti-slavery society, simply because he prefers to stand alone responsible for what he may say and do. . . . Nor does he go out to be a pecuniary burden or to make himself an unwelcome guest to any one; but he hopes that, by the sale of his Narrative, (the stereotype plates of which he takes with him,) he shall be able to meet such expenses as may arise beyond what the hospitality of friends may cover. His stay will be longer or shorter, as circumstances may determine.

Garrison also informed Miss Pease that Brown's appointment as a delegate to the Peace Congress had been officially made "by the Committee of the American Peace League, whose credentials he bears with him." Near the end of his letter Garrison revealed why the assembly of the preceding Monday evening had adopted two resolutions opposing the American Colonization Society and commissioning Brown to protest against it in Great Britain. "It appears," said Garrison, "that there is now in England, a 'Reverend' agent of the American Colonization Society, by the name of Miller, who is endeavoring to deceive the public and to get pecuniary aid for that Society, as did Elliott Cresson, many years ago; and it is one object of Mr. Brown, in going to England at this time, to meet and expose this wolf in sheep's clothing."[23]

22. *Narrative of William W. Brown, an American Slave, Written by Himself*, London, 1849, pp. 163–65.

23. Garrison to Elizabeth Pease, July 17, 1849, Anti-Slavery Letters Written by W. L. Garrison.

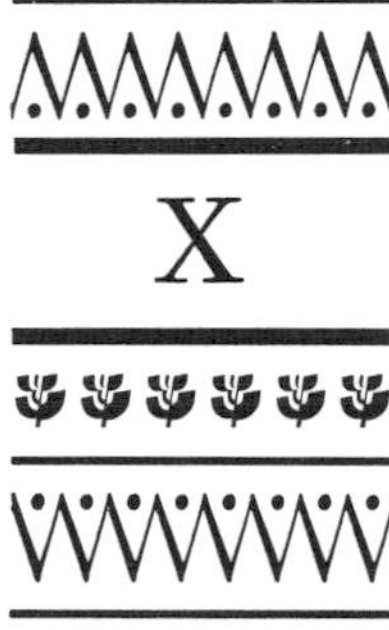

Freedom on British Soil

Brown sailed from Boston on July 18 on the Cunard steamship *Canada* bound for Liverpool. On this ship he found himself one of about a hundred passengers, many of whom, like him, were delegates to the forthcoming Peace Congress in Paris. When his presence on the ship became known, he said in a letter he wrote from London to Garrison on October 12,

> there was no little anxiety manifested on the part of the passengers to know something of the history of the fugitive. My Narrative,—a few copies of which I had with me,—was sought after, and extensively read, the reading of which produced considerable sensation among the passengers, especially the slaveholding and pro-slavery portion of them.[1]

1. *Liberator,* July 20, 1849, p. 114; *North Star,* August 3, 1849, p. 3; Brown to Garrison, October 12, 1849, *Liberator,* November 2, 1849, p. 175.

After a voyage of ten days the *Canada* arrived at Liverpool on the afternoon of July 28. During the customs inspection, which immediately followed debarkation, a customs official was amazed to find an iron collar in Brown's luggage. In answer to his questions about it, Brown explained that a female slave in the Mississippi Valley had been compelled to wear it, and he also gratuitously went into some details about American slavery—to the embarrassment of some of his fellow passengers and to the wry amusement of others. The discovery of this piece of apparatus from the laboratory of the "peculiar institution" brought an end to the inspection of Brown's luggage, in which the none-too-clean hands of the customs official had made "no improvement on the work of the laundress." Brown proceeded to Brown's Temperance Hotel, where he spent his first three nights in England.[2]

On July 30 Brown wrote from Liverpool to Elizabeth Pease, informing her of his arrival in England. Explaining that it would probably be some time before he would see her, he resorted to the questionable etiquette of sending by mail to her his letter of introduction from Garrison and also one from the Reverend Charles Spear.[3] The next day he went to Dublin, where he was hospitably received by Richard D. Webb and James Haughton, to whom he had letters of introduction from Garrison. In a letter he wrote on August 3 to Mrs. Maria Weston Chapman, who was then in Versailles, Webb said that Brown was currently his guest. When he first saw Brown, Webb confided to Mrs. Chapman, "I was fearful on his account—now I am full of hope. I think he will be able to do good service in a way of his own."[4]

Webb and Haughton sponsored a public meeting for Brown in the Rotunda in Dublin, and on this occasion, with Haughton as presiding officer, Brown had an audience of six hundred. In

2. *Three Years in Europe*, pp. 6–7.

3. Brown to Elizabeth Pease, July 30, 1849, Anti-Slavery Letters Written to W. L. Garrison and Others.

4. Webb to Mrs. Chapman, August 3, 1849, Anti-Slavery—Weston Papers.

his speech, which was his first one in the British Isles, he erroneously paid a tribute to Daniel O'Connell, the Irish patriot, for his rumored refusal to shake hands with "Stephenson," an American slaveholder; then he discussed at length slavery and Negro life in the United States mainly from an autobiographical point of view. Finally, he appealed to Irish Christians to add their influence to the antislavery movement and, according to Webb, "sat down amid loud cheering." To Haughton, Brown seemed to be "quite a superior man," one possessed of "much tact, as well as considerable power as a speaker, so that he greatly interested his audience."[5]

Brown having spent twenty days in Ireland, he and Webb left Dublin on the night of August 19 and went by way of Liverpool to London, where they arrived about midafternoon the next day. On the morning of August 21, at the London Bridge Railway Station, they joined about six hundred others who were en route to Paris. The departure of the group was delayed more than an hour by some confusion about tickets. On the passage from Folkestone to Boulogne there was more confusion, which resulted from the fact that many of the travelers, including Brown, had got on the wrong steamer. Arriving in Paris a little after midnight—about three hours late—Brown and his fellow delegates were welcomed by Elihu Burritt, who was the genius of the Peace Congress, and most courteously accommodated at Hotel Bedford.[6]

The Peace Congress was convened in the Salle de Sainte Cécile, with Victor Hugo as president, on August 22 and continued for three days. About eight hundred delegates were present, twenty of whom were from the United States. Among these were the Reverend James W. C. Pennington of Hartford, Con-

5. *National Anti-Slavery Standard*, September 13, 1849, pp. 62–63; James Haughton to Garrison, September 10, 1849, *Liberator*, October 12, 1849, p. 162.

6. Brown to Garrison, October 12, 1849; *Three Years in Europe*, pp. 22–23, 25–30; Merle Eugene Curti, *The American Peace Crusade, 1815–1860* (Durham, N. C.: Duke University Press, 1929), pp. 173–74.

necticut, and the Reverend Alexander Crummell of New York, both of whom were Negroes. Thirteen of the twenty were from Massachusetts, including Brown, Burritt, the Reverend James Freeman Clarke, and the Reverend William Allen of Northampton.[7] Many Americans who were not delegates were also present. Notable among these were Mrs. Maria Weston Chapman of Boston, her children, and two of her sisters.

The Paris police department, in cooperation with the French government, it was thought, had permitted the meeting to be held only on the condition that discussion of specific contemporary political and diplomatic questions would be avoided. Accordingly rule 7 of the eleven rules unanimously adopted early in the first session declared that "no speaker can be allowed to make any direct allusion to the political events of the day, or to discuss any questions of local interest." Any speaker who persistently violated this rule was to have the privilege of the floor withdrawn from him.[8]

As soon as Brown's identity became known, interest in him was intensified, not merely because he was a fugitive slave but also because he looked as much like an American white man as any of the slaveholders who were present. Indeed he was not the only fugitive slave who was a delegate to the meeting. Pennington, who was obviously a Negro, was both a fugitive slave and a delegate. Two of those who bestowed special attention upon Brown were Richard Cobden, the British statesman and economist, and Victor Hugo. They engaged him in a conversation immediately after the first session. Following that conversation, an American slaveholder whom Brown recognized as a former fellow passenger on the *Canada* came forward and spoke to him. This man, Brown remembered, had freely expressed his belief

7. *Report of the Proceedings of the Second General Peace Congress, Held in Paris, on the 22nd, 23rd, and 24th of August, 1849* (London, 1849), p. 99.

8. "Latest from Paris," *London Times*, August 21, 1849; "The State of Europe," *ibid.*, August 22, 1849; *Report of the Peace Congress, 1849*, p. 14.

in the inferiority of Negroes and would not condescend to speak to him while they were on the ship. Now, however, he introduced himself and requested Brown to introduce him to Cobden and Hugo. "I felt so indignant at the downright impudence of the fellow," Brown said in his letter of October 12 to Garrison, "that I left him without making any reply."[9]

The final session of the Peace Congress began at noon on August 24 and continued until after six o'clock. About midafternoon Brown succeeded in getting the floor, while the third resolution of the meeting was pending. This resolution urged

> all the friends of Peace to prepare public opinion in their respective countries, for the formation of a Congress of Nations, whose sole object it should be to frame a code of international laws, on just principles, and to constitute a Supreme Court, to which should be submitted all questions relating to the reciprocal rights and duties of nations.

Mrs. Maria Weston Chapman was present when Brown addressed the assembly. Writing from Versailles on August 28 to Sidney Howard Gay, she said that "our friend's *color* [his being a Negro] and his *cause*, the two very good reasons that would have prevented his obtaining a hearing in the United States, removed all the obstacles here." Athanase Josué Coquerel, a young

9. In his letter to Garrison, Brown told of the presence on the *Canada* and also at the first session of the Peace Congress of "a Judge Chinn, a Louisiana slaveholder, who had been appointed by our democratic government as Consul to Naples, and who was on his way out to occupy his post." This doubtless was Thomas Withers Chinn, a physician, lawyer, ex-judge, ex-congressman, and planter, of West Baton Rouge Parish, Louisiana. He had been recently appointed United States minister to the two Sicilies by President Zachary Taylor and was then en route by way of Paris to his new position. (*Biographical Directory of the American Congress, 1774–1961* [Washington, 1961], p. 688.) Most probably this was the man who Brown said asked him for an introduction to Cobden and Hugo. The *Liberator*, January 25, 1850, p. 15, carried a letter from Micajah T. Johnson of Short Creek, Warren County, New York, reprehending Brown for being unkind to the slaveholder as the slaveholder had previously been to him.

but already distinguished Protestant preacher, introduced Brown as a fugitive slave who had achieved his freedom by his own efforts. Again in the words of Mrs. Chapman,

> when he rose on the platform, the general feeling of the assembly sustained him, notwithstanding the efforts of the huissier, in the performance of his functions, to keep him down, his name not being on the list of speakers. He spoke about five minutes amid the most cordial applause.[10]

Brown began his speech by explaining that he was taking up the time of the meeting only because he fervently desired to protest at this Peace Congress against the war spirit by which slavery, although it had been abolished by almost every European nation, was still maintained in the United States, to the nation's shame. He avowed that he had spent twenty years in American slavery and therefore could speak authoritatively about it. He could express himself freely in Paris, the capital of France, against slavery, he said, but he could not do so in the capital of the United States without endangering his life. In his opinion it was impossible to maintain slavery without maintaining war, for slavery was essentially a war between the enslaver and the enslaved. "If therefore we can obtain the abolition of war," he concluded, "we shall at the same time proclaim liberty throughout the world, break in pieces every yoke of bondage, and let all the oppressed go free." Brown's speech was immediately translated into French by Coquerel.[11]

With its recognition of the need for a code of international laws based on just principles, the third resolution of the Peace Congress was broad enough to permit in the consideration of it some discussion of slavery and the war spirit. Even so, since American slavery was more or less generally considered an intranational problem, in discussing it Brown technically violated

10. *London Times,* August 27, 1849, p. 6; Mrs. Chapman to Gay, August 28, 1849, *National Anti-Slavery Standard,* September 20, 1849, p. 67; *Liberator,* September 28, 1849, p. 156.

11. *Report of the Peace Congress, 1849,* pp. 77–78.

rule 7 of the meeting. Nobody, however, seems to have raised such an objection, nor did any of the slaveholders present condescend—or dare—to defend their "peculiar institution" against his attack.

Brown's speech was favorably noticed by at least two important Parisian newspapers. As Mrs. Chapman observed, *Galignani's Messenger*, published daily in English, quoted it at length, and *La Presse*, edited by Emile de Girardin, one of the sponsors of the Peace Congress, was exuberant in praise of it. Brown, this newspaper said, "astonished the auditory by the abundance and the profoundness of his ideas." On the contrary a Paris correspondent for the *London Times* was apparently intentionally sarcastic—and unintentionally prophetic—in his comment on the speech. Said he,

> Mr. Brown, the black, certainly produced a feeling of intense hostility against the slave-holding states of America by his description of the horrors of slavery; and if war be not forthwith declared by one half of the union against the other, it is not to be attributed to Mr. Brown.[12]

On August 25 Alexis de Tocqueville, the French minister of foreign affairs, and Madame de Tocqueville gave a grand soiree in the Hôtel des Affaires Étrangères in honor of the Peace Congress and the various diplomatic legations then in Paris. Between 1,000 and 1,500 persons attended this reception. When Brown was introduced as an American slave to Madame de Tocqueville, she was surprised, for he did not fit into her conception of a slave. She became so curious about him that she not only transcended the ordinary custom by shaking hands with him but also engaged him in a brief conversation, thus making him the center of attention for a while.[13]

The British members of the Peace Congress honored "their

12. *La Presse* [Paris], quoted in Mrs. Chapman to Gay, August 28, 1849; *London Times*, August 27, 1849, p. 6.

13. Mrs. Chapman to Gay, August 28, 1849; Brown to Garrison, October 12, 1849; *Three Years in Europe*, pp. 50–52.

American brethren" with a breakfast in Versailles on August 27. This occasion became a sort of adjourned session of the Peace Congress, with Richard Cobden as master of ceremonies. About six hundred persons were present. Two American speakers who distinguished themselves were Elihu Burritt and the Reverend James Freeman Clarke. One American who embarrassed himself as well as his fellow Americans by saying more than he had to say was the Reverend William Allen of Northampton, Massachusetts. Speaking more or less apologetically about American slavery, Allen declared that the slave states alone were responsible for it—that neither the free states nor the federal government had anything to do with it. In the face of so much familiar evidence to the contrary, his declaration was astounding—so astounding that "the American delegation gathered round him in rebuke," and "the English shamed him into silence."[14]

Brown, nevertheless, did not let the matter rest thus. Having had no opportunity to reply to Allen at the breakfast, he wrote the preacher an open letter from London on September 2. His letter was published in several British newspapers, and it was also translated into French and published in *La Presse*. Brown also sent a copy of his letter to Garrison, who published it in the *Liberator* for October 12. In disproof of Allen's statement that the federal government had nothing to do with slavery, Brown reminded him that the Seminole War had been fought to safeguard property in slaves; that the Mexican War had been fought for the extension of slave territory; that in the District of Columbia, which was controlled by the federal government, both slavery and the slave trade flourished as vigorously as they did in any of the slave states; that the federal fugitive slave law of 1793 was still in force, as the successful prosecution of Thomas Garrett, the Delaware abolitionist, had recently shown; and that the Department of State arbitrarily denied that Negroes were

14. *Report of the Peace Congress, 1849*, p. 89; Mrs. Chapman to Gay, August 28, 1849; Brown to Garrison, October 12, 1849; *Three Years in Europe*, pp. 53–55.

citizens of the United States and refused to grant them passports unless they were traveling in the service of some white citizen. In proof of the last argument, Brown quoted John M. Clayton's letter refusing to grant a passport to Henry Hambleton of Philadelphia.[15] It does not appear that Allen ever replied to Brown's letter.

Although he had some profitable as well as pleasant experiences at the Peace Congress, Brown was doubtful about its effectiveness, as Mrs. Chapman was. For him the possibilities of the meeting had rendered it glorious, but the actualities had reduced it to "mere child's play." Having been permitted by governmental orders "to dwell on the blessings of peace," but prohibited from discussing any of the current events which were destroying or threatening to destroy peace, the congress was unable even to analyze many of the very problems for which it might have been expected to offer solutions. The planning committee had, Brown said, "permitted the Congress to be *gagged*, before it had met. They put padlocks upon their own mouths, and handed the keys to the government." Had he been fully aware, however, of the difficulties Burritt and a relatively small number of supporters had had to surmount to hold the meeting at all, he might have been less severe in his criticism of it.[16]

Brown was in Paris only about ten days, but he did a considerable amount of sight-seeing during that time. Like many other sight-seers he followed a guidebook, as he himself revealed. Yet unlike too many, doubtless, among the tourists who had preceded him and those who have followed him, he knew enough about the history of France to find more than a fleeting interest in what he saw. By chance he visited the Madeleine Church and was captivated by the grand and yet simple style of its architec-

15. Richard D. Webb to Gay, September 21, 1849, *National Anti-Slavery Standard*, October 18, 1849, p. 83; *Liberator*, October 12, 1849, p. 161.

16. *Three Years in Europe*, pp. 48–49; Mrs. Chapman to Gay, August 28, 1849. For an account of the difficulties Burritt and his supporters had, see Curti, *American Peace Crusade*, esp. chap. 8.

ture. He spent hours in the Louvre. When he walked through Versailles, Saint Cloud, the Tuileries, and Notre Dame, he was cognizant of the epoch-making events which had occurred in these places. He enjoyed strolling along the boulevards of the city. He was favorably impressed by the courtesy of the French people. Although he had gone to Paris a stranger to its people and its language, he thoroughly enjoyed his sojourn there.[17]

Upon returning to London, Brown took lodgings at 22 Cecil Street, Strand, and kept them during the five years he remained in Great Britain. Garrison had stayed in the same place in 1846, and Richard D. Webb and other abolitionists frequented it. On August 31 Brown called on George Thompson, then the most prominent British abolitionist, and presented to him a letter of introduction from Garrison. Before reading the letter, however, Thompson guessed who Brown was, for he had read in the *Liberator* the reports of the presentation and farewell meeting in Boston and of Brown's embarkation for England. Brown must have enjoyed his visit, for he prolonged it to three hours. Immediately afterwards Thompson wrote a letter to Garrison saying that he had given Brown "a hearty welcome" and promising to help him as much as possible to get on in England.[18]

In the opinion of Richard D. Webb, not the least of the advantages Brown had enjoyed at the Peace Congress was being introduced "to some of the best people in England, in a way that could not otherwise have been readily accomplished." Now in England to remain a while, he began, Webb continued, "reaping the fruits of the acquaintances he [had] formed in Paris." One of those acquaintances was Dr. John Lee of Hartwell

17. *Three Years in Europe*, pp. 30–82. Brown's remark on p. 83 that he had spent fifteen days in Paris on this his first visit is erroneous. He was back in London by August 31, and in his letter of October 12 to Garrison, he said that he had spent ten days in France.

18. Mary Anne Estlin to Mrs. M. W. Chapman, May 14, 1850, Anti-Slavery—Weston Papers; George Thompson to Garrison, August 31, 1849, *Liberator*, September 21, 1849, p. 150; Brown to Garrison, October 12, 1849; *Three Years in Europe*, pp. 85–86.

House near Aylesbury. With several other erstwhile delegates to the Peace Congress, Brown spent two days early in September as one of Lee's guests. Because Lee was "a staunch friend of Temperance, as well as of the cause of universal freedom," Brown felt especially welcome at Hartwell House.[19]

A welcome meeting for Brown was held in a lecture hall in Croydon on the evening of September 5. The sponsor of the meeting was John Morland of Heath Lodge, another English gentleman whom Brown had met at the Peace Congress. This was Brown's first public meeting in England and his second in the British Isles. Morland presided and Thompson introduced Brown. After complimenting the British people on what they had already done for abolitionism in America, Brown urged them to do more. They could do more, he explained, by refusing to hold fellowship of any kind with American slaveholders and by forestalling all efforts to make slavery appear innocuous. He repeated some autobiographical details, together with references to the laws and the horrors of slavery, and "concluded a long and eloquent speech amidst loud applause."[20]

In his letter of July 30 to Elizabeth Pease, Brown had said that he was going to Dublin the next day "for the purpose of getting out an edition of my book." While in Dublin in August, he had completed arrangements by which Webb and Chapman of that city were to print a thousand copies of his *Narrative.* The Webb in the partnership of printers was Richard D. Webb, who had been instrumental in getting the *Narrative of the Life of Frederick Douglass* published in the British Isles, and who had been Brown's host during his recent visit to Dublin.[21]

19. Richard D. Webb to "Mademoiselle," September 19, 1849, Anti-Slavery—Weston Papers; Richard D. Webb to Gay, September 21, 1849, *National Anti-Slavery Standard*, October 18, 1849, p. 83; *Three Years in Europe*, pp. 87–93.

20. *London Standard of Freedom*, September 8, 1849, quoted in *Liberator*, September 28, 1849, p. 154.

21. Richard D. Webb to Mrs. Maria Weston Chapman, August 3, 1849, Anti-Slavery—Weston Papers.

Chapter Ten

By the time Brown returned from Paris to London, the first British edition of his autobiography was off the press. The volume is entitled *Narrative of William W. Brown, an American Slave*, and it bears the imprint of Charles Gilpin, Bishopgate Street Without, London. The *London Standard of Freedom* for September 8 said that "a large number" of copies of it were sold at the close of the welcome meeting in Croydon.

The title page of this edition bears the number "Eleventh Thousand," ten thousand copies of the four American editions having been previously sold. It is said on the verso of the title page that the book was printed "chiefly from the American Stereotype Plates, by Webb and Chapman." With the exception of three additional introductory pages, the first 162 pages of this edition are exactly as they are in the fourth American edition, but these are followed by six additional pages which contain several "testimonials" and "opinions of the American press."

The twelfth thousand copies of Brown's *Narrative*, which were identical with those of the first British edition, were printed in 1850, and the thirteenth thousand were probably printed in the same year. In May, 1851, there appeared an *Illustrated Edition of the Life and Escape of Wm. Wells Brown from American Slavery*. Like the British editions of 1849 and 1850, of which it is only a shortened and slightly revised version, this also bears the imprint of Charles Gilpin. According to its title page, the copies of this edition were the fourteenth thousand of Brown's autobiography to be printed. This seems to have been the fourth printing of the *Narrative* in the British Isles and the eighth printing since 1847. This work hardly deserves its long title, for the only illustration in it which is not in all of the preceding editions of the *Narrative* beginning with the second one is an illustration on the title page. This is essentially the same as the figure which had been designed in October, 1787, for the seal of the Committee for the Abolition of the Slave Trade, and which had been used in various kinds of antislavery publications.[22] A variation of it is found at the top of the first page of Brown's *Anti-Slavery Harp*. After the publication of the *Illustrated Edition*, there seems to have been only one more edition of Brown's *Narrative*. This one "With Additions by the Rev. Samuel Green" was published by W. Tegg and Company of London in 1853.[23]

A public reception for Brown was held "in the spacious and elegant concert-room in Store Street," Tottenham Court Road in London on the evening of September 27. According to William Farmer, who reported the meeting especially for the *Liberator*, "The Hall was crowded in every part by a highly respectable audience." George Thompson spoke at length in introducing Brown. His speech was interrupted by George Jones, who said that he was a Bostonian and a friend of Daniel Webster. Jones not only asserted that American slavery was mild but also denied that race prejudice existed in Boston.

On this occasion Brown made his first noteworthy public speech in London. Speaking out of his own experience as a slave and the son of a slaveholder, he easily disproved Jones's assertion concerning the mildness of American slavery. He gave some details about the brutalities and the immorality inherent in it and also about the proslavery features of the Constitution of the United States. With regard to race prejudice in Boston, he reminded Jones that two years earlier, when the Rowe Street church was built, a provision in its deed prohibited Negroes from owning pews in it.

Before the meeting was adjourned, Jones spoke again. He reminded the audience that slavery had been established in the American colonies by the British government, and he praised

22. [Wendell Phillips Garrison and Francis Jackson Garrison], *William Lloyd Garrison, 1805–1879: The Story of His Life Told by His Children*, 4 vols. (Boston and New York, 1894), 1: 163.

23. See the *British Museum General Catalogue of Printed Books* (London, 1939), 26: 683.

the United States government for abolishing the African slave trade in 1808.

Brown said in rebuttal that Jones's argument concerning how slavery was established in the American colonies was commonly used by slaveholders; then he countered with the suggestion that if America had followed the British government in the bad example of fostering slavery for a while, it should now follow the good example that government had set in abolishing slavery from the West Indies. Brown found Jones's explanation concerning the abolition of the African slave trade misleading to those who did not know the pertinent facts. He explained that the United States government did not abolish the African slave trade in 1808, but had enacted in 1788 a law which allowed it to continue for twenty years, and that during that time the government had profited from a per capita tax which it had collected on the slaves who had been imported. Next he added the questionable explanation that the African slave trade had been discontinued so that Maryland, Virginia, and Kentucky might have "a monopoly in the trade of raising slaves to supply the Southern market." Surely, he insisted, Americans could claim no credit for abolishing the foreign slave trade if they did so in order that the domestic slave trade might flourish. Returning to Jones's assertion that American slavery was mild, Brown said that as far as he knew, the situation in slavery from which he had escaped was still open, and that he would be glad to recommend Jones for it, since Jones seemed to think that slavery was such a good thing. Brown's remarks were frequently interrupted by loud cheers, which indicated that the audience was deeply in sympathy with him.[24]

The next day Brown sent ten pounds to his daughters in New Bedford, Massachusetts; and after paying his rent the following

24. *Liberator*, October 19, 1849, pp. 166–67, October 26, 1849, p. 171, November 2, 1849, p. 173. An editorial note in the same newspaper for October 19, 1849, p. 166, said that "Of the Mr. Jones who figures in the meeting we know nothing, and no one we have seen has ever heard of him."

day, which was Saturday, he had only a few shillings left. He had an engagement to speak at a public meeting in Worcester the next Tuesday evening, and he expected to sell some copies of his *Narrative* on that occasion. He was not worried, therefore, about his temporary shortage of funds until he discovered that Worcester was not just ten miles from London, as he had been misinformed, but "above a hundred miles" away—a distance for which he was unable to pay traveling expenses.

After an impecunious weekend, Brown went out Monday morning and sought in vain for someone from whom he might borrow enough money to get to Worcester. Instead he met a destitute fugitive slave with whom he divided his last shilling. Although the day was very foggy, he walked a long time; and when he returned to his lodgings late in the afternoon, he had given up all hopes of getting to Worcester the next day.

Early in the evening, however, Providence not only surprised but also blessed him. Just after he had resolved, because he could not pay for a dinner, to be satisfied with tea provided by his landlord, the housemaid announced a visitor. It was Frederick Stevenson, a son of the minister of Borough Road Chapel, Southwark, in which Brown had recently lectured. Stevenson had taken it upon himself to sell copies of Brown's *Narrative* to members of the chapel and had come to bring him the money for the books—thirteen half-crowns. Brown was indeed grateful to Stevenson for being, albeit unknowingly, a very present help in a time of need. The sudden turn of affairs wrought radical changes in Brown's appetite and hopes. Instead of satisfying himself with the fare provided by his landlord, he went out to dine, and "With the means in my pocket of reaching Worcester the next day, I sat down to dinner at the Adelphi with a good cut of roast beef before me, and felt myself once more at home."[25]

The meeting in Worcester the next evening was held in the Guildhall and was attended by "from 2,000 to 3,000 persons."

25. *Three Years in Europe*, pp. 110–16.

The mayor of the city presided and introduced Brown. The speaker, "upon coming forward, was greeted with enthusiastic applause, which, for a time, prevented his speaking." When he did begin he went, as usual, into full details about American slavery. He "addressed the meeting for upwards of an hour and a half, being listened to during the whole time with the utmost interest, and on resuming his seat was loudly cheered."[26]

On the Tuesday after the meeting in Worcester, Brown was a dinner guest of one of the members of the Whittington Club. During this his first visit to a London club, he found there the kind of informality, freedom, and ease which to him seemed "unknown in the drawing-room of the private mansion." As he came to know London clubs better, his impression of them remained unchanged.

Towards the end of the 1840's it became a vogue for fugitive slaves who had acquired some education as well as their freedom to write open letters to their erstwhile masters. Brown made his contribution to the vogue with his "William W. Brown to His Master," which he wrote from London on November 23. Like other letters of its kind, Brown's letter combined personal references with antislavery arguments based on the doctrine of the inalienable rights of man, contempt for slaveholders' religion and morality, wry humor, defiance, and advice to the addressee to emancipate his slaves immediately. After discussing at length the immoral effects of slavery upon slaveholders as well as slaves, Brown continued in part as follows:

> Sir, you are a slaveholder, and by the laws of God and of nature, your slaves, like yourself, are entitled to "life, liberty, and the pursuit of happiness," and you have no right whatever to deprive them of these inestimable blessings which you

26. *Liberator,* October 26, 1849, p. 171. During the next week Brown had lecture engagements in Southwark and Colchester. (*London Morning Advertiser,* October 12, 1849, and *Essex Standard,* October 19, 1849, quoted in *Liberator* respectively for November 9, 1849, p. 178, and November 16, 1849, p. 181.)

> claim for yourself. Your slaves have the same right to develope their moral and intellectual faculties that you have; but you are keeping them in a state of ignorance and degradation; and if a single ray of light breaks forth, and penetrates to their souls, it is in despite of your efforts to keep their minds obscured in mental darkness. . . .
>
> In behalf of your slaves, I ask you, in the name of the God whom you profess to worship, to take the chains from their limbs, and to let them go free. It is a duty that you owe to God, to the slave, and to the world. . . . By your professed love of America, I conjure you to use your influence for the abolition of an institution which has done a thousand times more to blacken the character of the American people, and to render the name of their boasted free republic more odious to the ears of the friends of human freedom throughout the world, than all their other faults combined. . . .
>
> Sir, you may not be pleased with me for speaking to you in so plain a manner; but in this I have only done my duty. See that you do yours![27]

If Enoch Price ever received a copy of Brown's letter, he ignored it, for he remained a slaveholder until the time of the Civil War.

27. Brown to Price, November 23, 1849, *Liberator*, December 14, 1849, p. 199, and in Brown's *A Description of William Wells Brown's Original Panoramic Views* (London, [1850]), pp. 44–47.

Tours, Controversies, and Exhibitions

Before Brown left America, John Mawson of Newcastle upon Tyne had heard and read about him and had become interested in him. He and Brown had become acquainted in the office of the Peace Society in London in August, and they had kept in touch with each other since that time. A week after he wrote his open letter to Price, Brown went on a lecture trip to northern England. On December 1, "according to previous arrangement," as Mawson explained in a letter to Garrison two weeks later, "your friend and valued co-laborer in the great abolition cause, Wm. W. Brown, arrived at my house, and at once became a member of my family circle." Meanwhile Brown also spent some time in the home of Henry and Anna Richardson, who, like the Mawsons, had been hosts to Garrison and Frederick Douglass during their visits to Newcastle. He spent most of

December and the first week of the new year lecturing in Newcastle and its vicinity.[1]

Although more than four months had passed since Brown had forwarded to Elizabeth Pease of Darlington the introductory letters which Garrison and the Reverend Charles Spear had given to him, he had not yet visited her. On December 14 he wrote from the home of the Richardsons to Miss Pease, explaining that instead of visiting her on the fifteenth, as he had planned to do, he would have to postpone his visit for two more days. He went to Darlington on December 18 and remained there long enough to hold a public meeting. Soon afterwards Miss Pease informed Garrison that the fugitive "fully realized all that we had heard of him in public and private," and that he had made "a most excellent speech" to "a large and highly respectable audience, by whom he was warmly applauded."

From Darlington, Brown went on a brief lecture trip to York, arriving there on a moonlit night. Incongruously enough he said later that York Cathedral in the moonlight reminded him of "a mountain starting out of a plain, . . . looking down upon the surrounding buildings, with all the appearance of a Gulliver standing over the Lilliputians." The latter was the same inappropriate comparison he had previously made in speaking of Windsor Castle and its surroundings.[2]

Encouraged doubtless by Mawson, who had been most favorably impressed by his singing, Brown published in Newcastle early in 1850 a British edition of his *Anti-Slavery Harp*. The printing was done by J. Blackwell and Company of the same city. Bound in paper and consisting of forty pages, the booklet

1. Mawson to Garrison, December 14, 1849, and January 11, 1850, *Liberator*, January 4, 1850, p. 3, and February 8, 1850, p. 21; *Newcastle Guardian*, quoted in *Liberator*, January 4, 1850, p. 2, "William W. Brown," *Anti-Slavery Bugle*, February 9, 1850, p. 87.

2. W. Wells Brown to Elizabeth Pease, December 14, 1849, Anti-Slavery Letters Written to W. L. Garrison and Others; Elizabeth Pease to Garrison, *Liberator*, February 8, 1850, p. 23; *Three Years in Europe*, pp. 95, 134–37.

contains forty songs, all of which are among the forty-six found in the second American edition of the songbook. Among the six omissions is "Jefferson's Daughter"—an omission that did not improve the collection. Otherwise there were only minor changes in the work.

Whatever its fate was in Great Britain, the Newcastle edition of the *Anti-Slavery Harp* seems scarcely to have become known in America. In 1851 the third and last American edition of the work was published by Bela Marsh of Boston. This is only a reprint of the second American edition, and like the Newcastle edition, it seems never to have become widely known. By this time interest in Brown's antislavery songbook had spent itself.

On January 7 Brown went back to Yorkshire where he remained until the last week in the month lecturing and sightseeing. In Leeds he became acquainted with Wilson Armistead, the author of the voluminous *A Tribute for the Negro*, which had been published in both Manchester and New York two years earlier. In Sheffield he visited James Montgomery, "the poet of freedom," whose *Pelican Island* he had recently read. During the last week in January, he went a little farther south and visited Newstead Abbey and Hucknall, the home and the burial place respectively of Lord Byron, one of the English poets he liked best.[3]

Mawson said in his letter of January 11 to Garrison that Brown was going to Scotland after his tour of Yorkshire. Whether he spent February in Scotland or elsewhere, he was still in northern England in March; for he spent a considerable part of that month there, particularly in Lancaster County. On the twenty-second he addressed a "large and influential meeting" in Bolton, the county borough. After his speech a group of ladies presented to him a testimonial commending him for his exposure of the evils of slavery and resolving "to render what aid

3. *York Herald,* quoted in *Anti-Slavery Bugle*, February 9, 1850, p. 87; *Three Years in Europe,* pp. 142–43, 148–53.

we can to the cause which you have so eloquently pleaded in our presence."[4]

The officials of the British and Foreign Anti-Slavery Society had never welcomed Brown to Great Britain—a fact which Mawson had noted in his letter of December 14, 1849, to Garrison. Those officials had not done so because they were at odds with both the Massachusetts and the American Anti-Slavery Societies, and Brown was prominent in both, although he did not officially represent either in Great Britain. During his first six months there, those officials studiously ignored him. Then the Reverend John Scoble, Secretary of the British and Foreign Anti-Slavery Society, began to attack him directly, mainly on personal grounds. The bases of Scoble's attacks seem never to have been made public, but they made it necessary not only for Brown to defend himself but also for his friends to defend him, lest his antislavery work in Great Britain might be rendered futile. Fortunately, without searching for a champion, he found an able and influential one in Dr. John Bishop Estlin, the Bristol surgeon and philanthropist, whose generous support of abolitionism had long been well known.

On a trip to southwestern England early in April, Brown visited Bristol for the first time. A public meeting for him was held in the Broadmead Rooms in the city on the evening of the ninth. Almost two thousand people were present. The chairman of the meeting was Estlin, who took the occasion to censure the British and Foreign Anti-Slavery Society in general and Scoble in particular for their unfriendly attitude towards Brown.[5] Estlin's remarks won sympathy for Brown, but they did not stop Scoble's attacks on him. Indeed Scoble continued them for the next two years, until Brown threatened to prosecute him.

4. *Clotel*, pp. 42–44.

5. "A Friendly Address," *Liberator*, June 21, 1850, p. 99; "Memorial to the late Mr. Estlin," *ibid.*, November 30, 1855, p. 190. In the *Special Report of the Bristol and Clifton Ladies' Anti-Slavery Society* (London, 1852), p. 10, it is incorrectly implied that this meeting was held prior to April 3.

Estlin and Brown had already known each other by reputation, but they did not become personally acquainted until this visit of Brown's to Bristol. From the beginning, Estlin, a widower, and Mary Anne, his only child, were favorably impressed with Brown. On April 25 Estlin wrote to Mrs. Maria Weston Chapman as follows, not only giving his impression of Brown but also making some observations concerning Frederick Douglass which seem to have been left unnoticed by the latter's biographers:

> I am pleased with what I saw of W. W. Brown. He has not, I think, the talent of Douglass, nor his cultivated mind & refined habits, but I felt more sympathy with him than I did with F. D. There seemed an openness & confidingness about Brown that did not betray itself in D. Perhaps F. D. fancied *I* was not a person he could trust, tho' he *did* trust me very unreservedly as far as his pecuniary interests were concerned. Still I thought him naturally a cautious and suspicious man, which ought not to be any ground for censure considering how he was brought up. However, I regard him as a very interesting and remarkable character. Brown is not likely to be exposed to one danger by which F. D. was surrounded in this country—the being spoiled by the attentions of *ladies!* W. W. B. is certainly not such a "lady's man" as Douglass was. I must say[,] however, for the latter that, as far as my opportunity of [discovering?] went, "he was more sinned against than sinning"; indeed I was struck with his discretion & delicacy."[6]

Brown was in London during the latter half of April, but he was again in Bristol by the first week in May. One day early in that month, he went from Bristol to see the ruins of Tintern Abbey. He enjoyed his visit to the ruins, but less than he would have enjoyed it, no doubt, had he been better informed concerning the authentic and the traditional history of the Abbey than

6. Estlin to Mrs. Chapman, April 25, 1850, Anti-Slavery—Estlin Papers. See also Mary Anne Estlin to Mrs. Chapman, April 30, 1850, Anti-Slavery—Estlin Papers, and May 14, 1850, Anti-Slavery—Weston Papers.

he apparently was. Late in the afternoon he returned along a part of the same route that William Wordsworth and his sister Dorothy had followed from the Wye Valley to Bristol one afternoon in July fifty-two years earlier. He spent most of the next day "examining the interior" of the Church of Saint Mary Redcliffe in Bristol. He found this church especially interesting because of Thomas Chatterton's connection with it, and because of his familiarity with both the biography and the poetry of "the ardent boy," as he called the young and unfortunate poet.[7]

Returning to London about the middle of May, Brown preceded by a few days the Estlins, who expected to arrive on the twentieth to spend some time in the city, and who were doubtless members of the small audience Brown had at a lecture in Crosby Hall on the evening of May 30.[8] Meanwhile, for Brown the spring of 1850 became an open season for controversies. Scarcely had the controversy with Scoble begun when two old ones again claimed his attention. One of these was between him and the Reverend Artemas Bullard, pastor of the First Presbyterian Church of Saint Louis from 1838 until his death on November 1, 1855. As has been noted, in his *Narrative* Brown had adversely criticized Daniel D. Page of Saint Louis as a more or less typical Christian slaveholder. His controversy with Bullard resulted from the preacher's attempt to defend Page. This controversy, which was aired in the *Congregationalist* of Boston, continued almost two years without proving very much except, perhaps, the futility of argument.[9]

The second old controversy that claimed Brown's attention in the spring of 1850 was the one between him and his estranged wife. Although the Browns had not seen each other since September, 1848, they had heard much, indirectly if not directly,

7. *Three Years in Europe,* pp. 155–62.

8. Mary Anne Estlin to Mrs. Chapman, May 14, 1850; *Liberator,* June 28, 1850, p. 103.

9. For a full account of this controversy, see W. Edward Farrison, "A Theologian's Missouri Compromise," *Journal of Negro History* 48 (January, 1963): 33–43.

from and about each other; and what they had heard had not improved their attitudes towards each other. The husband had been informed that the wife had said she "would travel over the entire country to injure me," and he was convinced ere long that she had gone "as far as her means would permit" her to go. As he eventually discovered, in at least one instance she had sent a letter when and where she herself could not go.

The *New York Daily Tribune* for March 12, 1850, carried on its first page a short paragraph with the caption "A Stray Husband." Herein it was said that

> Mrs. Elizabeth Brown, wife of William W. Brown, a fugitive slave, (now stumping in England, we believe) sends us a long statement of her conjugal difficulties, the upshot of which is that, notwithstanding she is a very respectable woman and exemplary wife, (which she proves by "no end" of certificates,) her husband has deserted her and her youngest child, does nothing for their support, but on the contrary repudiates them both—the former as unfaithful, the latter as spurious. She says she is penniless and her child destitute, while the husband and father is living in clover.

The paragraph quoted Mrs. Brown as having said that "Mr. Brown has become so popular among the Abolition ladies that he did [*sic*] not wish his sable wife any longer." Finally it said that "We know none of the parties, but we suspect Elizabeth is slightly malicious."

Although it was brief, this paragraph refocused attention so directly upon Brown's marital difficulties that both he and the officials of the Massachusetts Anti-Slavery Society were constrained to break their silence of almost two years concerning the matter. Consequently Brown wrote in London on June 1 his article "To the Public," which was published in the *Liberator* for July 12, and which he concluded as follows:

> Had Mrs. Brown wished, she could still have had a home with my children; but she left, it is well-known, of her own ac-

> cord. I have declined giving any further support to a woman whose own misconduct has alienated her from me forever. Whether I have done right in this matter or not, I leave to a candid and impartial public to judge. In looking back upon the former part of this transaction, I see many acts of mine which I regret. But to do otherwise, at the time, was beyond my power. My attachment to my wife was too great to allow me to do what I saw clearly to be a duty to myself and my children. I have been blamed by many for my long silence upon this subject, and even now I give this statement with great reluctance. Nothing but self-defence could possibly have induced me to pen this article.[10]

Brown's article was followed by a brief statement from the officials of the Massachusetts Anti-Slavery Society. In this statement it was said that

> without intending to decide on the truth of all the facts mentioned above,—the truth of many of which can be known only to the parties themselves,—we and our friends were satisfied, from the investigations we were able to make here, and from all we could gather of the opinions of those, in whose neighborhood Mr. and Mrs. Brown resided at the time alluded to, that there was nothing in his [Brown's] conduct toward his wife worthy of censure; but that, on the contrary, he had shown her great forbearance—had endeavored to do his duty as a husband and father, watchful for the best interests of his children, for whom his exertions were untiring; and that he was entitled to the sympathy of his friends in the painful circumstances in which he was placed.

If Mrs. Brown ever saw Brown's article and the officials' statement, she probably did not reply to them; nor did she have to wait very long for fate to end the matter forever as far as she was concerned. In the memoir of Brown he wrote in 1852 for *Three Years in Europe*, William Farmer said that Mrs. Brown

10. William Wells Brown, "To the Public," *Liberator*, July 12, 1850, p. 111.

died in January of that year. But in the sketch of the author's life in *Clotel,* which was published late in 1853, it was said that she died in Buffalo in January, 1851.[11]

One day early in June, 1850, in pursuit of the pleasure which sight-seeing afforded him from time to time, Brown went to Westminster Abbey especially to visit the tomb of William Wilberforce, the great abolitionist. He told about this trip in an essay entitled "Visit of a Fugitive Slave to the Grave of Wilberforce," which apparently was not published until four years later.

About a third of this essay consists of an account of the author's visit to Nelson's monument at Trafalgar Square. The only connection this part of the essay has with what follows it is that while Brown was at the monument, he decided to visit the abbey again, having visited it in the preceding October. The middle third of the essay repeats much of what he said in *Three Years in Europe* about what he had seen on his first visit to the abbey. The last third consists of the quotation of the long inscription on Wilberforce's monument followed by an original paragraph of Brown's expressing appreciation for Wilberforce. Said Brown,

> No man's philosophy was ever moulded in a nobler cast than his; it was founded in the school of Christianity, which was, that all men are by nature equal; that they are wisely and justly endowed by their Creator with certain rights which are irrefragable, and no matter how human pride and avarice may depress and debase, still God is the author of good to man; and of evil, man is the artificer to himself and to his species. Unlike Plato and Socrates, his mind was free from the gloom that surrounded theirs. Let the name, the worth, the zeal, and other excellent qualifications of this noble man, ever live in our hearts, let his deeds be the theme of our

11. *Three Years in Europe,* p. xxvii; *Clotel,* p. 51. Official records of deaths in Buffalo go no further back than 1852, and no reference to Mrs. Brown's death has been found in the records for that year.

praise, and let us teach our children to honor and love the name of William Wilberforce.

Even though this essay is hardly a model of unified composition, its style is indeed simple, fluent, and dignified.[12]

On June 20 Brown delivered an antislavery lecture in the Whittington Club and Metropolitan Athenaeum, the first London club he had visited nine months earlier. Among the nearly two thousand members of this institution were Lords Brougham and Dudley Coutts Stuart, Charles Lushington and Richard Moncton Milnes, both of whom were members of Parliament, Charles Dickens, "and several other [*sic*] of the most distinguished legislators and literary men and women" of Great Britain. In addition to pleasing his audience, Brown must have proved himself to be what Dr. Samuel Johnson had called "a clubbable man"; for the next day he received a letter from William Strudwicke, the secretary of the club, thanking him on behalf of "the Managing Committee of this institution for the excellent lecture you gave here last evening" and "presenting you in their names with an honorary membership in the Club."[13]

Brown spent several days in July at the Polytechnic Institution in Southampton lecturing on slavery. His speeches there won the compliments of the *Hampshire Independent*. Later in July and in August he held meetings in Oxford, Reading, and neighboring towns, "with considerable effect he considers," said Mary Anne Estlin.[14] By this time, nevertheless, Brown had learned that the summer was by no means the best season in England for lectures, either antislavery or other kinds. He had also begun to realize that lest the public might lose interest in his lectures, he had better vary his activities for a while; so he began to suit his actions to a new idea.

12. This essay seems to have been first published in Julia Griffiths, ed., *Autographs for Freedom* (Auburn and Rochester, N. Y., 1854), pp. 70–76.

13. *Three Years in Europe*, p. xxiv; *Clotel*, pp. 45–46.

14. *Liberator*, August 9, 1850, p. 126; Mary Anne Estlin to Emma Weston, August 28, 1850, Anti-Slavery—Estlin Papers.

In the fall of 1847 Brown had seen a panorama of the Mississippi River on exhibition in Boston and had been "somewhat amazed at the very mild manner" in which it had portrayed slavery in what he considered the very valley of the shadow of death as far as the "peculiar institution" was concerned. That exhibition had brought to his mind the idea "that a painting, with as fair a representation of American Slavery as could be given upon canvass" might help to spread the truth about it and thereby help to hasten its destruction.[15] However good he thought the idea was, he let almost three years pass before doing anything about it.

In the summer of 1850, while his lecture engagements were not numerous, and after the India Route Panorama then on exhibition in London had begun to attract large crowds, Brown decided to carry out his original idea. Forthwith he employed "skillful artists in London" to portray scenes of various phases of American slavery—scenes based on his own experience and on what he had heard and read. In the meantime he busied himself with plans for his exhibition. About the middle of August he wrote to Estlin, who was back in Bristol, saying that the work on his panoramic views was progressing so rapidly and was demanding so much supervision from him, that he could not leave it to attend the International Peace Congress which was about to convene in Frankfort on the Main. His inability to attend the Peace Congress was "a circumstance on which my Father sees fit to congratulate him," wrote Mary Anne Estlin in her letter of August 28 to Emma Weston.

Even if he had not been busy with his panoramic views, Brown had no special reason to attend the Peace Congress. He was not a delegate, as he had been at the one in Paris in 1849; and although he was still interested in the peace crusade, he had not been sufficiently impressed by the achievements of the Peace Congress he had attended to go so far to attend another one. It

15. [William Wells Brown], *A Description of William Wells Brown's Original Panoramic Views* (London, [1850]), preface.

appears from the remark of Estlin's daughter quoted above that Estlin shared Brown's point of view.

By the middle of August, Brown had eighteen drawings for his panoramic views completed, and these had been pronounced good by competent judges. Within the next few weeks six additional drawings were completed, a descriptive catalogue of the drawings was printed, and the exhibition was ready to be opened. The catalogue is a small pamphlet consisting of forty-eight pages in paper covers. It bears the following title, whose length, plus its direct appeal to the British people, should have been sufficiently impressive: *A Description of William Wells Brown's Original Panoramic Views of the Scenes in the Life of an American Slave, from His Birth in Slavery to His Death or His Escape to His First Home of Freedom on British Soil.* The imprint, which includes no date, is that of Charles Gilpin, the publisher of most of Brown's other books published in England.

The sketches and stories in the catalogue are interesting in themselves as well as because of the information they give about the twenty-four panoramic views. This is especially true of the story pertaining to the eighth view, which portrayed an auction in New Orleans in which two white girls were being sold. Germinally a short story replete with romance and tragedy, it gives the following account of the two girls: A young physician from one of the free states went to New Orleans to practice medicine. Soon after his arrival there he fell in love with a young woman who was apparently white, but who was a slave. The physician bought her from her master, who was also her father, for $800 and married her; but to avoid publicizing the fact that she had been a slave, he never legally emancipated her. Meanwhile he and she lived happily together many years; then both of them died, leaving two beautiful teen-age daughters and a heavily encumbered estate.

The physician's brother went to New Orleans to act in the interest of the two girls. When the lawyers for the physician's creditors discovered that he had purchased but had never legally manumitted his wife, they argued that his daughters, having been born of a slave mother, were his slaves and should be listed in the inventory of his estate and sold at auction. Neither the physician's brother nor the girls themselves knew that the physician's wife had ever been a slave until they were thus informed by the lawyers. As the lawyers knew all too well, according to the laws in the several slave states, children born of slave mothers were slaves no matter who their fathers were. To the horror of the physician's brother and the girls, but in accordance with the law, the courts of Louisiana upheld the argument of the creditors' lawyers. One of the girls was sold, therefore, for $1,500 and the other for $2,000. "For what purpose such high sums were given," Brown commented, "all those who are acquainted with the iniquities of American Slavery will readily suspect."

This story is similar to one which had been synopsized in 1839 by Captain Frederick Marryat, and also to the last fifth of Mrs. Lydia Maria Child's "The Quadroons," which had been published in *The Liberty Bell* for 1842 and in her *Fact and Fiction: A Collection of Stories* in 1847.[16] It differs sufficiently from both Marryat's and Mrs. Child's versions, however, for Brown to be credited with some originality in his telling of it.

Four of the panoramic views were based on Brown's own life. The twelfth view portrayed Brown as a young fugitive treed by Benjamin O'Fallon's dogs in a woodland near Saint Louis after he had run away from Major Freeland to escape cruel treatment. This illustration had been first included in the second edition of Brown's *Narrative* opposite the first page of the first chapter. The seventeenth view pictured Brown and his mother in a boat crossing the Mississippi River by moonlight on their flight from Saint Louis. The nineteenth view illustrated the arrest of Brown and his mother in central Illinois, whence they were carried back into slavery. This picture had also been copied from one in the second edition of his *Narrative*. The

16. [Frederick] Marryat, *A Diary in America, with Remarks on Its Institutions*, 3 vols. (London, 1839), 3: 56–57.

twenty-first view showed Brown in southern Ohio on a cold night in January, 1834, following the North Star to freedom—a journey he had recounted in all of the editions of his *Narrative*.

The twentieth view portrayed a young woman with a child in her arms in flight from slavery in Kentucky crossing the Ohio River one morning in February, 1848, by jumping from one cake of ice to another. A report of such an incident had appeared in the antislavery press several times in 1848 and 1849.[17] Brown had doubtless read this report and had recognized the dramatic value of the incident. By making it the subject of one of his views and retelling it in his catalogue, he helped to publicize it a year before Mrs. Harriet Beecher Stowe made it famous as one of Eliza's experiences in *Uncle Tom's Cabin*.

It is doubtful that Brown's exhibition was remarkably successful, although Estlin and other friends helped him in every way they could to make the most of it. After keeping it in London five or six weeks, Brown took it to Newcastle upon Tyne, where he opened it during the last week in October. Six weeks later he was corresponding with William Smeal of Glasgow about the possibility of holding a public meeting and exhibiting his panoramic views in that city. Smeal was in favor of his doing both, as was Andrew Paton, also of Glasgow. Brown went to Scotland at the end of December and remained there about nine weeks, but whether he gave exhibitions there is unknown. He did not refer to his panoramic views in the letters he wrote from Edinburgh and Glasgow respectively on January 3 and 16, 1851, to Garrison, nor did he mention any exhibitions in any later accounts of his sojourn in Scotland.[18]

17. *True American*, reprinted in *North Star*, June 2, 1848, p. 2, and in *Liberator*, October 20, 1848, p. 166, and February 9, 1849, p. 21.

18. J. B. Estlin to "Miss Weston," October 30, 1850, Anti-Slavery—Weston Papers; "Extract from a letter from Mr. Wm. Smeal to W. Wells Brown . . . Decr. 12th 1850," *ibid.;* Brown to Garrison, January 3, 1851, and January 16, 1851, *Liberator*, January 24, 1851, p. 15, and February 7, 1851, p. 23.

Exiles from Tyranny

BROWN HAD ORIGINALLY INTENDED TO REMAIN IN GREAT Britain no more than a year, but circumstances not altogether unforeseen made him change his mind. In September, 1850, while he was busy with his panoramic views, the Fugitive Slave Law—one of the worst legal monstrosities imaginable—was enacted. Within the next two months the hunting of fugitive slaves and the more or less legal kidnapping of Negroes in the free states began to increase rapidly. Brown's friends feared—and their fears were later justified—that if he returned to the United States, he would be immediately arrested and remanded to slavery; for he was generally known to be a fugitive slave. Because of this fact Wendell Phillips, along with others who were concerned about him, advised him to stay in Great Britain, which he did.[1]

1. *Hereford* [England] *Times*, December 17, 1853; [Josephine Brown], *Biography of an American Bondman by His Daughter* (Boston, 1856), p. 73.

Naturally Brown felt that in effect he had been cruelly expatriated, but his feelings were somewhat assuaged by the new sympathy which his situation aroused for him among the British people. Moreover, although his exhibition was not achieving the success for which he had hoped, he had something else to which to look forward. This was the new lecture season which was about to begin. There were other facts which, if he was not slow to recognize them, must have emphasized for him as for others the irony with which human affairs are so often invested. The Fugitive Slave Law at once kept him in Great Britain and supplied him with new antislavery arguments to use there. What was vastly more important, attempts to enforce this law in the northern half of the United States were rapidly turning into abolitionists many who had been indifferent towards slavery, if not in favor of it. This was an instance in which what was foul in design was proving fair in effect.

A farewell meeting was held in the London Tavern on Wednesday evening, October 16, in honor of George Thompson, who was about to sail to America. Brown was one of the six hundred persons present, among whom were many women, and he was also one of the speakers for the occasion. After being presented by Thompson himself, he arose and "was received with the most enthusiastic cheers, again and again repeated, accompanied by the waving of hats and handkerchiefs." In a speech of about half an hour, he expressed appreciation for the numerous courtesies he had received from Thompson as a friend, and he also lauded Thompson for his courage and influence as an abolitionist. He remarked, perhaps wistfully, that it would be unsafe for him to return to the United States with his friend. Referring to the Fugitive Slave Law, he blamed "men pecuniarily interested" in slavery, "Northern dough-faces," and "certain Northern politicians, bidding for office" for colluding with proslavery leaders to get it enacted. He considered Daniel Webster especially notorious among the Northern senators who had voted for the law. Nevertheless he did not yet seem to be taking it very seriously. He even predicted, overoptimistically or naively, that because of the spirit of freedom prevailing in New England, the law could not be enforced there—certainly not in Boston, he thought.[2]

Alas Brown did not yet know about the danger of recapture then threatening his friends William and Ellen Craft, who were residents of Boston. These fugitives were sought and doubtless would have been arrested and returned to slavery if they had not been hidden and protected by abolitionists until they were spirited out of the United States.[3] Early in December the Crafts arrived in Liverpool. Brown, who was then in Newcastle upon Tyne, had been informed by correspondents in Boston that the Crafts were coming to England; and soon after their arrival in Liverpool, he heard that they wanted to get in touch with him. Forthwith he wrote to them, and without waiting for a reply, "made arrangements to give our friends a warm reception, at the place where I was then lecturing." But Mrs. Craft, who had been very sick on the voyage from America, was detained by illness for almost three weeks at the home of the Reverend Francis Bishop in Liverpool; so the reception had to be postponed.

Having previously planned to go to Scotland on a lecture tour at the end of December, Brown now considered the possibility of having the Crafts accompany him. He wrote to Henry Wigham of Edinburgh and to William Smeal and Andrew Paton of Glasgow, his sponsors in those cities, asking whether he might bring the Crafts with him. He received affirmative replies and informed the Crafts accordingly. Craft left his wife convalescing in Liverpool and joined Brown in Newcastle, whence the two men went to Edinburgh during the Christmas holidays.

2. *Liberator*, November 15, 1850, p. 182, November 22, 1850, p. 185.

3. "Slave-hunters in Boston," *Liberator*, November 1, 1850, p. 174; Vincent Y. Bowditch, *Life and Correspondence of Henry Ingersoll Bowditch*, 2 vols. (Boston and New York, 1902), 1: 205–09.

Brown and Craft spent their days in Edinburgh sight-seeing and their evenings attending antislavery and temperance meetings. On January 2, 1851, at a soiree given by the Edinburgh Temperance Society, they were not only "warmly greeted" but also voted life members in the organization "in the most enthusiastic manner, by the whole audience."[4]

Having become well enough to travel, Mrs. Craft went to Edinburgh on January 3. The next day Brown left the Crafts there and went to Glasgow. He went, he said, in acceptance of an invitation to be the guest of "a distinguished gentleman" he had met in London, and whose home was Laurel Bank at Patrick, about three miles from Glasgow. He probably went to Glasgow first to attend to last-minute details pertaining to the antislavery meeting which was to be held there on Monday evening, January 6. By that date the Crafts were also in Glasgow.[5]

The meeting was held under the auspices of the Glasgow Emancipation Society in the city hall. About three thousand persons were present, among them a large number of clergymen who sat on the platform. The Honorable Alexander Hastie, a member of Parliament, presided. After being introduced by Hastie, Brown spoke against the Fugitive Slave Law and also ridiculed the United States for welcoming so recently and so cordially "refugees from the banks of the Danube, the Tiber, and the Nile," while it so flagrantly belied its Declaration of Independence that two of its own citizens had to flee to monarchical England to escape from an exceedingly vicious form of tyranny in their native land. The two citizens he had in mind were, of course, the Crafts; but he might well have included himself, for the Fugitive Slave Law had put him in the same predicament with them. After his speech he publicly presented the

4. *Edinburgh Scottish Press,* January 1, 1851, reprinted in *Liberator,* January 24, 1851, p. 14; *Edinburgh Scotsman,* January 1, 1851, January 4, 1851; *Edinburgh Evening Courant,* January 2, 1851; Brown to Garrison, January 3, 1851, *Liberator,* January 24, 1851, p. 15; *Three Years in Europe,* pp. 164–74.

5. *Three Years in Europe,* pp. 174–75.

Crafts together, probably for the first time in Great Britain, as he had been the first person to introduce them in New England.[6]

For some time Brown had been possessed of the idea of establishing in Canada a manual-labor school for fugitive slaves. His idea was similar to one which had been held in the 1830's by Austin Seward and Josiah Henson, and which had been partially realized by Henson and others at Dawn, Ontario. At a meeting in Edinburgh on January 3, Brown had mentioned this idea, and it had been favorably although hardly enthusiastically received. When it was presented to the meeting in Glasgow, a resolution approving it was unanimously adopted. Although Brown's idea was approved on other occasions, it never received the actual support which was necessary for him to put it into effect.[7]

Brown and the Crafts spent more than two weeks attending meetings in Glasgow and its vicinity. At a meeting of the Glasgow Female Anti-Slavery Society on January 21, Brown concluded his speech by "singing in a fine, clear, full-toned voice, a beautiful anti-slavery melody, by John Quincy Adams, which was loudly applauded."[8]

From Glasgow Brown and the Crafts went to Dundee on January 23 to hold a meeting in that city that evening. Soon after their arrival at their lodgings, they were visited by Dr. Thomas Dick, the scientific writer and abolitionist. Feeling somewhat drowsy in a warm room after a cold ride, Brown was aroused to full attention only after he heard the name of the visitor, who was then very popular. It was another instance in which the

6. *Glasgow North British Mail*, January 7, 1851, reprinted in *Liberator*, February 14, 1851, p. 25; *Glasgow Herald*, January 10, 1851; Brown to Garrison, January 16, 1851, *Liberator*, February 7, 1851, p. 23; *Three Years in Europe*, pp. 175–76.

7. Austin Steward, *Twenty-two Years a Slave and Forty Years a Freeman*, 3d ed. (Rochester, 1861), pp. 185 ff; [Josiah Henson], *Truth Stranger than Fiction: Father Henson's Story of His Own Life* (Boston and Cleveland, 1858), pp. 168 ff; *Three Years in Europe*, p. xxviii.

8. Brown to Garrison, January 16, 1851; *Glasgow Herald*, January 24, 1851; *Liberator*, February 28, 1851, p. 33; Glasgow Female Anti-Slavery Society, *Sixth Report* (Glasgow, 1851), pp. 14–15.

presence of a celebrity brought everybody near him to life.

Both Dick and the Reverend George Gilfillin were on the platform at the meeting that evening. Gilfillin, a friend of Thomas De Quincey and Thomas Carlyle, was the author of *A Gallery of Literary Portraits.* It thus appears that Brown was by no means the most distinguished person present. Later, in what savored very much of rationalizing with regard to this fact, he referred to Napoleon's statement that the enthusiasm of others abated his own and then explained that "At any rate, the spirit with which each speaker entered upon his duty for the evening, abated my own enthusiasm for the time being."[9]

After holding a meeting in Perth, a short distance southwest of Dundee, the three fugitives went to Aberdeen, where they spent ten days and whence they returned to Edinburgh for a brief visit. During the last week in February, en route back to England, they stopped and held an evening meeting in Melrose. On their way back to their lodgings, they passed the ruins of Melrose Abbey. The moon was shining, and they stopped to view the ruins, thus following literally Sir Walter Scott's suggestion in *The Lay of the Last Minstrel* that whoever wishes to view the ruins of the abbey aright should visit them by moonlight. But realist that he was, Brown went alone early the next morning to see the ruins by daylight.

Later in the morning Brown spent three hours at Abbotsford, the estate on which Scott had spent his last twenty-one years. Brown and the Crafts finished their sight-seeing in the Scott country with an afternoon trip to Dryburgh Abbey, Scott's burial place. Forthwith they took a train from Melrose to Hawick, where they stopped overnight and held a meeting.[10]

The next day Brown and the Crafts proceeded by way of Langholm and Gretna Green to Carlisle, England. They had to travel by stagecoach from Langholm to Carlisle—a distance of

9. *Three Years in Europe,* pp. 177–84.

10. *Liberator,* March 7, 1851, p. 37; *Three Years in Europe,* pp. 185–96, 305–12; Brown to Douglass, March 26, 1851, *North Star,* April 17, 1851, p. 3.

twenty miles, according to Brown, and he was pleased to note that they covered it in two and one-half hours. But in spite of what seemed to him to be remarkably good speed on a road "as smooth as a mirror," he did not find the ride very pleasant. The inside of the stagecoach being full, he had to ride on the top, and the day was very cold. Consequently he was glad when the sight of "Four very tall chimneys, sending forth dense columns of black smoke, announced to us that we were near Carlisle," for "Ulysses was never more tired of the shores of Ilion," he confessed, "than I of the top of that coach."

Brown and the Crafts spent a night in Carlisle, "partaking of the hospitality of the prince of bakers." The next day, after "a cold ride of about fifty miles" they arrived at the Salutation Hotel in Ambleside, a village near the northern end of Lake Windermere. Although Brown had read but little of the poetry of Wordsworth, Coleridge, and Southey, he was aware that he and the Crafts were now in the center of the Lake District with which these authors' names were closely associated. He and the Crafts were there, however, for a reason which they considered more important than visiting the haunts of the Lake Poets. They had come in response to "a standing invitation to pay a visit to a distinguished literary lady," who was also a staunch abolitionist. This was Harriet Martineau, the author of *Society in America* and many other books which were once familiar to readers in both Great Britain and the United States. She lived in a cottage called The Knoll, which she had had built near Ambleside, "within half a mile of the residence of the late poet Wordsworth." The three visitors arrived at The Knoll a little after dark and were cordially welcomed by Miss Martineau.

Early the next morning Brown went on a jaunt up Loughrigg Fell. At the foot of the mountain he met a peasant who voluntarily lent him a donkey on which to make the ascent. Ignorant of donkey-riding but not averse to adventure, he mounted the donkey and started up the mountain. Before he had ridden very far, one of the donkey's hind feet slipped, and for a moment both the rider and the mount seemed to be in danger of precipitation into a chasm nearby. Fortunately, however, the donkey regained his foothold quickly enough to save the rider as well as himself from anything more tragic than quaking fright. After this experience Brown dismounted, having decided to trust himself to his own two feet rather than to the donkey's four for the remainder of the trip. For overcoming the difficulty he had in reaching the summit of the mountain, he was rewarded with a beautiful view of the surrounding territory. There were Rydal Mount, Wordsworth's last home, on his left; Dove's Nest, once the home of Mrs. Felicia D. Hemans, at some distance on his right; and Lake Windermere far down in front of him. Before descending he came close to blurring his judgment, if not the view, with some needless comparisons of the kind too many tourists have ever been too freely inclined to make. Lake Windermere looked more like a river than a lake, he opined, and "if placed by the side of our own Ontario, Erie, or Huron, would be lost in the fog." As it lay before him, nevertheless, he found it "beautiful in the extreme, surrounded as it is by a range of mountains that have no parallel in the United States for beauty."[11]

In the afternoon Miss Martineau took her guests on a drive to Dove's Nest and thence to Grasmere Church. There they saw the grave of Wordsworth, who had been dead less than a year, and the grave of Coleridge's son Hartley, who was also a poet, and whose life was said to have been blighted and shortened by intemperance. The visit to Hartley Coleridge's grave together with what Miss Martineau probably told about his last years, which he had spent in the Lake District, doubtless interested Brown in reading a new book which he saw in Miss Martineau's library.[12] The new book was a volume of Hartley Coleridge's

11. *Three Years in Europe*, pp. 196–203.

12. With regard to Miss Martineau's knowledge of Hartley Coleridge, see *Harriet Martineau's Autobiography*, 2 vols., ed. Maria Weston Chapman (Boston, 1877), 1: 511.

poems edited and supplied with a memoir by his brother, the Reverend Derwent Coleridge. Brown read this book while he was a guest at The Knoll or very soon afterwards. Ever zealous in the promotion of temperance, he found in Hartley Coleridge's life what he considered a veritable case history of the evils of intemperance. About two months after he and the Crafts visited Miss Martineau, in one of the letters he sent to Douglass for the *North Star*, he used that case history as an exemplum against the use of intoxicants. When in 1852 he compiled this letter and others like it in his *Three Years in Europe*, which was published in London in the same year, he omitted the exemplum, probably to spare the feelings of the poet's relatives who were still living in England. Three years later, however, he included it in the American version of that work.[13]

After a pleasant visit of three days with Miss Martineau, Brown and the Crafts left The Knoll but remained some weeks longer in northern England, holding antislavery meetings with special reference to the Fugitive Slave Law. By the first of April they were in London, which the Crafts now saw for the first time.

When the Crafts arrived in Liverpool early in December, 1850, they had a letter from Samuel May, Jr., general agent of the Massachusetts Anti-Slavery Society, introducing them to Dr. John Bishop Estlin. Before joining Brown in Newcastle, Craft had forwarded May's letter to Estlin along with an explanation of his intention to join Brown. Estlin had promptly written to Brown offering aid to the Crafts, as Harriet Martineau had done. Most probably he did not see them, however, until they went with Brown to Bristol early in April, 1851.[14]

On Wednesday evening, April 9, a public meeting was held

13. *Sketches*, pp. 188–91.

14. In his *Running a Thousand Miles for Freedom* (London, 1860), pp. 88–92, 108, Craft gave the impression that he and Mrs. Craft went directly to Bristol from Liverpool soon after their arrival there. This they did not do, as is evident from the references cited in my account of their first four months in Great Britain.

in the Broadmead Rooms in Bristol to welcome the Crafts along with Brown to the city. Incidentally it was exactly a year since Brown had been the guest of honor at a similar but larger meeting in the same place during his first visit to Bristol. The three fugitives next went to Plymouth, where they had a crowded meeting in "the large Theatre Royal." Subsequent to engagements in Exeter and Taunton, their itinerary, which became a sort of crisscross with Bristol as the center, next included Bridgewater, Gloucester, Cheltenham, and Bath. After "a short absence in Wales," they were back in Bristol by the first of May, as Estlin informed a Miss Wigham in a letter he wrote to her on the third.[15] In the same letter, in which he said that Mrs. Craft now called his house "home," Estlin confided in Miss Wigham thus:

> We have been endeavouring to improve the tone of Brown and Crafts [*sic*] Exhibition altering their *showman like* handbills, and securing a higher position for Ellen. She fully feels the propriety of all we have said and done and is very thankful to us.

Whether the exhibition Estlin mentioned was a new showing of Brown's panoramic views or simply Estlin's way of referring to the Brown and Craft meetings is not clear. If Brown's panoramic views were shown in Bristol in the spring of 1851, this was most probably the only revival of the exhibition after the preceding year.

Brown and the Crafts returned to London about the middle of May and remained inactive for some time with the exception of their participation in an antislavery meeting which the Unitarian Association held in the city on June 13.[16] Meanwhile, hav-

15. *Bristol Examiner*, reprinted in *Liberator*, May 9, 1851, p. 74; *Special Report of the Bristol and Clifton Ladies' Anti-Slavery Society* (London, 1852), p. 18; *Liberator*, May 30, 1851, p. 87; Estlin to Miss Wigham, May 3, 1851, Anti-Slavery—Weston Papers.

16. *London Inquirer*, reprinted in *Frederick Douglass' Paper*, July 24, 1851, p. 1, July 31, 1851, p. 2, and in *Liberator*, July 25, 1851, pp. 117–18.

ing said in his letter of March 26 to Douglass that "we also hope to get up an interest against the slaveholders who may make their appearance at the great Exhibition," Brown joined some fellow abolitionists in preparing to do just that.

On Saturday, June 21, Brown and the Crafts went with several of their friends to the International Exhibition, which had recently opened in the Crystal Palace. Among the friends were Estlin and his daughter, Mr. and Mrs. Richard D. Webb of Dublin, Mrs. George Thompson and her daughters, and William Farmer, who later sent Garrison a long report on the trip.[17]

Most prominent among the 15,000 persons who were there that Saturday were the members of the royal family and the Duchess of Sutherland, who was avowedly an abolitionist. The American visitors "were particularly numerous, among whom the experienced eyes of Brown and the Crafts enabled them to detect slaveholders by the dozens."

Conspicuous among the few American works of art displayed at the Exhibition was Hiram Powers' *The Greek Slave*. This was a life-size marble statue of "a young and lovely girl, standing in an attitude indicative at once of genuine modesty, keen suffering, and beautiful resignation," and "chained by the wrists to a column."[18] The display of such a work at that time, especially since it was the work of an American, afforded too great an opportunity for satire to be left unnoticed, an indeed it was not.

About a week before the fugitives and their friends went as a group to the exhibition, there appeared in *Punch, Or the London Charivari* a picture entitled "The Virginian Slave, Intended as a Companion to Power's [*sic*] 'Greek Slave.' " This was a picture of an abject-looking Negro woman wearing a headcloth and draped with a loincloth extending from her waist below her knees. She was leaning against a post not quite waist-high

17. "Fugitive Slaves at the Great Exhibition," *Liberator*, July 18, 1851, p. 116. In the memoir in Brown's *Three Years in Europe*, p. xxv, Farmer incorrectly said that the group made the trip in May.

18. *Literary World*, quoted in *Anti-Slavery Bugle*, August 27, 1847, p. 3.

which was draped with stars and stripes, and both the woman and the post were mounted on a pedestal decorated with catenaries of chain and around whose base was inscribed "E Pluribus Unum." The woman's hands were manacled, large links of chain hung from her wrists, and her ankles were fettered.[19]

When the fugitives and their friends arrived at Powers' masterpiece, one of them produced a copy of the picture in *Punch*, and some of them began comparing the two works quite audibly. They thus attracted a crowd including many Americans, as they wished to do; and they then talked *at* the Americans with the hope of provoking somebody into answering them. Withal nobody outside their group replied to anything they said. When words proved unavailing, one of the fugitives resorted to action. It was Brown. He ostentatiously placed the picture from *Punch* in the enclosure with *The Greek Slave*, saying loudly as he did so, "As an American fugitive slave, I place this Virginia slave by the side of the Greek Slave, as its most fitting companion." Nor did this bit of drama bring forth any replies. When, however, the fugitives and their friends had withdrawn only a little way from the statue, an American quietly removed the picture; and when the group returned and stood near him for a few minutes, he still kept silent.

The group spent six or seven hours at the exhibition, with no little satisfaction at being observed, they thought, as interracial companions who obviously considered each other social equals. Ironically enough, however, unless the identity of Brown and the Crafts was generally known, the interracial constituency of the group was scarcely noticeable, because Craft was the only one in it who could not have been taken for a white person.

On June 23 Brown went again to the Crystal Palace. This time he was accompanied only by "an English lady" and was much more interested in seeing the exhibits than in being a part of one. In a crowded omnibus in which he and the lady rode

19. *Punch; or, the London Charivari,* 20 (1851): 236.

homeward, he saw for the first time a famous British author who was by no means an idol of the abolitionists. In some of the best writing he ever did, Brown told of his sight of that man and also indulged in some frank and independent criticism of him:

> I had scarcely taken my seat, when my friend, who was seated opposite me, with looks and gesture informed me that we were in the presence of some distinguished person. I eyed the countenances of the different persons, but in vain, to see if I could find any one who by his appearance showed signs of superiority over his fellow-passengers. I had given up the hope of selecting the person of note when another look from my friend directed my attention to a gentleman seated in the corner of the omnibus. He was a tall man with strongly marked features, hair dark and coarse. There was a slight stoop of the shoulder—that bend which is almost always a characteristic of studious men. But he wore upon his countenance a forbidding and disdainful frown, that seemed to tell one that he thought himself better than those about him. His dress did not indicate a man of high rank; and had he been in America, I would have taken him for an Ohio farmer.
>
> While I was scanning the features and general appearance of the gentleman, the Omnibus stopped and put down three or four passengers, which gave me an opportunity of getting a seat by the side of my friend, who, in a low whisper, informed me that the gentlemen whom I had been eyeing so closely, was no less a person than Thomas Carlyle. I had read his "Hero-worship," and "Past and Present," and had formed a high opinion of his literary abilities. But his recent attack upon the emancipated people of the West Indies, and his laborious article in favour of the reestablishment of the lash and slavery, had created in my mind a dislike for the man, and I almost regretted that we were in the same Omnibus. In some things, Mr. Carlyle is right: but in many, he is entirely wrong. As a writer, Mr. Carlyle is often monotonous and extravagant. He does not exhibit a new view of nature, or raise insignificant objects into importance, but generally takes commonplace thoughts and events, and tries to express them

in stronger and statelier language than others. He holds no communion with his kind, but stands alone without mate or fellow. He is like a solitary peak, all access to which is cut off. He exists not by sympathy but by antipathy. Mr. Carlyle seems chiefly to try how he shall display his own powers, and astonish mankind, by starting new trains of speculation or by expressing old ones so as not to be understood. He cares little what he says, so as he can say it differently from others. To read his works, is one thing; to understand them, is another. If any one thinks that I exaggerate, let him sit for an hour over "Sartar [*sic*] Resartus," and if he does not rise from its pages, place his three or four dictionaries on the shelf, and say I am right, I promise never again to say a word against Thomas Carlyle. He writes one page in favour of Reform, and ten against it. He would hang all prisoners to get rid of them, yet the inmates of the prisons and "work-houses are better off than the poor." His heart is with the poor; yet the blacks of the West Indies should be taught, that if they will not raise sugar and cotton by their own free will, "Quashy should have the whip applied to him." He frowns upon the Reformatory speakers upon the boards of Exeter Hall, yet he is the prince of reformers. He hates heroes and assassins, yet Cromwell was an angel, and Charlotte Corday a saint. He scorns everything, and seems to be tired of what he is by nature, and tries to be what he is not.[20]

In the summer of 1851 Brown noted that there were hundreds of fugitive slaves in England, and that many of them had been reduced to beggary, including some who had "set themselves up as lecturers." Uneducated and unskilled in everything but the fundamentals of agriculture as these fugitives were, he observed, they could not compete with either native Englishmen or emigrants from continental Europe for jobs of any kind. In spite of the fact, therefore, that fugitive slaves were sympathetically and hospitably received by the British people, Brown considered it unwise for them to continue to migrate to England—only to join the ranks of the unemployed. He explained his point of

20. *Three Years in Europe*, pp. 216–19.

view in an open letter which he wrote from London on June 27 to *Frederick Douglass' Paper*. His letter was published in that journal under the heading "Don't Come to England." "If the climate in Canada is too cold, and you must leave the States," the letter concluded, "go to the West Indies. But, by all means, don't come to England."[21]

Six days later, on July 3, Brown wrote a letter to the *London Times*, enlarging upon his idea that it might be wise for fugitive slaves to migrate to the West Indies. He suggested that since most of the fugitives who could not find employment in England had had some experience raising cotton, sugar, rice, or other crops indigenous to the West Indies, perhaps they could be induced to go there to do farm work. He was convinced that if those who were interested in the West Indian estates would offer fair terms for such employment, their offers would be accepted by the fugitives and would prove beneficial to both the owners of the estates and the fugitives.[22]

Brown's suggestion resulted in several conferences between him and some of the West Indies proprietors and agents in London. Knowing, however, that many of the landowners in the West Indies had never been reconciled to the abolition of slavery and had tried to retain it in one form or another, Brown was suspicious of the proprietors and the agents from the beginning. His suspicion was intensified by a report that agents had already been employed to induce unsuspecting Negroes in Canada to migrate to the West Indies on questionable terms, that one of those agents was Josiah Henson, and that efforts had been made to keep the abolitionists in Great Britain ignorant of what those agents were doing. Brown pointed out all of this in a letter he wrote from London to Douglass on September 1. "As my letter in the *Times* first brought this subject before the people," he explained, "and fearing that some might be entrapped by this

21. *Frederick Douglass' Paper*, reprinted in *Liberator*, July 25, 1851, p. 118.

22. *London Times*, July 4, 1851, reprinted in *Liberator*, July 25, 1851, p. 118.

new movement, I take the earliest opportunity of warning all colored men to be on their guard, how they enter into agreements, no matter with whom, white or colored, to go to the West India Islands, least [*sic*] they find themselves again wearing the chains of slavery."[23]

Although Brown's suggestion in his letter to the *London Times* was interesting, little or nothing came of it, not only because of the danger it involved for the very people it was intended to help but also because its feasibility was questionable from the beginning. This fact was made clear in an editorial in the *New York Evening Post* for July 28. The editorial commended Brown for his "sensible letter" to the *London Times* and agreed with what he had said "in regard to the necessities and distresses of his brethren in exile." It doubted, nevertheless, that "the plan of sending them to the West Indies" promised "anything effectual for their relief." In a few more sentences the editorial noted that there was no actual shortage of labor in the British West Indies and that wages there were "now at the starving point;" then it bluntly warned that "it would be madness for colored people to go there in quest of labor."

On June 25 the Reverend Charles Spear sailed from Boston on the Royal British Mail steamship *America* bound for Liverpool. He was going as a delegate from Massachusetts to the General Peace Congress which was to convene in London during the last week in July. Pursuant to arrangements between him and their father, Spear took with him to London Brown's daughters Clarissa and Josephine, who had been in school in New Bedford several years. There was some annoyance for them before they left Boston. One Mr. Lewis, an agent in the city for the steamship company, refused to grant the girls passage unless they were entered on the passenger list as servants. His only reason for requiring that they be listed as such was that they were considered Negroes.[24]

23. Brown to Douglass, September 1, 1851, reprinted in *Liberator*, October 24, 1851, p. 169.

24. [Josephine Brown], *Biography*, p. 73.

Thus the iniquities of an irresponsible, proslavery father had again been visited not only upon his son but also upon his son's innocent children.

One of the fellow passengers of Spear and the Misses Brown was George Thompson, who was returning home after eight months of antislavery work in the United States. Finding that the vast majority of the passengers aboard the *America* were proslavery partisans, Spear and Thompson, with the two girls, isolated themselves as much as possible to avoid unnecessary unpleasantness. Even so there was an abortive threat of persecution for the girls. After the *America* had been at sea a few days, the apparently demure wife of a pious-looking preacher from Framingham, Massachusetts, complained to the captain of the ship about their presence in the ladies' cabin. She referred to them as "black girls" and "runaway slaves." The captain corrected the lady by referring to the girls as "dark-complexioned" and then explained that they had as much right to be in the ladies' cabin as she had. Having settled the matter thus, he casually told Thompson about it a day or two latter. After a voyage of eleven days, "prolonged, to some extent, by contrary winds," the *America* arrived at Liverpool on the morning of July 7. Late in the afternoon Spear, Thompson, and the two girls arrived in London, where they were met at the Euston Station by Brown, Mrs. Thompson, and Farmer.[25]

Brown had two reasons for having his daughters come to England. He had not seen them in two years, and this was the only way he could see them and keep them with him, since he could not yet return to the United States without risking reenslavement. Also, because of the prevalence of race prejudice in the schools in America and its absence from the schools in England and continental Europe, he could get his daughters better educated abroad than in their native land.

For the celebration of the eighteenth anniversary of emanci-

25. *Liberator,* June 27, 1851, p. 103; William Farmer to Garrison, July 8, 1851, *ibid.,* July 25, 1851, p. 118; *ibid.,* September 5, 1851, p. 142.

pation in the British West Indies and of the return of Thompson from America, the fugitive slaves and the Garrisonian abolitionists in London held a large public meeting on the evening of August 1 in the Hall of Commerce on Threadneedle Street. According to William Farmer, whose long report of the meeting was published in the *Liberator*, this was "the largest available room in the city of London, within a stone's throw of the Bank of England, the Exchange, and other public buildings—the terminus for omnibuses from all parts of the metropolis—in the very centre of its trade and commerce." To defray the expenses of the meeting, the sponsors of it charged an admission fee of one shilling. Despite this fact and the occurrence of other important meetings on the same evening, "nearly one thousand ladies and gentlemen were present." Surprisingly enough the Crafts were absent. They had previously assured Brown that they would be present, but "at a late hour" they had sent him a letter explaining that "unfortunate circumstances beyond their control prevented their attendance."[26]

At variance with Farmer's report that the meeting had been widely publicized, Brown's account of it which appeared a year later in his *Three Years in Europe* said that "little notice" of it had been given, "yet it seemed to be known in all parts of the city." Brown also noted that some distinguished persons whom Farmer did not mention were present, two of them being Macaulay, "the greatest critic of the age," and Tennyson, "England's best living poet." "The author of 'In Memoriam,' " Brown remembered, "had been swept in by the crowd, and was standing with his arms folded, and beholding for the first time (and probably the last) so large a number of coloured men in one room."[27]

"After tea was concluded," said Farmer's report, Brown, his two daughters, Thompson, the Reverend Edward S. Mathews,

26. *Liberator*, September 5, 1851, pp. 141–42.
27. *Three Years in Europe*, pp. 237–45.

and several others were seated on the platform; and the business of the meeting was begun with the formal election of Brown as chairman. Combining the roles of presiding officer and first speaker, Brown made enough remarks to fill almost two newspaper columns but said little or nothing he had not previously said many times. Finally he paid a brief tribute to Thompson and presented him to the audience.

Thompson in turn presented Mathews, who had been mobbed in Richmond, Kentucky, for preaching to slaves about freedom, and who had recently returned from the United States. Mathews spoke briefly but gave no details about his experience in Kentucky, since it had already been publicized in both American and British newspapers, notably in the *Liberator* for the preceding March 14 and 21. Thompson spoke next, eloquently and long as usual, telling about his recent sojourn in America and about the work of the American Anti-Slavery Society.

Prior to the meeting, Brown had written on behalf of the fugitive slaves in London an essay entitled "An Appeal to the People of Great Britain and the World." In this essay he urged the Christian world "to expostulate with the Americans, and let them know that you regard their treatment of the coloured people of that country as a violation of every principle of human brotherhood, of natural right, of justice, of humanity, of Christianity, of love to God and love to man." He also urged the British people to exclude from their religious fellowship proslavery preachers and laymen who might visit the British Isles. Apparently, still trusting in the power of moral suasion, he thought that Christian nations might create a world opinion that would compel the United States to abolish slavery.[28]

Having been approved by a committee of fugitive slaves, Brown's essay was presented to the assembly, by which it was unanimously adopted. The evening was now far spent, but Thompson took a few minutes to introduce Brown's daughters

28. *Ibid.*, pp. 246–50.

and to tell about the preacher's wife who had spoken contemptuously of them on the steamship *America.* Resolutions were then adopted commending Garrison and his fellow abolitionists for their antislavery work and thanking Brown for presiding so ably, and at last the meeting was adjourned.

XIII

From Journalist to Author

On August 19 Brown wrote to Anne Weston, one of Mrs. Maria Weston Chapman's sisters, who was then in Hampshire. In his letter he thanked her for a note which she had written to him on August 16 and also for 110 pounds which he had recently received from her.[1] Coincidentally, as he informed her, his daughters had gone on August 13 to Calais, France, where they were enrolled in a seminary in which they spent a year. Perhaps the money Brown mentioned was a loan or a contribution from the Westons towards the education of his daughters.

A large antislavery meeting at which Dr. John Bishop Estlin, George Thompson, and the Reverend Edward S. Mathews were the principal speakers was held in the Broadmead Rooms in Bristol on September 4. Many of the American abolitionists who

1. Brown to Anne Weston, August 19, 1851, Anti-Slavery—Weston Papers.

were then in England as well as many of the British abolitionists who were not residents of Bristol were present. Brown, however, was absent. In his letter of August 19 to Anne Weston he had said that he was planning to visit his daughters in Calais within a few weeks. He was a guest at the wedding of one of Thompson's daughters in London on August 20, but presumably he was in Calais when the meeting in Bristol was held. Otherwise he most probably would have been present, as so many of his friends and associates were.[2]

Again in England, during the second week in September, Brown went to Oxford not only to lecture, as he had done a year earlier, but also as a tourist. He spent the most of two days seeing the city and its famous university. In Christ's Church Chapel one morning, he heard Dr. Edward Bouverie Pusey preach. To him Pusey's appearance was anything but that of one who might have been expected to become the influential churchman that he was, and his preaching seemed "cold and tame."

Brown's visit to the university reimpressed upon him the value of education and the necessity for diligence in pursuit thereof. "It is not always those who have the best advantages, or the greatest talents, that eventually succeed in their undertakings," he remarked, "but it is those who strive with untiring diligence to remove all obstacles to success, and who, with unconquerable resolution, labour on until the rich reward of perseverance is within their grasp."[3]

When Brown spoke of the necessity for diligence and perseverance in the pursuit of education, he was talking out of his own experience. Whatever learning he had acquired by this time—and he had acquired a considerable amount—he had achieved by constant efforts often put forth when things more mundane than studying books were clamoring for his attention.

2. *Liberator*, September 12, 1851, p. 146, and October 3, 1851, pp. 157–58; [George Thompson], *Speech of George Thompson . . . Broadmead, Bristol, September 4th, 1851,* [Bristol, 1851], p. 3.

3. *Three Years in Europe*, pp. 227–35.

He had long been in the habit of carrying books with him wherever he went and devoting to them such time as he could in waiting rooms, omnibuses, railway cars, and steamboats, in addition to hours in his home at night. He could now contemplate with pardonable pride what he had accomplished, for in the opinion of others whose judgment commanded respect, he had become "an educated man." During the preceding two years he had learned to read French well, had made "considerable progress in Latin," and had begun to study German without a teacher.[4]

Aside from the fact that Brown was in France during January, 1852, nothing is known of his activities from the fall of 1851 to the spring of 1852. It was probably during this period that he traveled in Germany and Italy as well as in France, as he was said some years later to have done.

Wherever Brown was, he was not merely loafing and inviting his soul, for he was still faced with the necessity of providing for his two daughters as well as for himself. What he could do to secure the income he needed was an ever-pertinent question. When, therefore, he became sufficiently prominent in London to gain access to newspapers there as a paid contributor, he welcomed the opportunity thus afforded him to supplement his income.

In the spring of 1852 Brown began writing for London newspapers—probably for the *Daily News*, the *Leader*, of which Leigh Hunt's son Thornton was the editor, and the *Morning Advertiser*. His daughter Josephine said later that because of his want of a classical education, he sometimes had to work all night to get his articles into acceptable form, but that his efforts were well rewarded by the liberal remuneration he received. Miss Brown also said that he devoted himself primarily to American subjects, three of the most notable of these being the deaths of

4. "William Wells Brown," *The Public Good; Devoted to the Advocacy of Great Principles, the Advancement of Useful Institutions, and the Elevation of Man*, 2 (1851): 223–26.

Henry Clay and Daniel Webster and the remanding of Anthony Burns to slavery.[5] She did not identify the newspapers in which her father's articles on these subjects appeared. She probably had in mind, however, none of the newspapers mentioned above, but instead the *Antislavery Advocate*. This was a small monthly periodical, whose publication was begun in London in October, 1852, with Brown as a prominent member of its staff.

The first number of this periodical carried articles with the captions "Daniel Webster" and "Henry Clay." The number for December carried an article entitled "The Death of Daniel Webster." All three of these articles expressed some of the unfavorable opinions of Webster and Clay which were shared not only by the Garrisonian abolitionists but also by many other Americans. At the time of the publication of these articles, Brown was the only American on the staff of the *Anti-Slavery Advocate* and doubtless felt freer than anyone else on the staff to speak so frankly about the two famous American statesmen. Moreover, in style as well as in subject matter, these articles remind one of Brown's writing.

How much and how long Brown wrote for London newspapers can hardly be determined, but it is probable that he occasionally contributed articles to some of them from the spring of 1852 until September, 1854, when he returned to America. An article entitled "American Prejudice Against Colour" was reprinted from the *London Morning Advertiser* in the *Anti-Slavery Advocate* for May, 1854. This article gave some information about the educational, religious, and political proscription Negroes experienced in the Northern states because of their race. Then by way of contrast it referred briefly to the warm welcome Brown's two daughters had received at schools in both France and England, and to the fact that both of the girls were now successful schoolmistresses in England. The details concerning Brown's daughters, together with the rest of the

5. [Josephine Brown], *Biography of an American Bondman, by His Daughter* (Boston, 1856), p. 82

subject matter and the tone of the article, all strengthen the probability that Brown was the author of it.[6]

An article with the heading "Man Hunting and Attempted Rescue in Boston" was published in the same periodical for the following July. The middle half of this article is a reprint of the *New York Daily Tribune's* report of the rendition of Anthony Burns to his claimant. The remainder of it consists of two paragraphs in criticism of the affair.[7] Presumably this is the article Josephine Brown had in mind when she credited her father with writing for a London newspaper an article dealing with the remanding of Burns to slavery. At least the new paragraphs in this article are characteristic of Brown's writing.

Brown was briefly distracted in the spring of 1852 by an unpleasant matter involving his reputation. For no good reason as far as he and his friends and associates could see, there had arisen early in 1851 the rumor that he had deserted his wife and was then going around in Great Britain with another woman. The other woman was alleged to be Mrs. Ellen Craft. Brown ignored the rumor until it had persisted for almost a year. During that time he became convinced that the Reverend John Scoble, with whom he had already had trouble, was its chief promulgator if not its originator. In the spring of 1852, therefore, he threatened to sue Scoble for slander if Scoble continued to spread the rumor.[8] Whether because of a want of a factual basis —a want which has not always kept rumors from circulating— or because of Brown's threat to prosecute the suspected promulgator, the spreading of the rumor soon ceased.

Brown had never gone around with only Mrs. Craft. In fact he had made only a few trips with only William Craft. Usually, if one of the Crafts was with him, both of them were, as they

6. "American Prejudice Against Colour," *London Morning Advertiser*, reprinted in *Anti-Slavery Advocate*, May, 1854, p. 159.

7. *Anti-Slavery Advocate*, July, 1854, pp. 171–72.

8. John Bishop Estlin to Garrison, June 7 and 11, 1852, Anti-Slavery Letters Written to W. L. Garrison and Others.

had been with him in New England during the first five months of 1849 and in Great Britain during the first six months of 1851. Since the latter period Brown and the Crafts had not traveled together and had seen each other only infrequently.

In his speech at the emancipation celebration on August 1, 1851, Thompson had emphasized the need in London for a working Garrisonian antislavery society. By the spring of 1852 Estlin had decided to take the initiative in organizing such a society, and during the first week in June he held two meetings in his lodgings at 22 Cecil Street, Strand, London, where Brown was living. Other participants in the meetings were Brown, Thompson, Farmer, Mathews, and Robert Smith. This group organized "a humble" society, which they named the Anglo-American Anti-Slavery Association, and they limited its immediate objective to the publication of the *Anti-Slavery Advocate.* Within a week after the meetings, Estlin wrote to Garrison telling him about them. "Brown is an excellent fellow," he commented. "I look to him for the success of the 'Advocate' as he will keep parties *up to their work.*" Whether because Brown failed to do this or for some other reason, publication of the periodical was not begun until the following October.[9] From that time it was continued at least until May, 1863.

With his daughters, who had recently returned from France, Brown attended the anniversary celebration of emancipation in the British West Indies which was held in Saint Martin's Hall in London on August 2, but he had no prominent part in it. Early in September he spent two days visiting and sight-seeing in the vicinity of London. On one of these days he took a boat on the Thames to Twickenham to fulfill his long-held intention to visit Alexander Pope's villa. After his visit, somewhat under the influence of Dr. Samuel Johnson, he praised Pope highly as a poet. With unintentionally ironic exactness of diction, Brown asked rhetorically, "Where can be found a finer effusion than

9. John Bishop Estlin to Garrison, June 7 and 11, 1852; *Anti-Slavery Advocate,* October, 1852, p. 1.

the 'Essay on Man'?" Also, in ignorance of both the Greek language and authoritative opinions to the contrary, he asserted that Pope was still "the unsurpassed translator of Homer."[10]

Especially during his first three years in Europe, Brown sent to Frederick Douglass's newspapers and also to personal friends letters recounting his experiences and observations abroad. Unfortunately the originals of these letters seem to have been lost, but fortunately for posterity, in the summer of 1852 Brown gave many of them a permanent as well as coherent form by collecting and publishing them in an octavo volume of 344 pages. The full title of this book is *Three Years in Europe; or, Places I Have Seen and People I Have Met.* It came forth with the imprint of Charles Gilpin of London and also with that of Oliver and Boyd of Edinburgh.[11]

The frontispiece in *Three Years in Europe*, which is the only illustration in the volume, is an engraving of the bust of the author—a more recent likeness than the one in the several editions of his *Narrative*. Twenty-nine of the thirty-two introductory pages consist of William Farmer's "Memoir of William Wells Brown." In his two-page preface which follows, Brown explained that he had compiled the book from the letters mentioned above and had published it by subscription. He also reminded those who might find errors in it that he had been a slave during his first twenty years, that he had been denied all educational opportunities during that period, and that he had no education except what he had got "by his own exertions, he never having had a day's schooling in his life."

The main body of the work, which fills 312 pages, consists of twenty-three letters. All but two of these—numbers 21 and 22—are devoted to accounts of places Brown had seen, people

10. *National Anti-Slavery Standard*, August 26, 1852, p. 55; *Sketches*, pp. 243-46, 296.

11. An advertisement in *Athenaeum, Journal of Literature, Science, and the Fine Arts*, September 25, 1852, p. 1045, said that the book was "just published." The advertisement also named W. and F. G. Cash, publishers, as successors to Charles Gilpin.

he had met, and meetings in which he had participated during his first two and a half years in Europe. As a matter of fact the first half of the title of the book is inaccurate, for only the period just mentioned is covered in it.

Letter 21 is inappropriately entitled "A Chapter on American Slavery," for it is much less a discussion of slavery than a series of thumbnail sketches of twelve American reformers, one of whom was Gerrit Smith. In his sketch of Smith, Brown gratefully referred to that philanthropist's gifts of land to him and many others. Surprisingly enough, withal, when Brown's book was published, taxes for as far back as 1849 were still due on his grant, and the county treasurer had advertised it for sale. The sale was prevented, however, by the payment of the taxes for 1849 and 1850 in Brown's name on October 5, 1852, probably by Smith himself.[12]

Letter 22, entitled "A Narrative of American Slavery," represents Brown's first attempt to write an antislavery romance. According to the story, one of the participants in Nat Turner's insurrection of August, 1831, was a white slave named George, the nineteen-year-old son of a mulatto slave woman and "a member of the American Congress." For some time he had been the more or less favored property of a gentleman named Green of Richmond. Green also had among his possessions Mary, a quadroon about seventeen years of age, who was his daughter as well as his slave, and who was in love with George.

Having been tried and found guilty as an insurrectionist, George was sentencd to be hanged. Three nights before he was to be executed, Mary, who had been permitted to visit him daily in prison, persuaded him to exchange clothes with her and to flee to freedom, leaving her in his cell. Once out of prison, George tarried in Richmond only long enough to avail himself of "a small parcel of provisions which she [Mary] had placed

12. New York State Department of Taxation and Finance to me, July 9, 1951.

in a secluded spot." He then set out for Canada, following a route which led through what is now West Virginia.

In a boat which he appropriated for the purpose, the fugitive ferried himself across the Ohio River one morning and landed near Mount Pleasant, Ohio. Although he was now in a free state, he was so swiftly pursued by two slave catchers who had discovered him by chance, that he was saved from capture only by the ingenuity of a Quaker, who sped him on his way to Canada.

After six months of working and saving on a farm near Saint Catherines, George sent "an English missionary" to Richmond to investigate the possibility of purchasing Mary's freedom. The Englishman returned to Saint Catharines with the news that because Mary had helped George to escape, her father had been compelled to sell her out of Virginia, and she had been taken by a slave trader to New Orleans to be sold there. Discouraged by this news, George decided to quit America forever, and soon afterwards he embarked on a freight ship bound for Liverpool.

At the end of ten prosperous years in England, which he spent principally in Manchester working and educating himself, George went on a vacation to Dunkirk, France, in October, 1842. There fate smiled benignly upon him—having guided him there, one may suppose. One afternoon he strolled into a cemetery and sat on a marble tomb to read a book which, coincidentally, Brown himself had spent some time reading three years before he published George's story. It was William Roscoe's *The Life and Pontificate of Leo the Tenth.* Before George had read more than half a page, a veiled widow who was walking with her five-year-old son happened to come along. At a glance she recognized him and fainted—but not until her father-in-law, Monsieur J. Devenant, fortuitously appeared. He was to become the *deus ex machina* by which George and the widow were to be brought together later under the proper circumstances.

The next day, having found George's name and local address

in the book he had inadvertently left in the cemetery, Devenant invited him to dinner. In the Devenants' drawing room, when George saw the widow without her veil, he immediately recognized her as Mary; and in the best tradition of moonlight and wisteria romances, *he* fainted. When he was revived, he was eager to hear the story which he knew Mary had to tell.

On a Saturday, the second day she was on display in a slave market in New Orleans, said Mary, she had been seen by Devenant's son, who had fallen in love with her at first sight, because she resembled very closely his recently deceased sister. After the slave trader had shown him two certificates from Richmond attesting to her good character, he had resolved to free her "from the condition of a slave."

On Monday she had been purchased by a gentleman in the city and had been carried very soon afterwards as his wife's maid on a steamboat trip to Mobile. With the hope of winning her, young Devenant had taken passage on the same steamboat. By the time the steamboat arrived at Mobile, he had wooed her and persuaded her to flee with him to France. They had embarked on the steamship *Utica* which had sailed from Mobile at midnight and had arrived at Le Havre five weeks later. Young Devenant had married her upon their arrival in France, as he had promised to do, and they had lived together happily in the Devenants' home in Dunkirk until he died, leaving her with one son.

Two weeks after their meeting in Dunkirk, George and Mary were married. At last love, faithful even when seemingly hopeless, had triumphed. In concluding the story Brown explained that without assuming responsibility for its truthfulness, he had retold it "as it was told to me in January last [1852], in France by George Green himself."

The reason for this explanation is easily discernible. In writing the story Brown was, of course, less interested in achieving a literary success than in developing a persuasive antislavery argument. As he was doubtless aware, however, although the story portrayed various evils which were inherent in slavery, it was also a love story abounding in surprising incidents motivated only by chance. He could hardly have missed foreseeing, therefore, that as a whole it might be considered not much more than a romance in the popular sense of the word. If it was taken for that, his explanation implied, it should at least be considered a romance with a factual basis.

Writing from London to Garrison on September 24, George Thompson noted that *Three Years in Europe* was comparatively expensive—its price was three shillings and six pence—but he was glad that it was finding purchasers and hoped that it would be "a source of profit to the author." That Thompson was not absolutely satisfied with the work was evidenced by his expression of a wish that it contained "more anti-slavery matter, and less of what can be found in our 'guide books' & 'travelling companions.' " His final remark concerning the book indicated that it had already achieved enough popularity to make a cheap reprint of it profitable. He said that a London bookseller had offered Brown $250 for the right to publish a one-shilling edition, but that Brown's agreement with the original publishers did not permit him to accept such an offer.[13]

Generally speaking, *Three Years in Europe* was as well received by British reviewers as by ordinary readers. Having seen most of the book while it was still in press, a writer for the *British Friend* commented quite favorably upon it. To him it was "really wonderful how one who has had to surmount so many difficulties in his literary career, should have been able to produce a volume of so sparkling a character." The *London Daily News* for September 24 said in concluding its review that "He [Brown] writes with ease and ability, and his intelligent observations upon the great question to which he has devoted, and is devoting, his life, will command influence and respect." Understandably the *Anti-Slavery Advocate* had nothing but congratulations for the author. Brown's book, said the *Critic*, was

13. Thompson to Garrison, September 24, 1852, Anti-Slavery Letters Written to W. L. Garrison and Others.

without a display of "literary talent or skill" but "is not devoid of a certain interest, and is for the most part unaffectedly and often pleasingly written."[14]

The *Athenaeum* found "a simplicity and an ingenuousness in these confessions which make us merry and sad by turns." One of the occasions for sadness, it observed, was Brown's failure to maintain "the chivalries" in refusing to introduce the slaveholder to Cobden and Hugo. "Indeed throughout the book," the *Athenaeum* continued, "Mr. Brown scarcely makes so heroic a figure as the injudicious flatterers of the black men would have him believe. He is evidently very ill informed; and pronounces judgments on men and things of which he knows very little with the forwardness of a schoolboy. But when he writes of the wrongs of his race or the events of his own career he is always interesting or amusing." Observing that this was the first book of travels by a fugitive slave to be published in England, the *Literary Gazette* considered its appearance "too remarkable a literary event to pass without notice." It also pronounced Brown's sketch of Carlyle "good and just." The *Eclectic Review* commented favorably on the book but also noted some errors of fact and taste which needed to be corrected.[15]

Only the antislavery segment of the American press seems to have noticed *Three Years in Europe*. The *National Anti-Slavery Standard* gave it considerable attention; but instead of producing an original review, it reprinted a favorable one from the *London Morning Advertiser* and quoted profusely from the book. The *Liberator* emphasized the novelty of the world's having had "submitted to its perusal a volume of travels from the pen of a fugitive slave," and it also noted that the book was

14. *British Friend* 10 (July, 1852): 187–88; *Anti-Slavery Advocate*, October, 1852, p. 8; *Critic, London Literary Journal*, 11 (October 1, 1852): 508–09.

15. *Athenaeum, Journal of Literature, Science, and the Fine Arts*, October 2, 1852, pp. 1056–57; *Literary Gazette and Journal of Belles Lettres, Science, and Art*, October 2, 1852, pp. 741–42; *Eclectic Review*, n. s., 4 (November, 1852): 616–17.

written "in a style and with an ability evincing much cultivation of mind and unusual intellectual development."[16]

Except in occasional statements and in two passages in which the differences between American slaves and British peasants and laborers were discussed (pages 91–93 and 139–41), this book did not argue directly against slavery. Yet as Garrison and many others realized, the writing of such a book by a fugitive slave was in itself a forceful argument against the "peculiar institution." If at the age of thirty-eight Brown had accomplished as much as he had after a handicap of twenty years in slavery, how much more might he have achieved if slavery had not deprived him of the rights and opportunities which were enjoyed from the beginning by many who were born when he was born? And how many people of rare intelligence and genius had slavery destroyed before the world had an opportunity to learn anything about them?

Three Years in Europe is the very kind of book by which many journalists since Brown's time have been heralded as promising authors. Although Brown did not write it primarily to win distinction as an author, and although he seems not to have claimed authorship as his profession until 1860, this book may be said to have launched him on his career as a professional writer. It was indeed a good beginning—one which, alas, gave promise of more than Brown ever achieved as an author. Because of its simplicity and fluency of style and its quality of perennial human interest, it is still a good example of travel literature.

In a letter he wrote from London to Garrison on November 6, Farmer said that because *Uncle Tom's Cabin* had created "a deep interest in American Slavery in this country," Brown was "doing very well"—that his lectures were "well attended" and *Three Years in Europe* was "having an extensive sale." About the time Farmer wrote his letter, Brown went on a lecture trip

16. *National Anti-Slavery Standard,* October 14, 1852, p. 84, October 28, 1852, p. 92, November 4, 1852, p. 96, November 25, 1852, p. 108; *Liberator,* November 19, 1852, p. 186.

to Scotland. While he was there his "A True Story of Slave Life" appeared in the *Anti-Slavery Advocate* for December.[17] In this short story Brown again experimented, although briefly, with factual matter suitable for an antislavery romance, as he had recently done in letter 22 in *Three Years in Europe*.

According to this story, at an auction in Richmond one Saturday in October, 1844, a quadroon slave and her daughter, both of whom were the property of a Mr. Carter of that city, were offered for sale. The quadroon, who was then twenty-eight years of age, had been a housekeeper for Mr. Carter and ten years earlier had borne him the daughter, whose name was Elizabeth. Mr. Carter, who was now about fifty years old, "had formed a matrimonial alliance with a lady in the neighbourhood, one of the conditions of which was that the housekeeper and her child should be sent off before the arrival of the bride." The bidding on the quadroon was begun at $500. When the auctioneer exhibited a certificate saying that she had "a good moral character," the bid was raised to $700; when the auctioneer explained on the basis of the same certificate that she was "very intelligent," the bid was raised to $800; and when he added that she was "a devoted Christian and perfectly trustworthy," the bid was rapidly increased until she was sold to a speculator for $1,000.

"This was a southern auction," Brown commented, "at which the bones, muscles, sinews, blood, and nerves of a young lady of twenty-eight years of age sold for five hundred dollars; her moral character for two hundred dollars; her improved intellect for another hundred, and her Christianity—the person of Christ in his follower—for two hundred more." With others purchased by the speculator, the quadroon was taken to "the cotton, sugar, and rice district" of the deep South and presumably lost in the inferno of slavery there.

Since nobody had bid on Elizabeth at the sale, Mr. Carter

17. Farmer to Garrison, November 6, 1852, Anti-Slavery Letters Written to W. L. Garrison and Others; *Liberator*, December 17, 1852, p. 202; *Anti-Slavery Advocate*, December, 1852, pp. 23, 24.

took her back with him, whence he soon sent her to Philadelphia along with a family going on a trip to the North. The family left her forlorn on Lombard Street in the city, without even a change of clothing. Fortunately she was rescued by Robert Purvis, a wealthy Negro abolitionist, who took her into his family and began to educate her. In 1848 Purvis transferred her to the home of his mother-in-law, Mrs. James Forten. After two years of efforts repeated by letters, Mrs. Forten succeeded in interesting Mr. Carter in his daughter enough for him to stop in Philadelphia to see her while he was en route to Saratoga Springs. When in Mrs. Forten's drawing room he saw his daughter for the first time after six years, beautiful, well-mannered, and accomplished as she was, the love of the father overcame the prejudices of the slaveholder; and Mr. Carter not only recognized Elizabeth as his child but also paid for her maintenance for the years she had been in Philadelphia and "amply" provided for "her future support and education."

At the end of the story Brown said that while he was in Philadelphia in "the summer of 1848," he was introduced to Elizabeth Carter—two years before her father visited her. Since Brown was in Great Britain from the middle of the summer of 1849 through the summer of 1854, he must not have heard the last part of Elizabeth's story until he had been there more than a year—perhaps not until shortly before he put the story into print. It must have been a noteworthy coincidence that the histories of Mary Green and Elizabeth Carter, which began so similarly in the same city at times so close together, were both told to Brown within a few years.

There is a partial analogue to Brown's story of Elizabeth Carter in the reminiscences of Captain Edmund Bacon of Trigg County, Kentucky, which were recorded by Hamilton W. Pierson in 1861 and published in 1862. Bacon said that he was born "within two or three miles of Monticello" in 1785, and that his oldest brother, William Bacon, "had charge of his [Thomas Jefferson's] estate during the four years he was Minister to France."[18] According to what Bacon told Pierson, he had been Jefferson's overseer at Monticello from 1804 to 1824, but this part of his account is somewhat inaccurate. He was employed in various capacities at Monticello beginning at least as early as 1804, but he was overseer there only from 1806 to 1822. After the last-mentioned year, he moved to Kentucky.[19] As Bacon remembered,

> He [Jefferson] freed one girl some years before he died, and there was a great deal of talk about it. She was nearly as white as anybody, and very beautiful. People said he freed her because she was his own daughter. She was not his daughter; she was ———'s daughter. I know that. I have seen him come out of her mother's room many a morning, when I went up to Monticello very early. When she was nearly grown, by Mr. Jefferson's direction I paid her stage fare to Philadelphia, and gave her fifty dollars. I have never seen her since, and don't know what became of her. From the time she was large enough, she always worked in the cotton factory. She never did any hard work.[20]

For obvious chronological reasons, if for no others, Elizabeth Carter could not have been the girl Bacon sent to Philadelphia. Nor had Bacon's reminiscences been recorded when Brown wrote his story, so that Brown could not have known anything about them. Whatever similarities there are between the two stories most probably resulted from familiar practices incident to the "peculiar institution."

En route from Scotland back to London, probably late in December, Brown stopped in Leeds long enough to deliver three

18. Hamilton W. Pierson, *Jefferson at Monticello. The Private Life of Thomas Jefferson. From Entirely New Materials* (New York, 1862), p. 28.

19. *Thomas Jefferson's Garden Book*, annotated by Edwin Morris Betts, (Philadelphia, 1944), pp. 312, 601, 605; *Thomas Jefferson's Farm Book*, ed. *Edwin Morris Betts* (Princeton, 1953), p. 149; Pierson, *Jefferson at Monticello*, pp. 22, 29.

20. *Pierson, Jefferson at Monticello*, p. 110.

lectures. In January and February, 1853, he was busy filling engagements in London and its vicinity and also in southwestern England, averaging three lectures a week.[21]

Brown wrote from London on May 17 to Garrison, telling him about the anniversary meeting of the British and Foreign Anti-Slavery Society which had been held in Exeter Hall the preceding evening. Neither Brown nor any other Garrisonian abolitionist was on the program, but several of them were present, including William and Ellen Craft as well as Brown himself. Brown thought that his being jostled as he was by the vast crowd in the hall was compensated by his hearing the opening speech of the Earl of Shaftesbury and seeing for the first time Mrs. Harriet Beecher Stowe, who was a guest of honor. Her husband, the Reverend Professor Calvin Ellis Stowe, was one of the speakers. Brown was displeased, as were many others who were present, by Stowe's more or less apologetic remarks about American slavery; but he was not surprised, for he had come to expect American preachers, as a rule, to say just what this one said about the subject on this occasion. Samuel Ringgold Ward, an American Negro preacher, delivered what Brown considered the best speech of the evening. "Mr. Ward did himself great credit," Brown informed Garrison, "and exposed the hypocrisy of the American pro-slavery churches in a way that caused Professor Stowe to turn more than once upon his seat."[22]

On July 29 Brown wrote hurriedly to Mary Anne Estlin. The next day, acting as his amanuensis, his daughter Josephine wrote another letter for him to the same lady. Both of these letters referred casually to plans for the forthcoming celebration of the anniversary of emancipation in the British West Indies, which was held in London on August 1, and at which Brown was one

21. *National Anti-Slavery Standard,* March 3, 1853, p. 162; *Anti-Slavery Advocate,* February, 1853, p. 37, March, 1853, p. 45; *Liberator,* March 18, 1853, p. 42.

22. "Letter from William W. Brown," *Liberator,* June 3, 1853, p. 97; *London Morning Advertiser,* May 18, 1853, reprinted in *Liberator,* June 10, 1853, p. 99.

of the speakers. The second letter also expressed hopes for improvement in the health of Dr. Estlin, who was then ill.[23]

With the exception of a brief trip to southwestern England, Brown spent August and September filling lecture engagements in London and its vicinity and in Kent. On the evening of September 21, he lectured in Sittingbourne, one of the villages in which Chaucer's pilgrims had stopped to dine; and the next evening he lectured in the Guild Hall in Canterbury. He was said to have had enough engagements in Kent to keep him there "for some weeks to come."[24] Within two weeks, however, he was again in London for at least a few days on business pertaining to the publication of his next book.

23. Brown to Mary Anne Estlin, July 29, 1853, and July 30, 1853, Anti-Slavery—Weston Papers; "Letter from William Wells Brown," *National Anti-Slavery Standard,* August 20, 1853, p. 51; Excerpt from a letter from the Reverend Edward Mathews, *American Baptist,* reprinted in *Liberator,* November 25, 1853, p. 185.

24. Edward Mathews to unidentified man, September 2, 1853, Anti-Slavery—Weston Papers; *London Morning Advertiser,* reprinted in *Anti-Slavery Bugle,* October 29, 1853, p. 1; *Anti-Slavery Advocate,* October, 1853, p. 104.

"Clotel; or, The President's Daughter"

ON OCTOBER 3 BROWN WROTE FROM LONDON TO SAMUEL May, Jr., and sent his letter by one of the Chapmans who was then returning to Boston. Although May considered the letter private, he published a part of it in the *Liberator* for November 4 in order to gratify the desires of Brown's friends in Boston for news about him. In the part of the letter May published, Brown said, among other things, "I am now looking over the proof-sheets of 'Clotel, or the President's Daughter,' a new work of mine now going through the press." Early in November, *Clotel; or, The President's Daughter: A Narrative of Slave Life in the United States* was published in London by Partridge and Oakey. The time of publication is indicated by the fact that on November 12 Brown autographed copies of the book for several of his friends. Notable among these were Dr. John Bishop

Estlin and his daughter Mary Anne, William Lloyd Garrison, John Mawson, and Samuel May, Jr.

There are four full-page illustrations in the book. The most important of these, which is entitled "The Death of Clotel," shows the heroine leaping from the Long Bridge at Washington, D. C., into the Potomac River to avoid recapture by slave catchers. In some copies of the work this is the frontispiece; in others it is opposite page 218, on which the suicide of Clotel is recounted.

This octavo volume consists of 253 pages, but the story itself fills fewer than 200 of these. In the preface of three pages, Brown explained that the Constitution of the United States together with the Fugitive Slave Law protected slavery everywhere in the nation; that slaveholding was common among all classes in the South; that since slavery had been introduced into the American colonies while they were controlled by the British government, "Englishmen should feel a lively interest in its abolition"; and that if his story "should add anything new to the information already given to the Public through similar publications, and should thereby aid in bringing British influence to bear upon American slavery, the main object for which this work was written will have been accomplished."

The first fifty-two pages of the text proper consist of a "Narrative of the Life and Escape of William Wells Brown," which has for a motto at its head the fifth stanza of John Greenleaf Whittier's "Stanzas for the Times." This "Narrative" contains some details not found in other sketches of Brown's life and also some noteworthy errors. On the eighteenth page it is incorrectly said that the steamboat on which Brown worked during the summer of 1833, while he belonged to Samuel Willi, was the *Saint Louis* and that Enoch Price was its owner. By what is said further on the same page and the next, the false impression is given that Brown escaped from Price in Louisville instead of in Cincinnati.

Brown not only gave titles to the several chapters of the

story but also prefaced most of them with quotations for mottoes, most of which are in verse. He took some of these quotations from the several editions of his *Anti-Slavery Harp* and others from well-known American and British writers.

In "A True Story of Slave Life," published less than a year earlier, Brown had related what was germinally the principal story he told in his novel. That story, which he had averred was founded on fact, ended tragically enough for the quadroon slave mother, but for her daughter it ended too happily to arouse the strong antislavery sentiment Brown wanted to arouse. Moreover, even if the Carter in that story was a real person, he was not known widely enough to attract attention as a typical American slaveholding democrat, moralist, and statesman. But there was the famous Thomas Jefferson, who had been President of the United States, and whom tradition had credited with begetting slave children and forgetting them. One of his alleged slave daughters was the quadroon young woman whose sale Otis Reynolds of Saint Louis said he had witnessed in New Orleans. For Brown, facts and tradition thus made Jefferson an example par excellence of the American democrat whose professions and practices were altogether inconsistent—an example which would be sure, Brown thought, to shock readers into attention. Accordingly he replaced the Mr. Carter of the "true story" with the Thomas Jefferson of a traditional one and combined the details of these stories with many others, some factual and some fictitious, into an episodic narrative abounding in tragedy and melodrama.

Brown never claimed personal acquaintance with any slave children of Jefferson, nor is it probable that he knew any more about such children than he had read in abolition newspapers and had heard in antislavery circles. He was aware, however, that such reports concerning Jefferson's fathering and neglecting such children could have and even might have been true. He knew that similar reports certainly were true of many other slaveholders, some of whom he had known personally. He did not worry, then, about whether the reports concerning Jefferson were literally true in every detail; he merely used them for their sensational value to illustrate the ironical inconsistencies that existed between the theories and the practices of soi-disant democratic American slaveholders, of whom the famous author of the Declaration of Independence and *Notes on the State of Virginia* with its especially remarkable "Query XVIII" might be taken, he thought, as an archetype. Brown's novel grew out of his desire, not to attack the character of Thomas Jefferson per se, but to win attention, by means of an entrancing story, to a comprehensive and persuasive argument against American slavery.

Clotel is principally the story of the fortunes and misfortunes of Currer, a mulatto slave of Richmond, Virginia, her quadroon daughters, Clotel and Althesa, and Clotel's daughter Mary. Currer, who was an expert laundress, had hired her time from her owner, John Graves, "for more than twenty years" before the beginning of the action in the story. During these years she had lived in Richmond, and for several of them she had been the housekeeper and mistress of Thomas Jefferson, who was the father of her two daughters. But "Jefferson being called to Washington to fill a government appointment, Currer was left behind, and thus she took herself to the business of washing, by which means she paid her master, Mr. Graves, and supported herself and two children." At the beginning of the action, Currer was "nearly forty years of age," Clotel was sixteen, and Althesa was fourteen.

As Brown might or might not have known, Jefferson resided in Washington during a part of his fourth year as Vice-President and during his eight years as president—from June, 1800, when Washington became the nation's capital, until March, 1809. If his alleged affair with Currer preceded his removal to Washington, Althesa's age dates the beginning of the action in the novel not later than about 1814. This date is inconsistent, however, with others found in the work—dates which make it impossible to fit the story chronologically into the history of Jefferson's life. Brown could hardly have been well informed concerning that history when he wrote *Clotel*, for no comprehensive biography of Jefferson had yet appeared, nor was such a biography published until Brown's novel was five years old.[1]

At the beginning of the action in the novel, John Graves having been dead for some time, his thirty-eight slaves including Currer and her daughters were sold at auction in Richmond on Monday, November 10, of a year Brown did not specify. The year could not have been 1814, however, for November 10 was not on Monday in that year. The closest Monday, November 10, to that year occurred in 1817, which was reasonably close to the inferable time of the beginning of the action, but it is no more consistent with other dates in the novel than is 1814. Clotel, the last of the slaves to be sold, was purchased for $1,500 by Horatio Green, a young gentleman of Richmond, for the purpose of making her his mistress. Currer and Althesa were bought by Dick Walker, a speculator. Soon afterwards, along with thirty-eight others they were transported westward by land and then by way of the Ohio and Mississippi Rivers to the deep South.

In telling about the group's trip down the Mississippi River, Brown drew liberally upon his memory of what he himself had experienced and observed while he was in the service of James Walker, the Missouri slave trader, in 1832–33; and he repeated much of what he as well as others had previously said about the recklessness of life on the Mississippi, which was the main thoroughfare of the interstate slave traffic. Dick Walker sold Currer to the Reverend John Peck, a Methodist preacher of Natchez, Mississippi, thus separating her and Althesa forever. Currer's family was now completely disintegrated, as slave families often were by sales.

The introduction of Currer into Peck's service and her residence in Natchez provided the author with occasions for por-

1. The first comprehensive biography of Jefferson was Henry S. Randall's *The Life of Thomas Jefferson*, 3 vols. (New York, 1858).

traying various phases of slavery. A few days after Currer arrived in the city, said Brown, a slave hunt occurred there, and one of the victims of the hunt was burnt alive for running away and fighting to avoid recapture. Brown did not completely originate his account of this episode; he quoted the report of the burning from the *Natchez Free Trader* for July 16, 1842, as he had previously done in the second edition of his *Narrative*.[2] The only connection between Currer and this episode was that she was one of four thousand slaves who witnessed the burning, "and it gave her no very exalted opinion of the people of the cotton growing district."

In using the article from the *Natchez Free Trader* as he did, Brown gave the impression, perhaps unconsciously, that the action in his novel began in 1841 or 1842. Neither of these dates is consistent with the impression he had already given that Jefferson had become the father of Clotel and Althesa before he became President, if not before he became Vice-President, since Clotel was only sixteen years of age and Althesa was only fourteen at the beginning of the action. Herein is one of several anachronisms found in *Clotel*.

In the story, Peck, who was a native of Connecticut, had gone to Mississippi many years earlier and had "succeeded in captivating a plantation with seventy slaves, if not the heart of the [consumptive and now deceased] lady to whom it belonged." His plantation, called Poplar Farm, was in a valley nine miles from Natchez, situated like Dr. John Young's plantation near Marthasville, Missouri, on which Brown had spent a part of his boyhood. Peck left the management of his plantation to an overseer named Ned Huckelby, and he and his daughter Georgiana, his only child, lived in a house in the city. Currer became one of five servants in that house. In Peck, Brown portrayed the so-called Christian slaveholder who was enough of a casuist to defend slavery on apparently convincing biblical grounds. As a

2. *Natchez Free Trader,* July 16, 1842, quoted in *Narrative,* 2d ed. (Boston, 1848), p. 123.

slaveholding preacher, nevertheless, who pretended that everything he did was "for the glory of God," he was no better than his neighbor Jones, a non-Christian slaveholder who did not profess to do anything for God's glory.

At an auction in New Orleans—an event that gave Brown a good reason for describing a slave prison and market he had seen in that city—Althesa was purchased by James Crawford, a teller in a local bank, who had recently married. A native of Vermont, Crawford was opposed to slavery, but his wife had convinced him that owning a slave was not worse than hiring one from somebody else. As Brown must have been aware, this reasoning, on which he made Crawford act in buying Althesa, was questionable at best, for surely nobody was compelled either to hire a slave from somebody else or to buy one. This is a good example of what critics of fiction call unconvincing motivation. Nevertheless it helped to get Althesa into what proved to be a fortunate situation.

When the Crawfords purchased Althesa, Henry Morton, also a native of Vermont, was boarding with them. Morton had gone to New Orleans only a few weeks earlier to practice medicine. Having been told in his native state that slaves were Negroes, he was surprised to find that Althesa, who from all appearances was white, was really a slave. Six months later, induced first by pity and then by love, he purchased Althesa, married her, and established a home in another part of the city, where nothing about his wife was known. Within five years the couple became the parents of two daughters—Ellen and Jane.

As soon as Morton became prosperous, he and Althesa sent an agent to Natchez to purchase Currer's freedom, but Peck refused to sell her because he had found her "such a good housekeeper." Currer survived Peck, who suddenly died of cholera; but while Peck's daughter Georgiana and her newly acquired husband Miles Carlton, both of whom were abolitionists, were preparing to emancipate the deceased preacher's slaves, Currer contracted yellow fever and died.

Beginning with their getting acquainted in the home of the Crawfords, the story of Henry and Althesa Morton is an expansion of the story related in *A Description of William Wells Brown's Original Panoramic Views*, View Eighth. In retelling this story Brown not only included the reference to Currer for the sake of coherence in the plots of his novel but also added some new details and a new although not entirely original ending. The most remarkable addition was this introduction of the story of Salome Miller, which he altered considerably for no apparent reason, unless he was unfamiliar with its details at the time of the writing of his novel. After the Mortons had been married five years, he said, Althesa discovered that Salome Miller, a white slave she had hired to do some housework, had been treacherously and illegally reduced to slavery. When by chance Salome's identity was ascertained by a former acquaintance, Althesa supplied some of the money for the lawsuit by which Salome regained her freedom. Brown related the story of Salome Miller, not to arouse special sympathy for white slaves, but to illustrate one of the most striking peculiarities of the "peculiar institution." That peculiarity was that with their insatiable lust for victims, the demons of slavery were respecters of neither persons nor races—that in the land of King Cotton, a breath might make one a slave as easily as Oliver Goldsmith had said it could make one a lord.

Salome Miller, whose surname was originally Müller, was a native, not of Germany, as Brown said she was, but of Alsace. In a trial held in New Orleans in May, 1844, she lost her suit to regain her freedom, but she appealed to the state's supreme court and won her suit in June, 1845. Her case, therefore, was no longer in the New Orleans newspapers in 1845–46, as Brown said it was. There were articles about it, however, in the *National Anti-Slavery Standard* for July 31, 1845, and for January 1, 1846. These could have been the articles Brown had in mind, but as familiar as he was with the *National Anti-Slavery Standard*, it would have been surprising for him to confuse it with the New Orleans newspapers.[3]

According to the story, Henry and Althesa Morton died of yellow fever in the summer of 1831. If they did, obviously Althesa could not have aided Salome Miller in 1844–45. On the contrary, if Mr. and Mrs. Morton died after 1845, and if their daughters, who survived them, were less than five years old, as inferentially they were when their mother aided Salome Miller, they could not have been in their teens when their parents died, as Brown said they were. Herein is another of the anachronisms in *Clotel.*

After Henry and Althesa Morton died, the physician's creditors discovered all too soon, as in *A Description of William Wells Brown's Original Panoramic Views,* that he had never legally manumitted his wife. But unlike his prototype, Morton had failed to manumit Althesa, not because of fear of embarrassment, but because of ignorance of the laws of the several slave states. Apparently he had assumed incorrectly that his purchase of Althesa and formal marriage to her had freed her from slavery. Consequently he died without knowing that his marriage was one "which the law did not recognize; and therefore she whom he thought to be his wife was, in fact, nothing more than his slave." Now, when upon his creditors' insistence the daughters were inventoried as slaves and auctioned off, they were purchased obviously for concubinage—one for $2,300 and the other for $3,000.

In his first version of this story, Brown did not tell what became of the two girls after the sale, but in *Clotel* he did. Preferring death to the sordid life into which she was about to

3. George W. Cable, ed., "'Salome Müller.' Strange True Stories of Louisiana," *Century Magazine*, N. S. 16 (May, 1889): 56–69; Helen Tunnicliff Catterall, ed., *Judical Cases Concerning Slavery and the Negro* (Washington, 1932), 3: 570–71; *National Anti-Slavery Standard,* July 31, 1845, p. 33, January 1, 1846, p. 121.

be forced, Ellen committed suicide the night after her purchaser, "an old gentleman," took her to his home nine miles from the city. In relating Jane's fate, Brown used much of the language as well as many of the details of the last fifth of Mrs. Lydia Maria Child's "The Quadroons" with a change in the setting. Jane's purchaser, a wealthy young man, took her to his home near the mouth of the Mississippi River and virtually made her a prisoner in order to overcome her resistance to his advances. When her legitimate lover attempted to rescue her, the young man killed him instantly, and Jane died of a broken heart a few days afterwards.

As is inferable from the title of the novel, Brown intended to make the Clotel–Horatio Green affair the main plot of it. In beginning the development of this plot, however, he did not proceed originally. Instead he reproduced most of the details and most of the language verbatim of the first two-thirds of Mrs. Child's "The Quadroons," shifting the setting from the vicinity of Augusta, Georgia, to that of Richmond and changing the names of the characters. Slavishly following Mrs. Child, he invested the story of Clotel and Horatio Green with the sentimentalism and the rosewater atmosphere characteristic of so many of the antebellum romances of the South.

After purchasing Clotel, Horatio "hired" a secluded cottage "about three miles from Richmond" for her, "and the quadroon girl soon found herself in her new home." Horatio made Clotel his wife in almost every respect save in name, and for some time he and she spent many hours together in what was at least quasi happiness, especially after their daughter Mary was born. From time to time, nevertheless, Clotel was not only concerned about her own precarious position but also apprehensive about the future of her daughter; for she knew that both of them were still slaves and were, therefore, subject to the sudden reversals of fortune which slaves in situations like theirs frequently experienced.

Ere long Clotel's fears and scruples, as Banquo would have

called them, proved to be well founded. In order to succeed in politics, in which he had become interested, Horatio found it expedient to marry a wealthy and influential man's daughter whom Brown identified only as Gertrude. During what proved to be his last visit to the secluded cottage, Horatio pled "the necessity of circumstances" as the reason for his decision to marry, soothingly professed "that as he still loved her [Clotel] better than all the world, she would ever be his real wife," and also expressed the hope that "they might see each other frequently." Clotel indignantly as well as immediately rejected his last-mentioned idea, partly because she loved him too much to share him with another woman and partly on ironically high moral grounds. Amid their kissing, sighing, and crying, she told him that this must be their last meeting, because "To meet thus is henceforth crime"; and a few minutes later they parted never to meet again in such lovingness.

For some time after his marriage, Horatio showed his want of moral principles by repeatedly but futilely entreating Clotel to receive him as of old. Contrariwise he showed himself possessed of some sense of responsibility by regularly sending to Clotel allowances for the support of herself and Mary. This unhappy state of affairs continued until Gertrude by chance discovered the existence of the inhabitants of the secluded cottage and her husband's relationship to them. When she did she proceeded exactly as Brown had known the wives of slaveholders to proceed in such situations. She compelled Horatio to sell Clotel for transportation out of the state; then she took Mary, now ten years old, into her home as a special object of persecution.

Clotel, "now nearly thirty years of age," was purchased and carried to the Mississippi Valley by Dick Walker, who "a few years previous" had purchased and carried away Currer and Althesa. She was sold by Walker in Vicksburg, Mississippi, where she remained about a year, and whence she and a fellow slave named William escaped in the identical way in which William and Ellen Craft had escaped. Upon arriving in Cincinnati, the two fugitives separated, and William set out for Canada. Meanwhile Clotel continued by steamer to Wheeling and thence by stagecoach to Richmond to find her daughter Mary. During the stagecoach ride Clotel heard discussions about the possibilities of Martin Van Buren, William Henry Harrison, and Henry Clay as candidates in the forthcoming presidential election. The time of her ride, therefore, must have been in the fall of 1839, for that was the only time during which the three persons mentioned were simultaneously considered as possible presidential candidates by their respective political parties. This date is not consistent, however, with Brown's most recent reference to Clotel's age. If Clotel was born before Jefferson became President, she must have been considerably more than thirty years old in 1839.

Clotel, so the story goes, arrived in Richmond late one evening during the excitement that followed Nat Turner's insurrection. This account is inconsistent with both the last reference to Clotel's age and the time of her stagecoach ride. In 1839 Nat Turner's insurrection was eight years old, and the excitement it had caused hardly lasted eight years. Furthermore Clotel herself had been out of Richmond only about a year, it seems, and apparently the city was not excited about the insurrection when she was carried away. Herein are still more anachronisms in Brown's novel.

In spite of Clotel's disguise as a young gentleman, her identity was discovered within three days after her arrival in Richmond, before she heard any news about Mary. She was arrested and imprisoned, and her last owner was notified concerning her whereabouts. Brown recounted the remaining few days of her life in chapter 25, which he cryptically entitled "Death Is Freedom." Upon her owner's request she was transferred to Washington and put in a slave prison midway between the Capitol and the president's house to await transportation by steamboat to New Orleans. "At dusk of the evening prior to the day when she was to be sent off, as the old prison was being closed for the night, she suddenly darted past her keeper, and ran for her life." She made her way to the Long Bridge over the Potomac River but was trapped on it between her pursuers from Washington and three Virginians approaching from the south. Realizing that escape was now impossible, she needed only a moment to make a final choice. Then, "within plain sight of the President's house and the capital [*sic*] of the Union," after breathing a prayer, "with a single bound, she vaulted over the railings of the bridge, and sunk [*sic*] for ever beneath the waves of the river."

Two years before the publication of *Clotel*, Grace Greenwood had published her *Poems*, in which she had included a poem of six eight-line stanzas entitled "The Leap from the Long Bridge. An Incident at Washington" with the following introductory note: "A woman once made her escape from the slave-prison, which stands midway between the Capitol and the President's house, and ran for the Long Bridge, crossing the Potomac to the extensive grounds and woodlands of Arlington Place."[4]

It is indeed probable that the setting of Clotel's fatal flight and the idea of her dramatic death were suggested by Miss Greenwood's introductory note and poem. The third stanza of the poem even refers to the men who approached the slave woman from the Virginia end of the bridge. Brown ended chapter 25 with the poem, saying not very convincingly that it had been published in a newspaper a few days after Clotel's death. In his version of the poem there are differences in the wording of ten lines, and there is a seventh stanza containing the ironic idea that Clotel could find only in death the freedom that George Washington was supposed to have won "for our land."

Thus ends Clotel's story but not the novel. In three more chapters (26–28) Brown completed the story of Clotel's daughter Mary. In doing this he simply retold verbatim the story he had already told in *Three Years in Europe*, letter 22. But in order to connect this story with Clotel's, he added a few minor details and identified the Mary in it as Clotel's daughter and George Green as Horatio Green's slave until he fled to freedom.

4. Grace Greenwood, *Poems* (Boston, 1851), pp. 80–82.

In chapter 29, which is entitled "Conclusion," Brown affirmed that "the various incidents and scenes" in his novel were "founded in truth," that many of them were based on his own experience and observations, and that others had been related to him by fugitive slaves he had helped while he was employed on Lake Erie steamers. He acknowledged his indebtedness to the various abolition journals for information about some of his characters and to Mrs. Child for the use of her story. He did not identify the story, however, as he might well have done since he had used it so freely. Finally, after quoting statistics giving estimates of the number of slaves held by the members of the several religious denominations in the United States, he besought British Christians to do two things—to hold no fellowship with slaveholders who called themselves Christians, and to urge the slaveholders for the sake of "*the* common salvation, which knows no distinction between the bond and the free, to proclaim the Year of Jubilee."

Although *Clotel* was potentially sensational, it created no sensation, partly, no doubt, because it was brought out scarcely more than a year after *Uncle Tom's Cabin*, with which it invited comparisons to its disadvantage. Indeed it cannot be said to have won acclaim, but it was found worthy of some commendation. Both the *London Daily News* and the *Leader* were said to have commented favorably on it; and according to the *Hereford Times* for December 17, 1853, "the neat little book" was "pleasing evidence that he [Brown] knows how to wield the pen of a ready writer. . . . In 'Clotel,' " the *Times* continued, "the writer has touched lightly upon his dreadful subject, yet, writing upon a matter of which he has had such painful experience, he could hardly fail to be interesting."[5]

Said *The Literary Gazette* for December 31,

5. [Josephine Brown], *Biography of an American Bondman, by His Daughter* (Boston, 1856), p. 89; "*Clotel; Or, The President's Daughter*," *Hereford* [England] *Times*, December 17, 1853.

> This tale of American slavery is one of deep interest. The writer has not the literary art and dramatic skill which have gained for the story of Uncle Tom its world-wide popularity, but he writes with the force and earnestness of one who has himself been a slave, and who keenly feels the wrongs of the coloured race.

In the *Anti-Slavery Advocate* for January, 1854, a critic remarked that "the book contains material amply sufficient, if artistically treated, to fill a three volumed [*sic*] novel." The *Athenaeum* for January 21 said that "The story of Mr. W. Wells Brown told, in half a line, on his title-page." Forthwith this periodical dismissed the work with the notation that it was "a voice to swell the chorus which Mrs. Beecher Stowe has raised," but that the "literary merits" of this and several other current books by American authors "are such as can only claim a local—as distinguished from a general—success."[6]

The *National Anti-Slavery Standard* for December 31, 1853, commended the book to readers in America by means of a favorable article about it reprinted from the *London Eastern Star*. To the writer of this article, Brown's novel was an attestation of the truths *Uncle Tom's Cabin* had told about American slavery—an attestation all the more convincing because its basis was the author's experience rather than information received from others. The *Liberator* for February 3, 1854, expressed the wish that the book "might be reprinted in this country"; for there was much in it, this newspaper said, "calculated to intensify the moral indignation of the world against American slavery."[7]

Although John Herbert Nelson considered Brown an "unpolished and ignorant negro writer," he credited Brown with

6. *Literary Gazette and Journal of Belles Lettres, Arts, and Sciences*, December 31, 1853, p. 1263; *Anti-Slavery Advocate*, January, 1854, p. 125; *Athenaeum, Journal of Literature, Science, and the Fine Arts*, January 21, 1854, p. 86.

7. *National Anti-Slavery Standard*, December 31, 1853, p. 128; *Liberator*, February 3, 1854, p. 19.

occasionally introducing in *Clotel* "scraps of genuine dialogue and characters that he [Brown] knew at first hand."[8] Nelson seems, however, to have missed discovering the main purpose of the novel, which was not to evoke pity for white and near-white slaves, as he seems to have thought it was, but to expose the evils of slavery in their various forms and to show that slavery was based as much on caste as on race.

Had Nelson read *Clotel* more discerningly than he seems to have done, he probably would have discovered that there is little or nothing racially remarkable about the "negro dialogue and characters" in it. As to the dialect, that is easily recognizable mainly as mutilated English, which so much of literary dialect is. As to what is said, one can find nothing remarkably Negroid about that. Brown simply made his characters say what, in his opinion, the circumstances in the story occasioned or necessitated on the part of such characters from time to time.

As many of its readers have doubtless observed, the novel suffers from sketchiness in the development of its plots and in the portrayal of characters, as well as from defects in style. "The great weakness of *Clotel*," said Vernon Loggins, "is that enough material for a dozen novels is crowded into its two hundred and forty-five pages."[9] Loggins's statement may well be considered extravagant, but the book does contain too much subject matter for full treatment in one novel.

In reference to the anachronisms in *Clotel*, Brown's failure to remove them might have been due to carelessness or inadvertence, but it might also have been due to a much better reason. Brown had doubtless learned from his reading that neither historical fiction nor historical drama strictly regarded chronological details as history itself must regard them. He had read Scott and Shakespeare, and from their works he could hardly have

8. John Herbert Nelson, *The Negro Character in American Literature* (Lawrence, Kan., 1926), pp. 83–85.

9. Vernon Loggins, *The Negro Author: His Development in America* (New York, 1931), p. 166.

missed perceiving that if an historical story presented a true and vivid picture of a certain period, errors in calendar dates which did not becloud the picture were relatively unimportant. The anachronisms in Brown's novel detracted nothing from his portrayal of American slavery as he had come to know it. Presumably, therefore, they were from his point of view ultimately inconsequential. Brown's *Clotel* is generally considered the first novel written by an American Negro; and although it abounds in imperfections, it is a memorable effort of a pioneer among Negro authors.

XV

Glory Exchanged for Hope

After more than a month devoted to intermittently filling lecture engagements in southeastern England and attending to details incident to getting *Clotel* off the press, Brown went on a lecture tour of the northwest Midlands. About a year afterwards he gave a sketchy account of this tour, implying that he began it late in December. He began it early in that month, however, if not before that time. He went from London directly to Ludlow, traveling 150 miles by railway "and twenty miles on the top of a coach, in a drenching rain." He spent most of December lecturing "to advantage," said the *Anti-Slavery Advocate*, in small as well as in large towns, principally in Shropshire and Herefordshire.[1]

As usual Brown lectured in the evenings and spent some of the days sight-seeing. In Ludlow he visited the ruins of the famous

1. *Sketches*, pp. 223–39; *Anti-Slavery Advocate,* February, 1854, p. 132.

castle of the same name, but he did so much more like an historically uninformed tourist than he ordinarily seemed to be. He said, among other things, that John Milton wrote *Comus* in the castle and that King Charles I saw it performed there in 1631. "Little did the king think," Brown remarked, "that the poet would one day be secretary to the man who should put him to death and rule his kingdom." Here Brown was probably more interested in the irony of history afforded by the juxtaposition of Charles I and Milton in the same imaginary scene than he was informed concerning the facts. *Comus* was first performed in Ludlow Castle on Michaelmas Night (September 29) in 1634. The king almost certainly was not present, nor is there any proof that Milton either wrote the masque in the castle or witnessed its performance there.[2]

More entertaining than what Brown told about his sightseeing in Ludlow is his story—whether true or apocryphal—of a farcical episode in which he starred during his stay of one night at "the principal hotel in the town." When at twelve o'clock at night he left the fireside in the parlor of the hotel and went to bed, he found himself shivering between damp sheets. In a childish fit of disgust he took the sheets off the bed, balled them up, and threw them through a window into the street below; then he slept between blankets the remainder of the night. The next day, after returning from a trip to the castle, he asked for his bill. The landlady of the hostelry, "the finest specimen of an English landlady that I had seen for many a day," he said, "nearly as thick as she was high, with a red face, garnished around with curls," asked him about the missing sheets. When he told her what he had done with them, she threatened to charge him for them; whereupon he threatened to publicize her bill in the *London Times* so as to "let the travelling public know how much you charge for wet sheets!" The threat and the counterthreat seem to have neutralized each other; and without being

2. David Masson, *The Life of John Milton*, new and rev. ed., 7 vols. (New York, 1946), 1: 604–23.

charged for the sheets, Brown left the hotel as a patron in good standing.[3]

About ten years later Brown added a sequel to this story. When he returned to the hotel as a guest a week after his first stay there, he remembered, he learned that he had been suspected of stealing the sheets, and that while the landlady was questioning him about them, a policeman was concealed nearby. Nevertheless all that had ended well was still well; and when on the night of his second visit, he retired, "I found two jugs of hot water in the bed," he was glad to say, "and the sheets thoroughly dried and aired."[4]

From Ludlow Brown went to Hereford, in whose vicinity he spent several days lecturing and sight-seeing. He made an extraordinarily favorable impression with his comprehensive lecture on "Slavery in the United States" in the Theatre in that city on the evening of December 12. The *Hereford Times* for December 17 commented in part thus on its sixth page:

> There was a very numerous attendance, comprising members of almost all denominations of Christians in the city, testifying by their presence their abhorrence of this monstrous system. Mr. Brown can scarcely be called a man of colour. His complexion nearly approaches white, and except for some slight traces of negro blood, [he] would scarcely be recognised as a descendant of that degraded and much persecuted race.

Also, in its review of *Clotel* on the twelfth page of the same number, this newspaper described the lecture as "lucid and powerful" and complimented the lecturer as follows:

> Mr. Brown occupies a position in public esteem only second to that of his powerful-minded compatriot, Frederick Douglass. Without Mr. Douglass's vivid imagination, deep pathos, and wealth of language, Mr. Brown has achieved not less an honour by the clearness of his statements, his generally happy

3. *Sketches*, pp. 230–36.
4. *Black Man*, 2d ed. (New York and Boston, 1863), p. 30.

choice of language, and the calm power of his appeals to the reason of his auditors.

Returning northward Brown filled lecture engagements in Shrewsbury and also in Wellington, about ten miles east of that city. In a letter he wrote from Alnwick, Northumberland County, on February 21, 1854, to Sarah H., he said, "Some few weeks since I gave a lecture in your old town Shrewsbury—'Lion Assembly Rooms,' and regretted you were not there." Both the addressee of this letter and "dear Blanche" who is referred to twice in it remain unidentified.[5]

From Wellington Brown proceeded to Coventry, where he spent several days as a guest of Joseph Cash of Sherbourne House. One day while he was Cash's guest, he went on a visit to Leamington. When in that town he found himself only a short distance from Stratford on Avon, he followed the suggestion of an acquaintance and went sight-seeing there apparently for the first time. He enjoyed visiting Shakespeare's birthplace, but he was wisely skeptical as to how authentic many of the mementos in it were. He was much more favorably impressed with the dramatist's burial place in the parish church than with the birthplace, for the church had not been especially prepared for tourist trade as the house seemed to him to have been. By evening he was again in Coventry.[6]

Brown spent the Christmas holidays with his daughters in London. In January, 1854, after lecturing several times in the metropolis, he visited Nutcham and the island of Jersey. Late in January or early in February, he went to northern England and spent most of the latter month "lecturing with much success to full houses" in small towns in Durham, Northumberland, and Cumberland Counties.[7] During most of March he was in southern

5. Brown to Sarah H., February 21, 1854, Henry P. Slaughter Collection.

6. *Sketches,* pp. 223–25.

7. *Anti-Slavery Advocate,* February, 1854, pp. 132–33, April, 1854, p. 152.

Scotland, where he lectured in several towns which he and William and Ellen Craft had visited together early in 1851. He also lectured in many of the villages in Aryshire and Dumfriesshire which he had not previously visited. Finding himself in the area in which Robert Burns had spent most of his life, he naturally went to see the places associated with the life and works of that poet. While in Dumfries he "lodged in the same house with Robert Burns, the eldest son of the Scottish bard," and also visited the bard's grave. A few days later, during his sojourn in Ayr, he visited Burns's birthplace at Alloway, the Doon bridge on which Tam o'Shanter's mare lost her tail, and the Burns monument nearby.

In his comments on what he saw in the area and on Burns himself, Brown evinced considerable familiarity with the poet's biography as well as with his best-known poems. Whether altogether apt or not, his criticism of Burns was original. To him Burns not only "surpassed Sir Walter Scott and Lord Byron" in song-writing but also was "a more than Simonides in pathos, as in his 'Highland Mary;' a more than Tyrtaeus in fire, as in his 'Scots wha ha'e wi' Wallace bled;' and a softer than Sappho in love, as in his 'Had we never loved so kindly.' "

On his way southward from Scotland, Brown traveled through the Lake District of England, as he had first done three years earlier. He tarried long enough to lecture in several towns in the district, notably in Kendal "by invitation of the Ladies Anti-Slavery Committee of the latter place."[8]

As Brown was aware long before he left America, the business of selling and buying slaves, diabolical as it was, could be carried on in effect anywhere in the United States. If during his sojourn in Great Britain he had forgot this fact, he was forcefully reminded of it in the spring and summer of 1854. During that time he himself was a commodity in that business although he was three thousand miles from America.

8. *Anti-Slavery Advocate,* May, 1854, p. 160; *Sketches,* pp. 247–53, 259–61.

In his letter of January 10, 1848, to Edmund Quincy, Enoch Price had offered to sell Brown to himself or his Boston friends for $325. Brown had summarily rejected Price's offer with the explanation that "God made me as free as he did Enoch Price, and Mr. Price shall never receive a dollar from me or my friends with my consent." After the enactment of the Fugitive Slave Law, however, Brown was confronted with a simple, unavoidable alternative. To be sure of avoiding reenslavement, he must either agree to the purchase of his freedom or stay out of the United States. That he would not have been safe from recapture as a fugitive slave even in Boston, "the cradle of liberty," had been proved by the experience of Thomas Simms there in April, 1851. Thus, although he appeared to be forsaking the principle of natural rights on which he had previously rejected Price's offer, Brown eventually permitted his freedom to be formally purchased for a practical reason. He wanted to return to his native land and rejoin the struggle for liberty which his fellow abolitionists were carrying on there. This he explained again and again in speeches he delivered after he returned to America.[9]

Doubtless with Brown's consent, the Reverend Edward Hore of Ramsgate, Kent, had written to Price on January 6, 1852, in an effort to negotiate Brown's manumission. After referring to Price's offer of January 10, 1848, Hore had offered him fifty pounds if he would relinquish all claims upon Brown and supply the fugitive with a bona fide deed of emancipation. Price had replied to Hore on the following February 16. In his letter he had acknowledged his first offer and had straightway renounced it, adding the following explanation:

> The Fugitive Slave Bill has been passed since then. I can now take him [Brown] anywhere in the United States, and I have everything arranged for his arrest if he lands at any port in the United States. But I will give him papers of emancipation, properly authenticated by our statutes, for the sum of five

9. See, for example, "The Reception at the Meionaon," *Liberator*, October 20, 1854, p. 166; *New York Daily Tribune*, December 20, 1854.

> hundred dollars (or £100) that will make him as free as any white person. If this suits your views, you can let me know, and I will have the papers made out and forwarded to Boston, to Joseph Gruley [Greely], of the firm of Charles Wilkins and Co., 33, Long Wharf. The money must be paid before the papers are handed over to your agent.

With an amazing show of courtesy and humility, Price had closed this mercenary and vindictive letter with "Respectfully your obedient servant."[10]

Nothing seems to have come of the Hore-Price correspondence for more than a year—except, perhaps, more correspondence between them and between other friends of Brown and Price. During that time Price a fortiori had come to realize anew that he could, of course, get nothing for Brown if Brown stayed in Great Britain, as an exorbitant price for his ransom might compel him to do. But even if Brown had returned to the United States without first getting his freedom legalized, there was another circumstance which a practical businessman like Price would not have overlooked. In spite of the Fugitive Slave Law, attempts to recapture fugitive slaves might prove ridiculously expensive, as Simms's owner had found, or both dangerous and futile, as the claimants involved in the Christiana, Pennsylvania, encounter of September, 1851, and in the Jerry rescue in Syracuse, New York, in the following October had learned. Accordingly it must have dawned upon Price that the best he could do was to bargain on the basis of Brown's desire to return to the United States. And having found that he had overestimated that desire, Price had concluded that the proverbial half-loaf would be better than no loaf at all. Strictly speaking, he got more than half a loaf. He eventually settled the business for three-fifths of the price he had demanded from Hore. Before the fall of 1853, he had written to Hore offering to reduce the price of Brown's ransom to three hundred dollars.[11] Many months were

10. *Clotel*, pp. 51–52.
11. *Hereford* [England] *Times*, December 17, 1853, p. 6.

to pass, however, before anything definite was done about Price's new offer.

By the spring of 1854, Ellen Richardson of Newcastle upon Tyne had begun negotiations with Price to secure Brown's freedom. Miss Richardson was a member of the same family which had been instrumental in purchasing the freedom of Frederick Douglass.[12] On April 24 Price wrote a deed of emancipation—less euphemistically, a bill of sale—setting Brown free "for and in consideration of the sum of three hundred dollars, to be paid to Joseph Greely, my agent in Boston, Mass., by Miss Ellen Richardson, or her agent, on the delivery of this paper." The next day he acknowledged the deed before William J. Hammond, clerk of the circuit court of Saint Louis; and that official forthwith wrote a certificate validating Price's acknowledgement, copied the deed, and wrote a certificate authenticating his copy. On April 26, Alexander Hamilton, "sole judge of the Circuit Court within and for the Eighth Judicial Circuit of the State of Missouri, (composed of the County of St. Louis,)" issued a certificate verifying the clerk's second certificate.[13] In due time Price forwarded the deed and the three certificates to his agent in Boston, where they waited for the next step in the transaction.

It was announced in the *Liberator* for May 26 that friends of Brown in England had contributed "the amount necessary to secure his ransom from bondage," and that in a recent letter to William C. Nell, Brown had intimated that he might arrive in Boston in the following June or July. If Brown had any expecta-

12. *Life and Times of Frederick Douglass, Written by Himself*, new rev. ed. (Boston, 1895), pp. 314–16. Lawrence Richardson to me, September 5, 1949. Mr. Richardson is a collateral descendant of Ellen Richardson. His letter refers to the fact that Miss Richardson, her brother Henry, and his wife Anna "raised a fund to buy the freedom of Frederick Douglass" but tells nothing about the purchase of Brown's freedom.

13. Circuit Court of the City of St. Louis, Permanent Record Book Number 24, p. 150; *Sketches*, p. 304; [Josephine Brown], *Biography of an American Bondman, by His Daughter* (Boston, 1856), pp. 96–98.

tions of returning to America so soon, they were premature, unless he was willing to risk returning before negotiations to guarantee his freedom were completed. For reasons still undiscovered, the negotiations were not completed for more than two months after Price wrote the deed of emancipation. It was not until July 7 that William I. Bowditch, acting as agent for Miss Richardson and Brown, paid Joseph Greely $300 and received the deed and the three certificates along with a receipt.[14] Thus, in accordance with the slavocracy's proclivity towards legal dialectics, it may be said that an American slave three thousand miles from America was sold in Saint Louis, where slavery was legal, and was finally bought in Boston, where slavery was not legal.

Whether because Bowditch delayed sending Brown's free papers to him or because of some other reason, Brown was still without them or even definite information about the progress of the negotiations more than three weeks after they had been completed. This fact was revealed by some remarks of his in Manchester on August 1 at an antislavery conference and celebration of the anniversary of British West Indian emancipation. The meeting was held under the auspices of the North of England Anti-Slavery and India Reform League. Brown's daughters, the Reverend Samuel Ringgold Ward, Parker Pillsbury, and several other Americans as well as Brown himself were present. At the afternoon session of the meeting, somebody said that Brown's freedom had been bought "by the liberality of the English people." In a speech during the evening session, which was held in the town hall, Brown referred briefly to the remark concerning the purchase of his freedom. Said he, among other things, "I know not that such a purchase has taken place; I know it is in contemplation, and many suppose it may have been accomplished by this time, but I do not know that such is the case."

14. *Liberator*, May 26, 1854, p. 82; [Josephine Brown], *Biography*, p. 98.

He affirmed, therefore, that by the laws of the United States he was still a fugitive slave.[15]

Near the end of his speech, however, Brown said that this might be "my last opportunity of speaking publicly in this country." Although he did not know that negotiations for the purchase of his freedom had been completed, he must have been expecting as well as hoping to be soon informed that they had been, for as the last-quoted remark implied, he was then preparing to leave Great Britain. Apparently the speech of August 1 was his last public speech there before he returned to the United States.

As usual the coming of the summer had brought an end to the lecture season, and Brown was left with a considerable amount of leisure. He had spent most of the two preceding summers writing books, but he seems to have done but little writing of any kind during the summer of 1854, even for the *Anti-Slavery Advocate.*

There was always sight-seeing to be done, of course, when one had time to do it, as Brown now had. Late in June he witnessed a session of the House of Commons while that assembly was discussing the Crimean War. From the visitors' gallery in the chamber of the house, he recognized many of the members and also heard Benjamin Disraeli and William Ewart Gladstone speak. On July 18 he went to Kensal Green Cemetery "to attend the inauguration" of Matthew Noble's monument to Thomas Hood. The occasion prompted him to set down some original reflections on Hood and his work in particular and on authors in general—reflections characteristic of the nationalistic and pragmatic school of criticism.

> Hood [he said] was not a merely ephemeral writer. He did not address himself to the feelings which were passing events

15. *Liberator*, August 25, 1854, p. 135, September 1, 1854, p. 138; *Report of the Proceedings of the Anti-Slavery Conference and Public Meeting, Held at Manchester, on the 1st of August, 1854* (London and Manchester, 1854).

generated in the minds of his readers. He smote deep down into the hearts of his admirers. Had he been nothing more than a literary man, the ceremony on this occasion would have been an impertinence. The nation cannot afford to have its time taken up by eulogiums on every citizen who does his work well in his own particular line. Nevertheless, when a man not only does his own work well, but acts powerfully on the national mind, then his fame is a national possession, and may be with all propriety made the subject of public commemoration. A great author is distinguished from the merely professional scribe by the fact of adding something to the stock of national ideas.

Without explaining how Hood acted powerfully on the national mind or what he added to the stock of national ideas, Brown attempted to exemplify the last-quoted generalization with a reference to Shakespeare. "Who can tell," he queried, "how much of the national character is due to the operation of the works of Shakspeare [*sic*]? The flood of ideas with which the great dramatist inundated the national mind has enriched it and fertilized it. We are most of us wiser and better by the fact of Shakspeare having lived and written. . . . A great author, such as Shakspeare, is, then, a great public educator." Returning to Hood, Brown said that he "was one of those who not only enriched the national literature, but instructed the national mind. . . . His labors were not, like those of Shakspeare, colossal," Brown admitted; but he averred that Hood "has produced as permanent an effect on the nation as many of its legislators," and that "Englishmen are wiser and better because Hood has lived."[16] Here again Brown unfortunately neglected to be specific about what either Shakespeare or Hood taught, what political effects the latter had produced, or how either had made Englishmen wiser and better by living. This commendable attempt at criticism thus leaves the reader where critical pronouncements have too often left readers—in a chilly fog of generalities.

16. *Sketches*, pp. 276–95.

During his five years in Great Britain, Brown traveled more than 25,000 miles, "addressed more than one thousand public meetings, lectured in twenty-three mechanics' and literary institutions, and gave his services to many of the benevolent and religious societies on the occasion of their anniversary meetings." Instead of soliciting contributions from audiences, he explained some years later, "I charged an admission fee at the door, except when I was engaged to lecture before a lyceum." In the latter event he charged the lyceum a specific fee. Meanwhile the sale of the four books he published in England—the British editions of his *Narrative* and his songbook, his *Three Years in Europe*, and his *Clotel*—netted him about $3,000.[17] From both his friends' point of view and his own, he was now justified in viewing with satisfaction the five years of anti-slavery work abroad which he had completed, and he was prepared to render a good account of himself when he returned to America.

Brown must have heard from Bowditch soon after the meeting in Manchester, and he must have forthwith informed Garrison as to when he expected to leave England, for at first Garrison expected him to arrive in Boston by the middle of September. But because of his inability to obtain immediate passage on a steamship bound for Boston, he did not leave England as soon as he had hoped to leave. On August 29 he wrote to Garrison explaining why he had been delayed and that he expected to leave Liverpool on the steamer *City of Manchester* on September 6 bound for Philadelphia, with the hope of arriving in that city about fourteen days later.[18] He did not, however, arrive in Philadelphia on time and probably did not get to Boston until the first week in October.

Before circumstances made it feasible for Brown to return

17. *Ibid.*, p. 32; William Wells Brown to *Frederick Douglass' Paper*, September 27, 1859, reprinted in *Weekly Anglo-African*, October 22, 1859, p. 3.

18. William Lloyd Garrison to the Reverend Samuel J. May, September 11, 1854, Anti-Slavery Letters Written by W. L. Garrison; "Letter from W. W. Brown," *Liberator*, September 22, 1854, p. 151.

to the United States, other circumstances made it desirable for his daughters to remain in England. After a year in a seminary in Calais, Clarissa and Josephine had entered the Home and Colonial School in London, where they had studied for eighteen months. The respectability of this teacher-training institution was evidenced by the fact that it numbered among its "members" Queen Victoria, Prince Albert, the Duchess of Sutherland, the Earl of Derby, and many other peers and peeresses, as well as "bishops, baronets, members of Parliament, clergy, magistrates, and merchants." In December, 1853, the two girls had passed an examination by which they had been qualified as schoolmistresses, and both had been appointed to teaching positions. Clarissa had become mistress of a school at Berden, Essex County, about forty miles from London. Being well-pleased with her situation, she had decided to remain in England.

Josephine, at less than fifteen years of age, had become mistress of East Plumstead School, Plumstead, Woolwich. At this school, in which more than a hundred students were enrolled, Josephine had an assistant who was her senior by two years, and several of her students were older than she was. Realizing that she held a position the like of which she could not get in America, she had informed Samuel May, Jr. in a letter of April 27, 1854, that she wished to remain in England, "for I am fond of teaching," she explained. In spite of her fondness for teaching, withal, she gave up her position and returned to France late in the summer to continue her education. She was there when her father returned to America.[19]

On September 4 or 5 Brown took leave of his daughter

19. William Farmer, "Education of Colored Refugees in England," *Liberator*, January 14, 1853, p. 7; *Anti-Slavery Advocate*, February, 1854, pp. 132–33, May, 1854, p. 159 (The latter is an article, probably written by Brown himself, reprinted from the *London Morning Advertiser*.); Josephine Brown to Samuel May, Jr., April 27, 1854, reprinted in *Liberator*, May 26, 1854, p. 82; "Letter from W. W. Brown," *Liberator*, September 22, 1854, p. 151.

Clarissa in London and entrained for Liverpool. With 174 other cabin passengers and more than 500 in steerage, he left Liverpool aboard the *City of Manchester.* He had previously become acquainted with John Mirehouse, one of the ship's officers, and "To this gentleman I am much indebted," he said later, "for kind attention shown me on the voyage." The trip was long and stormy but otherwise uneventful, except that a small leather trunk of Brown's was stolen and ransacked and was found only after he offered a reward for its recovery. The steamship arrived at Philadelphia about midafternoon on September 26. At last Brown was again in his native land—the land in which he had been worked as a slave and in which a proslavery government had denied him citizenship. To him it was no land of glory, as Great Britain had been, but it was, nevertheless, a land of hope. Otherwise he would not have returned to it to rejoin on the home front the crusade against slavery and its by-product, racial proscription.[20]

Incidentally, Brown brought with him from William Craft a letter for Garrison and money for a subscription to the *Liberator.* By some mischance Craft's letter was lost for several months, but it was eventually found and published on the thirty-first page of the *Liberator* for February 23, 1855.

20. *Sketches,* pp. 307–11, 314–15.

XVI

America, but Not Yet the Beautiful

If perchance Brown had forgot while he was abroad what being a Negro in America meant, he did not have to wait very long after his return to his native land to have his memory jolted. Soon after their debarkation he and two foreigners who had traveled with him from London to Philadelphia hailed an omnibus on Chestnut Street. The two foreigners were immediately taken aboard, but he was bluntly told that Negroes were not allowed to ride in that omnibus.[1] This was indeed America, but for him and many others it was certainly not yet the beautiful.

Upon his arrival in Philadelphia, if not before he left England, Brown was informed that a special meeting of the American Anti-Slavery Society together with a celebration of the anniversary of the Jerry rescue was to be held in Syracuse, New

1. *Liberator,* November 10, 1854, p. 178; *Sketches,* pp. 312–14.

York, on September 29–30. He was also informed that he was expected to be present and to address the meeting. On September 11 Garrison had written to the Reverend Samuel J. May of Syracuse expressing doubts that the meeting should be held because of "the prospective and probable lack of effective speakers."[2] But eventually Garrison's doubts proved to be groundless. Brown went directly from Philadelphia to Syracuse, where he found Garrison, Frederick Douglass, Charles Lenox Remond and his wife, and other old faithfuls of the antislavery cause.

The sessions of the first day were held in the city hall—a fact which suggests that the city officials were not opposed to abolitionism if they were not actively in favor of it. At the first evening session the hall "was crowded to its utmost capacity by a very large and brilliant audience." After being introduced by Garrison, who presided, Brown spoke optimistically of the progress of abolitionism in Great Britain and related several of his and his daughters' experiences abroad.[3]

On the evening of October 4, Brown, Remond, and probably William C. Nell held a meeting in Corinthian Hall in Rochester. Church services and capricious weather kept their audience small, but not too small for Brown to speak for about an hour. In his speech he said that while he was living in Buffalo, he and other abolitionists retained Millard Fillmore as counsel for an alleged fugitive slave, and that Fillmore served without accepting a fee, explaining that he considered it "his duty to help the poor fugitive." This was the same Fillmore who as President of the United States had signed the Fugitive Slave Bill of 1850. Here was a notable instance, Brown thought, in which a man had sacrificed his moral convictions for a political advantage.[4]

Brown returned with the Remonds from Rochester to Boston; thence on Saturday, October 7, he went with them to Salem

2. Garrison to May, September 11, 1854, Anti-Slavery Letters Written by W. L. Garrison.

3. *Liberator,* October 6, 1854, p. 158, October 13, 1854, p. 161.

4. *Ibid.*, October 27, 1854, p. 171.

to be their guest for one or two days. The next day he participated in a quarterly meeting of the Essex County Anti-Slavery Society, of which Remond was president. The youthful Charlotte L. Forten was then living with the Remonds and attending the Higginson Grammar School in Salem. In 1848, when she was about eleven years old, she had first seen Brown in the home of her grandmother, Mrs. James Forten, in Philadelphia. Now, six years later, she noted in her journal that Saturday evening that Brown "has improved greatly both in appearance and conversation during his residence in England."[5] Since she was so young when he went to Europe, it is doubtful that she knew much about him then, and it is still more doubtful that she remembered him well enough to distinguish him as he was in 1854 from what he was in 1848. Her opinion alone, therefore, hardly merited more than casual consideration.

Nevertheless, as those who knew Brown much better than Miss Forten doubtless observed, he had indeed greatly improved himself during the preceding five years. He had extended his knowledge of the world by study, travel, and contact with many classes of people; and he was now better prepared to deal with men and issues than he was when he left America in 1849.

On the evening of October 13, a well-attended public meeting was held in the Meionaon in Boston to welcome Brown to America. Francis Jackson, president of the Massachusetts Anti-Slavery Society, presided but had very little to say. Nell introduced Brown with remarks which were appropriate, and which were certainly long enough for an introduction. Referring to the fact that Brown's freedom had been recently purchased from Enoch Price, he punned on that slaveholder's name. "Let us thank God," he said, "that Enoch cannot translate you, our brother, back to slavery. You are now beyond *Price*."

Upon the cessation of the "long and loud applause" with which he was greeted when he arose, Brown delivered his first

5. *Ibid.*, October 20, 1854, p. 167; [Charlotte L. Forten], *The Journal of Charlotte L. Forten* (New York, 1953), pp. 49–50.

speech in Boston since his return to America. He took cognizance of the progress of slavery during the years he was abroad and predicted that ere long efforts would be made by American slaveholders to establish their "peculiar institution" in Cuba and even in Haiti. The menace he envisioned for Haiti prompted him to repeat some of what he had said in his *St. Domingo: Its Revolutions and its Patriots*, a lecture which he had delivered at the Metropolitan Athenaeum in London on the preceding May 16. He now spoke enthusiastically, as he had spoken in the lecture, about the successful struggle of the Haitians against Napoleon Bonaparte, and he predicted defeat for American slaveholders if they ever attempted to possess Haiti.

Wendell Phillips next delivered a brief but characteristically eloquent speech. He welcomed Brown back to America although he was aware that Brown had come "home to no liberty but the liberty of suffering—to struggle in fetters for the welfare of his race." After paying "a warm tribute" to Brown, Garrison spoke at length against proslavery interpretations of the Bible.[6]

Brown had an engagement to lecture in the town hall in Abington on Sunday evening, October 15, "at the usual time for religious service." The next day he and Garrison went to Philadelphia to attend a public reception for him on the following Tuesday evening and the Women's Rights Convention which began the next day. The reception, sponsored by the Vigilance Committee of Philadelphia, was held in the Brick Wesley Church. It was an "enthusiastic" and "delightful" occasion, Garrison informed his wife in a letter he wrote to her from Philadelphia on October 19. "The church was so crowded that it was with extreme difficulty I could get up to the pulpit."

Upon arising to speak, Brown began with a reference to a storm which the *City of Manchester* had encountered on its recent voyage from Liverpool to Philadelphia. He recalled that rough weather had kept the ship's captain from ascertaining "the latitude in which he was, or the distance he had run," until the sun

6. *Liberator,* October 13, 1854, p. 162, and October 20, 1854, p. 166.

shone again and enabled him to take his bearings. In an attempt to draw an analogy between this event and the situation of Negroes in America during more than two centuries, Brown now advised that they "stop and take the sun, and see where we are." After this beginning, which reminds one of the exordium of Daniel Webster's *The Reply to Hayne*, he did not take the sun. Instead he said essentially the same things he had already said in two or three of the speeches he had delivered since his return to America.[7]

Garrison went from Philadelphia to Cincinnati, in fulfillment of plans he had explained in his letter of September 11 to the Reverend Samuel J. May. Meanwhile Brown remained in the city and its vicinity about a week—at least long enough to attend the seventeenth annual meeting of the Pennsylvania Anti-Slavery Society, which was held in Westchester on October 23-24. Having recently accepted an appointment as a lecturing agent for the American Anti-Slavery Society, he returned to New England and began in his new position with a lecture in Pawtucket, Rhode Island, on October 29. Between that date and December 8, he had at least nineteen engagements in cities and towns in Rhode Island, including two in Providence.[8]

Interrupting his lecture tour briefly, Brown went to Salem on Saturday, November 18, where he remained as the Remonds' guest until the following Monday. According to Miss Forten, during this time he talked so much about his daughters that she began to wonder whether they were prodigies, became "extremely curious to see them," and hoped that "they are as finely

7. *Ibid.*, October 13, 1854, p. 163; *National Anti-Slavery Standard*, October 28, 1854, pp. 2–3; Garrison to Mrs. Garrison, October 19, 1854, Anti-Slavery Letters Written by W. L. Garrison.

8. *Proceedings of the Massachusetts Anti-Slavery Society at the Annual Meetings Held in 1854, 1855, & 1856* (Boston, 1856), p. 26; *Liberator*, October 20, 1854, p. 167, October 27, 1854, p. 171, November 3, 1854, pp. 174–75, November 10, 1854, pp. 178, 179, November 17, 1854, p. 183, November 24, 1854, p. 187, December 1, 1854, p. 191; *National Anti-Slavery Standard*, December 4, 1854, p. 3.

educated and accomplished as he evidently thinks they are." After hearing him lecture in Salem on Sunday evening, Miss Forten commented in her journal as follows: "I thought that he spoke much better than he usually does. His manner was more animated. But although in private conversation he has improved, I do not think he is a very good lecturer."[9]

As busy as he was traveling and lecturing during the first six weeks after his return to America, Brown found time to revise and enlarge his *Three Years in Europe* for publication under a new title—*The American Fugitive in Europe. Sketches of Places and People Abroad.* This work has been generally referred to only by the second half of its title. There appeared in the *Liberator* for November 10 an advertisement of John P. Jewett and Company, publishers, of Boston announcing that they would issue the new volume about November 25. The *Liberator* for December 2 informed its readers that the book had been recently published, and the same newspaper for December 15 quoted favorable comments on it from five other New England newspapers.[10]

Sketches of Places and People Abroad is a duodecimo volume of 320 pages. Its frontispiece is the same as the one in *Three Years in Europe.* The publishers' imprint contains not only the name of John P. Jewett and Company but also those of Jewett, Proctor and Worthington of Cleveland, and Sheldon, Lamport and Blakeman of New York. The date in the imprint is 1855, but the copyright date is 1854.

"A Memoir of the Author" fills twenty-six pages. This is a reproduction of the first forty-six pages of the autobiographical sketch in *Clotel* with some omissions and changes in wording here and there. The only new item in the memoir is the one with which it ends, namely, the Reverend Edward S. Mathews's stanzas "To William Wells Brown," which Mathews had pre-

9. [Charlotte L. Forten], *Journal,* p. 53.

10. *Liberator,* November 10, 1854, p. 179, December 8, 1854, p. 195, December 15, 1854, p. 198.

sented at a soiree in Brown's honor in Bristol, England, early in April, 1850.

In a "note to the American Edition," Brown said that he was offering the revision "to the American public, with a dozen or more additional chapters," as the divisions in this edition are designated. His statement, however, was not altogether accurate. The first eleven chapters are the same as the first eleven letters in the original work. The next nine chapters were altered not only by additions and omissions but also by changes in wording and paragraphing which proved to be of no special value to readers. Chapter 27 is letter 23 renumbered and thus left as far out of place as it originally was. Only eleven new chapters were added, making a total of thirty-two. These chapters, which comprise about one-third of the text itself, give information, although not in chronological order, about Brown's activities from the fall of 1852 until his return to America. Best among the additions are Brown's account of his visit to Ludlow (chapter 22) because of its anecdotal excellence, his résumé of his tour of the Burns country (chapter 24) because of its vividness in the presentation of details, and the sketch of the versatile and ubiquitous Joseph Jenkins of London (chapter 28) because of its human interest.

Sketches of Places and People Abroad seems to have been the first of Brown's books to be reviewed by an American metropolitan daily newspaper, and the first newspaper of this kind to review this book was apparently the *New York Daily Tribune.* "Apart from the merits of this volume as a lively and entertaining record of foreign travel," said that newspaper, "its peculiar origin makes it a novelty in literature worthy of the attention of our modern D'Israelis." The newspaper reminded its readers that the book was the work of a fugitive slave "who never enjoyed the advantages of a day's schooling in his life," and it further observed that "Without respect to its authorship, the volume is far superior to the ordinary run of books of foreign travel."[11]

11. *New York Daily Tribune,* December 12, 1854.

A brief complimentary notice concerning the book appeared under the heading "New Publications" on the third page of the *National Anti-Slavery Standard* for December 23, 1854. Eight additional newspaper criticisms of it were quoted on the fifth page of the *Liberator* for January 12, 1855. All of these were favorable except one from the *New York Independent*. The "chief interest" that journal found in the book was the fact that it was written by "a colored man" who had spent his first twenty years in slavery, and who had never gone to school. The journal also seemed inclined to attribute whatever artistic genius Brown had to the influence of his white ancestry.

Sketches of Places and People Abroad is not a remarkably good revision of *Three Years in Europe*. In it Brown corrected some of the imperfections of the first version, left some as they were, and added some new ones. He did not arrange the new chapters in chronological order. In fact he seems to have left them without order, unless it was the order in which he happened to write them. They are arranged as if he might have written some of them hurriedly in response to his printers' requests for more copy while other things were demanding his attention. Had time together with inclination permitted him to reorganize the subject matter as he might well have reorganized it, and to improve the style of the work as he presumably could have improved it, he might have made this not only his best book but also an American classic. As it is, it is not a much better book than *Three Years in Europe*.

On Saturday evening and Sunday, December 9 and 10, 1854, the Worcester County South Division Anti-Slavery Society held its annual meeting in the city hall in Worcester. Brown as well as Garrison was present. At the session Saturday evening, Brown commented adversely although briefly upon *A South-Side View of Slavery; or, Three Months at the South, in 1854.*[12] This apologetic discussion of slavery by the Reverend Dr. Nehemiah Adams of Boston had been recently published in that

12. *Liberator,* December 15, 1854, p. 199.

city. For a long time afterwards Brown and other abolitionists frequently ridiculed or otherwise criticized "South-Side Adams," as he came to be called, and his views concerning slavery. In his speeches Brown pointed out repeatedly that whereas Adams had spent only three months in the South, he himself had spent twenty years in slavery and was sure, therefore, that he knew at least as much about the "peculiar institution" as Adams did.

Brown had a few engagements in Rhode Island for the second week in December, after which he spent the last two weeks of the year lecturing in New Jersey, Philadelphia and its vicinity, and New York City. On the evenings of December 18, 20, and 21, he delivered "a course of three lectures" in Saint Thomas' Episcopal Church in Philadelphia. The first lecture, whose title was "Places and People Abroad," was a digest of *Sketches of Places and People Abroad.* The second was the one on St. Domingo which Brown had delivered on the preceding May 16 in London, and which had been only recently published in Boston. The third lecture, the only new one in the series, had for its title "The Humble Origin of Great Men." Among those Brown referred to in exemplifying his central idea were Virgil, Cervantes, Defoe, Toussaint L'Ouverture, Dumas, and Charles Dickens.[13]

About the middle of December Brown's lecture on St. Domingo had been published by Bela Marsh of Boston in a pamphlet of thirty-eight pages with the title *St. Domingo: Its Revolutions and its* [*sic*] *Patriots. A Lecture, Delivered Before the Metropolitan Athenaeum, London, May 16, and at St. Thomas' Church, Philadelphia, December 20, 1854.* The pamphlet was copyrighted in 1854. The date in the publisher's imprint is 1855, but that the work was published about the time men-

13. *Ibid.*, December 8, 1854, p. 195; *National Anti-Slavery Standard*, December 9, 1854, p. 3, December 16, 1854, p. 3, January 6, 1855, p. 2. "This, we believe," said the last-cited article, "is the first attempt of a colored man to give a course of Lectures, embracing other topics than the anti-slavery subject, and we are glad to learn that these lectures have been very successful."

tioned above is proved by the fact that the *Liberator* for December 22 announced its recent publication and commented favorably upon it.[14] The reference in the title to the delivery of the lecture in Saint Thomas' Church was, of course, anticipatory.

In this work Brown intended to make the history of the Haitian revolution serve the United States as a warning and a reminder—a warning that Negroes, like other human beings, not only desired freedom but would fight unto death to win and maintain it, and a reminder that a slave revolt had actually succeeded. In four places in the pamphlet, he sounded a tocsin for American slaveholders. In one of these places he asked rhetorically, "Who knows but that a Toussaint, a Christophe, a Rigaud, a Clervaux, and a Dessalines, may some day appear in the Southern States of this Union? That they are there," he continued, "no one will doubt. That their souls are thirsting for liberty, all will admit. The spirit that caused the blacks to take up arms, and to shed their blood in the American revolutionary war, is still amongst the slaves of the south; and, if we are not mistaken, the day is not far distant when the revolution of St. Domingo will be rëenacted in South Carolina and Louisiana."[15]

Having adapted passages from the Reverend John R. Beard's *Life of Toussaint L'Ouverture* in his *Clotel*, Brown used that biography much more extensively in his *St. Domingo*. In many instances he quoted or adapted Beard's sentences, changing them only to facilitate his own sentence structure, or shortening them by eliminating words not needed in his context. He changed words in some places apparently for the sake of simplicity, but without necessarily achieving that to any greater extent than Beard had already achieved it.

For Brown, as for others who have written about the Haitian revolution, Toussaint L'Ouverture was, of course, chief among the Haitian patriots. Near the end of his pamphlet, Brown com-

14. *Liberator*, December 22, 1854, p. 202.
15. William Wells Brown, *St. Domingo* (Boston, 1855), p. 32.

pared Toussaint and Napoleon Bonaparte in the following passage, which he borrowed almost verbatim from Beard:

> The history of Toussaint, placed by the side of that of Napoleon, presents many striking parallels. Both born in a humble position, they raised themselves to the height of power by the force of their character. Both gained renown in legislation and government, as well as in war. Both fell the moment they had attained supreme authority. Both finished their career on a barren rock [*sic*].
>
> The parallels, however, have their contrast. Toussaint fought for liberty; Napoleon fought for himself. Toussaint gained fame by leading an oppressed and injured race to the successful vindication of their rights; Napoleon made himself a name and acquired a sceptre by supplanting liberty and destroying nationalities, in order to substitute his own illegitimate despotism.[16]

Anticipating an idea expressed by Wendell Phillips seven years later in his lecture on Toussaint L'Ouverture, Brown finally compared Toussaint with George Washington to the disadvantage of the latter. Said he,

> Toussaint's career as a Christian, a statesman, and a general, will lose nothing by a comparison with that of Washington. Each was the leader of an oppressed and outraged people, each had a powerful enemy to contend with, and each succeeded in founding a government in the New World. Toussaint's government made liberty its watchword, incorporated it in its constitution, abolished the slave-trade, and made freedom universal amongst the people. Washington's government incorporated slavery and the slave-trade, and enacted laws by which chains were fastened upon the limbs of millions of people. Toussaint liberated his countrymen; Washington enslaved a portion of his, and aided in giving strength and vital-

16. John R. Beard, *The Life of Toussaint L'Ouverture, the Negro Patriot of Hayti* (London, 1853), pp. 281–83; Brown, *St. Domingo*, pp. 36–37.

ity to an institution that will one day rend asunder the UNION that he helped to form.[17]

Although *St. Domingo* was Brown's first attempt to write history, it is as good writing of the kind as he ever did; and it is far from being an example of the worst kind of popular historical writing. Especially remarkable is the human interest with which its subject matter is endued, as well as its simplicity of diction and sentence structure and its freedom from rhetorical flourishes, even though it was originally prepared for the platform in the age of Delsartian oratory. Because of these qualities it was probably easy to listen to, and it still makes easy as well as interesting reading.

About the middle of November, Brown had accepted an invitation to deliver a lecture in New York City under the auspices of the New York Anti-Slavery Society on Tuesday evening, December 19. His was to be one of a series of lectures sponsored by the society during the lecture season of 1854–55. The other lecturers being who they were, he had a good reason to consider his invitation a distinction. Among others engaged to speak in the series were Joshua R. Giddings, Charles Sumner, the Reverend Antoinette L. Brown, Cassius M. Clay, Wendell Phillips, Henry Ward Beecher, and Ralph Waldo Emerson.[18] The place provided for the lectures was the Broadway Tabernacle, the scene of many of the annual meetings of the American Anti-Slavery Society. Before Brown went to Europe, he had spoken extemporaneously at meetings of that society in that building as well as in others in the city, but he was now to appear for the first time as a lyceum lecturer in the American metropolis.

Whether by chance or unavoidable circumstances, Brown's engagement in New York and his series of lectures in Philadelphia almost conflicted. As it was he had to go from Philadel-

17. Brown, *St. Domingo*, p. 37.
18. *National Anti-Slavery Standard*, November 25, 1854, p. 2.

phia to New York on December 19 to lecture there that evening and return to Philadelphia on the twentieth to lecture there that evening and the next.

Brown's lecture was the fourth in the series. A report on the fifth page of the *New York Daily Tribune* for December 20 said that his audience was "a fair one, though not so numerous as at the previous lectures, owing, perhaps, to the extreme coldness of the evening." The *New York Herald*, morning edition, for December 21 said on its second page that "At half-past seven o'clock there was a very fair audience assembled, and in a short time after, Mr. Brown, accompanied by Mr. Oliver Johnson and two other gentlemen, ascended the platform, and were [*sic*] received with much applause." This newspaper next opined that "Mr. Brown is a gentleman of pleasing appearance and good address. He is far removed from the black race, being just the 'color of mahogany,' and his distinct enunciation evidently showed that a white man 'spoke' within, although the words were uttered by the lips of a redeemed slave."

The subject of Brown's lecture was "Our National Character, and How It Is Viewed from a Distance." America had been "signally successful as a national power," he observed, but had failed to establish within its boundaries the liberty professed in its creed. He said that people abroad were too familiar with the inconsistency between actual American slavery and theoretical American republicanism to take the latter very seriously. He declared that proslavery American ambassadors had done the national reputation much more harm than good. As examples of diplomats who "sunk our national character lower and lower," he cited Andrew Stevenson of Virginia, Abbott Lawrence of Masachusetts, James Buchanan of Pennsylvania, and Pierre Soulé of Louisiana. Stevenson had been minister to Great Britain from 1836 to 1841. He was, doubtless, the "Stephenson" to whom Brown had erroneously referred in his lecture in Dublin in August, 1849. Lawrence had been minister to Great Britain from 1849 to 1852. At the time of Brown's lecture, Buchanan and

Soulé respectively had been minister to Great Britain and minister to Spain a little more than a year.

Brown had previously said many times most of what he said in this lecture. Although not much of what he said was new, from the applause he received during and after his speech, it appears that he pleased his audience very well. The final statement in the *Herald's* report of his lecture was, "The meeting separated, evidently highly pleased, at 9 o'clock."

Within the next few days after he completed the course of lectures in Saint Thomas' Episcopal Church in Philadelphia, Brown lectured in the city one evening on slavery and in Chester on December 24 on the same subject. During the Christmas holidays, by invitation he lectured before the Banneker Institute, "one of the literary Associations among the colored people of Philadelphia." On this occasion he spoke on "Mahomet and Confucius," and the subject was "ably handled by the lecturer."[19]

19. *National Anti-Slavery Standard,* December 23, 1854, p. 3, and January 6, 1855, p. 2.

XVII

With Eloquence, Wit, and Pathos

BROWN SPENT MOST OF JANUARY AND FEBRUARY, 1855, LECturing principally in the eastern half of Massachusetts and in Rhode Island. At the twenty-third annual meeting of the Massachusetts Anti-Slavery Society, which was held in the Meionaon in Boston on January 25–26, he was rather prominent, as he was doubtless expected to be after an absence of five years from such meetings. In a speech at one of the sessions, he asserted that it was the policy of the slave power "to buy up whatever stood in its way—politicians and ministers especially." He then citen the Reverend Dr. Nehemiah Adams as an example of a minister who had been bought and criticized him severely for writing appeasingly and ignorantly about slavery. "Had Dr. Adams been present," said the official report of the meeting, "we think he would have felt himself to be a very insignificant personage before this graduate of the plantation, and we could wish him no greater *justice* than to have to meet Mr. Brown on the anti-slavery platform." Alas the wish expressed in the report seems never to have been fulfilled. It is indeed doubtful that Brown and Dr. Adams ever met on any occasion. At the final session Brown limited himslf to a half-hour of remarks concerning slavery, the purchase of his freedom by British friends, and his experiences and observations abroad.[1]

In order to keep an engagement he had made in the preceding November, Brown had to interrupt for a day or two his activities in Rhode Island, where he was lecturing in the middle of February. The Worcester City Anti-Slavery Society, of which Thomas Wentworth Higginson was then president, sponsored a course of lectures which were given in the city hall on successive Friday evenings from December 1, 1854, to March 2, 1855. Among those who were engaged to lecture were the Reverend John Pierpont, the antislavery poet, Salmon P. Chase of Cincinnati, Ralph Waldo Emerson, David Wilmot of Towanda, Pennsylvania, and Brown, whose engagement was for February 16. Although no Worcester newspaper seems to heve reported his lecture, Brown doubtless kept the engagement.[2]

Early in 1855 a controversy between Brown and Frederick Douglass, which had been smoldering for some time, suddenly flared up and subsided equally as suddenly. What amounted only to hints concerning it reached the public in two contributions to the antislavery press. The first of these was a paragraph entitled "William Wells Brown" on the second page of *Frederick Douglass' Paper* for March 2. The second was an open letter from

1. A. Firth to Samuel May, Jr., January 9, 1855, Anti-Slavery Letters Written to W. L. Garrison and Others; *Liberator,* January 12, 1855, p. 11 [7], January 26, 1855, pp. 14, 15, February 2, 1855, pp. 18–19; *Proceedings of the Massachusetts Anti-Slavery Society at the Annual Meetings Held in 1854, 1855 & 1856* (Boston, 1856), pp. 33–36, 42.

2. *Liberator,* February 9, 1855, p. 23, February 16, 1855, pp. 27, 28; [Charlotte L. Forten], *The Journal of Charlotte L. Forten* (New York, 1953), p. 58. The *Worcester Daily Spy,* February 16, 1855, announced that Brown would lecture in the city hall that evening.

Brown "To Frederick Douglass" in the *National Anti-Slavery Standard* for March 10.

While Brown was still in Great Britain, he had most probably been informed about the estrangement between Douglass and the Garrisonians, which by the fall of 1853 had become almost irreconcilable. After his return to America he had doubtless heard talk about it in the antislavery office in Boston.[3] Talk among the Garrisonians about Douglass had probably led Brown to tell about an uncomplimentary letter which he said Douglass had written to an Englishwoman about him before he left America; and what Brown had told had been perchance relayed to Douglass by rumor. Upon hearing that Douglass had heard of what he had said and had been displeased by it, Brown had attempted to deal roundly with the matter by writing Douglass a letter about it on January 20, 1855. In this letter he had gone into details about the alleged uncomplimentary letter.

Instead of publishing Brown's letter of January 20, as Brown thought he should have done together with "such comments as you thought best," Douglass kept silent more than a month and then published the paragraph mentioned above. In this paragraph Douglass informed the public that he did not regret commending Brown repeatedly while Brown "was abroad, laboring, with admirable industry in the cause of human freedom, and adding to his stock of knowledge of men and things." He said that he regretted, nevertheless, that Brown "should feel called upon, to show his faithfulness to the American Anti-Slavery Society, by covering us with reproach and dishonor." He advised that if Brown had any charges against him and would put them "in suitable shape," he would see that they were set forth "not only in the anti-slavery office at Boston, in the private ear of prejudice" but also in print. As an honest man Brown was obli-

3. For brief accounts of this estrangement, see Benjamin Quarles, *Frederick Douglass* (Washington, 1948), pp. 70–79; and Philip S. Foner, *The Life and Writings of Frederick Douglass*, 4 vols. (New York, 1950–55), 2: 48–66.

gated to do this, he said, "or cease circulating as facts, what we know can be shown to be the merest fictions."

It was this paragraph that provoked Brown into writing the open letter to Douglass which appeared in the *National Anti-Slavery Standard* for March 10. A few months after his arrival in England, Brown said in this letter, he had visited an Englishwoman, "a distinguished Abolitionist," who was a friend of Douglass. During his visit he had been informed by the lady herself of the contents of the uncomplimentary letter Douglass had written to her about him. Having been influenced by the letter, the lady had given him, Brown remembered, "a cold reception." He did not name the lady, he explained, because he was sure that Douglass remembered who she was—"unless you wrote to more than one." Brown insisted that the controversy between him and Douglass had nothing to do with the American Anti-Slavery Society. He also took Douglass to task for blandly ignoring his letter of January 20, which in his opinion contained in a suitable form his charges against Douglass. Finally he explained that he had written the open letter because he considered it his duty to tell the public the truth, but that "no future insinuation of yours, no matter how false or unjust, shall provoke from me a reply."

Apparently Douglass never publicly denied nor affirmed that he had written a letter disparaging Brown to an Englishwoman. Indeed he seems to have said nothing more publicly about the affair. Thus, for want of further attention from the parties most concerned, another controversy, in which very little had been proved or disproved, was ended.

The Englishwoman to whom Brown said Douglass had written the uncomplimentary letter could have been either Ellen Richardson of Newcastle upon Tyne or Elizabeth Pease of Darlington, both of whom Brown visited for the first time in December, 1849. During the remainder of his sojourn in Great Britain, Brown kept in touch with Miss Richardson as well as with her brother Henry and his wife Anna, and he was their guest on several occasions. It should also be remembered that Miss Richardson was instrumental in the purchase of his freedom. On the contrary he seems to have had little or no contact with Miss Pease after December, 1849. These facts lead—or at the worst, tempt—one to conjecture that it was Miss Pease who, under Douglass's influence, had given Brown a cold reception.

By the middle of February it had been decided that Brown would spend most of March and April in Ohio lecturing for the American Anti-Slavery Society. Meanwhile ten conventions under the sponsorship of the society were "projected" for four urban centers in west central Massachusetts and Vermont for March 3–11, and Brown was expected to participate in all of them.[4]

En route from Boston to Ohio, Brown stopped in west central Massachusetts long enough to attend most of these meetings. In a letter he wrote on March 19 from Salem, Ohio, "the centre of radical anti-slavery in the Buckeye State," to the editors of the *National Anti-Slavery Standard*, he gave some details about his trip westward from Springfield. On the morning of March 10 he left Springfield by railway for Albany, New York. Within ten miles of Pittsfield his train had a minor wreck—an incident he related in a seriocomic narrative which amounts to about half of his letter. Some of the cars, including the one in which he was riding, ran off the track and jolted many of the passengers not only out of their seats but also at least momentarily out of their wits. Brown himself did not know that anything had gone wrong "until the classic Dante I was reading was fairly shaken out of my hand." Fortunately matters were soon set right, and the train proceeded on its way, arriving in Albany only a few hours late. Brown spend tthe night there and lectured to "a large audience." The next day he continued his journey westward.

After spending a night in Buffalo, where he saw "some old and attached friends," Brown went to Cleveland. This was his

4. *Liberator*, February 16, 1855, p. 27, February 23, 1855, p. 31, March 2, 1855, p. 35, March 9, 1855, p. 39.

first time in Ohio in almost eleven years. From Cleveland he went to Salem, whence he wrote the previously mentioned letter of March 19.[5] Afterwards he lectured "in most instances to large audiences, in a number of towns between New Lisbon and Massillon." Thence he went by way of Crestline and Dayton to Cincinnati, where he arrived at the end of March. It was his first time in southern Ohio since he passed through it on his flight to freedom twenty-one years earlier. Because of the rapid growth of Cincinnati and the changes which had taken place in it, he could hardly recognize the scenes of his experience of January 1, 1834; and as he lived again in memory that crucial day in his life, he found himself without words to express his feelings.

Although the local abolitionists had not planned to have Brown deliver an antislavery lecture in Cincinnati before the forthcoming antislavery convention there, he lectured in the Baker Street Baptist church on Sunday evening, April 1, mainly against slavery. This was a Negro church, and the presiding officer for the evening was Bishop Daniel Alexander Payne of the African Methodist Episcopal Church. The next day Brown went on the steamboat *Bostona* up the Ohio River to New Richmond, about twenty miles from Cincinnati, to visit some abolitionist friends. On the steamboat he "lost my dinner, or rather failed to get it, because I would not eat with the servants." After more than a week of lecturing in New Richmond and neighboring towns, he returned to Cincinnati.[6]

The Cincinnati antislavery convention was held on April 25–27. Brown made several speeches during the three days. At one of the sessions he regaled his audience with a tale as amusing as convincing. The tale was that while in London—the time implied was the summer of 1852—Enoch Price called on him; that after receiving Price most graciously, he introduced one of his daughters, who had recently returned from a boarding school

5. *National Anti-Slavery Standard,* March 31, 1855, p. 3.
6. *Ibid.*, April 21, 1855, p. 3.

in France; and that Price considered his actions the very height of impudence.[7] If this tale had any foundation in fact, it is surprising that neither Brown nor any of his friends had put it into print before the Cincinnati convention.

From the time it was announced, the convention had been plagued by insinuations especially from clergymen in Cincinnati that it would be devoted to infidelity. To those whose beliefs were easy to win, some of the discussions of the second day relative to what the Bible taught about slavery seemed to justify the insinuations. In a letter published on the third page of the *National Anti-Slavery Standard* for May 12, Brown endeavored to absolve the convention from the charge of infidelity. Going further he voiced the suspicion that the Cincinnati preachers who were critical of the convention were, in spite of their avowed antislavery sentiments, either too unwilling or too weak to do anything toward the abolition of slavery.

On his way back to the East, Brown stopped in Cleveland and lectured on slavery on May 1, thereby winning a compliment from the *Cleveland Morning Express* of the next day. Whether he arrived in New York in time for the American Anti-Slavery Society's celebration of its twenty-second anniversary on May 9 or did not, he was there for its annual meeting of the next two days. In a speech during the evening session of the first day, he dwelt on what he considered the worthlessness of the Union to the North on the one hand and to the slaves on the other. Indeed he thought that if the South had been left to itself, without the support of the strong federal government, it could not have maintained slavery—the slaves would have effected their own deliverance. As to free Negroes, he could see no value whatever in the Union for them, and he was convinced, therefore, that they ought to have been unanimously opposed to it.

When Brown concluded his speech, Frederick Douglass arose, according to the report of Samuel May, Jr., temporary

7. *Anti-Slavery Bugle,* May 5, 1855, pp. 1–2.

secretary of the meeting, "to say a word in vindication of the colored people who vote under and support the Constitution of the United States. He spoke at considerable length, indulging in some personalities."[8] Here was a renewal of the argument concerning political versus nonpolitical abolitionism, perhaps with casual references to the recent Brown-Douglass controversy. Since nobody answered Douglass directly, however, the argument was not continued.

Brown spent most of May and June holding meetings in New Hampshire and the eastern half of Massachusetts, including Cape Cod. His arrangement with the American Anti-Slavery Society must have been flexible enough to permit him to lecture occasionally for other societies, for his lectures on the cape were under the auspices of the Massachusetts Anti-Slavery Society. In fact he continued to lecture as an agent of first one and then the other of these societies for at least two more years.[9]

At the celebration of July 4 which the Massachusetts Anti-Slavery Society held in the Grove in Framingham, Brown was one of the principal speakers. During the morning's program he argued from an historical point of view that wherever the enslavement of a part of a people was allowed, the freedom of the other part did not prosper—that, in other words, a nation could not endure half slave and half free. Having thus anticipated Abraham Lincoln's famous argument, he deduced from it a proposal which eventually proved to be absolutely unacceptable to Lincoln. "He urged the necessity of an entire separation of the Free States (so called) from the Slave States, as affording the

8. *Liberator,* May 18, 1855, pp. 78–79; American Anti-Slavery Society, *Annual Report* (New York, 1855), pp. 123–147. This report said on p. 142 that Douglass' speech was brief, and it did not say that Douglass indulged in personalities.

9. *Liberator,* May 18, 1855, p. 79, May 25, 1855, p. 83, June 8, 1855, pp. 89, 91. Between January 1, 1855, and January 1, 1856, the Massachusetts Anti-Slavery Society paid Brown $265.55 "for Services and Expenses as Agent." (*Proceedings of the Massachusetts Anti-Slavery Society at the Annual Meetings Held in 1854, 1855, & 1856* [Boston, 1856], p. 46.)

only possible opportunity of securing the blessings of liberty to ourselves and our posterity; and equally to the slaves of the South."[10]

Beginning with Sunday, July 15, Brown had engagements to hold meetings for a month in Maine. On the day just mentioned, he lectured twice in the city hall in Portland—in the afternoon and again in the evening. For his evening lecture "the hall was crowded to a jam," he told Samuel May, Jr. in a letter he wrote from Portland on July 18. In the same letter he wrote as follows about a rascally though somewhat laughable trick played at the evening meeting by John Randolph, an imposter:

> Did you ever see an empty headed, slim, thin faced, gaunt looking, well dressed coloured man who calls himself John Randolph, son of the original of old Virginia? I remember to have seen him in the office, previous to my going to England. On Sunday night last, while Newell Foster was looking after the "*Spirits*," this scamp looked after the contribution box, or rather hat, helpped [*sic*] himself, and went home. He spirited away the money, some ten or twelve dollars, in silver, and left five dollars in coppers and five cent pieces. Foster found him but could get no money from him without taking him up, and that, it was thought best not to do. But the way in which he took it was really laughable. He set himself on the platform, and when Dr. Grandin and Mr. Morrill took up the collection and came to the platform with it, Randolph held out both hands, took the two hats, picked out the bills and large coin, put the leavings in his own handkerchief, handed it to me and walked off with his own share. I had to laugh at the fellows [*sic*] boldness.[11]

Brown gave a more detailed but not essentially different account of this incident in a letter which he wrote to Garrison on August 6, and which was published in the *Liberator* for Au-

10. *Liberator*, July 6, 1855, p. 106, July 13, 1855, p. 110.

11. *Ibid.*, July 13, 1855, p. 111, July 27, 1855, p. 119, August 3, 1855, p. 123; Brown to May, July 18, [18]55, Anti-Slavery Letters Written to W. L. Garrison and Others.

gust 17. He had heard of Randolph's charlatanry, he told Garrison, in almost every town he had recently visited. One of the reports he had heard was that a few days before he arrived in Portland, Randolph had "made himself very officious with the collections" taken at meetings held there by Sojourner Truth and, of course, had cheated her.[12]

In a letter he wrote from Bangor to May on July 28, and in his letter of August 6 to Garrison, Brown admitted that he was "not a little surprised at the advanced state of public opinion on the subject of slavery in Maine," and also at the state's comparative freedom from race prejudice. He was cognizant, nevertheless, that anti-slavery sentiment was much further advanced in Maine than in Massachusetts, for instance, not because the people of Maine were better, "but because they are further from the South, and have not so much dealing with slaveholders, as in Massachusetts." The last statement in Brown's letter of August 6 to Garrison was, "Unless the return of my daughters should call me out of the State, I shall spend the remainder of the month here." Meanwhile it was reported in the *Liberator* for August 10 that one of Brown's daughters "arrived in Boston yesterday from England"; and doubtless Brown himself returned soon afterwards to the city.[13]

If Brown was disappointed because only one of his daughters had returned, he was probably glad that Josephine, whom he seemed to idolize more than he did Clarissa, was that one. Among the first places to which he took her visiting out of Boston was Salem. There at the home of Mrs. Caroline Putnam, Charlotte L. Forten became acquainted with her on August 17. From the beginning Miss Forten was favorably impressed with her but found her father's fondness for her "rather too demonstrative. I guess she is a sensible girl," Miss Forten judged cautiously. "I enjoy talking with her about her European life. —She is pleasant and communicative, and though coming lastly from England,

12. *Liberator*, August 17, 1855, p. 132.

13. Brown to May, July 28, 1855, Anti-Slavery Letters Written to W. L. Garrison and Others; *Liberator*, August 10, 1855, p. 127.

has, I think, lived in France too much to acquire a great deal of that reserve which characterizes the manners of the English."[14]

During the next three months, Brown was so busy filling lecture engagements that he had not much time for Josephine. Occasionally, however, he took her on trips with him and permitted her to speak at his meetings. Beginning with the second week in October, Brown spent a month in eastern and central Vermont. This was his first extensive lecture trip in that state, and on it he held about twenty meetings in as many towns from Saint Johnsbury westward to Montpelier and southward to Brattleboro. On October 18 he lectured in Peachum in the afternoon and again in the evening. A correspondent for the *Liberator* who heard him both times said that "None could fail to be impressed with the eloquence, wit and pathos with which friend Brown addressed us, and his dignified, gentlemanly deportment won all hearts."[15]

A lecture Brown delivered in Framingham on December 3, about three weeks after his return from Vermont, was preceded by occurrences whose kind had been common at the beginning of the antislavery crusade in Massachusetts as well as elsewhere, but which by this time had become unusual in that state, especially so close to Boston. Prior to the day of Brown's lecture, notices concerning it were sent to the several churches in the town to be posted on their bulletin boards. As soon as the notice was posted in the entry to the "Orthodox" church, the sexton tore it down and boasted that he would tear down all such notices. The sexton of the Baptist church obviated matters by refusing to post the notice, explaining that he already knew "*the views of the Church Committee*."[16] Such occurrences, however, did not discourage the abolitionists. They merely emphasized

14. [Charlotte L. Forten], *Journal*, p. 62.

15. *Liberator*, August 24, 1855, p. 134; September 7, 1855, p. 143, September 14, 1855, p. 146, September 21, 1855, p. 151, September 28, 1855, p. 155, October 5, 1855, p. 159, October 26, 1885, p. 171, November 2, 1855, p. 175, and November 9, 1855, p. 179; *Vermont Christian Messenger*, October 19, 1855, *National Anti-Slavery Standard*, October 20, 1855, p. 3.

16. "Letter to Parker Pillsbury," *Liberator*, January 4, 1856, p. 4.

the fact that the work which the abolitionists were doing in the free states was necessary to bring public opinion to the point from which it could be transformed into action destructive of slavery.

Probably because of difficulties of travel and uncertainties about lodgings, Josephine Brown did not accompany her father on his trip to Vermont. Instead she remained in Boston and finished writing her *Biography of an American Bondman, by His Daughter*, which, according to its preface, she had begun while she was in school in France. This duodecimo paperback booklet of 104 pages was published in Boston about the middle of December by Robert F. Wallcut. It was copyrighted by Josephine herself in 1855 and was advertised under the heading "Just Published" in the *Liberator* for December 21. The date in its imprint, however, is 1856. Wallcut, a Unitarian clergyman, was recording secretary of the Massachusetts Anti-Slavery Society, and as publisher of the booklet he probably represented that society.

Biography of an American Bondman recounts Brown's life, although by no means in detail, from its beginning to the fall of 1854. Chronologically it is more extensive than any of the preceding autobiographical or biographical sketches of Brown, but it only supplements rather than supersedes them. This work contains some information not found in any other sketch of his life, but it does not contain some information found in previously published sketches. It follows, nevertheless, Brown's *Narrative* as far as that goes and draws freely upon the biographical and autobiographical data found in *Three Years in Europe*, *Clotel*, and *Sketches of Places and People Abroad*. In many instances it follows its sources almost verbatim.[17]

17. There is in my collection of Brown's works a copy of the second edition of his *Narrative* which Brown seems to have kept in his possession until his death in 1884. From his widow it passed to one of her nieces, and from that relative to the person from whom I received it. The first chapter in this copy contains penciled changes in Brown's handwriting—changes which were included in what Josephine quoted from this chapter in her first chapter.

During the last week in December and the first three weeks of 1856, Brown and Josephine had engagements in at least fifteen towns within a radius of forty miles from Boston. On the evening of January 16, "by express invitation" Josephine lectured before the Millbury Lyceum on "The Bards of Freedom." Brown spent two hours on Sunday afternoon, January 20, in a meeting with "a few but earnest friends of freedom in the Town Hall at South Reading," said a correspondent for the *Liberator*. That evening in the same hall, he spoke briefly "on the truly religious character of the anti-slavery movement," said the same correspondent, "and then introduced his daughter, who is very prepossessing in her appearance. Her theme was the reformatory influence of literature: and her apt selections from standard poets and authors clearly proved her extensive acquaintance with the classics; but the charm of all was her chaste and clear enunciation, which acted like a spell upon the large audience."[18]

The twenty-fourth annual meeting of the Massachusetts Anti-Slavery Society was convened in Williams Hall in Boston on January 24-25. At the opening session Stephen S. Foster asserted in a speech, perhaps more pessimistically than realistically, that the number of abolitionists had diminished, and that as a group they were now weaker than they were ten years earlier. This situation, he said, resulted from the fact that although people recognized the truth of the Garrisonian principles, they found them impracticable. As if to substitute one group of impracticalities for another, albeit unconsciously, Foster proposed that the Garrisonians organize disunion churches and a disunion political party to replace the churches and the political parties from which they had urged people to withdraw.

Straightway Garrison attempted to vanquish pessimism with optimism. He assured Foster and the others present that abolitionism had never been better off than it was then, and that it was not the function of the abolitionists—at least not of the

18. *Liberator*, December 21, 1855, p. 203, December 28, 1855, p. 207, January 11, 1856, p. 7, January 25, 1856, p. 14

Garrisonian abolitionists—to organize churches and political parties, but "to convert and change the public sentiment," so that it would speedily abolish slavery. This he thought they were doing, and from his point of view their progress had been sufficient to stimulate hope.[19]

Brown was present but did not join in the discussion. At the final evening session, however, in a long speech he returned to the Foster-Garrison argument and supported Garrison's point of view. An experience of the preceding evening, he explained, had impressed upon him anew the importance of creating an active public opinion against slavery. He had gone "with many other blockheads," he confessed, to Tremont Temple the preceding evening to hear Senator Robert Augustus Toombs of Georgia speak. He had been surprised to find that far from receiving that archdefender of slavery with silence—if not with hisses—the audience had actually applauded him. "I felt last night," Brown complained, "the want of that public opinion in Massachusetts which shall sustain anti-slavery, and condemn slavery in every form." He considered it the principal duty of the abolitionists "to create that public opinion that shall do the cause of liberty justice," that would prepare the people of Massachusetts, for example, to treat slaveholders who came among them to defend slavery "as any one who goes into any community for the purpose of vindicating an atrocity equal to that of enslaving men ought to be treated." He was aware, he admitted, that the abolitionists had not yet succeeded in creating such a public opinion, but he shared Garrison's optimism enough to believe that they could and would create it.[20]

Continuing his efforts to help create this public opinion in New England, Brown devoted most of the next four months to lecturing in eastern Massachusetts, Rhode Island, and Connecticut. He had more than fifty engagements during that period in

19. *Proceedings of the Massachusetts Anti-Slavery Society, at the Annual Meetings Held in 1854, 1855, & 1856*, Boston, 1856, pp. 57–58.
20. *Liberator*, February 8, 1856, p. 22.

about forty cities and towns in the areas just mentioned. His lectures were variously sponsored, most of those in Massachusetts by the Massachusetts Anti-Slavery Society, most of those in Rhode Island and Connecticut by the American Anti-Slavery Society, and some by local groups. Again and again he found himself not only in the same town but also in the same hall in which he had lectured more than once. But in Greemanville, Noank, Mystic, and Naugatuck, Connecticut, where he had engagements between April 30 and May 13, he was in territory relatively unfamiliar to him.[21] Apparently Josephine ceased traveling with her father after February and returned to England soon afterwards.

21. *Ibid.*, January 18, 1856, p. 11, January 25, 1856, p. 15, February 1, 1856, p 19, February 8, 1856, p. 23, February 15, 1856, p. 27, February 22, 1856, p. 32, March 7, 1856, pp. 38, 39, March 21, 1856, p. 47, April 11, 1856, p. 59, April 18, 1856, p. 63, April 25, 1856, p. 67, and May 2, 1856, pp. 70, 71.

The Play's the Thing

BROWN HAD LEARNED BY EXPERIENCE THAT IN ORDER TO WIN and hold the attention of possible converts to the antislavery cause, he must vary from time to time the form in which he presented his antislavery arguments. He had repeatedly tried direct argument; he had exemplified arguments by means of autobiography; he had presented arguments in songs; he had resorted to prose fiction as a medium of argument and had become a pioneer among Negro authors in that literary form; he had also essayed historical writing as a means of crusading against slavery. But there was still another well-established literary form which remained to be tried. He tried it and became a pioneer among Negro authors in that form, namely, the drama.

Early in 1856 Brown wrote his first drama, a satire on the Reverend Dr. Nehemiah Adams and his *A South-Side View of Slavery*. On the evening of April 9, Brown read his drama in

Brinley Hall in Worcester. According to the *Worcester Daily Spy* of three days later, his reading "was a highly entertaining performance." It was reported in the *Liberator* for April 25 that Brown had read his drama "to great acceptance in some of the surrounding towns," and that he intended to read it in Boston "during Anniversary week."[1] That was the last week in May, during which the annual New England Anti-Slavery Convention was usually held.

This work was eventually entitled *Experience, or, How to Give a Northern Man a Backbone.* It is not improbable, however, that Brown at first gave the drama another title by which it might have been occasionally identified afterwards. In his "Memoir of the Author" which was included in Brown's *The Rising Son,* Alonzo D. Moore credited Brown with writing a play entitled "The Dough Face." Moore said that Brown wrote this play soon after the publication of *Sketches of Places and People Abroad,* and that he read it before lyceums, giving "general satisfaction wherever it was heard." William J. Simmons said later that Brown had written a drama entitled "Doe Face"—which is obviously Simmons's form of the title Moore had mentioned.[2] This title is more or less applicable to *Experience,* since the principal character in the drama typified the kind of Northern preacher known in the slang of the time as a doughface. It is doubtful that Brown ever published this drama, but he frequently presented it as a dramatic reading for more than a year, even after he had written another and perhaps better play.

An advertisement on the third page of the *National Anti-Slavery Standard* for May 9, 1857, announcing a reading Brown expected to give in Samson Street Hall in Philadelphia on May 15, included the following synopsis of *Experience:*

1. *Worcester* [Massachusetts] *Daily Spy,* April 12, 1856; *Liberator* April 25, 1856, p. 66.

2. *Rising Son,* p. 23; William J. Simmons, *Men of Mark: Eminent, Progressive and Rising* (Cleveland, 1887), p 449.

Act I. Scene 1: Thanksgiving Day. Return of a Boston D. D. to the Parsonage; his remarks on his own sermon; thinks his future prospects very fair; his "South-side View of Slavery." Deacon Harris and Lady [visitors]. Scene 2: The Doctor, in his study, meets his publisher. Departure of the Doctor on his second visit to the "Sunny South."

Act II. Scene 1: A Southern Hotel; the Doctor and the Landlord. The Slave-Trader; sale of the Doctor; he is gagged, chained and carried to the slave market. Scene 2: Mr. Patterson's plantation; the Doctor's sermon; he refuses to submit, and is whipped in. The Doctor and Dinah. Scene 3: The Northern man at work in the field. Sam's Toast. Scene 4: The negro quarters; the Doctor cooking his supper; Sam's remarks. Scene 5: The repentance; he hates slavery, and thinks he will never go South again if he succeeds in getting his liberty.

Act III. Scene 1: The Doctor's release and return home. Scene 2: Meets his parishioners; sister Harris's congratulations; he resolves to oppose slavery. Marcus, the fugitive slave; his eloquent appeal. Grand Poetical Finale.

Brown had read a considerable number of dramas, including many of Shakespeare's, and he had seen many plays on the stage in both America and Great Britain. Accordingly, whether he had any noteworthy genius or not for writing plays, he was not ignorant of the exigencies of the stage. His plot, it may be observed, was compact and full of dramatic situations. In the first scene, for example, he gave himself an excellent opportunity to let the Boston D. D., Jeremiah Adderson, reveal himself in a soliloquy. In act 2 there were the quirky circumstances under which Adderson was kidnapped and sold into slavery—a transaction in which the landlord of the Southern hotel and the slave trader presumably colluded; there was the breaking of the new and apparently recalcitrant white slave; there were the more or less farcical situations in which Adderson, Dinah, and Sam were involved; there was the climactic scene in which Adderson repented for formerly condoning slavery and avowed his hatred of it. Finally, in act 3, Adderson having got out of slavery and returned home, there was the scene in which he took the first opportunity to become an agent on the Underground Railroad. Marcus, a fugitive slave, arrived at Adderson's home at an opportune time and spoke so eloquently of human freedom that Adderson immediately resolved to help him achieve it in Canada. The erstwhile doughface had at last become possessed of a backbone as well as a conscience.

One can only wish that he knew what the "Grand Poetical Finale" mentioned at the end of Brown's synopsis was. Considering Brown's recorded efforts at original poetry, one must be extremely optimistic to suppose that originality and grandeur coexisted in this part of the drama.

On the first day of the twenty-third annual meeting of the American Anti-Slavery Society, which began in New York on May 7, 1856, Brown was present, but he must not have remained there very long, unless a statement made subsequently by Mrs. Lucretia Mott was erroneous. In a letter she wrote from Philadelphia on Wednesday, May 14, to her sister, Mrs. Martha Coffin Wright of Auburn, New York, Mrs. Mott said that Brown "spoke nicely" at a meeting which a local women's antislavery society held "for our young Friends" on the preceding Wednesday. Whether Brown went to Philadelphia on May 7 or later, he spent most of the week of the fourteenth there. During that time he held meetings "which were well attended," and he also read his drama to a Philadelphia audience for the first time.[3]

Brown was expected to read his drama for the first time before a Boston audience on the evening of May 26 in Tremont Temple. He did not read it, however, until the following evening. It was the first day of the New England Anti-Slavery

3. *Liberator*, May 16, 1856, p. 79; *National Anti-Slavery Standard*, May 24, 1856, p. 3; American Anti-Slavery Society, *Annual Report* (Boston, 1856), p. 62. Mrs. Mott to Mrs. Wright, May 14, 1856, Sophia Smith Collection.

Convention, which was held in the Melodeon, and Brown's reading took the place of an evening session. A report in the *Liberator* for June 13 said that his audience was "highly appreciative and delighted" and his drama "first rate." At the final session of the convention on the evening of the twenty-ninth, Samuel May, Jr. offered a resolution paying a tribute to Dr. John Bishop Estlin, who had died on June 10, 1855—not long after the last convention. Brown spoke briefly in support of the resolution, which was adopted, of course, and also in criticism of Preston Smith Brooks's recent assault upon Charles Sumner in the Senate chamber of the United States Capitol.[4]

On June 4 Brown read his play to an audience in Groveland, about thirty miles north of Boston. The next day a resident of the town who had heard the reading wrote enthusiastically to Garrison, saying that "The drama is not only extremely amusing, but is really a very effective plea for the cause of anti-slavery." The Grovelander's letter, which was included in the report in the *Liberator* for June 13, perhaps contains the earliest published reference to the play by title.

Brown had planned to spend June lecturing in Vermont, but he found it necessary to change his plans and did not go to that state again until July.[5] On Monday evening, July 7, he lectured in Vergennes, and on the following evening he read his play there. From the vantage point of the editorial plural, the *Vergennes Citizen* for July 11 admitted on its second page that

> seldom have we listened to a lecture by a white man surpassing it [Brown's lecture] in interest, eloquence, and feeling. Mr. Brown's appearance as a lecturer is rather prepossessing although you feel better prepared to listen to a narrative than a lecture, and it is not until he warms up with the theme that you lose sight of the speaker, and flashes of wit and sparkling gems of thought scattered with rapidity and force convince

4. *Boston Evening Transcript*, May 26, 1856; *Liberator*, June 6, 1856, pp. 89–90, June 13, 1856, p. 95.

5. *Liberator*, May 30, 1856, p. 87, June 27, 1856, p. 103.

> you that no ordinary man is swaying the feelings of the deeply interested and breathless auditory.

With regard to Brown's reading of his play, the same newspaper observed that

> There are many vivid, graphic and thrilling passages in the course of the reading and they are brought out by Mr. B. with telling power. It was no matter of surprise to us that in the last act when the trembling fugitive burst forth into a peroration towering and noble in language and sentiment in favor of freedom as it SHOULD be, that scarcely a dry eye was to be seen in the room. No man of ordinary ability could originate so truthful a picture, and few, very few have the capacity requisite to do justice to the subject before an appreciative audience.

The next Monday evening Brown lectured in the town hall in Burlington, whose *Free Press* for July 15 said on its second page that Brown's speech "was uncommonly interesting, both for its matter and for the manner of its delivery," and that "Mr. Brown's address as a public speaker is uncommonly pleasing." During the second and third weeks of August, Brown lectured in New York counties adjoining Vermont. By the first of September he was back in eastern Massachusetts, where he remained until the end of the year.[6]

Early in October, Brown became a temporary agent for the Old Colony Anti-Slavery Society of Plymouth County and held about twenty meetings in a dozen towns in the county and elsewhere in the eastern half of the state between the middle of that month and the middle of the next one. In the meantime his frequent readings of his drama brought so many additional requests for readings, that he decided to relinquish his position as an official antislavery agent so as to devote himself to lecturing and

6. *Ibid.*, August 1, 1856, p. 124, August 15, 1856, p. 131, August 22, 1856, p. 139; *National Anti-Slavery Standard*, August 16, 1856, p. 3; *Liberator*, September 5, 1856, p. 147, September 12, 1856, p. 151, September 26, 1856, p. 159, October 3, p. 159 [163], October 17, 1856, p. 167; [Charlotte L. Forten], *The Journal of Charlotte L. Forten* (New York, 1953), p. 72.

reading his drama before lyceums. By the middle of November he had "more than twenty engagements to give his recitation before lyceums and independent courses." Moreover, encouraged by the success of his first drama, he had completed another.[7] This was doubtless the work now known as *The Escape.* At the time it was probably complete only in a rough draft—in a form still too rough for a public reading. Anyway, Brown let almost three months more pass before he read it publicly.

Meanwhile, Brown kept on reading *Experience.* On the evening of November 12 he read it in Lyceum Hall in Salem under the auspices of the Salem Female Anti-Slavery Society. His performance proved so pleasing that he was invited to repeat it, which he did on the twenty-first in the same hall before "a large and discriminating audience, who received it with much applause." Between this time and the end of the year, he still had about twenty engagements for readings in as many different towns and villages spread all over eastern Massachusetts exclusive of Cape Cod. To keep even a majority of these engagements, he had to do a considerable amount of traveling over the same routes and often in bad weather. He read his drama in Lynn on the evening of December 11. "It rained quite hard, but he had a pretty good audience. Everybody liked it; and he will repeat it next night after Christmas." Thus wrote William Lloyd Garrison, Jr. in a letter from Lynn on December 15 to his brother Wendell Phillips Garrison. Brown's last engagement in New England for five months was one to read his drama before the Chebacco Library Association in Essex on Wednesday evening, December 31.[8]

Before the end of November, Brown had decided to go on a

7. *Liberator,* October 10, 1856, p. 163, October 24, 1856, p. 171, October 31, 1856, p. 175, November 7, 1856, p. 179, November 14, 1856, p. 183, November 21, 1856, p. 186.

8. *Salem* [Massachusetts] *Register,* November 10, 1856, November 20, 1856; *Liberator,* November 21, 1856, p. 187, November 28, 1856; p. 191, December 5, 1856, p. 195, December 12, 1856, p. 199, December 26, 1856, p. 207; W. L. Garrison, Jr. to W. P. Garrison, December 15, 1856, Sophia Smith Collection.

lecture trip in the following January through New York to the Middle West and to return eastward through Pennsylvania. He left Boston on January 2, 1857, and stopped first in Little Falls, New York, to read *Experience* on January 3. He spent the next ten days in central New York, giving readings notably in Syracuse, Port Byron, and Skaneateles. He went on to Ohio, and during the next two weeks he lectured and gave readings in Painesville, Oberlin, Salem, and elsewhere. On February 4 he read *The Escape* in Salem.[9] This was probably the first public reading of this drama.

Brown read *Experience* before a small audience in the courthouse in Elyria on the evening of March 5. According to the *Elyria Independent Democrat*, the reading "was decidedly the richest treat of the season, and had our citizens known the character of the Drama, and the genius and learning displayed in its production, the Court House would have been filled to its utmost capacity." Upon "the unanimous request" of those who had heard his reading of March 5, Brown read the drama in Elyria again on the evening of March 27, this time "to a large and delighted audience" in the local Baptist church. In accordance with the vote of the last-mentioned audience, he read *The Leap for Freedom*, as the *Independent Democrat* called *The Escape*, "before a large audience" in the courthouse on the evening of April 4. "No description which we could give," the newspaper commented, "would convey an adequate idea of the beauties of this Drama. It must be heard to be appreciated."[10]

By the last week in April, Brown was again in central New York. Mrs. Martha Coffin Wright of Auburn recorded in her diary that he was one of her visitors on April 24. She also said in

9. *Liberator*, November 28, 1856, p. 190, December 26, 1856, pp. 206, 207, January 2, 1857, pp. 2, 3, January 9, 1857, pp. 5, 6; *Anti-Slavery Bugle*, February 7, 1857, p. 2; *National Anti-Slavery Standard*, February 21, 1857, p. 3.

10. *Elyria* [Ohio] *Independent Democrat*, March 11, 1857, March 24, 1857, March 31, 1857, April 7, 1857; *National Anti-Slavery Standard*, April 11, 1857, p. 3.

the same place that on Sunday, the twenty-sixth, she "went in the rain" to hear him lecture, had him as a guest at tea on Monday, and heard his public reading of one of his dramas that evening. Mrs. Wright did not tell which drama Brown read, nor did she mention the fact that he gave another reading Tuesday evening.[11]

The drama Brown read Monday evening was *Experience*, and the one he read Tuesday evening was *The Escape*. The reading of the first drama, said the *Auburn Daily Advertiser* for April 28, "was well attended, and gave the most unbounded satisfaction. Mr. Brown's Drama," this newspaper continued, "is, in itself, a masterly refutation of all apologies for slavery, and abounds in wit, satire, philosophy, argument and facts, all ingeniously interwoven into one of the most interesting dramatic compositions of modern times. His personations were many of them admirable, and all of them good." In reference to the second work, the *Daily Advertiser* for April 29 remarked that "Though this drama is not equal to the one entitled *Experience*, it is an able production, and was rendered with excellent effect." That the Tuesday evening's audience shared the newspaper's opinion as to which was the better drama is inferable from the fact that by its vote Brown was invited to read *Experience* again in Stanford Hall on May 8.

In the meantime Brown read *Experience* to "a small but very attentive and highly interested audience" in Concert Hall in Seneca Falls on April 29 and *The Escape* in the same place on the thirtieth. The *Seneca Falls Courier* for the latter date credited him with exhibiting "a dramatic talent possessed by few who have, under the best instruction, made themselves famous on the stage."[12]

From central New York, Brown went to New York City, where he attended the twenty-fourth annual meeting of the

11. Mrs. Martha Coffin Wright, Diary, Sophia Smith Collection.

12. *Auburn Daily Advertiser,* April 28, 1857, April 29, 1857; *Seneca Falls Courier,* April 30, 1857, quoted in *National Anti-Slavery Standard,* May 9, 1857, p. 2.

American Anti-Slavery Society on May 12–13. After the meeting he went to Philadelphia to keep engagements for lectures and readings which had been advertised on the second and third pages of the *National Anti-Slavery Standard* for May 9. He expected to deliver three lectures while in the city—one on "The Dred Scott Decision," one on "The Influence of Slavery on the Whites of the South," and one on "Woman and Her Influence." He read *Experience* in Sansom Hall on Friday evening, May 15, and expected to read *The Escape* in the same hall the following Monday evening. The *Philadelphia Daily Evening Bulletin* for May 16 said on its fifth page that his reading of his first drama the preceding evening "was highly entertaining and well received by an intelligent and appreciative audience. The drama is very laughable, and had our citizens been aware of its character, the hall would have been crowded."

In Brown's audience on the fifteenth were Mattie Griffiths, whose *Autobiography of a Female Slave* had been recently published, William Lloyd Garrison, and Oliver Johnson. Garrison and Johnson had stopped in Philadelphia overnight en route to the Fifth Yearly Meeting of the Progressive Friends of Pennsylvania, which was to be held at Longwood in Chester County on May 17–19. In a letter he wrote to his wife from Longwood on May 18, Garrison said that Brown's drama "was well delivered and well received; but the number present was very small, and the expense must have been beyond the receipts."[13]

Brown was again in Boston in time to participate in the annual New England Anti-Slavery Convention, which was held in the Melodeon on May 27–28. At the afternoon session of the first day, he offered a resolution asserting the slaves' right to obtain their freedom by revolution. Affirming that everyone had a right to life and liberty, he argued that if white men were justified in fighting for their rights, colored men were justified in fighting for theirs—that if it was right for the American colonies to rebel

13. *Liberator*, May 29, 1857, p. 86; Garrison to Mrs. Garrison, May 18, 1857, Anti-Slavery Letters Written by W. L. Garrison.

in 1776, it was right for the American slaves to rebel in 1857. Brown's resolution was adopted along with others at the final session of the convention on the evening of the twenty-eighth.[14]

Although Brown's resolution was obviously inconsistent with the Garrisonian principle of nonviolence, it provoked little or no criticism among his fellow abolitionists—certainly not such as it would have provoked in 1837 or even in 1847. The reason for the change thus evidenced was easily discernible. Instead of meeting the opponents of slavery in free and fair discussion, the exponents of slavery had resorted more and more to violence not only to defend their "peculiar institution" but also to prevent discussion of it. Their employment of *argumentum ad baculum* —presumably their best argument—had reached a new low a year earlier in Brooks's cowardly attack on Charles Sumner. As a result even such a believer in nonviolence as Senator Henry Wilson had found it necessary to prepare for violence as a means of self-defense because he had frankly condemned Brooks's conduct.[15] Moreover, by 1857 it was clear to many Americans that because of the half-slave and half-free situation in the United States, the nation was on the verge of civil war—a tragedy of retribution to which the then recent struggle in Kansas had been the prologue. Amid such circumstances as then prevailed, it must have been extremely difficult if not impossible for even the most ardent believers in nonviolence to cling to their belief. Certainly they could no longer counsel the enslaved, who had been the victims of so much force and violence, to refrain from such if thereby they might gain their freedom.

Now again under the auspices of the Massachusetts and the American Anti-Slavery Societies, Brown had numerous engagements for lectures in Massachusetts and New Hampshire during July and August. On several occasions Frances Ellen Watkins,

14. *Liberator,* May 22, 1857, p. 83, June 5, 1857; pp. 89–90; *National Anti-Slavery Standard,* June 6, 1857, p. 2.

15. Henry Wilson, *History of the Rise and Fall of the Slave Power in America,* 3 vols. (Boston, 1872–1877), 2: 486–87.

the mulatto poet and lecturer, who later became Mrs. Harper, was a fellow speaker. The two of them gave a series of lectures in the Joy Street and Twelfth Baptist Churches in Boston during the latter half of July, "treating prominently," said William C. Nell in the *Liberator* for July 31, "of slavery, temperance, and the elevation of colored Americans."[16]

Early in August, Brown decided to set out before the end of the month on another western trip. This time he was going as an agent of the American Anti-Slavery Society to participate in a series of conventions which that organization had scheduled in New York, western Pennsylvania, and Ohio. At first he had planned to stop en route westward to hold meetings in western Massachusetts and eastern New York; but probably because he could not leave Boston as soon as he had hoped to leave, he had to make some changes in his itinerary.[17]

With Susan B. Anthony, Aaron M. Powell, and others, Brown participated in a convention in Brigham Hall in Binghamton on September 2 and 3. This was the first of the series of conventions the American Anti-Slavery Society had planned for the fall in the three states mentioned above. From a report on the third page of the *Binghamton Daily Republican* for September 3, it appears that Miss Anthony and Brown made the most impressive speeches on the first day. "The remarks and anecdotes of Mr. Brown, who is a bright and handsome mulatto, were exceedingly eloquent, humorous and interesting, showing clearly the white blood of his father. . . . He has much dramatic power, and a very agreeable voice and manner." In a letter he wrote to Garrison the day after the convention closed, Brown said that "the audiences were not large, still there was much interest manifested by those who attended."[18]

16. *Liberator,* June 26, 1857, p. 102, July 3, 1857, p. 106, July 10, 1857, pp. 110–11, July 17, 1857, p. 115, July 24, 1857, p. 119, July 31, 1856, p. 122, August 7, 1857, p. 127, August 14, 1857, p. 131.

17. *Ibid.,* August 7, 1857, pp. 126–27, August 21, 1857, p. 135, August 28, 1857, p. 139.

18. *Ibid.,* September 11, 1857, p. 146.

Brown spent Saturday and Sunday, the fifth and sixth, holding meetings in Windsor, a village on the Susquehanna River fifteen miles southeast of Binghamton. As he explained in his next letter to Garrison, which he wrote a week later probably from Corning, his visit to Windsor proved most opportune. He was there in the nick of time to counteract some of the propaganda of the American Colonization Society. One Mr. Avery of Syracuse, a superannuated clergyman and agent of the society, lectured in its behalf in the Presbyterian church in Windsor Sunday morning and received contributions for it.

Having heard Avery's lecture, Brown answered it with one of his own in the local Methodist church at five o'clock in the afternoon. "My audience was very much larger than attended the Colonization lecture," he assured Garrison, "and I never had a more attentive hearing." He explained to his audience that far from being the friend of Negroes, which Avery had said it was, the society was their enemy, "supported by slaveholders and pro-slavery people; that it created and kept up prejudice against the free colored people"; that instead of approving its objects, as Avery had said they had done, "Thomas Clarkson and all other friends of freedom had condemned the course and aims of the society"; and that Negroes of Boston, Philadelphia, and other cities in the United States had "especially" repudiated it. With regard to its purposes and methods of operating, Brown adduced the startling fact "that at the instigation of the Colonization Society of Maryland, the Legislature of that State had imposed a tax of one dollar upon the head of every free colored person in the State, and those who could not pay the tax were to be sold into slavery"; and that by this means fifty thousand dollars "had been wrung from the poor defenceless free colored population of Maryland" for the support of the society. The pastor of the church in which Avery had spoken was present at Brown's lecture "and seemed not a little surprised," Brown observed, "at the revelations I made."[19]

19. *Ibid.*, September 18, 1857, p. 152.

After three weeks in south central New York holding meetings in Owego, Corning, Elmira, and Penn Yan, Brown, Miss Anthony, and Powell proceeded to the western end of the state, where they spent three weeks more participating in conventions. The three lecturers were to begin a convention in Girard in Erie County, Pennsylvania, on October 15, but upon their arrival there, they found that plans for the convention had been abandoned. In a long letter he wrote from Linesville on October 20 to Garrison, Brown explained that "For want of interest in Girard, our friends changed the arrangements, and advertised us to lecture in separate places [in the northwestern corner of Pennsylvania], which, upon the whole, worked well, for we found crowded houses and willing listeners in all of the gatherings."[20]

Brown lectured twice in Lockport, probably on October 15 and 16. He went thence to Linesville, whither Miss Anthony and Powell had preceded him. There the three of them held a convention on the seventeenth and eighteenth. "We could not have wished," Brown said in his letter of October 20 to Garrison, "for a more enthusiastic or better attended meeting than we had at Linesville. The place of the meeting was a double school-house, with the partition opened, and the two rooms thrown into one. The Baptist church, the only religious building in the town, was shut against us." Once again the speakers severely criticized the church, the Union, and the Republican party, especially the Republicans of Pennsylvania, for their want of antislavery enthusiasm. Brown noted, however, that "The better portion of politicians of the Republican or Free Soil stamp attend our Conventions, and some help in getting up meetings."

By Saturday, October 24, the three lecturers were in Painesville, Ohio, where they held a two-days convention, which

20. *Owego* [New York] *Times*, September 10, 1857; *Yates County Chronicle* [Penn Yan, New York], September 17, 1857, September 24, 1857; *Liberator*, September 25, 1857, p. 155, October 9, 1857, p. 163, October 16, 1857, p. 168, October 30, 1857, p. 175.

Brown said "was well attended throughout." On the following Monday, Miss Anthony went to hold a meeting in Mentor, about seven miles southwest of Painesville; and Brown and Powell went to hold one in Kirtland, now Kirtland Hills, a few miles south of Mentor. As Brown knew, Joseph Smith and his followers had built their first Mormon temple at Kirkland twenty-four years earlier. The temple was still there and Brown went to see it. Experienced sight-seer that he was, he seemed to have been almost as much impressed by the temple as he was by the meeting. To him the structure looked "very much like Faneuil Hall."

The next day Brown, Miss Anthony, and Powell went to Cleveland to attend a Northern disunion convention which had been called to be held in that city on October 28 and 29. Having seen an advertisement in the *Anti-Slavery Bugle* saying that delegates to the convention would be accommodated at the Bennet House, the three lecturers went to that hostelry. There they found a considerable number of their fellow abolitionists. When dinner was served and Brown along with others started into the dining room, he was stopped at the door and told "that I must wait, and eat at the second table." Upon seeing Brown thus rebuffed, Powell, Miss Anthony, Mrs. Lucy Newhall Colman, then of Rochester, New York, and Andrew T. Foss refused to enter the dining room without him. During an hour's conference with the abolitionists, the landlord of the hostelry offered to serve them at a separate table or in their rooms—in any way except letting Brown go to the first table. But the abolitionists remained uncompromising until the landlord apologized to Brown, permitted him to eat at the first table, and agreed not to discriminate against him anymore.[21]

A "circular call" for the disunion convention had been signed and issued in July by a committee of five abolitionists, including Garrison, Thomas Wentworth Higginson, and Wendell Phillips. The purpose of the convention was "to consider the practicability, probability, and expediency of a separation of the Free and

21. Brown to Garrison, *Liberator,* November 6, 1857, p. 179.

Slave States, and to take such other measures as the condition of the times may require." Because of the financial panic that struck the United States early in the fall, the call for the convention had been withdrawn. Nevertheless, in accordance with an explanation Garrison had made in a letter to Samuel J. May on October 18, "an informal convention" was held at the appointed time "so as not to create too great a local disappointment."[22]

During the two days of the convention, there was much discussion pro and con of the desirability and the practicability of the dissolution of the Union, of the effect such an act might have on slavery, of the question as to whether the Constitution was a proslavery or an antislavery document, and of the right of the American slaves to free themselves by rebellion. Brown took no part in the discussion until the final session. Then in a speech about twenty minutes long, he expressed himself in favor of disunion. He believed that the dissolution of the Union would end slavery, because in his opinion the South was too weak to maintain slavery without the military support of the North. He referred to "an influential journal of the South" whose editor had expressed the same opinion. Referring to Nat Turner's insurrection, he observed that "the brave and chivalrous Virginians were compelled to acknowledge their weakness by calling in the United States troops to put down the outbreak." He was convinced that the slaves had a right to free themselves by force, as he thought they could have done had they not been deterred by the power of the United States government. He alluded to the Haitian revolution and to the history of Solon and Pisistratus, of William Tell and Gesler, and of Cromwell and Charles I—all of which he considered instances in which tyranny had been overcome, as he was sure American slavery would be, since it was one of the world's worst forms of tyranny.[23]

22. *Ibid.*, September 11, 1857, p. 146, October 23, 1857, p. 170; [Wendell Phillips Garrison and Francis Jackson Garrison], *William Lloyd Garrison, 1805–1879: The Story of His Life Told by His Children*, 4 vols. (Boston and New York, 1894), 3: 460, 463.

23. *Liberator*, November 6, 1857, p. 180; *Anti-Slavery Bugle*, November 7, 1857, p. 1, November 14, 1857, pp. 1–2, November 28, 1857, p. 2.

Immediately after the convention, Powell was compelled by poor health to return home, and Miss Anthony went to fill engagements in eastern New York. Their places as lecturers with Brown were filled by Joseph A. Howland of Worcester, Massachusetts, and Mrs. Colman. Severeal times alone but usually with these two new colleagues, Brown filled engagements in towns in northeastern Ohio during November, sometimes with extraordinary discomfort. His "almost iron frame," as he called it, having been debilitated by "a twenty-seven miles' ride over a rough road, through a drenching rain," he had to let his colleagues do almost all of the speaking at a convention in Windsor on the seventh and eighth.[24]

While Brown, Howland, and Mrs. Colman were in Ohio as agents of the American Anti-Slavery Society, they were more or less responsible to Marius R. Robinson of Salem, who was the editor of the *Anti-Slavery Bugle* and the head of the society in that state. Apparently Howland and Mrs. Colman departed from northeastern Ohio at the end of November, while Brown was faced with the necessity of changing plans he had made to spend a part of December in Ohio and a part in western Pennsylvania. Sometime during the week of November 15, while Brown was in Kinsman, about twenty-five miles north of Youngstown, he received a letter from Robinson advising him not to go to either Cincinnati or Pittsburgh, as Brown had thought of doing. In addition to explaining that Charles Lenox Remond and his sister Sarah, both of whom had attended the convention in Cleveland, had recently lectured in both Cincinnati and Pittsburgh, Robinson objected to Brown's giving dramatic readings instead of lecturing.

From Hartford, a short distance south of Kinsman, Brown wrote to Robinson on November 29. He agreed that it was useless for him to lecture in either Cincinnati or Pittsburgh so soon after the Remonds' lectures in those cities. He explained that when he planned to visit those cities, he did not know that the Remonds had recently visited either of them. But to him, Robin-

24. Brown to Garrison, *Liberator*, November 20, 1857, p. 187.

son seemed not to understand the situation pertaining to the dramatic readings—that there were places in which these were far more effective than lectures. "People will pay to hear the Drama [presumably *The Escape*]," he said, "that would not give a cent in an anti-slavery meeting." Yet he assured Robinson that "I have no wish to Read the Drama if you are opposed to it. For I had rather give two lectures than to give one Reading. We had meetings in Hartford last Sunday," he continued, "and after three speeches, took up *Ninety Five Cents*, on Wednesday Evening I read the Drama in the same place, charged 10 cents at the door, paid $2.00 for the Hall, and had 5.00 over all expenses. Now, this is more than Mrs[.] Coleman [*sic*], Mr. Howland and myself have taken up in Collections for the last ten days." Brown concluded his letter with a tentative itinerary for lectures during December in Youngstown and neighboring towns and also in towns in western Pennsylvania. Assuming that Robinson would approve the itinerary, he requested that it be advertised in the *Anti-Slavery Bugle;* but he also suggested that if Robinson did not approve it, he should "lay out" another for the lecturer.[25]

No advertisements nor reports of lectures by Brown were published in any of the numbers of the *Anti-Slavery Bugle* for December or the next few months. Presumably, therefore, Brown did not remain in northeastern Ohio very long after he wrote his letter of November 29 to Robinson.

25. Brown to Robinson, November 29, 1857, Schomburg Collection.

"The Escape; or, A Leap for Freedom"

If Brown returned to Boston before the end of 1857, he either went away again soon after the beginning of the new year or remained inactive in the city for a month or more. For a short time he was expected to participate in the annual meeting of the Massachusetts Anti-Slavery Society on January 28–29, 1858, but the *Liberator's* report of the meeting does not refer to his being present.[1]

Late in February a resident of Cortland, New York, informed Garrison concerning the antislavery lecturers who had recently visited that town. He said that in addition to Wendell Phillips,

> Charles C. Burleigh and Wm. Wells Brown have also been with us, and done good service, each in his own way, for the Anti-Slavery movement. Mr. Burleigh's lectures were, of

1. *Liberator,* January 22, 1858, p. 14, January 29, 1858, p. 18, February 5, 1858, pp. 21–23.

> course, admired for their logical, rhetorical and critical ability; and Mr. Brown's Dramas have compared favorably with the most attractive Lyceum entertainments of the season. . . . Mr. Brown is still hereabouts, working industriously, and, I think, profitably, both for himself and the cause of the slave. I saw him yesterday at the Academic Exhibition of Central College, McGrawville, which was, by the way, a fine affair, and very creditable to the students and institution—nearly a thousand persons being present as spectators. Mr. Brown gave one of his Dramas, in the evening, to a large and appreciative audience in the College Hall.[2]

The statement concerning Brown's working industriously and profitably for himself as well as for the cause of the slave probably implied that he was then working, not as an agent for any antislavery society, but independently as a lecturer and dramatic reader.

During most of the following spring, Brown was more or less active in Boston and its vicinity. He had an engagement to lecture in the Joy Street Baptist Church on Sunday evening, April 11, on "The Great Men of the St. Domingo Revolution." Obviously this was to be his old lecture on Haiti somewhat remodeled. The next day he wrote to William Lloyd Garrison, Jr., who was then in Lynn, saying, "You will see by the hand bill I send you, that I am reading my new drama, which I consider far superior to the one I gave in Lynn." The new drama was *The Escape*, and Brown inquired about the possibility of reading it in Lynn. Garrison, Jr. must have replied favorably as well as promptly, for on April 17 Brown wrote him another letter, along with which he sent three hundred handbills for distribution. It appears from this letter that Brown was to read the drama in Sagamore Hall in Lynn on the evening of the nineteenth. In the letter he requested Garrison, Jr. to make some of the final

2. Letter from W. H. F., *Liberator*, March 5, 1858, p. 39.

arrangements for the reading, explaining that he would not get to Lynn "till six or seven o'clock," and that "I shall drive back the same night, as I shall have a lady with me that must be returned."[3] The lady Brown had in mind was probably Annie Elizabeth Gray of Cambridgeport, who became his second wife two years later.

Late in the spring, the public having been apprised that it was forthcoming, Brown's new play entitled *The Escape; or, A Leap for Freedom: A Drama in Five Acts* was published by Robert F. Wallcut of Boston.[4] This, of course, was not Brown's first play and was not, therefore, the first play written by an American Negro, as it has been frequently said to have been. Until evidence to the contrary is discovered, however, it may still be considered the first play by an American Negro author to be published.

The Escape is an octavo pamphlet of fifty-two pages. Brown said in his preface that he wrote the play "for my own amusement and not with the remotest thought that it would ever be seen by the public eye," that he read it "privately, however, to a circle of my friends, and through them was invited to read it before a Literary Society. Since then," he continued, "the Drama has been given [presented as a dramatic reading by himself] in various parts of the country. By the earnest solicitation of some in whose judgment I have the greatest confidence, I now present it in a printed form to the public." With unnecessary bluntness he explained that never having aspired to be a dramatist, he had "little or no solicitude" for the fate of the work, but was content to let it stand on whatever merits it might have. He also attested that "The main features in the Drama are true," that his hero and heroine—Glen and Melinda—were still living

3. *Liberator,* April 9, 1858, p. 59, April 23, 1858, p. 67, June 4, 1858, p. 90; Brown to Garrison, Jr., April 12, 1858, April 17, 1858, Sophia Smith Collection.

4. *Liberator,* May 7, 1858, p. 75, June 4, 1858, p. 91.

in Canada, and that "Many of the incidents were drawn from my own experience of eighteen years at the South." With something less than good grace, he ended his preface with the assertion that he owed the public no apology for the defects in the drama, because as he had reminded his audiences on many occasions, "I was born in slavery, and never had a day's schooling in my life."

Apparently Brown was prone to forget that not everyone who had been formally educated either spoke or wrote well, and that some of the celebrated authors he had read and admired had had but little formal education. Otherwise he might have recognized the fact that there was not necessarily any direct causal connection between his want of formal schooling and the imperfections in his works.

Whatever might have been his original purpose in writing *The Escape*, Brown made it primarily an antislavery argument. The subject matter of the drama belonged to the same department of the "peculiar institution" as did much of the subject matter of *Clotel*—the department of romances between masters and beautiful slave women, usually mixed breeds. The course reviewed in the drama, however, was successful only in reverse. The master-professor flunked, and the unwilling slave-student passed, but without the usual grade—a mulatto or quadroon offspring.

The time of the action in the drama might have been any time after the 1830's—after the Underground Railroad began doing a remarkably large amount of business. In addition to being a physician and politician, Dr. Gaines of Muddy Creek and Poplar Farm, Missouri, was a connoisseur of beautiful slave women. In the opinion of Mrs. Gaines, his wife, he had long ago succeeded embarrassingly well in at least one master-slave romance. For on his first visit to the Gaineses' home, a certain Major Moore noticed the striking resemblance between Dr. Gaines and Sampey, a mulatto house slave in his teens. Moore assumed that the boy was the son of both Mrs. Gaines and the physician and complimented him accordingly to Mrs. Gaines, very much to her annoyance.[5]

Dr. Gaines was now enamored of Melinda, one of his mulatto slaves—not without being suspected by Mrs. Gaines. Melinda, nevertheless, had bravely withstood his blandishments. For some time she had been in love with Glen, the property of the physician's brother-in-law, and had recently been secretly married to him in a moonlight ceremony conducted by "Old Uncle Joseph," the plantation slave preacher.

Meanwhile, when Walker, a slave trader, visited Muddy Creek, Mrs. Gaines insisted that her husband sell Melinda, as Wildmarsh, a neighbor who happened to be present, admitted to Dr. Gaines that he had sold his own mulatto daughter a week earlier because of his wife's jealousy of him. Instead of selling Melinda, however, as he led his wife to believe he had done, Dr. Gaines hid her in a cottage on Poplar Farm. A night later he went to the cottage and again importuned Melinda to become his mistress. The frigid style with which her replies were invested, of which the following is representative, must have been as devastating as their content:

> Sir, I am your slave; you can do as you please with the avails of my labor, but you shall never tempt me to swerve from the path of virtue. [act 3, scene 5, p. 33.]

In less artificial language Melinda finally told the physician about her marriage to Glen four weeks earlier, whereupon he went away determined to get even with both her and Glen—with the young woman for spurning him and with the young man for successfully rivaling him. The means by which he chose to get even was to have Glen imprisoned and whipped.

5. In both *The Black Man*, pp. 18–19, and *The Negro in the American Rebellion* (Boston, 1867), pp. 363–64, Brown related the incident involving Major Moore, identifying Mrs. Gaines as Mrs. Young and Sampey as himself. In the later work he said that he was about ten years old when the incident occurred, but in neither work did he say that Dr. Young was his father.

Dr. Gaines left the cottage just in time to avoid being caught there by Mrs. Gaines, who, like a horsewoman of the Apocalypse, descended upon the place bent on destruction. She had decided to terminate her husband's pursuit of Melinda by putting the young woman beyond pursuit forever. In soap opera fashion—whether intentional on Brown's part or not—she tried in vain to compel Melinda to commit suicide by drinking poison. Then in a frenzy of anger she attempted to stab Melinda with a dagger. The soap opera now reduced itself to slapstick comedy. In the ensuing battle far from royal between the two women, Melinda's weapon of both defense and offense was a broom with which, according to Brown's stage directions, she "sweeps off Mrs. Gaines—cap, combs and curls" as the scene ends.

A day or two later, while Glen was in prison soliloquizing about the wrongs he had suffered at the hands of Dr. Gaines, Sampey came and informed him of Melinda's whereabouts. When soon after Sampey's visit, Scragg, the overseer, arrived to flog Glen as Dr. Gaines had requested him to do, Glen overpowered him and escaped. The following night, while he and Melinda were searching for each other, they fortuitously met in a forest (act 4, scene 3) and immediately set out together for Canada. In telling Melinda about his escape from prison, Glen said in English more colloquial and more natural than he ordinarily used, "I pounded his [Scragg's] skillet well for him, and then jumped out of the window. It was a leap for freedom. Yes, Melinda, it was a leap for freedom. I've said 'master' for the last time."

Brown did not develop his plot involving Dr. Gaines, Melinda, and Glen as rapidly as the synopsis of it thus far may lead one to suppose. From the beginning he introduced a variety of characters and incidents which he did not fuse into subplots, but which he obviously intended to exemplify the brutalities and grotesqueries of slavery. There was Cato, the clownish slave who assisted Dr. Gaines in his office and practiced medicine on fellow slaves. There was the occasion on which Mrs. Gaines entertained the Reverend Mr. Pinchen in her dining room and pretended to saintly piety while planning to whip the slave Hannah for no good reason. There was the appallingly ignorant Big Sally, whom Dr. Gaines sold to Walker. At the same time the doctor sold Hannah's husband to the slave trader, thus separating the husband from his wife forever. There was Tapioca, whom Cato described as a "mulatter gal," and who was a refinement of Topsy in *Uncle Tom's Cabin.*

Near the beginning of a kitchen scene, Cato, who was indeed no less knave than fool, belied the belief that he was a contented, happy-go-lucky slave by soliloquizing about his wish to escape to Canada. He ended his soliloquy with a part of "A Song of Freedom," one of the selections in all of the editions of Brown's *Anti-Slavery Harp.*

Ignorant of Cato's real attitude towards his situation, as Price was of Brown's in December, 1833, Dr. Gaines took Cato along with himself and Scragg in pursuit of Glen and Melinda. One night in a hotel in a town in Ohio, while Dr. Gaines and Scragg were asleep, Cato dressed himself in the doctor's clothes and escaped. Cato's scheme was not new in Brown's writing. Brown had already told in *Clotel* about a fugitive slave who escaped from his captors in southeastern Ohio by the same scheme. Cato joined Glen and Melinda, apparently by chance, in the home of a Quaker in northern Ohio, whence after being refreshed, all three of the fugitives were sped on their way to freedom. But they were not yet completely out of danger. Their pursuers caught up with them at noon one day just as they were about to be ferried across the Niagara River to Ontario. At the ferry there was a fight between Dr. Gaines and his official slave catchers on the one hand and the fugitives and their friends, including two comical peddlers, on the other. The latter group won, and amid cheers the fugitives were ferried across the river to a haven in Canada.

One of the contributions to *The Liberty Bell* for 1858, which was actually published by the middle of December, 1857, was

Mrs. Lydia Maria Child's *The Stars and Stripes*, an antislavery melodrama in eight scenes. There are obvious similarities between Brown's drama and Mrs. Child's in characterizations and plots, though in neither setting nor style. Dr. Gaines, Melinda, Glen, and Cato have their counterparts respectively in Mr. Masters, Ellen, William, and Jim in *The Stars and Stripes*. The action in Mrs. Child's drama began on Mr. Masters' plantation in South Carolina and ended at a ferry at Detroit. The time of the action was fixed by Mr. Masters' reference in scene one to how "our brave Brooks served that miserable traitor Sumner."

With regard to the similarities in the dramas, if Mrs. Child was not indebted to Brown, it is not likely that Brown was indebted to her. By the end of 1856 *The Escape* existed in a more or less complete version, and early in 1857 Brown began presenting it in dramatic readings, some of which Mrs. Child might have witnessed. On the contrary, even if Mrs. Child's drama already existed in manuscript when Brown began reading his publicly, it is hardly any more probable that Brown had seen her manuscript than it is that she had seen his. The similarities between the dramas could have resulted, of course, from the writers' drawing upon a common stock of antislavery literature, as Mrs. Child seems to have drawn upon the story of William and Ellen Craft not only in choosing names for her hero and heroine but also in having them escape from slavery disguised as a servant and his master. Brown himself had contributed much from his own experience to the stock of antislavery literature and was familiar with it, therefore, from personal experience as well as from reading.

The similarity between the last scenes of the dramas is traceable to the kind of incident which had become a part of the stock of antislavery literature. This was the vain attempt of slave catchers to recapture slaves at an American-Canadian ferry. One such incident had been related by Alvan Stewart of Utica, New York, at the annual meeting of the American Anti-Slavery

Society in New York City in May, 1836.[6] A similar incident, it should be remembered, had been related by Brown himself in the fourth American edition of his *Narrative*. The last scene in Mrs. Child's drama is obviously an adaptation of the incident related by Stewart. The last scene in *The Escape* was doubtless based on the incident related by Brown himself.

By the time Brown wrote *The Escape*, the subject matter of which he composed it had become so familiar and indeed so stereotyped that it needed a newer and more original treatment than he gave it. All of the principal characters in the drama are stock characters. Their being such is not a fault in itself, but it is a fault that there is little or no character development as the action proceeds except in one instance. That is the one involving Mrs. Gaines, who at first tried to appear as the very soul of piety, but who appeared more and more as the termagant she really was. Among the numerous dramatic situations in the play, those most effectively realized are the farcical ones—the kind most easily portrayed. Much of the dialogue in the comical scenes consists of the speech of illiterate slaves, which Brown represented by what has traditionally become known as dialect writing. His representations are more or less typical of that kind of writing; this is to say, they are as much mutilated English as anything else.

By far the worst defect in the drama is the artificial dialogue in which it abounds. In many places in this work, as in many places especially in the latter half of *Clotel*, Brown seems to have made special efforts to write beautifully instead of simply and effectively; and like others who have indulged in such misdirected efforts, he succeeded in writing much worse than he otherwise might have written. In act 1, scene 3, for example, and again in act 3, scene 4, he seems to have tried, although vainly, to model Glen's soliloquizing after Hamlet's first two soliloquies;

6. American Anti-Slavery Society, *Third Annual Report* (New York, 1836), pp. 19–20.

and in act 3, scene 5, he tried to make Melinda soliloquize about sleep somewhat as Macbeth talked about it. In all of these instances he doubtless would have written less artificially and more convincingly had he tried to make his hero and heroine talk like themselves rather than like Shakespearean characters. In spite of its defects, however, *The Escape* is indeed distinctive as an authentic and vivid portrayal of slavery because of its human-interest appeal, and as a pioneering effort among Negro authors in the writing of dramas.

Brown spent most of the summer of 1858 lecturing in eastern Massachusetts, presumably again under the auspices of the Massachusetts Anti-Slavery Society. The numbers of the *Liberator* from June 9 to September 17 carried reports of his speeches in some instances and announced more than twenty engagements for him—most if not all of them in towns in which he was well known as a lecturer—in Natick, Groveland, Marlboro, Feltonville, and Abington among others. Not that he had altogether new arguments to present, but as an apostle of abolitionism he repeatedly preached the same gospel of freedom to the same people to keep converts steadfast in the antislavery cause as well as to win supporters for it.

On July 13 Brown attended a meeting held in the A.M.E. Zion church in Worcester for the purpose of planning for "the Mass Convention of Colored Citizens" which was to begin in New Bedford on August 2. He served as secretary for the meeting and as one of the three members of a committee on finance, but he refused to accept an appointment as a delegate to the convention. Nevertheless he was not only present during the two days of the convention but also served as its presiding officer. Meanwhile "eloquent and stirring addresses were delivered by C. L. Remond, Robert Morris, Father Henson," and others.[7]

Apparently, during the summer Brown gave but few if any dramatic readings, but early in September he again began in-

7. *Liberator*, July 30, 1858, p. 123, August 6, 1858, p. 126.

terspersing his lecture engagements with them. Frequently he lectured in a hall in the afternoon and read one of his plays in the same hall in the evening, as he had engagements to do in several towns in Plymouth County between September 12 and 22. During the last week in the month, he went to Utica, New York, where he read *The Escape*. Henry C. Wright, who witnessed the reading, sent a complimentary account of it to the *Liberator*. "The audience," said Wright, "listened to his reading —or, rather, *reciting*—with deepest interest, and the only regret seemed to be, that it was too short, though the delivery of it occupied an hour and a quarter."[8]

After another month of lecturing and dramatic readings principally in eastern Massachusetts, Brown went to New Jersey and thence to eastern Pennsylvania, where he remained at least until the middle of December. He lectured in Temperance Hall in Trenton on Sunday evening, November 7, and read one of his plays in the same hall the next evening. The *Trenton Daily State Gazette and Republican* for November 9 took cognizance on its third page of the "large audience" he had on both occasions and also remarked that "Mr. Brown possesses a high order of intellect, and is a fine orator." At one of the sessions of the Twenty-third Anti-Slavery Fair and Convention which was held in Samson Street Hall in Philadelphia on December 14–17, he spoke on the progress of the antislavery movement, as did Mrs. Lucretia Mott and James Miller McKim. He also read one of his plays one evening. In a letter written from Philadelphia on January 4, 1859, Ellen Wright told her mother, Mrs. Martha Coffin Wright, about the fair and convention. Referring to Brown's reading, she said, "I didn't hear W. W. Brown's drama which was considered fine by Emma Parker and others whom I heard speak of it."[9]

8. *Ibid.*, September 10, 1858, p. 147, October 8, 1858, p. 163.

9. *National Anti-Slavery Standard*, December 25, 1858, p. 3; Ellen Wright to Mrs. Martha Coffin Wright, January 4, 1859, Sophia Smith Collection.

XX

Author and Bridegroom

Brown's whereabouts between the middle of December, 1858, and the last of April, 1859, seem not to have been reported in the antislavery newspapers. During the intervening months, he might have made his second trip to the West Indies. Anyway he was in Massachusetts by May 1. On that day the Essex County Anti-Slavery Society held a quarterly meeting in Westbury. In his report of the meeting, Moses Wright, its secretary, said that at the afternoon session Brown "addressed the meeting at some length, and made a humorous and interesting speech, which put the audience in good condition for contribution [*sic*], which occasion was improved to good effect."[1]

For the next two months Brown was more active among the Negroes of Boston as a group than among the organized abolitionists. He served as chairman of meetings held in Twelfth

1. *Liberator*, May 13, 1859, p. 75.

Baptist Church on May 23 and June 1 to sympathize with and aid the Oberlin-Wellington rescuers. One evening early in June he gave in the Joy Street Church what William C. Nell described in a report in the *Liberator* for June 17 as "an entertaining and instructive dissertation on Love, Courtship, and Marriage." More important, one may suppose, was the public discussion which was begun in Twelfth Baptist Church on the evening of June 28 and continued the following evening. The question considered was "Is the condition of the colored people of the United States worse now than it was fifteen years ago?" The Reverend John B. Smith, then of New Bedford, upheld the affirmative, and Brown upheld the negative. Nell deemed the question out of date as far as the abolitionists "and all other discerners of the signs of the times" were concerned, but he noted that the discussion "created much interest, and drew crowded and intelligent audiences both evenings," and that both speakers "acquitted themselves with great ability, and received a unanimous vote of thanks." At the Massachusetts Anti-Slavery Society's celebration of July 4 in Framingham, Brown repeated much of what he had said in the recent discussion in Twelfth Baptist Church and avowed his confidence that the end of American slavery was near.[2]

Pursuant to the consensus reached at a public meeting in Bethel Church on West Centre Street in Boston on May 3 and a call issued a month later by Brown, Nell, and others, "a Convention of the Colored Citizens" of New England, New York, New Jersey, Pennsylvania, Ohio, and "the far West" was held in Tremont Temple on August 1–2. The purpose of the convention, the call had explained, was "to take into consideration the Moral, Social, and Political elevation of those with whom we are identified, by complexion and condition, in the New England and other States."

At the opening morning session Brown called the meeting to order, and while a committee appointed to nominate permanent

2. *Ibid.*, May 27, 1859, p. 83, June 10, 1859, p. 90, June 17, 1859, p. 94, June 24, 1859, p. 99, July 8, 1859, p. 107, July 15, 1859, p. 111.

officers for the convention was deliberating, he addressed the assembly.

> I confess [he said] that I am unfavorable to any gathering that shall seem like taking separate action from our white fellow-citizens; but it appears to me that just at the present time, such a meeting as this is needed. The colored people in the free States are in a distracted and unsettled condition. The Fugitive Slave Law, the Dred Scott Decision, and other inroads made upon the colored man's rights, make it necessary that they should come together that they may compare notes, talk over the cause of their sufferings, and see if any thing can be done to better their condition.

He spoke against the emigration of Negroes from the United States under the sponsorship of the American Colonization Society and the African Civilization Society. For in his opinion those organizations were proceeding on the assumption that Negroes could never be integrated into the American body politic. He asserted that "Our right to live here is as good as the white man's." It was his hope, he explained, "that this Convention will stimulate our people to self-elevation. . . . We must educate our children," he said, "give them professions or trades, and let them have a capital within themselves, that shall gain them wealth and influence. We must recommend to our people," he advised like a forerunner of Booker T. Washington, "to become possessors of the soil, to leave the large cities, take to farming, and make themselves independent."

In accordance with the report of the committee on nominations, George T. Downing of Newport, Rhode Island, was elected president of the convention; and as was customary for such meetings, a multiplicity of vice-presidents was elected. One of these was the Reverend John Sella Martin, formerly of Buffalo, New York, and then of Lawrence, Massachusetts. With about fifteen others Brown served on the business committee. He and two others constituted the committee on rules and order, and his ladylove, Annie Elizabeth Gray of Cambridgeport, served as one of the seven members of the committee on finance. The numerous and indeed voluminous resolutions which were devised by the business committee and presented by Nell near the end of the first session provoked considerable discussion throughout the convention. At various times some of the speakers found their tempers out of joint, as did Remond at the morning session of the second day. He was "aggrieved at some allusions made by Mr. Wm. Wells Brown to the fault-finding spirit which had characterized the remarks of Mr. Remond. He (Remond) felt an utter contempt for his (Brown's) remarks."

The last afternoon and evening sessions were devoted principally to the discussion of a resolution denouncing the American Colonization Society and the African Civilization Society. During the afternoon session, Brown spoke on the resolution. He repeated his objections to the organizations and also criticized the African Civilization Society for what he considered its degrading system of begging for support. The last-mentioned society was defended not very successfully by Martin and the Reverend John B. Smith, and near the end of the final session, the resolution denouncing both societies was adopted.[3]

Towards the end of August, Brown went on a lecture trip to New York and remained away from Boston about a month. Meanwhile he found himself briefly involved in a newspaper controversy with Henry Highland Garnet, with whom he had had his first controversy in print sixteen years earlier. On August 30 Garnet, who was president of the African Civilization Society, delivered a lecture in the Joy Street Church in Boston. In his lecture he answered Brown's criticism of the society for begging by accusing Brown of begging extensively in Great Britain as well as in America. He said that when he went to England, "there was Mr. Brown, and after one of his spirited lectures, and before

3. *Ibid.*, June 3, 1859, p. 87, July 22, 1859, p. 115, August 19, 1859, p. 132, August 26, 1859, p. 136; *Weekly Anglo-African*, August 6, 1859, pp. 2–3.

he closed, he said he should have to crave a collection to pay expenses."[4]

An extract of Garnet's speech including his reference to Brown was published in *Frederick Douglass' Paper* for September 23. After reading that extract, Brown sent a reply to the same newspaper from Buffalo on September 27. He ended his reply with the request, "Will the 'Anglo-African' do me the justice to copy this?" His reply was published in *Frederick Douglass' Paper* and was reprinted thence on the third page of the *Weekly Anglo-African* for October 22. He denied that he had ever tried to support himself by accompanying his lectures with begging. When he lectured before a lyceum, he explained, he charged the lyceum a specific fee; and when he sponsored his own lectures, he charged an admission fee. He challenged Garnet "to name the time and place where he had heard me 'crave a collection to pay expenses.' " Finally he assured Garnet that "If he will come to Boston, he shall have half the time in the meetings"—meetings in which he and Garnet might discuss matters of public interest.

It does not appear that Garnet ever accepted either Brown's challenge or his invitation. Within the next seven months, nevertheless, Brown had an occasion to comment again on the African Civilization Society. In March, 1860, George T. Downing and Charles L. Reason of New York City sent letters to several abolitionists asking them to express their opinions of the society and its efforts to promote the immigration of Negroes to Africa. On April 12, under the sponsorship of Downing, Reason, and others, a public meeting was held in an A. M. E. Zion church in the city. The meeting had been called to give "the colored people of New York and vicinity" an opportunity "to pass judgment on the African Civilization Society . . . and to declare openly whether they approve or condemn that society." Between 1,000 and 1,200 persons were present. Downing read to the assembly nine replies

4. *Liberator*, September 2, 1859, p. 138, September 23, 1858, p. 151.

which he and Reason had received in answer to their letters. Among these were replies from Brown, Gerrit Smith, Oliver Johnson, and Robert Purvis of Byberry, a suburb of Philadelphia.

Brown's opinion was one with those expressed in the other letters Downing read. Writing from Boston on April 6, he had said, among other things, "My main objection to the movement lies in the fact that its agents both in this country and in England, in their appeals to the public for funds to carry on the operations of the society, represent that there is no hope for the moral, social or political elevation of the free colored people in the United States, and that this association will open a home for us in Africa." Whether Downing and Reason had received only letters opposed to the society, or whether Downing read only letters opposed to it was not made clear during the meeting—which, having been threatened with disorder from the beginning, was eventually terminated in disorder.[5]

On October 16, 1859, John Brown led an abortive raid on Harper's Ferry. Within a comparatively short time, he and all of his followers who were captured alive were tried and executed. William Wells Brown knew John Brown but was not known to have had any close contact with him or any of his followers; hence he was never suspected of being involved in the activities that culminated in the raid, as Frederick Douglass was suspected. Like other abolitionists, however, he was deeply concerned about the effect the raid and the trials and executions might have on the antislavery crusade. Stimulated by the public interest in the aftermath of the raid, he announced in the *Liberator* for November 25 that he would lecture in the Joy Street Church on the evening of November 28 on "The Harper's Ferry Heroes." Instead he lectured on "The Heroes of Insurrection," dividing his subject into "heroes of the pen, the platform, and the sword" and including "personal reminiscences of John Brown." He lectured on the same subject to an audience that

5. *Weekly Anglo-African,* April 21, 1860, p. 2.

filled Pratt's Hall in Providence on the evening of December 2, the day before John Brown's execution. "His allusion," said the *Liberator* of two weeks later, "to Captain Brown's invasion of Virginia, to give freedom to the bondmen, and [to] the present tottering condition of the Slave Power, was well received."[6]

Late in the fall of 1859 there was printed in Boston the *Memoir of William Wells Brown, an American Bondman, Written by Himself*. This is a duodecimo pamphlet of thirty-six pages bound in paper covers and bearing the imprint of the Boston Anti-Slavery Office. There is no copyright statement in the pamphlet. There are four full-page illustrations in it—the same four found in *Clotel*, with minor differences in the wording of their titles. This work is principally a condensation in the first person of Josephine Brown's *Biography of an American Bondman*. In the condensation, in recounting his first thirty years, Brown made numerous incorrect statements involving names and events, or at least statements inconsistent with what he had said in the several editions of his *Narrative*, when those years were much fresher in his memory than they were in 1859. This work gave little or no new information about Brown's life—certainly not enough to justify its publication.

The annual meeting of the Massachusetts Anti-Slavery Society was held in Tremont Temple on January 26–27, 1860. At the final evening session, in a brief address, Brown spoke too optimistically of the prospective disappearance of race prejudice from America, but he recognized the fact that John Brown had sounded a tocsin of war between the North and the South over slavery. He spoke especially of the good that had been done for the antislavery cause by Mrs. Lydia Maria Child's open letter of December 17, 1859, to Mrs. J. C. Mason of Alto, King George's County, Virginia. Mrs. Child had written in reply to an open letter Mrs. Mason had addressed to her on the preceding November 11 condemning her for sympathizing with John Brown. As

6. *Liberator*, November 25, 1859, p. 187, December 16, 1859, p. 199; *Weekly Anglo-African*, December 24, 1859, p. 1.

William Wells Brown had doubtless observed, Mrs. Mason's letter had given Mrs. Child an occasion to set forth succinctly and unanswerably many of the best arguments against slavery and to get them read where antislavery lecturers could not get them heard; and Mrs. Child had indeed made the most of the occasion.[7]

Brown had engagements for lectures in western Massachusetts from early in February to the first of April. Within two weeks thereafter a most important change was made in his private life. On April 12 he was married in Boston to Annie Elizabeth Gray, the daughter of William H. and Harriet Gray of Cambridgeport. The marriage ceremony was performed by the Reverend Leonard A. Grimes, Pastor of Twelfth Baptist Church, with the assistance of the Reverend David Stevens. In the official registration of the marriage, both the groom and the bride were described as "col[ore]d." Brown was also listed as a resident of Cambridgeport, his age was set down as forty-one years—whereas he was at least forty-five—and his occupation was given as "author." This seems to have been the first time that he officially referred to his occupation thus. The bride's first name was recorded as Anna, her birthplace as Baltimore, and her age twenty-five years. According to the registration this was Brown's second marriage and Annie's first.[8]

A few days after their wedding, the Browns went to Pennsylvania and spent most of the week of April 22 in Harrisburg. There on the evening of that day, which was Sunday, Brown lectured in the Second Presbyterian Church on "practical Christianity." On the following Tuesday and Wednesday evenings respectively, he read what a correspondent of the *Weekly Anglo-African* identified as "his celebrated dramas entitled 'Life

7. For the correspondence between Mrs. Mason and Mrs. Child, see *Letters of Lydia Maria Child* (Boston, 1883), pp. 120–37.

8. *Liberator*, January 27, 1860, p. 15, March 16, 1860, p. 43, March 30, 1860, p. 51, April 20, 1860, p. 63; Massachusetts, 19th Registration, 1860, Marriages, vol. 137, Suffolk-Worcester, p. 32, no. 574, State House, Boston, Massachusetts.

at the South' and 'Experience; or how to give a Northern man a backbone.' " After talking as if the subject matter of the two dramas was the same and commenting favorably on Brown's reading of them, the correspondent said, "It is regretted that he did not arrive here during the lecturing season, when his readings would have been more largely attended."[9] This was probably the correspondent's euphemistic way of saying that the reader had very small audiences both evenings.

The title *Life at the South* was new, but the drama to which it referred need not have been. This title was more or less appropriate for *The Escape*, and that, perhaps somewhat altered, might well have been the first of the two dramas Brown read in Harrisburg.

When the American Anti-Slavery Society held its annual meeting in New York on May 8–9, it also celebrated its twenty-seventh anniversary. A part of the anniversary celebration was an afternoon session at Cooper Institute on May 9. Brown was one of the principal speakers at that session. Beginning on a somber note of pessimism, he took cognizance of the progress of American slavery, especially as that progress was evidenced by the recent illegal but none the less actual reopening of the African slave trade and the rising prices of slaves. He referred to the serpentine logic by which slaveholders rationalized concerning free Negroes in the South. They declared as occasion seemed to dictate, he observed, that free Negroes were "a nuisance and ought to be driven out," or that they were "a very orderly class of people," among whom were some of the best mechanics and artisans available. The latter opinion, he remembered, had been expressed by John Catron of Tennessee, one of the justices of the United States Supreme Court who had concurred in the majority opinion in the Dred Scott decision. Catron had recently expressed this opinion of free Negroes in a letter to the legislature of Tennessee, and the letter had been published in the *Nashville Union.*

9. *Weekly Anglo-African,* May 12, 1860, pp. 2–3.

Brown noted, in passing, the pernicious influence of slavery on the status of Negroes in the free states and condemned American historians, particularly George Bancroft, for ignoring the services rendered by Negroes in America's wars. The reign of terror resulting from John Brown's raid, he said, and the chasing of white men out of the Carolinas, Virginia, Kentucky, and other Southern states for speaking against slavery showed that slavery was no respecter of persons—that ultimately it cared "no more for the rights of the white man than for those of the black man."

Animadverting upon the idea of the colonizationists and even of some Republican politicians that Negroes should be expatriated, Brown provoked applause by exclaiming that although some individuals might emigrate to improve their condition, Negroes as a group were determined to stay in America and work for the abolition of slavery. He referred to the extensive racial amalgamation which had been carried on principally by slaveholders and asserted that Negroes were too closely connected by blood with the white people especially of the South to leave their native country so lightly, as some seemed to think they would. With wry humor he cited by way of example his own blood relationship to some of the best white families in Kentucky. Blending humor and seriousness, he managed nonetheless to emphasize the fact that generally Negroes regarded without pride their illicit blood relationships to white people. Then, rising to a diapason note of optimism, he avowed that Negroes still had faith in the antislavery movement, that the movement would eventually abolish slavery, that although slavery was progressing on one hand, the cause of freedom was advancing on the other, and that "We have the truth on our side, and that shall make us free." His speech was followed by "prolonged cheering."[10]

This was indeed one of Brown's best oratorical efforts, not only because of what he said but also because of the facility with which he made the most of the occasion. From the begin-

10. *National Anti-Slavery Standard,* May 26, 1860, p. 4.

ning he established rapport with his audience; and by the earnestness with which he spoke, coupled with his sallies of wit and humor, he prevented the familiar from becoming trite and the serious from becoming depressing. He kept his audience in a sympathetic as well as receptive mood to the end.

By the middle of June the Browns had established their home next door to that of Mrs. Brown's parents on Webster Avenue in Cambridgeport. A census taker found them living there on June 19. That functionary incorrectly described both of them as "B[lack]" and also incorrectly recorded Brown's age as forty years and his occupation as "Laborer." The Browns maintained their home there eighteen years.[11]

Whether the Browns ever owned this home is uncertain. Brown was not listed in the manuscript schedules of the census of either 1860 or 1870 as the owner of any real estate or even personal property. Nor was his name in the list of taxpayers published in the several editions of the *Cambridge Directory* during his residence in Cambridgeport. The absence, however, of references in the manuscript schedules to any property of Brown's is less significant than it would be if the schedules pertaining to the Browns for both of these censuses did not contain so many errors. The omission of Brown's name from the list of taxpayers in the *Cambridge Directory* might also have been erroneous, as the omission of the name of his father-in-law, William H. Gray, must have been for the years during which he was known to have owned real estate in Cambridgeport.

On June 4, 1860, Charles Sumner delivered in the United States Senate his famous philippic entitled "The Barbarism of Slavery." In appreciation for his fearless exposure of the "peculiar institution," Negroes of Boston held a meeting in the Joy Street Church on the evening of June 18 and paid him a tribute in absentia. Brown was one of the principal speakers for

11. U. S. Bureau of the Census, Eighth Census, 1860, Free Inhabitants, Massachusetts, vol. 16, p. 218; *Cambridge Directory, 1861–1878; Boston Directory 1865–1877.*

the occasion. A few days later he went on a lecture tour of Vermont, visiting some of the same towns in which he had spoken on his previous trips to the state. He remained on this tour about four weeks, after which he returned home in time to participate in the Massachusetts Anti-Slavery Society's celebration of emancipation in the British West Indies, which was held in Abington on August 1.[12]

After about two weeks at home, Brown set out on another tour of Vermont, stopping on his way to lecture in villages in northcentral Massachusetts. He went on this tour as well as on the one of June and July under the auspices of the American Anti-Slavery Society. That organization had come to regard Vermont as a Macedonia, in which the antislavery cause needed the help of an apostle from the outside.[13] That its judgment of at least the eastern half of the state was correct was verified by Brown's experiences there between August 17 and September 13.

At Topsham, where Brown lectured at least twice, his first lecture "stirred up the pure minds of the Democracy, and the following morning I received a note, through the post office, warning me to leave the town, and threatening that if I was not out of the place in twenty-four hours, I would be waited on by a 'committee appointed for the purpose.' The only attention that I paid to this was to criticise [*sic*] the writer and his party." With the aid of Leonard Johnson, a brother of Oliver Johnson, he gained access to the Congregational church in Peachum for a lecture, "though the Rev. Mr. Boutwell, the minister in charge, gave the meeting a poor reception, and me a worse name when the lecture was over. He thought me too severe on the pro-slavery religion of the country, North and South." Thanks again to Johnson's "untiring energies," Brown lectured a second time in the same church in spite of efforts to keep him from doing so.

12. *Liberator*, June 29, 1860, p. 103, July 20, 1860, p. 115, August 17, 1860, p. 130; *Weekly Anglo-African*, July 7, 1860, p. 2.

13. *Liberator*, August 3, 1860, p. 123, August 10, 1860, p. 127, August 17, 1860, p. 131.

Thanks further to Johnson's influence, the Methodist church in Danville, "a superannuated village, five miles from Peachum," was made available to him, and he lectured in it one Sunday afternoon at five o'clock. "This was said to have been the largest anti-slavery meeting held in the place for years," he noted.

Having been engaged to deliver two lectures in a church in South Ryegate, Brown delivered the first lecture one afternoon and therewith so thoroughly stirred "the bad feeling[s]" of the local Democrats that when he returned to deliver the second lecture, he found the church closed against him. The only other place available for a meeting in the village was a schoolhouse. Upon inquiry he was informed that he would be permitted to use the building if he paid a rental fee for it and supplied lights himself. The trustees of the school admitted that a rental fee was demanded because he was speaking on slavery. He found their terms unacceptable; and "As there was no hotel in the town at which I could stop, and no offer of hospitality from the inhabitants, I shook the dust from my feet, and walked five miles to McIndoes [*sic*] without my supper." Soon afterwards a friend in Bradford informed him that he might be permitted to lecture in the Methodist church there if he would promise not to speak about politics nor against the Methodist church. He promptly refused to make such a promise. Nevertheless he lectured in the town hall one Sunday "and had a good attendance."[14]

After his return from Vermont about the middle of September, Brown spent most of the next two months lecturing in Rhode Island, Maine, and eastern Massachusetts.[15] Meanwhile, on Friday evening, October 12, with many others he heard William Lowndes Yancey, a United States senator from Alabama, popularly known as "one of the fire-eaters of the South," lecture in

14. William Wells Brown, "The Cause in Vermont," *Liberator*, September 21, 1860, p. 151.

15. *Liberator*, September 21, 1860, p. 151, September 28, 1860, p. 155, October 5, 1860, p. 159, October 12, 1860, p. 163; October 19, 1860, p. 167, November 2, 1860, p. 175, November 9, 1860, p. 179.

Faneuil Hall. In a speech fraught with words offensive not only to Negroes but also to others in his audience, Yancey repeated the familiar arguments in defense of slavery, including the doctrine of the natural inferiority of Negroes and the right of the superior race to govern the inferior race.

Brown wrote to Yancey the next day inviting him to attend a meeting the Negroes of Boston were planning to hold in the Joy Street Church the following Monday evening. The business of the meeting was to be a review by Brown of Yancey's speech, and in his letter to Yancey, Brown promised that the senator would have an opportunity to reply to the review before the meeting was adjourned. Not surprisingly at all Yancey neither acknowledged receipt of Brown's letter nor attended the meeting.

The meeting having been opened at the appointed time with remarks by the Reverend John Sella Martin, then pastor of the church, Brown presented his review. In answer to Yancey's "long argument" that slave labor was more beneficial to the country than free labor, he cited by title Hinton R. Helper's *The Impending Crisis*, a book then three years old. He then said more or less casually, "It has been shown that the product of the hay crop alone in the Free States is worth more than the entire products of the South," but he gave no proof for this statement. The mere reference to Helper's book was hardly convincing, for as Brown himself must have been cognizant, probably very few members of his audience were even generally informed concerning it. When, however, in rebuttal to Yancey's denial that slavery was a demoralizing institution, he referred to the large number of white slaves in the South and queried as to whence they came, his argument was specific and irrefutable.

With regard to racial inequalities, Brown denied on historical grounds that there were master races and slave races. He reminded his audience that various races had been enslaved in different periods of history, and that among these were the Britons and the Anglo-Saxons, whom he identified as the ancestors of the American white people. Principally on the authority of David Hume's and Thomas B. Macaulay's histories of England, he said that the Britons had been savages for a long time and had also been slaves of the Romans, and that the Anglo-Saxons had been slaves of the Normans. He said that, on the contrary, three thousand years earlier "the antecedents of the Negro" had been the leaders of civilization. Assuming that the ancient Ethiopians and Negroes were ethnologically identical, and fusing—if not confusing—history and tradition, he asserted that Euclid, Homer, Plato, and Terence were Ethiopians and that Hanno, the grandfather of Hannibal, was a Negro. "The Romans, Saxons and Normans," he declared, "who swallowed up the Britons, and gave them a name and a language, received their civilization from Egypt and Ethiopia. When Mr. Yancey's ancestors were bending their necks to the yoke of William the Conqueror, the ancestors of his slaves were revelling in the halls of science and learning."[16]

Brown cited no authorities for his assumption that the ancient Ethiopians and Negroes were racially identical nor for his assertion concerning the racial identity of Euclid, Homer, Plato, Terence, and Hanno. He could have referred, however, to R. B. Lewis' *Light and Truth*, in which both of these ideas are repeated several times.[17] Lewis, who was identified on the title page of his book as "A Colored Man," copyrighted the work in 1836, but it was not published until 1844, when it was brought out in Boston "by a Committee of Colored Gentlemen." Most probably Brown was familiar with this book but did not refer

16. *Ibid.*, October 26, 1860, p. 172. Brown quoted from Hume's *The History of England from the Invasion of Julius Caesar to the Abdication of James the Second, 1688*, vol. 1 (1754), chap. 1, and from Macaulay's *The History of England from the Accession of James the Second*, vol. 1 (1848), chap. 1.

17. R. B. Lewis, *Light and Truth; Collected from the Bible and Ancient and Modern History, Containing the Universal History of the Colored and the Indian Race, from the Creation of the World to the Present Time* (Boston, 1844), esp. pp. 15, 61, 125, 193, 283, 314.

to it perhaps because he was aware that it was too curious a compound of biblical lore, history, tradition, and fancy to be taken seriously.

On Wednesday afternoon, October 17, the Prince of Wales arrived in Boston for a royal visit which lasted until the next Saturday morning. Negro citizens seem to have had no part in the two days of festivities held in his honor in the city. A group of Negroes collaborated, however, in preparing an "Address" to him as an expression of "their profound and grateful attachment and respect for that Throne which you represent here, under whose shelter so many thousands of their race, fugitives from American Slavery, find safety and rest; and of their love for that realm which, noblest among modern nations, first struck off the fetters of her slaves." The "Address" was obviously intended to be, and indeed was, not only a compliment to Great Britain but also an adverse criticism, at least by implication, of the proslavery American government. Among the numerous signers of it were Brown and Nell. Having no opportunity to present it publicly to the prince, the group had to content themselves with presenting it to him during a private audience at the Revere House, where he was a guest during his visit to the city.[18]

18. *Boston Daily Evening Transcript,* October 16, 1860, October 18, 1860, October 19, 1860; *Liberator,* December 31, 1860, p. 210.

"Miralda"— but Little Time for Art

AN ANNOUNCEMENT ON THE SECOND PAGE OF THE WEEKLY *Anglo-African* for November 24, 1860, said that in its next number this newspaper would begin publishing "an interesting and thrilling anti-slavery story" entitled *Miralda; or, The Beautiful Quadroon* by "that able and popular writer, William Wells Brown, of Cambridgeport, Mass." The announcement also said that the story had been written "expressly" for the *Anglo-African Magazine* but was about to be published in the newspaper because publication of the magazine had been suspended. The magazine had been published monthly in New York by Thomas Hamilton, the owner and editor of the *Weekly Anglo-African*, from January, 1859, to March, 1860, at least, but no writing of Brown's had appeared in it. As the author of the announcement presumably did not know, Brown had only rewritten the story for the periodical, for the work proved to be only an extensively altered version of *Clotel.*

Miralda; or, The Beautiful Quadroon. A Romance of American Slavery, Founded on Fact, as it was fully entitled, was published in sixteen front-page installments in the *Weekly Anglo-African,* beginning in the number for December 1, 1860, and ending in the number for March 16, 1861. The numbers of the newspaper for December 1 and 8 seem not to have been preserved, but the numbers containing the remaining fourteen installments have been. Each installment has for its motto Alexander Pope's *Epilogue to the Satires,* "Dialogue II," lines 197–200. The work abounds in misprints and misspellings which must have been embarrassing to both the printers and the author. In many instances the same word is spelled in different ways in the same column.

The first two installments consisted of six and a half chapters—about one-seventh of the work. The want of these two installments would be a much greater loss than it is except for one fortunate circumstance. In 1864 Brown published the same version of the novel under the title *Clotelle: A Tale of the Southern States* with Miralda's name changed to Clotelle and with some other changes. The first six and a half chapters of this version fit very well into the context of *Miralda*—a fact which suggests that they originally belonged to it—and from them one can get an idea of the contents of the first two installments.

In transforming *Clotel* into *Miralda,* Brown did several remarkable things. For no discernible good reason, he changed the names of almost all of the important characters and of some of the minor ones. Among the changes in names are the following, the first name in each pair being the one used in *Clotel* and the second being the one used in *Miralda:* Currer—Agnes, Clotel—Isabella, Althesa—Marion, Horatio Green—Henry Linwood, Mary—Miralda, Henry Morton—Adolphus Morton, George Green—Jerome Fletcher, and the Reverend John Peck—the Reverend James Wilson. The only important characters whose names were not changed were Georgiana, the daughter of the slaveholding preacher, Gertrude, the wife of Linwood, and the Devenants, father and son.

In *Miralda,* Brown changed the setting and the order of several of the events in *Clotel* and rearranged its division into chapters, omitting all or parts of some chapters and adding new ones or new parts to old ones. He had introduced most of the chapters in *Clotel* with quotations in verse. In *Miralda* he not only replaced most of those quotations with different ones but also quoted poetry profusely, or made different characters quote it, within the chapters themselves. This extensive quoting, which, alas, abounds in minor errors, reflected much more light on the author's reading than splendor on either his thought or his style. Generally he repeated verbatim the phraseology he had used in the corresponding parts of *Clotel,* but here and there he eliminated or added sentences or parts of sentences. He appropriately omitted some of the rhetorical flourishes found in the original work and inappropriately added new purple passages, where their supposed beauty is their only excuse for being—and theirs is seldom if ever a good excuse. Unfortunately he omitted all of the part of the original chapter 6 in *Clotel* which tells about the Reverend Hontz Snyder's sermon to the Reverend John Peck's slaves—one of the most satirical passages in the novel.

The first half of *Miralda,* chapters 1–16, consists principally of adaptations of the stories of Currer and the Reverend John Peck, Althesa and Henry Morton, and Clotel and Horatio Green. These are identifiable in the newspaper serial as the stories of Agnes and the Reverend John Wilson, Marion and Adolphus Morton, and Isabella and Henry Linwood. In recounting the Clotel–Horatio Green romance as that of Isabella and Linwood, Brown wisely eliminated the artificial language which he had previously borrowed from Mrs. Lydia Maria Child's "The Quadroons." He refined Gertrude into a sentimental and demure near-heroine and introduced a new character in the person of her mother, Mrs. Miller, whom he made the evil genius of Isabella and Miralda. Being "a woman of little or no feeling, proud, peevish, and passionate," Mrs. Miller was only another Mrs. Gaines. Her husband, Gertrude's father, was now altered into a Dr. Gaines with an emaciated will, "a mere cipher about his premises . . . with seven mulatto children who claimed him as their father."

Interestingly enough Brown slightly altered the statement he had made in his account of the death of Clotel identifying her as Thomas Jefferson's daughter. In *Miralda* he said, "Thus died Isabella, a descendant of Thomas Jefferson, the immortal author of the Declaration of Independence." In the last fourteen installments of *Miralda,* this is the only reference, whether intentional or inadvertent, to Jefferson as an ancestor of Agnes's children.

The second half of *Miralda,* chapters 17–36, is mainly an expansion of the Mary–George Green story into that of Miralda and Jerome Fletcher. Brown related in alternate chapters or groups of chapters the adventures of Miralda and Fletcher during their more than ten years of involuntary separation. Presumably he proceeded thus for the purpose of achieving order in time in the development of his plot. He can hardly be said, however, to have succeeded very well. The second half of *Miralda* is as episodic as is the major part of *Clotel.*

In *Clotel* what happened to Mary between the time George Green left her in prison in Richmond and the time of their fortuitous meeting in Dunkirk was related to Green by Mary herself. In *Miralda* all of this, with some additions and a few minor changes in details, was related by the author himself. This change in the method of narration made it possible for the author to comment on the action or indulge in pertinent reflections, as he could not have made his heroine do naturally.

Brown, however, did not end the story of Miralda and Fletcher with their reunion in Dunkirk. Instead he continued it through four new chapters (33–36). A few hours after their marriage on "a bright day in the latter part of October," the

Fletchers set out on a wedding tour, whose terminus was Geneva. While they were in Switzerland, the course of their lives was interrupted by a chance as freakish as any they had previously experienced either separately or together. On a stormy night in a small hotel on Lake Leman, they found themselves in a room next to one occupied by a demented man, whose groans and shrieks kept them awake all night, and whom they found the next morning to be Henry Linwood, Miralda's father! A train of misfortunes, including the death of his wife three years earlier and the death of his mother-in-law during the preceding winter, had very badly undermined his health of body and mind; and his physician had advised him to seek recovery by traveling. He had been out of America two months; but instead of improving he had been suffering more and more from a guilt complex, the result of his consciousness that he had abandoned Miralda to Mrs. Miller's tyranny. Thus the Furies, those goddesses of retribution, had driven him to madness. But behold, "The presence of his long absent child had a soothing effect upon Mr. Linwood, and he now recovered rapidly from the sad and almost hopeless condition in which she had found him."

There are obvious similarities between Linwood's experience of madness and King Lear's with regard to cause, course, and cure. These similarities could have resulted from coincidence since the two characters were briefly afflicted with the same kind of mental disorder. Brown, however, was doubtless as familiar with Shakespeare's *Tragedy of King Lear* as he was with the then prevailing knowledge of insanity. It is at least probable, therefore, that in writing his account of Linwood's madness, he was influenced by the former as much as by the latter, if not more.

Although Linwood was glad to be with his daughter again, he was displeased to find her married to a black man. His frank and rather tactless expression of this fact gave the Fletchers an occasion to begin a process of educating him not only out of his race prejudice but also away from slaveholding. Supported by the influence of an environment from which race prejudice was absent, they succeeded more rapidly than they might have expected at first to do; and when they returned home, they took him with them. "After a stay of four weeks at Dunkirk, the home of the Fletchers, Mr. Linwood set out for America, with the full determination of freeing his slaves, and settling them in one of the Northern States, and then to return to France to end his days in the society of his beloved daughter." Thus said Brown near the end of chapter 36, which is entitled "Conclusion," and which is principally an argument summarizing the irreconcilable conflict between human nature and slavery.

Presumably Brown altered this second version of his novel as he did with the hope of improving the work as art if not as argument. But as is evidenced by a careful study of the two versions, he did not improve it in either way. Like *Clotel*, *Miralda* suffers from a plethora of subject matter, sketchiness in the development of plots and the portrayal of characters, and ineffectiveness of style. In too many instances the action is still unconvincingly motivated by manipulated, freakish chance. Although Brown had recently officially identified himself as an author, he was still much more an abolitionist than a writer, as he continued to be until American slavery was abolished.

Brown had engagements to lecture twice in North Abington, Massachusetts, on Sunday, December 16, 1860.[1] None of the abolition journals seem to have given any information about any lectures of his on any other days in December or during the next two months. His lecturing was most probably interrupted by the fact that the general excitement resulting from secession and the disruption of business was too easily provocative of mob violence to make the holding of antislavery meetings propitious in either small towns or cities. The annual meeting of the Massachusetts Anti-Slavery Society, for instance, was begun in Tremont

1. *Liberator*, December 14, 1860, p. 199.

Temple in Boston on January 24, 1861, but was terminated after two sessions because of the interference of a mob.[2]

Moreover, Brown had a personal reason for remaining near his home during the first two months of the new year. He and Mrs. Brown were expecting their firstborn ere long. In fulfillment of their expectations, William Wells Brown, Jr. was born in Cambridgeport late in February. The exact date of his birth seems not to have been recorded. His life, alas, was very short. He died in Cambridgeport on the following July 25 of cholera infantum and was buried in the Cambridge Cemetery.[3]

Meanwhile on February 6, 126 Negro citizens of Massachusetts presented to the state legislature a memorial opposing the Crittenden Compromise. Being uncertain about what the legislature would do with regard to this notorious attempt to appease the South, the Negroes met in the Joy Street Church on the evening of February 14 to consider appealing directly to the white citizens of the state. Following the preliminaries of the meeting, the Reverend John Sella Martin bitterly denounced the compromise, and George T. Downing read the proposed "Appeal to the White Citizens of the State" urging them to oppose it.

Brown, who was present, then said that he considered the "Appeal" premature. For reasons which he apparently failed to explain, he predicted that the Crittenden Compromise would not be adopted by either the so-called Peace Congress or the United States Congress, both of which were then in session in Washington. He also said that if it was adopted by the United States Congress, it would have to be submitted to the people of the several states, since it had been proposed as an amendment to the

2. [Wendell Phillips Garrison and Francis Jackson Garrison], *William Lloyd Garrison, 1805–1879: The Story of His Life Told by His Children*, 4 vols. (Boston, 1894), 4: 4–8.

3. Massachusetts, 20th Registration, 1861, Births, vol. 142, Hampshire-Plymouth, p. 72, no. 935; Deaths, vol. 148, Hampshire-Plymouth, p. 64, no. 313, State House, Boston, Massachusetts; records in the office of the Cambridge Cemetery; *Liberator*, August 2, 1861, p. 123.

Constitution. He thought it well, he explained, for Negro citizens to be alert to their situation, but not to act too hastily with reference to it. In a flush of optimism hardly justified by the time, he declared that he had never felt more buoyant than he did then. Negroes had only to sit still, he said, and the law of progress would bring freedom to them. He considered the recent actions of antiabolition mobs the final struggles of tyrants. Reverting to the "Appeal," he repeated that he saw no reason to send it out so soon, since the compromise could not be presented to the people until the next fall. It did not occur to him, perhaps, that even if such an appeal did no good, it was not likely to do any harm.

In rebuttal Downing said he was convinced that Brown's point of view was erroneous, and that the matter was of immediate as well as of the greatest importance, for the rights of all Negroes were involved in it. There were brief speeches in favor of the "Appeal" by Martin, Robert Morris, and others, after which it was adopted, and the meeting was adjourned.[4] It may be noted in passing that Brown's prediction concerning the compromise was at least half-wrong, for the Peace Congress adopted what was essentially the same thing, although the United States Congress never voted on the report it received from that group.

The indecision and inaction of James Buchanan during his last three months in the Presidency, the servile concessions proffered by Northern politicians to appease, the slaveholders, the hauteur with which Southern leaders ignored—if they did not spurn—Northern proposals for compromises, the secession of seven slaveholding states between December 20, 1860, and February 1, 1861, and their formation of the Confederate States of America—these events were sufficient to convince the North that the Union could not be saved by the mobbing of abolitionists into silence and the enactment into laws of one "forever" after another in favor of slavery. By the time of Lincoln's first

4. *Liberator*, February 22, 1861, p. 31.

inauguration, this fact was becoming clearer and clearer to all who could perceive what George Thompson called "the inevitable tendency of events, and their resistless influence."[5] And while Lincoln girded the North for the now unavoidable Civil War, the abolitionists continued with renewed determination their crusade against slavery. As was obvious to everyone who understood much about American affairs, slavery was the basic cause of the war, and it was the new mission of the abolitionists to convince the nation that the war could end not to be renewed only when the basic cause of it was removed.

Four days after Lincoln's first inauguration, the *Liberator* announced a lecture by Brown for the first time since the preceding December. Brown was expected to speak in Groveland on March 10 on a subject which had been provided for him by the time. It was "Slavery and the Present Crisis," and he doubtless dwelt on that subject on many occasions, as he was engaged to do in Taunton and three other towns in southeastern Massachusetts in the middle of April.[6]

On the evening of April 23, in the wake of the fall of Fort Sumter and Lincoln's call for 75,000 volunteers, Negroes held a meeting in Twelfth Baptist Church in Boston to express their sentiments concerning the incipient war. There were some oratorical preliminaries, after which Robert Morris read the report of the three-members committee on resolutions. The report, which exulted in patriotic sentiments, consisted of a preamble in two parts and five resolutions. Assuming that victory for the Union would terminate slavery, the resolutions avowed, among other things, that Negroes were ready to defend the Union "as the equals of its white defenders" and to raise an army of 50,000 men if state and federal laws were changed so as to allow them to enlist; that "the colored women would go as nurses, seamstresses, and warriors, if need be, to crush the rebellion and

5. [Garrison and Garrison], *William Lloyd Garrison*, 4: 28.
6. *Liberator*, March 8, 1861, p. 39, April 12, 1861, p. 59.

uphold the Government;" that Negroes were "ready to go at a moment's warning, if they were allowed to go as soldiers," the implication being that they did not wish to be only common laborers and servants; and that Negroes should immediately organize themselves into drilling companies "to the end of becoming better skilled in the use of fire-arms; so that when we shall be called upon by the country, we shall be better prepared to make a ready and fitting response."

In a long, eloquent, and patriotic speech, Morris urged the adoption of the resolutions. Brown "then spoke at length" against them "amid manifestation of disapproval" of his point of view. He argued that although freedom for the slaves was of prime importance, the federal government had yet done nothing to indicate that it would do anything about slavery. He was aware, he admitted, that the general excitement of the time made his point of view unpopular, but he insisted that his many years of labor on behalf of the slaves had merited for him the right to express himself freely as well as frankly with regard to their interests. Above all else he thought that self-respect should keep Negroes from begging the government for opportunities to defend it.

Not only was Brown interrupted by opponents of his point of view, but he also became momentarily the object of abuse. With the kind of obtuseness which amounted to genius for confusing issues and men, "One venerable gentleman denounced him as a slaveholder, and another as a liar."

After some more speeches in support of the resolutions, Brown again addressed the meeting in an effort to clarify some ideas concerning which he thought he had been misunderstood. He was, he declared, "in favor of preparation, organization, arming; he had never been a peace man;" but he did not want Negroes to rush blindly into the situation before them. He warned his hearers that even if the Union accepted Negroes as soldiers, it might put them to guarding forts and arsenals in the North and thus keep them from getting in the way in the South as well as prevent them from fighting directly for the freedom of the slaves.

Finally the Reverend John Sella Martin, the presiding officer, spoke in support of the resolutions. His speech "was full of eloquent hits, sharp sarcasm, well managed but false argument, and some pertinent statements." He thought that Negroes should voluntarily join in the war, because they would thus entitle themselves to claims on the gratitude of the whites when the conflict ended. He predicted correctly that the South would fight desperately at the beginning with the hope of winning quickly, because it was not financially able to carry on a long war. He predicted also correctly that the South would at first be victorious, and that when the North was gravely endangered, it would welcome the services of Negro soldiers. It was his opinion, therefore, that Negroes should by all means be prepared to fight when they got the opportunity to do so. In spite of Brown's opposition, the resolutions were enthusiastically adopted, and the meeting was adjourned "at a late hour." Pursuant to the adoption of the resolutions, a drilling company of 125 Negroes was organized on April 29.[7]

Not long before the Civil War began, there was stimulated anew the interest of American Negroes in immigrating to Haiti in quest of the freedom their native land denied them because of their race. Upon assuming the presidency of Haiti in 1858, Fabre Geffrard invited American Negroes to settle there, and many did or at least thought seriously of doing so. Within the next three years, "Haytian Emigration," as it was then called, gained considerable impetus under the sponsorship of James Redpath, the Scottish-American roving editor and abolitionist. Having recently visited Haiti three times, Redpath announced in a circular dated at Boston, November 3, 1860, that Geffrard had appointed him "General Agent of Emigration" for the Haitian government, and that he had established his office in Boston. In

7. *Ibid.*, April 26, 1861, p. 67, May 3, 1861, p. 71, May 31, 1861, p. 86; *Weekly Anglo-African,* May 4, 1861, p. 3.

a second circular dated January 8, 1861, he designated agents for several cities and for regions including most of the free states.[8]

Although Brown was ever opposed to the schemes of the American Colonization Society for the expatriation of free Negroes, he was never opposed to voluntary emigration by those who thought that they could improve their situation by such a change. In accordance with the latter fact, at least for a year he found less of a reason to oppose Redpath's promotion of Haitian immigration than to support it—in his own way. His first way was to prepare a lecture on Haiti for the enlightenment of prospective immigrants[9]—or to refurbish his old lecture on the subject—and to deliver it on opportune occasions. Early in May he went on a lecture tour in central and western New York. He delivered his lecture on Haiti in Rochester on the fifteenth and in Elmira within the next week. In the opinion of Frederick Douglass, who was in his audience in Rochester, but who considered Haitian immigration unwise, "His lecture was replete with instruction, and quite eloquently delivered."[10]

In the masthead of the first numbers of the *Pine and Palm*, a weekly newspaper which Redpath began publishing in Boston and New York on May 18, Brown's name was listed among those of the "Special Contributors." His first special contribution to the publication, a contribution exemplary of his second way of supporting Haitian immigration, was an article entitled "Opposition to Emigration" on the second page of the number for June 1. This was an effort of his to explain, for he could not explain

8. James Redpath, ed., *A Guide to Hayti* (Boston, 1861), pp. 5, 9–10, 63–126.

9. *Weekly Anglo-African*, April 13, 1861, p. 4. An editorial entitled "The Haytian Movement" in this number noted that "The Haytian Fever is spreading far and wide," but refrained from unequivocally approving or disapproving of the movement.

10. "All Going to Hayti," *Douglass' Monthly*, May, 1859; see also *ibid.*, June, 1861, p. 468; *Liberator*, April 26, 1861, p. 66; *Pine and Palm*, June 8, 1861, p. 4, June 15, 1861, p. 4.

away, the mounting opposition to "the splendid offer," as he described it, "now made by the Haytian Government, to induce colored Americans to emigrate to that beautiful Island." Naively enough he found the first of three reasons for the opposition in the pseudoanthropological assumption that "every race has its peculiarities," and that one of those of his race was a disinclination to migrate—"and this is our greatest misfortune," he opined. In proof of his assertion that Negroes disliked migrating, he cited the situation of free Negroes in the slave states. In those states oppressive laws against free Negroes gave them good reasons to migrate, but the thought that they did not do so because of their "love of home, and fear of adventure." He found the second reason in "the prejudice which the Colonization scheme has created in our minds against everything that would induce us to leave our native land." He considered the colonization scheme and the Haitian movement too different, however, for anybody to confuse them. He found the third reason in "the feeling that we ought not to quit the land of our birth, and leave the slave in his chains." This feeling prompted him to observe that the vast majority of Negroes in the United States were in menial positions which commanded for them no influence in the controversy over slavery or in public affairs in general.

Brown was convinced, he said, that Negroes could become independent and influential only by becoming prosperous landowners and farmers. They had but few opportunities, however, to become such in the United States, he thought, for the majority of them were too poor to buy land; and "The inducements held out to other people, to take up the Western lands, are denied to the descendents of Africa, for the government has decided that colored men have not the right of preëmption in the occupancy of the public lands." On the contrary Haiti, he said, was generously offering Negroes opportunities to become prosperous, independent landowners as well as participants in the building of a great republic. Echoing in part Redpath's editorial in the first number of the *Pine and Palm,* he said that "To emigrate to Hayti, and to develop the resources of the Island, and to build up a powerful and influential government there, which shall demonstrate the genius and capabilities of the Negro, is as good an Anti-Slavery work as can be done in the Northern States of this Union."

Brown's current advocacy of the mass immigration of Negroes to Haiti was not altogether consistent with what he had said about emigration in his speech at Cooper Institute in May, 1860. He had said in that speech that aggressive Negroes should and would stay in America and work for the abolition of slavery. He must have been aware, of course, that only aggressive people would ever be likely to emigrate. Was he not now advising aggressive Negroes to do exactly what he had advised them against doing a year earlier? He had said that Negroes still had faith that the abolition movement would eventually achieve its great purpose. He must have realized that even with the aid of numerous aggressive immigrants, it would take Haiti many years to develop into an influential state—many more years than most Americans expected in the spring of 1861 that slavery would last. Was he now growing doubtful of the efficacy of the antislavery crusade, when its success was almost in view? Perhaps his judgment was again beclouded by the uncertainty of the time, as it seems to have been at the meeting in the Joy Street Church on February 14 and at the one in Twelfth Baptist Church on April 23.

Probably very few if any of Brown's acquaintances of the time knew about his trip to Haiti twent-one years earlier. If they had known about it, they might have embarrassed him with a forceful *argumentum ad hominem.* Since he had already visited Haiti and thought so well of Geffrard's offer, why, they might have asked, did he not immigrate to that country? Whether he ever was asked or ever answered such a question in public seems to have remained unrecorded.

Brown returned home from western New York about the

middle of June and remained in the vicinity of Boston about six weeks. During that time he delivered no lectures on Haiti—probably because of a want of interested audiences—but he spoke occasionally on the relationship between slavery and the war.[11]

An opportunity to discuss Haitian immigration came incidentally to Brown on Sunday evening, July 21—a few hours after the defeat of the Union army at Bull Run in the first battle of the Civil War. Garrison spoke in Twelfth Baptist Church that evening on "The War and the Haytian Emigration Movement." After his speech, while a collection was being taken, he invited questions.

George T. Downing said that like the American Colonization Society, the promoters of Haitian immigration seemed "to desire to create in the minds of the colored people the impression that they cannot be anything in this country." He then asked Garrison whether he had discovered this similarity between the desires of the two groups. Garrison replied that he had not, but that if he did, he would certainly oppose the movement for Haitian immigration.

Instead of asking a question, Brown made a brief speech. He did not want those present to get the impression, he protested, that the movement for Haitian immigration advocated "the doctrine, that colored men cannot rise in this country." He avowed that if the movement espoused such a doctrine, he would immediately oppose it. "I am glad," he continued, "my friend Garrison has not seen any thing of the kind, for we all know he would oppose it, if he saw it manifested." Brown said that it was wise for Negroes to be cautious about proposals for them to emigrate; "but," he contended, "when such a movement as this by the Haytian government is inaugurated, and taken up by people here, we ought to do them justice, and give justice to those who are interested in the movement here."

Before the meeting was adjourned, Garrison spoke again

11. *Liberator*, July 5, 1861, p. 107, July 12, 1861, p. 111, July 26, 1861, p. 119.

briefly and earnestly. Said he to the Negroes present, "I would not have you leave this country on any account; and yet, I admit, it requires almost or quite an apostolic self-sacrifice for you to remain." Nevertheless he said emphatically that instead of emigrating, Negroes should remain in America and continue in the crusade against slavery and other kinds of racial injustice.[12] Clearly, if he did not specifically oppose Haitian immigration, it was because he did not favor any kind of mass emigration of Negroes from America.

Brown had recently written two narratives for the *Pine and Palm*. One of these was an account of Nat Turner and his insurrection of August, 1831, in Virginia. The other was an account of Madison Washington and the mutiny on the *Creole*, a coastwise steamer, early in November, 1841. These narratives were published under the heading "Celebrated Colored Americans" on the second page of the newspaper for August 3 and 17 respectively.

During the first three or four days of November, 1831, while Turner was in prison awaiting trial, Thomas R. Gray, his court-appointed quasi-counsel, interviewed him at least three times and recorded verbatim, Gray said, what Turner voluntarily told about his early life and about his insurrection. Early in the following December, Gray published in Baltimore a pamphlet of twenty-three pages entitled *The Confessions of Nat Turner, the Leader of the Late Insurrection in Southhampton, Va.* Fifty thousand copies of this pamphlet were printed, said the *Liberator* for December 17. This work has remained the principal source of information about Turner and his insurrection. Before the end of 1831 a pamphlet on the same subject was published in New York. This one was entitled *Horrid Massacre. Authentic and Impartial Narrative of the Tragical Scene Which Was Witnessed in Southhampton County (Virginia) on Monday the 22nd of August Last.* Also, there appeared in the *Atlantic Monthly* for August, 1861, Thomas Wentworth Higginson's

12. *Ibid.*, August 9, 1861, p. 127.

"Nat Turner's Insurrection," an article much longer and much better written than Brown's. Higginson had never seen Gray's pamphlet, but he owned a copy of the one which had been published in New York. He had drawn upon that, "But the greater part of the facts which I have given," he said, "were gleaned from the contemporary newspapers."[13]

Unless Brown saw Higginson's article in manuscript, he could not have seen it at all before his own was published. Whether he had seen either Gray's or the New York pamphlet is uncertain, but he had read the *Anglo-African Magazine* regularly and most probably was directly indebted to the version of Gray's pamphlet which had been published in the number of that periodical for December, 1859. The first and last thirds of Brown's article are rather unskillful condensations of parts of his source. The middle third consists of a quotation from Gray's version of Turner's confessions. Nowhere in the article was Brown critical of Gray's pamphlet, as he might well have been since Gray's was the work of a man who doubtless felt much more obligated to be loyal to slaveholders than considerate of Turner. Brown's last four paragraphs, which are very brief, reminded his readers that such uprisings as Nat Turner's taught an important lesson concerning the human will to freedom—that, thanks to thirty years of free discussion of slavery, public opinion in the North was now more sympathetic toward such uprisings than it was in 1831, and that the war which had recently begun in the United States afforded an opportune occasion for the coming forth of another Nat Turner.

The article on Madison Washington and the mutiny on the *Creole* is shorter and less informative than the one on Turner and his insurrection. The most probable reason for this fact is that not much information about Washington and the mutiny was

13. *Ibid.*, December 17, 1831, p. 202; Benjamin Brawley, *A Social History of the American Negro* (New York, 1921), pp. 406–07; Thomas Wentworth Higginson, "Nat Turner's Insurrection," *Atlantic Monthly*, 8 (August, 1861): 185.

available to Brown. During the first two months after the mutiny, two articles about it from the *New York Journal of Commerce* had been reprinted in the *Liberator*. Only the second of these articles, which was originally an editorial in the *New York Evangelist*, referred to Washington by name. In Julia Griffiths' *Autographs for Freedom* for 1853, Douglass had published a stilted story of Washington under the title "The Heroic Slave." Although the case of the *Creole* had remained a subject for argument between the United States and Great Britain for more than a decade, Washington himself seems to have been lost in obscurity within a short time.[14]

Brown adapted the facts known about Washington's life before the mutiny into a more or less conventional story of a slave who escaped to Canada, returned to Virginia to get his wife, and was recaptured and sold to be taken to the deep South. Brown gave but few details about the mutiny itself and none about the slaves involved in it after they disembarked at Nassau and were liberated. Nor did he remind his readers of the significance which the story of Washington and the mutiny had in common with the story of Nat Turner and his insurrection. He included, however, an account of a fortuitous reunion of Washington and his wife at breakfast on the *Creole* on the morning after the mutiny. It was the same kind of chance reunion, whether actual or only imaginary, by which the stories of George Green and Mary and Jerome Fletcher and Miralda were made to end happily.

14. *Liberator*, December 24, 1841, p. 206, January 7, 1842, p. 1; Julia Griffiths, ed., *Autographs for Freedom* (Boston, 1853), pp. 174–239.

XXII

An Odyssey without Splendor

Early in August, Brown set out on a trip to Ontario—probably his first trip there since 1843. The *Liberator* for July 26 had informed its readers that he intended to spend "a few weeks in Canada, and will lecture at Toronto, and other important places, on the elevation of the colored population."[1] He went, however, primarily as a field agent in the interest of Haitian immigration.

En route to Toronto, Brown stopped in Troy, New York, and delivered a lecture on Haiti. The "Conclusion" to his lecture was published "by request"—whether his or somebody else's is not known—on the fourth page of the *Pine and Palm* for August 31. Most of this conclusion, which fills almost two newspaper columns, is a verbatim selection of passages from the latter half of his *St. Domingo: Its Revolutions and its Patriots.*

1. *Liberator*, July 26, 1861, p. 119.

This fact suggests that the major part of the lecture was a partial repetition of the first half of the work just mentioned. Indeed it would have been unlike Brown to prepare a new lecture on Haiti when his old one a little remodeled would have done just as well. In the last third of the conclusion, Brown turned to "the present prospects of the Republic of Hayti." He promised not to make "an appeal in favor of emigration," but he did propose "to lay before you merely the advantages which that Government in its liberality holds out to all colored persons to become citizens, and to share with them the blessings of liberty."

Brown was in Ontario from the second week in August until the middle of October. During that time he lectured and held emigration meetings in cities and towns from Toronto westward to Windsor. He recorded his experiences and observations in these places in seven articles entitled "The Colored People of Canada" and published them severally in the *Pine and Palm* for September 7, 14, 21, and 28, October 19, November 30, and December 7. He spent the middle third of August in Toronto, whence he dispatched to Redpath two reports of his activities in that city in behalf of Haitian immigration. The first report was discouraging because he had at first found little or no interest among the Negroes of the city in emigration. The second report, however, was quite optimistic because he had succeeded meanwhile, he thought, in stimulating considerable interest in Haitian immigration.[2]

From Toronto, Brown went to Hamilton and thence to Saint Catharines. Having long been an important terminus on the Underground Railroad, Saint Catharines had become the center of a community of prosperous Negro farmers. Brown arrived there on August 23, and during a sojourn of several days, he lectured four times. Principally because of his efforts, many Negroes in the community seemed to have become interested in immigrating to Haiti, but most of them were prevented from do-

2. *Pine and Palm*, August 31, 1861, p. 4, September 14, 1861, p. 4.

ing so because they owned property which they could not sell advantageously.

If Brown was inclined to forget that there was nothing in a name, he was emphatically reminded that there was not when he visited London, about a hundred miles west of Saint Catharines. It did not take him long to discover that this city was as different from the British metropolis of the same name as Beelzebub was from his former self when he awaked at the bottom of the nether world. The physical features of the city were, of course, immediately obvious to everyone; the spirit of the city soon became equally obvious to Brown while he tried to get on with the business for which he was there.

Prominent among the Negro citizens of London was an old acquaintance of Brown's. This was the Reverend L. C. Chambers, pastor of the Methodist church, one of the two Negro churches in the city. Upon the pastor's invitation Brown spoke at both the morning and evening services in the church on Sunday, September 1, "to a crowded house on both occasions." He lectured in the city again the following Monday evening and was accorded therefor a complimentary if somewhat belated report in the *London Daily Prototype* for September 7. According to that newspaper he had a large audience and his lecture was "very interesting."[3]

So disturbed was Brown by the anti-Negro sentiment he discovered in London, that he devoted almost all of his third article on the colored people of Canada to the discussion of race prejudice therein with special reference to London. Having for a long time heard the name Canada closely associated with the North Star and freedom, he was not prepared for the manifestations of race prejudice he encountered here and there in that country. He found, for instance, that as a rule white artisans refused to work on jobs with Negro artisans no matter how

3. *London* [Ontario] *Daily Prototype*, September 7, 1861, quoted in *Pine and Palm*, September 28, 1861, p. 4.

skillful the latter might be, and that hotels and inns either refused to accommodate Negroes or accorded them inferior accommodations. "Most of the towns have excluded the colored children from the schools," he said; and when he arrived in London, that city was about to follow suit. From the *London Free Press,* the "liberal paper of this section of Canada," he quoted an editorial which advocated the exclusion of Negro children from the public schools. He noted that the principal reason which the editorial gave for its point of view was the same as that which a mob had given for disrupting Prudence Crandall's school in Canterbury, Connecticut, twenty-eight years earlier, namely, that integration would produce "amalgamation."

Brown next visited Chatham, the quasi capital of fugitive slaves in Canada. He arrived there during the first week in September and kept his headquarters there several weeks. His fourth article on the colored people of Canada, which is the longest one in the series, deals with Negro life in Chatham. On the evening of September 6, he lectured in Chatham in the interest of Haitian immigration. The reaction to his lecture was sufficiently favorable to lead him to believe that several of the leading men of the community intended to immigrate to Haiti very soon. As he discovered before very long, however, he was much more optimistic about emigration from that community than he had reasons to be.

With his tongue in his cheek, Brown wrote at length about one of the local Negro physicians and leaders, who was also well known in the United States. Said he, "Dr. M. R. Delany, though regarded as a man high in his profession, is better and more widely known as a traveller, discoverer, and lecturer. His association with professor [*sic*] Campbell in the 'Niger Valley Exploring Expedition' has brought the doctor very prominently before the world, and especially that portion which takes an interest in the civilization of Africa." Characterizing Delany as both tactless and self-conceited, Brown quoted Delany's honors and titles from a handbill he said he had seen on which Delany himself had listed them along with an announcement that he would lecture on Africa. In summarizing his opinion of Delany, Brown said, "Considered in respect to hatred of the Anglo-Saxon, a stentorian voice, a violence of gestures, and a display of physical energies when speaking, Dr. Delany may be regarded as the ablest man in Chatham, if not in America."

On the date of the *Pine and Palm* containing Brown's remarks, September 28, Delany, who was then in New York, wrote a letter concerning them to the *Weekly Anglo-African.* His letter was published on the second page of that newspaper for October 5. Hitherto, he said, he had regarded Brown as a gentleman and a friend and was now writing only to correct what he considered Brown's several misrepresentations concerning him.

Beneath Delany's letter appeared an editorial entitled "Who Made Thee a Prince and Judge?" the title having been taken from Exodus 2: 14. The editorial accused Brown of ridiculing Delany because of "his association with some of the first Scientific and Literary Institutions in Europe"—because of his achievement of equality with some of the best white people. According to the editorial, Brown seemed to consider such an achievement impossible in America but possible in Haiti. Hence his advocacy of the immigration of Negroes to that country—something he was being paid to advocate. The editorial concluded with a reminder that Brown could ill afford to ridicule Delany for listing the honors he had received, since Brown himself had earlier publicized in antislavery newspapers the fact that in Paris he had shaken hands with de Tocqueville and his wife and with Victor Hugo. Apparently, by not replying to either Delany's letter or the editorial, Brown avoided a new newspaper controversy in which he would have been on the defensive.

About the middle of September, Brown visited the Buxton Settlement in Raleigh Township, about ten miles southeast of Chatham and near Lake Erie. This colony had been established in 1849 by the Reverend William King, an Anglo-Scotchman who had been born in Ireland and educated in Scotland, and who had lived for a while in northern Ohio, whence he had migrated to the South. While he was headmaster of a school in Jackson, Louisiana, he had married a local slaveholder's daughter. Upon the death of his wife and their only child, he had become the owner of his wife's slaves. These he had emancipated as soon as possible and had established them in the settlement, which he had also opened to other Negroes who could give evidence of good character and habits of temperance. Legal authority over the land had been vested in 1850 in a corporation called the Elgin Association, named for James Bruce, the Eighth Earl of Elgin, who was then governor-general of Canada. Soon afterwards, when King had a post office established in the settlement, he had named the postal station Buxton in memory of Thomas Fowell Buxton, the English abolitionist.[4] Thus the settlement had become known both as the Elgin and as the Buxton Settlement, but better known, perhaps, by the latter name.

In his account of his visit there, in his fifth article on the colored people of Canada, Brown called it the Elgin Settlement and apparently mistook Buxton for the name of the township. At the time of Brown's visit, King was not only still the sponsor of the settlement but also the pastor of one of its churches. To Brown, who spent some time as King's guest, King was "a kind-hearted and benevolent man, and deserves the respect and esteem of friends of freedom and justice everywhere."

According to Brown, in spite of King's philanthropic efforts, the Buxton Settlement had not become an ideal community as far as racial matters were concerned. Sometime before his visit, Brown said, the Negro voters in the township had become sufficiently influential to elect two of their number to the township council. Along with their political success had come the appointment of a Negro teacher for the district school, where-

4. Annie Straith Jamieson, *William King: Friend and Champion of Slaves* (Toronto, 1925), pp. 72–131.

upon the white parents had withdrawn their children from the school and had kept them out of it ever since. Apparently no questions concerning the efficiency of the teacher had been raised; the objections were all complexional. Presumably those parents were convinced, as some of their spiritual descendants in the southern United States still seem to be, that learning, whether the entity or the process, is somehow adulterated by pigmentation.

The next place Brown visited was the community of Dresden, about fifteen miles north of Chatham. Altogether unfavorable was his opinion of what he found at what had been Dawn Institute on the Sydenham River less than a mile from Dresden. This was the manual-labor school which had been founded about twenty years earlier by Josiah Henson. Although it had been generously supported by both British and American philanthropists, the institute had suffered so badly from mismanagement, if nothing worse, that it was no longer a school. In fact Brown found nothing of the school remaining except the three hundred acres of "beautiful and well cultivated land" which had once belonged to it. This land, Brown was informed, was "now in the hands of Mr. John Scoble, the superannuated secretary of the British and Foreign Anti-Slavery Society, London, England," and was being farmed by a son of Scoble's "for the sole use of his father." Brown doubtless remembered the elder Scoble as something less than a friend if not an avowed enemy during the preceding ten years. From the beginning he had been uncertain about Scoble's interest in either abolition or Negroes, and what he heard about the management of the Dawn property made him suspicious about both the father and the son. That his suspicion was well founded was proved by events of the next few years—events which, however, are no part of Brown's history.[5]

5. For an account of these events, see "*Uncle Tom's Story of His Life.*" *An Autobiography of the Rev. Josiah Henson*, ed., John Lobb (London, 1867), pp. 164–72.

Chapter Twenty-Two

By the end of September, Brown had transferred his headquarters from Chatham to Windsor on the Detroit River opposite Detroit, Michigan. Windsor was a well-known terminus of the Underground Railroad, but Brown found nothing especially noteworthy about it. Nor did he find much more to praise than to decry in Amherstburg, a town on the Detroit River eighteen miles south of Windsor and long a receiving station on the Underground Railroad. In his opinion, however, Colchester Township on the shore of Lake Erie about eight miles southeast of Amherstburg was "the warmest section of Canada, and the land here, is the best I have yet seen." To him it was indeed a land of wonders—or a subject for hyperboles. "Sweet potatoes of good size," he averred, "pumpkins three feet high, and watermelons two feet long, are all brought to perfection in this climate." One of the colored persons who he said owned farms in the township was Joseph Mason, whom he identified as an ex-slave and son of ex-Governor Mason of Virginia. Although the people in the township were apparently in good circumstances, many of them seemed to Brown "anxious to make their homes in Hayti, for the benefit of their children."[6]

Late in October, Brown submitted to Redpath a report on "my labors" from September 29 to October 18. This report, which was first published on the first page of the *Pine and Palm, Supplement* for January 2, 1862, told briefly of Brown's lectures from September 29 to October 4 inclusive to large audiences in Refugee House near Windsor and in Amherstburg and Colchester. It also told of his return to London, Hamilton, and Toronto early in October "to facilitate the departure of emigrants from those places." He arranged for the emigrants to form a group in Toronto, and he himself returned to Cambridgeport.

Brown probably wrote his sixth and seventh articles on the colored people of Canada while he was still in Ontario, but the sixth was not published until more than a month after he re-

6. *Pine and Palm*, December 7, 1861, p. 2; *Pine and Palm, Supplement*, January 2, 1862, p. 1.

turned home, and the seventh not until still later. In the sixth article he did not talk about specific places he had visited and persons he had met. Instead he returned to the consideration of how Negroes in Canada were victimized by race prejudice—the subject to which he had devoted almost all of the third article in his series. He observed that Negro immigrants were often overworked and underpaid by "the mongrel whites, half French, Indian and Spanish on the one side, and Irish, Scotch, German and English, on the other," who, nevertheless, called themselves natives. He dwelt at length on how "a set of land speculators, under the guise of philanthropy, owning larg tracts of wild, heavy timbered, and low, wet land, which has been purchased for a shilling an acre, or thereabouts," managed to make illiterate Negroes pay several times for farms before they received clear titles to them. He identified the Benevolent Land Association as one of the groups engaged in such exploitation, apparently in collusion with certain lawyers. He also said that Negroes suffered at the hands of "political jugglers." When after an election, he was informed, it was found that Negro residents of the Refugee Home lands held the balance of power in their district, the property qualification for voting was so maneuvered that they were disfranchised. "The more I see of Canada," Brown concluded, "the more I am convinced of the deep-rooted hatred of the negro here."

In his seventh article, which told mainly of his visits to Amherstburg and Colchester, Brown commented favorably on the morals and half-seriously on some of the mores of the colored people of Canada. "Everywhere," he said, "the whites testify to the high moral standing of the colored people; and this is the more commendable from the fact that so many of them are from slavery, where there is no inducement for them to be chaste and virtuous." He was favorably impressed by their abstention from the use of intoxicants, but he was humorously critical of the smoking and chewing of tobacco which he said were all too common among men, women, and children.

Since Brown went to Ontario in the interest of the movement for Haitian immigration, presumably he intended for his articles to contribute to that movement. Thus he might have had a two-fold reason for speaking unfavorably of Canada as he did in his third and sixth articles. Perhaps in addition to telling the truth as he saw it, he made the most of the opportunity to portray Canada as less of a haven for Negroes than Haiti seemed to be.

Aside from any ad hoc purposes Brown might have had in writing them, these articles have remained valuable for other reasons. They constitute a pioneering study in regionalism—in this instance the analysis of the status of a small regional class. Needless to say, Brown was not a professional social scientist. He was, nevertheless, a careful observer of people and their ways, and he possessed sufficient common sense and insight to comprehend what he saw. As he traveled from one community to another, he observed Negroes as a class with regard to population, economic conditions, religion, education, morality, etc. and endeavored to record and interpret his observations systematically.

Because the vast majority of Negroes in Canada lived in southern Ontario, Brown had limited his tour, but not the title of his series of articles, to that area. Consequently the title he gave the series is far more inclusive than is justifiable. For the sake of accuracy he might well have entitled it "The Colored People of Southern Ontario." Although these articles are here and there sketchy, superficial, and wanting in objectivity, they have preserved a segment of enlightening as well as interesting local history which otherwise might have been lost in oblivion.

By the time Brown finished his tour of Ontario, he had discovered that there was increasing opposition in the province to the movement for Haitian immigration. Most prominent among its opponents was Mrs. Mary Ann Shadd Cary of Chatham, whom Brown had characterized in his fourth article as "the most intelligent woman I have met in Canada." Mrs. Cary wrote at least three letters in criticism of the movement to the *Weekly*

Anglo-African. These were published severally in the numbers of that newspaper for October 19 and 26 and November 9. To Mrs. Cary the movement was only a recrudescence of the old colonization scheme in a new guise, the promised land now being what she described in her second letter as "an island where six hundred thousand people now revel in worse than heathen superstition, make 'sacrifices to the God that gives them rain,'—practice polygamy, and die both natives and emigrants in frightful numbers with malignant fevers." She suspected that the ultimate aim of the movement, as of the old scheme, was to rid North America of free Negroes, "the disgraceful work in which Clay and Webster failed." She accused Redpath and especially his Negro agents, whom she called Judases, of misrepresenting the situation in Haiti and thereby inducing unsuspecting Negroes to immigrate there. In referring to some of the agents by name, she threw a rosy brick at Brown by saying that "Mr. Brown did not utterly disregard the twinges of conscience in his advocacy" of the movement, although he had overtaxed the credulity of the people of Chatham with an account of the enormous sizes to which sweet potatoes grew in Haiti. Following Mrs. Cary's second letter was an editorial comment expressing doubt concerning the wisdom of the movement.

Brown returned home from Ontario just in time to encounter mounting opposition in Boston to Haitian immigration. According to a report on the front page of the *Weekly Anglo-African* for November 16, antiemigration meetings were held in the city on October 16 and 23. At both of these meetings John A. Coleman, who "with what remains of his family" had recently returned from Haiti, spoke quite unfavorably of conditions there. Coleman's testimony was corroborated by that of Jacob R. Andrews, who had recently returned from a visit to Haiti. Brown was present at the second meeting. He "plead [*sic*] well for Mr. Redpath and his cause," said the report in the *Weekly Anglo-African*, "but Boston refused to hear or even believe that his heart was in his speech." Especially notable because of its wording was the first of four antiemigration resolutions which were introduced during the second meeting. It proposed that "certain intelligent, but misguided colored men and white men" who were trying to promote Haitian immigration be regarded with suspicion and their counsel deprecated. Another of the resolutions opposed the emigration of Negroes from America until after the abolition of slavery. After being ably supported by Robert Morris, the Reverend Leonard A. Grimes, and others, all of the resolutions were adopted.

Whether his heart was in his speeches or not, Brown continued to travel and lecture during the next two months in the interest of Haitian immigration. He spent the first half of November lecturing in towns in eastern New York. He had a very small audience in the A. M. E. Zion church in Poughkeepsie on the evening of November 6. In a letter dated November 20, a local correspondent for the *Pine and Palm* who identified himself as "A Friend to Humanity" blamed the darkness of the night for the small attendance at the lecture.[7] Brown, said the same correspondent, "gave us a history of his life, and a history of his tour of Hayti, and the advantage of those who go, over those that will remain in the United States to be trodden under foot by the white man." On the day after his lecture, while still in Poughkeepsie, Brown sent Redpath an optimistic but general report of his recent activities in eastern New York. He said that in all of the towns he had visited—thus far he seems to have visited only Fishkill Landing, Newburgh, Baxtertown, and Poughkeepsie—"I gained the interest of the right kind of persons in favor of Hayti."[8]

Brown's lecture in the A. M. E. Zion church in Poughkeepsie on November 6 interested his audience enough for them to invite him to lecture again in the same church a week later. At that time he addressed "a large audience" on "Revolutions of Hayti

7. *Pine and Palm,* November 3[2], 1861, p. 3, November 9, 1861, pp. 3 and 4; *Pine and Palm, Supplement,* January 2, 1862, p. 2.

8. *Pine and Palm,* November 30, 1861, p. 4.

or San Domingo." Thus reported "A Friend to Humanity," who said that Brown delivered the second lecture on November 13. Brown himself said in a letter he wrote from Boston on December 9 to Redpath that he delivered the second lecture on November 16, and that he held a second meeting with "a large attendance" in a Baptist church in Newburgh on the seventeenth.[9] Since the correspondent wrote his letter a few days after the second lecture in Poughkeepsie, and Brown did not write his until almost a month afterwards, the former is more likely to have given the correct date of the lecture than the latter. This is especially probable since Brown had held meetings and had lectured in many places in the meantime and therefore might have confused the dates of some of his lectures.

There appeared on the second page of the *Pine and Palm* for December 14 a sort of by-product of Brown's tour of eastern New York. This is his article entitled "Colored People of the Empire State." It is similar to his articles on the colored people of Canada but inferior to the several installments in that series. The title is extravagantly comprehensive for the subject matter under it. The first part of the article consists of two paragraphs of generalizations about the history of Negroes in New York—generalizations which are too broad to be very enlightening. The remainder, which amounts to more than two-thirds of the article, deals with three towns in the Hudson Valley—Newburgh, Fishkill Landing, and Baxtertown. The comments on these places are neither extensive nor thorough enough to arouse the reader's curiosity, not to speak of satisfying it. On the whole the article is possessed of considerably more ephemeral interest than of any other kind of value.

After his tour of eastern New York—principally of the Hudson Valley—Brown went to New Jersey to continue his efforts to promote Haitian immigration. During the week of November 19–25, he had engagements for seven meetings in six different

9. Brown to Redpath, December 9, 1861, *Pine and Palm, Supplement,* January 2, 1862, p. 1.

cities and towns in the state, notably in Newark, Paterson, Princeton, and as far south as Mount Holly. In all of these places, he assured Redpath in his letter of December 9, "the meetings were well attended, and the people seem interested in the cause of emigration."[10]

Having lectured in Paterson on November 20, Brown lectured there again on the twenty-seventh. The *Paterson Daily Guardian* for the twenty-eighth briefly but favorably noticed his speech, reporting that he had "a large audience of our colored population," and that he "presented the emigration movement in a favorable light."[11] As Brown informed Redpath in his letter of December 9, at the conclusion of his lecture an emigration club was formed, "and twenty-six names were at once given in. Those who joined in the club," he explained, "were amongst the most industrious and influential persons of Paterson, the Rev. Mr. Scudder, the presiding minister of the Zion Methodist church, being one of them."

Brown lectured in a Congregational church in Paterson on the evening of December 6, this time not on Haiti but on "Wit and Humor." After noting that he had "an appreciative audience" without referring to its size, the *Paterson Daily Guardian* for the following day remarked that "We do not hazard anything in saying that those who failed to attend, lost one of the richest treats of the season." The lecture, the newspaper also reported, was "full of hits and amusing reflections on affected and hypocritical foibles." When it was concluded, several gentlemen in the audience engaged "the talented gentleman" to repeat the same lecture or give another one in Continental Hall during the forthcoming Christmas holidays.[12]

Within the next two days Brown returned to Cambridge-

10. *Pine and Palm*, November 16, 1861, p. 3, November 23, 1861, p. 3; *Weekly Anglo-African*, November 30, 1861, p. 2; *Pine and Palm, Supplement*, January 2, 1862, p. 1.

11. *Paterson* [New Jersey] *Daily Guardian*, quoted in *Pine and Palm*, December 7, 1861, p. 3.

12. *Paterson* [New Jersey] *Daily Guardian*, December 7, 1861, quoted in *Pine and Palm*, January 9, 1862, p. 3.

port after an absence of more than a month from the city. In due time, however, he went back to Paterson to keep his holiday lecture engagement there. The *Paterson Daily Guardian* for December 24 announced on its third page that Brown would deliver a lecture in Continental Hall on Christmas Day at three o'clock in the afternoon—"an humorous and highly entertaining lecture, calculated to send everybody away with a broad grin however ruefully they appear on entering." Brown was no Artemus Ward, the newspaper admitted, "but a regular genius in his way and worth your while to study as a character. We have heard this Brown and can certify to the fact that he is a 'GOOD EGG.'" His program was to consist of "classical, humorous and sentimental recitations." Apparently it was not to consist of a lecture at all. A "Grand Concert, comic and sentimental, under the direction of Mr. Charles Atherton, assisted by the best amateurs in the city," was to be presented in the same hall at seven o'clock in the evening, and Brown was expected to fill the "intervals between the pieces" of the concert with individual presentations. The same newspaper for December 26 reported, again on its third page, that Brown's "suddenly acquired popularity in this place, secured him a good audience yesterday afternoon. . . . His hearers gave abundant evidence of their pleasure, and the speaker was greeted after his performances were ended, and personally introduced to many of our citizens. He has a noble intellect, and considering the disadvantages under which he has risen to his present position, [he] deserves commendation."

Writing from Paterson on December 30 to the *Weekly Anglo-African*, a correspondent who called himself "Occasional" said that "In my last I informed you of the formation of a Haytian Emigration club; now I have the pleasure of recording its utter disbandment. The common sense of the people here arrays them against the scheme heartily and universally, and if Mr. Redpath or his mercenaries want to speculate on colored people, they will have to go elsewhere."[13]

13. *Weekly Anglo-African,* January 11, 1862, p. 4.

Chapter Twenty-Two

As Brown must have been aware by this time, the movement for Haitian immigration was doomed to failure almost from its beginning by several circumstances. From the beginning many people suspected it of being nothing more than the old, discredited colonization scheme disguised, and nothing had occurred in the meantime to allay their suspicion. Rather, the interest manifested in the movement by former supporters of colonization, together with the mystery that surrounded its financing, had increased suspicion concerning it. From the testimony of an increasing number of emigrants who had returned from Haiti, it appeared that that country was not the paradise it had been said to be. Moreover, by the end of 1861 it was becoming more and more evident that the Civil War would not be a brief, inconsequential episode in American history, but indeed a long and difficult struggle between liberty and despotism, and that it was to the best interests of Negroes to remain in America, join in the struggle, and do all that they could to insure the victory for liberty. Because of these circumstances, although Brown's efforts in behalf of the movement were persistent and extensive, inevitably his wanderings in quest of Haitian immigrants became only an odyssey without splendor.

XXIII

Freedom for Victory

BROWN HAD AN ENGAGEMENT TO LECTURE IN THE MEIONAON in Boston on Sunday evening, January 12, 1862, on "The Black Man's Future in the Southern States"—an engagement which he presumably filled. By the middle of February he was again touring the Hudson Valley, this time principally as a lyceum lecturer. On the twenty-sixth, according to the *National Anti-Slavery Standard* of ten days later, he delivered "his new Lyceum Lecture, on 'Life in the Southern States' " in the A. M. E. Zion church in Poughkeepsie. It was the same church in which he had lectured twice during the preceding November.[1]

An announcement in the *Poughkeepsie Daily Eagle* for March 11 said that Brown would repeat his new lecture in the local Universalist church on March 12 and urged the public to

1. *Pine and Palm,* January 9, 1862, p. 3; *Liberator,* January 10, 1862, p. 3; *National Anti-Slavery Standard,* March 8, 1862, p. 3.

attend the lecture, assuring them that it would be an occasion for both "Fun and Benevolence." It would present, said the announcement, "the humorous side of slavery on a Southern plantation"—which was certainly something less than Brown intended to portray. The net proceeds from the lecture were to be given to the "Contrabands"; hence "Those wishing to laugh and do good at the same time" were especially invited to be present. A report in the same newspaper for March 13 said that "The lecture of W. Wells Brown, last evening at the Universalist Church, on 'Fun and Benevolence' was well attended and highly applauded by those present, who went home apparently well satisfied with their evening's entertainment."[2]

The *Daily Eagle* mistook for the title of the lecture a phrase which the newspaper itself had used in its announcement of March 11. Since the proceeds from the lecture were intended for a charitable cause, the occasion afforded its patrons an opportunity for fun and benevolence; but "Fun and Benevolence" was not the title of the lecture. The title, which the *National Anti-Slavery Standard* had quoted almost correctly as "Life in the Southern States," was actually "Life at the South." This, of course, was not a new title; nor was the lecture really a new lecture, but most probably a dramatic reading adapted from *The Escape*. In an article entitled "Tour of William Wells Brown," the *Liberator* for April 4 said that Brown had complied with a request that he "give a reading of his new Drama on 'Life at the South' " in Poughkeepsie, but this newspaper incorrectly reported that he had given after March 12 what was actually his second reading of the work in the city within a month.

In compliance with a request from his audience of March 12, Brown delivered a free lecture in the Universalist church on Monday evening, March 17. His subject was "What ought to be done with the Traitors and the Slaves." The *Daily Eagle* for the next day said that the lecture "was attended by a very large audience." Brown, the newspaper explained, "thought the diffi-

2. *Poughkeepsie Daily Eagle*, March 11, 1862, March 13, 1862.

culty in settling our national difficulties was not so much what to do with the slaves as what to do with the masters. He argued that the rebellion could never be suppressed until slavery was abolished and he complimented President Lincoln's message proposing gradual emancipation."[3]

The presidential message which Brown had complimented was Lincoln's message of March 6 to Congress. The proposal it contained was so indefinite that it might well have been taken to mean almost anything to almost anybody. The best that even the most optimistic abolitionists could see in it was, in the words of Wendell Phillips, "one more sign of promise."[4] It must have been surprising to many of Brown's contemporaries, therefore, that he found the message worthy of a high compliment.

Brown was at home again before the end of March. He witnessed, if he did not actually participate in, two literary programs given by the Union Progressive Association of Boston in the Joy Street Church on March 24 and 25. The purposes of these programs were respectively to raise funds to increase the association's library and to benefit "the fugitives in Kansas." Brown also had an engagement to lecture in the city hall in Charlestown on Sunday evening, March 30, on "What shall be done with the Traitors, and what shall be done with their slaves?"[5]

In December, 1861, a bill was introduced in the United States Senate proposing the immediate abolition of slavery in the District of Columbia. While this bill was pending, several unsuccessful attempts were made to saddle it with an amendment by which $100,000 would be appropriated for the president to use in colonizing somewhere outside the United States the already free Negroes in the district and those who would be set free by the bill, whether they wanted to be expatriated or not. As the bill was passed by Congress in April, 1862, and signed by Lincoln

3. *Ibid.*, March 13, 1862, March 17, 1862, March 18, 1862.

4. *The Collected Works of Abraham Lincoln*, 9 vols., ed. Roy P. Basler (New Brunswick, N. J., 1953–55), 5: 144–46; *Liberator*, March 14, 1862, p. 42.

5. *Liberator*, March 28, 1862, p. 51, April 4, 1862, p. 54.

on the sixteenth of that month, it authorized the expenditure of $100,000 for the colonizing of Negroes who might voluntarily accept colonization.

This scheme of colonization had no more to recommend it than did the old one. In fact Lincoln, who highly favored it, posited his point of view on the same false assumption which the American Colonization Society had long promulgated, namely, that Negroes and white people could not live together as equals in the United States. As might have been expected, therefore, this scheme was also opposed by Negro leaders. Typical of their opposition was that voiced by a "large number of the colored citizens of Boston" at a meeting in Twelfth Baptist Church on the evening of April 28. In a series of resolutions which were supported by Brown, the Reverend John Sella Martin, and others, the group opposed the colonization of Negroes in any territory set apart for them "either in the United States or elsewhere." With other abolitionists Brown had consistently opposed the old scheme of colonization; somewhat inconsistently he had espoused Redpath's abortive movement for Haitian immigration; but again consistently he now opposed the new scheme of colonization, which indeed was only the old one now under the aegis of the federal government.

Within three months Negroes in Boston found it necessary to hold another meeting of the same kind. On the evening of July 20, they assembled in the same church to voice again their opposition to colonization, because "certain influential colored men, connected with the Liberia Commission, had been of late quite active in endeavoring to impress members of Congress and others with the idea that the colored citizens of the United States have been favorably disposed towards Liberia [*sic*] colonization." After some discussion a committee consisting of Brown, William C. Nell, and three others was selected to publish a report of the anticolonization views of the assembly.[6]

6. *Collected Works of Lincoln,* 5: 370–75; *Liberator,* May 2, 1862, p. 71, August 1, 1862, p. 123, August 22, 1862, p. 133, August 29, 1862, p. 140.

Freedom for Victory

The twenty-ninth annual meeting of the American Anti-Slavery Society was held in New York on May 6 and 7. At the first day's morning session, which was held in the Church of the Puritans, Garrison presented Brown, explaining that the latter would answer two questions. The questions proved to be the same two that Brown had discussed several times during the preceding two months: What should be done with the slaves, and what should be done with the slaveholders?

With regard to the first question, Brown pronounced false the oft repeated assumption that some slaves would not appreciate liberty and could not take care of themselves if they were set free. Said he, "It has been clearly demonstrated, I think, that the enslaved of the South are as capable of self-support as any other class of people in the country." In proof of this fact he cited examples of slaves who, having hired their time from their owners, had earned and saved considerable amounts of money. He took some of his examples from the Reverend Dr. Nehemiah Adams's *A South-Side View of Slavery*, a well-known proslavery book. He also cited from Southern newspapers favorable comments concerning the thrift and industry of free Negro artisans in the slave states. Among these comments was one by John Catron of Tennessee, to which he had referred in his speech at Cooper Institute in New York in May, 1860. To Brown the testimony of Adams and Catron was especially convincing, because at best they could be considered only reluctant witnesses in behalf of either free Negroes or slaves. Most surprising of the examples Brown cited was one involving Stephen A. Douglas. This senator, Brown remarked—"a man who never lost an opportunity to vilify and traduce the colored man, and who, in his last canvass for a seat in the United States Senate, argued that the slaves were better off in slavery than they would be if set free, and declared that the blacks were unable to take care of themselves while enjoying liberty—died, a short time since, $12,000 in debt to a black man, who was the descendant of a slave."

Brown assured Northern white laborers that they had no need

to fear competition from emancipated slaves, for there was no prospect that emancipation would be followed by an exodus of freedmen from the South. The fact was evidenced, he said, by circumstances that prevailed in the South prior to the beginning of the war. In spite of the cruel laws against free Negroes in the slave states, many free Negroes had remained in those states, "Because they were unwilling to leave the congenial climate of the sunny South for the snowy hills of the rugged North." And he predicted that "what has kept the free colored people in the Southern States will prevent the slaves [from] coming here, if slavery is abolished." Individuals had fled to the North, he explained, because they could secure their freedom only by flight, but the vast majority of Southern Negroes would remain in the South, he was sure, if they could remain there and be free. With reference to the slaves' will to freedom, he ridiculed the threat of Robert Toombs of Georgia and other slaveholders to arm their slaves and turn them against the North. He did not doubt that Toombs and his compeers knew very well that such slaves would turn against the slaveholders and free themselves as soon as they could do so.

In answer to the second question, Brown said, "The only recommendation I have to make in regard to that is, that you shall take the slave from the slaveholder, and let the slaveholder go to work and labor for himself, and let him keep out of mischief." Brown concluded with the same optimistic expressions concerning the abolition of slavery with which he had ended his speech at Cooper Institute in May, 1860.[7]

On May 8, the day after the meeting in New York was adjourned, the Brown's daughter Clotelle was born in Cambridgeport. The baby was named by her father after the heroine of *Clotel*, but the spelling of the name was lengthened—and was thereby made a problem in orthography for the scribes who had to enter it a few times in official records. The local numerator for

7. *Liberator*, May 16, 1862, p. 77. Brown's speech was reprinted in the *Anti-Slavery Advocate*, July, 1862, pp. 535–37.

the only national census in which Clotelle lived long enough to be counted, the census of 1870, not only recorded the name as "Clotilde" but confused matters completely by listing the mother under that name and the daughter under the name "Annie G." Clotelle died in Cambridgeport on October 1, 1870, of typhoid fever and was buried in the Cambridge Cemetery. In the state registration of deaths, her name is recorded as "Clotilde" and in the index to that registration as "Clotisde."[8]

From the middle of May until late in the following summer, Brown lectured frequently in New England on what should be done with the slaves if they were emancipated. As might have been expected, he usually said the same things on the subject. From time to time, however, he varied his discussion with ideas which he considered especially pertinent for specific audiences or occasions. This he did at the evening session of the New England Anti-Slavery Convention in the Melodeon in Boston on May 28. On that occasion he began by refuting the doctrine of the natural inferiority of the Negro race—a doctrine espoused by many otherwise well-informed Americans and promulgated by such influential newspapers as the *Boston Courier*, the *Boston Post*, and the *New York Herald*. Brown argued that admittedly two and a half centuries of slavery had left American Negroes in a condition incomparable with that of white people, but that in earlier periods of history Negroes had been the leaders of civilization, as he had said in his review of Senator Yancey's speech in Boston in October, 1860. Finally he denounced "those Union-savers, speakers and writers, who say one word in favor of the

8. Massachusetts, 21st Registration, 1862, Births, vol. 151, Hampshire-Plymouth, p. 116, no. 666, State House, Boston, Massachusetts; Brown's dedication to his wife in his *Clotelle; or, The Colored Heroine* (Boston, 1867), p. [3]; U.S., Bureau of the Census, Ninth Census, 1870, Population, Massachusetts, vol. 12, Middlesex County, part 1, p. 206; Massachusetts, 29th Registration, 1870, Deaths, vol. 230, Hampshire-Plymouth, p. 111, no. 639, State House, Boston, Massachusetts; records in the office of the Cambridge Cemetery; *Boston Daily Evening Transcript*, October 4, 1870, p. 2.

Constitution and the Union and ten against the negro and his friends"—those who professed themselves lovers of the Union but who did not perceive or pretended not to perceive that the Union could not be saved without the abolition of slavery. He considered such individuals among the worst enemies of liberty in the Union.[9]

In a speech at the Massachusetts Anti-Slavery Society's celebration of July 4 in Framingham, Brown began by announcing that he was going to speak "concerning the black man's future in this country"—a subject which obviously involved consideration of the question as to what should be done with the freedmen after emancipation. In contrast to his point of view of a year earlier, he now advised Negroes against immigrating to Haiti, Jamaica, and the Danish West Indies even though they might be welcome in those places. Addressing himself specifically to the factory workers in Massachusetts, he repeated much of what he had said at the meeting of the American Anti-Slavery Society in New York in May. This time, however, he carried his argument further by predicting that the freedmen would remain in the South and become consumers of goods manufactured in the North, and consequently would increase the demand for factory workers by increasing the demand for consumers' goods. Thus their fredom would prove a boon not only to themselves, he was sure, but also to Northern factory employees. Two days later he had occasions to repeat much of what he said in Framingham in speeches in Feltonville and Marlboro.[10]

During the next few weeks Brown repeated this argument for labor many times, but he did not limit his speeches to it. At the Massachusetts Anti-Slavery Society's celebration of emancipation in the British West Indies in Abington on August 1, he said, in agreement with many others, that there now seemed "not to be a possibility of putting down the rebellion without

9. *Liberator*, March 14, 1862, pp. 41, 42, March 21, 1862, p. 45, May 23, 1862, p. 83, May 30, 1862, p. 87 June 6, 1862, p. 92, June 13, 1862, p. 96.

10. *Ibid.*, July 4, 1862, p. 107, July 18, 1862, pp. 114, 115.

giving the black man his freedom." He also voiced the opinion that if the federal government would proclaim emancipation and remove racial restrictions upon enlistment in its army, Negroes from both the North and the South would promptly as well as gladly join the army to fight for freedom.[11]

Most probably not many if any of the Garrisonian abolitionists yet knew that during a meeting on July 22, Lincoln's cabinet had discussed the recruiting of Negroes for military service, and that at the same meeting Lincoln had read to his cabinet the first version of his Emancipation Proclamation.[12] For all of the abolitionists it was indeed a time of generally uncertain waiting and hoping—until September 22. Lincoln's Preliminary Emancipation Proclamation of that date was much less than Brown and the other Garrisonians had hoped for, because it was fraught with contingencies. They accepted it, nevertheless, as still another sign of promise and endeavored to make the most of it.

Between October 19 and the end of the year, Brown had at least twenty engagements to lecture in Massachusetts, New Hampshire, New York, and New Jersey. His subject for all of these occasions was "The President's Proclamation, and its effect on the Slaves of the South, and the Laborers of the North." Needless to say, he expected the effect to be unquestionably wholesome for both classes. A Haverhill correspondent for the *Liberator* reported that on Sunday evening, October 26, Brown lectured in the Music Hall in that town "to a good house, notwithstanding the severe rain storm which began just on the eve of the meeting." Four evenings later, according to the same correspondent, Brown lectured in the new town hall in Haverhill to "a crowded and attentive audience." After a collection of approximately twenty dollars was taken, a gentleman who was a

11. *Ibid.*, July 25, 1862, p. 119, August 1, 1862, p. 123, August 15, 1862, p. 131; Garrison to Wendell Phillips Garrison, August 1, 1862, Anti-Slavery Letters Written by W. L. Garrison.

12. *Collected Works of Lincoln*, 5: 336–38.

manufacturer of shoes, and who had been most favorably impressed by Brown's lecture, had himself introduced to the speaker and shook five dollars "with his heart in it" into the latter's hand. Whatever Brown had said about the effect of the Emancipation Proclamation upon Northern laborers was evidently pleasing to that representative of capitalism. On the evening of November 6, the same correspondent informed the *Liberator*, "Mr. Brown again occupied the Town Hall, and gave us his literary and humorous entertainment, in aid of our Soldiers' Relief Society and the contrabands." As Brown had previously suggested, the society sponsored his program and charged an admission fee from which there was a profit of eighty dollars—forty for the society and forty for the relief of the contrabands.[13]

For some time Brown had been working on a new book—*The Black Man, His Antecedants, His Genius, and His Achievements.* By the end of the summer of 1862, he had progressed far enough with it to seek Gerrit Smith's aid in getting it published. In a letter of September 4 accompanied by a one-page prospectus of the work, he told Smith that "we think here [in Boston] that it is just the work needed for the hour, to place the Negro in a right position before the country, especially the working classes." After remarking that "I have spent in it what little I had and need more funds to bring it out," he strained the quality of tact by avowing that "I have never asked a donation for myself from any one, and do not ask it for myself now. If you feel," he continued, "that you can give me any assistance in getting out the book, I will send you enough copies to make the *advance* good, at least in paper." The prospectus contained the names of twenty-two biographees whom Brown had already

13. William Wells Brown to B. Cheever, October 14, 1862, Henry P. Slaughter Collection; *Liberator*, October 17, 1862, p. 167, October 24, 1862, p. 171, November 7, 1862, p. 179, November 14, 1862, p. 183, November 21, 1862, p. 187, November 28, 1862, p. 191, December 12, 1862, p. 199; *Herald of Progress*, December 27, 1862, p. 5.

selected, and it also said that sketches of twenty additional "well-known persons of color" would be included. In spite of the tone of the letter, an endorsement on it in Smith's handwriting shows that he responded with a contribution of five dollars—enough to pay for five copies of the book.[14]

As early as October 24, readers of the *Liberator* were apprised that the book would be published on December 1. Although the date in its imprint and copyright is 1863, the book was published early in December, 1862. A complimentary note in the *Liberator* for December 12 referred to it as a work "just published," and the *National Anti-Slavery Standard* for December 20 commented favorably upon it as a new publication.[15] An octavo volume of 288 pages, it was published jointly in New York by Thomas Hamilton and in Boston by R. F. Wallcut. In a preface of one and a half pages, Brown set forth the two purposes of the work. To refute the doctrine of the "natural inferiority" of the Negro, he explained, "and to supply a deficiency, long felt in the community, of a work containing sketches of individuals who, by their own genius, capacity, and intellectual development, have surmounted the many obstacles which slavery and prejudice have thrown in their way, and raised themselves to positions of honor and influence, this volume was written." Before addressing himself to his purposes, Brown devoted nineteen pages to an autobiographical "Memoir of the Author," sketching his life from his birth to his return from England to America in 1854, but giving no important new information about himself.

Brown sought to achieve his first purpose by means of an historical essay of twenty pages entitled "The Black Man and His Antecedents." Herein he again argued that the Negro race had not always been considered inferior, nor had the Anglo-

14. Brown to Smith, September 4, 1862, Gerrit Smith Miller Collection.

15. *Liberator*, October 24, 1862, p. 170, November 21, 1862, p. 187, December 12, 1862, p. 198; *National Anti-Slavery Standard*, December 20, 1862, p. 3.

Saxons always been the leaders of civilization, but that on the contrary there had been periods of history when Negroes were the leaders of civilization and when the Anglo-Saxons were slaves. In defending this thesis he reiterated with some additions what he had previously said on it on many occasions. With regard to the slaves' desire for freedom, their ability to take care of themselves as freemen, and their right to equality in American life, he repeated verbatim much of what he had said about these things in his speech of May 6 in New York. Referring several times to Lincoln by name in the essay, he ridiculed the president for espousing the doctrine of the inferiority of the Negro, as that executive had done in his conference with a deputation of Negroes on the preceding August 14.[16]

Near the end of the essay Brown repeated in substance what he had said on several occasions since the preceding spring against colonization and about the economic advantages to Northern industry the four million slaves would bring as freedmen and consumers. Finally he said, as he had said many times before and was to repeat many times afterwards, that by their industry, thrift, and patriotic activities in all of America's wars, Negroes had merited not only freedom but also all other rights possessed by other Americans.

The part of the book in which Brown endeavored to accomplish his second purpose is entitled "The Black Man, His Genius and His Achievements." This part, which amounts to more than four-fifths of the work, consists of biographical sketches of fifty-three persons generally classified as Negroes. The biographees. about two-thirds of whom were still living, were principally Americans and Haitians. Brown did not arrange the sketches in any specific order, unless it was the order in which he wrote them.

The first sketch is that of Benjamin Banneker (1731–1806), the Maryland mathematician, astronomer, and inventor. At the

16. *Collected Works of Lincoln,* 5: 370–75; *Liberator,* August 22, 1862, p. 133, August 29, 1862, p. 140.

time Brown was writing *The Black Man*, one of the two most easily available sources of information about Banneker was John H. B. Latrobe's *Memoir of Benjamin Banneker, Read Before the Maryland Historical Society, at the Monthly Meeting, May 1, 1845*, a pamphlet of sixteen pages, which had been published in Baltimore in 1845. The other source was *A Sketch of the Life of Benjamin Banneker; From Notes Taken in 1836. Read by J. Saurin Norris, Before the Maryland Historical Society, October 5th, 1854*, a pamphlet of twenty pages, which had been printed in Baltimore for the society soon after it was presented. Brown had long been familiar with Latrobe's pamphlet, but whether he had read Norris's is uncertain. Anyway he related nothing important about Banneker which was not in Latrobe's pamphlet, and he repeated most of the errors in it.

The second and third sketches are those of Nat Turner and Madison Washington, which had been published in the *Pine and Palm* in August, 1861. They were reprinted in the book with only minor changes. Incidentally, the sketch of Nat Turner is the longest one in the work.

Another insurrectionist whom Brown made the subject of a sketch was Denmark Vesey, the leader of the abortive insurrection in Charleston, South Carolina, in the summer of 1822. Contrary to his usual practice, Brown cited specifically the source of his information about Vesey. It was Thomas Wentworth Higginson's "Denmark Vesey," which had been published in the *Atlantic Monthly* for June, 1861. Brown quoted three passages from Higginson's article—two from Higginson himself and one which Higginson had quoted from Lionel H. Kennedy and Thomas Parker's *An Official Report of the Trials of Sundry Negroes, Charged with an Attempt to Raise an Insurrection in the State of South Carolina*, which had been published in Charleston in the fall of 1822. The three passages amount to half of Brown's sketch. Brown told much less about Vesey's personal life than Higginson had told. Rather he devoted most of his sketch to the insurrection itself—a fact which perhaps indicates that he was more interested in that than in biographical details.

Scattered through the series of sketches are those of seven Haitian leaders, including Toussaint L'Ouverture, Jean Jacques Dessalines, Henri Christophe, and Fabre Geffrard. Brown based these sketches principally on his *St. Domingo: Its Revolutions and its Patriots* and on the work to which this lecture was indebted, namely, the Reverend John R. Beard's *The Life of Toussaint L'Ouverture.* He also drew upon Redpath's *A Guide to Hayti* and possibly upon St. Amand's *A History of the Revolutions of Hayti,* which had been at least partially serialized in the *Pine and Palm* beginning with the number of that newspaper for October 5, 1861.

Brown commemorated Crispus Attucks and Phillis Wheatley, two of the most famous early American Negroes, in brief sketches which one wishes were much better than they are. He said little or nothing more about Attucks than Nell had said in his *The Colored Patriots of the American Revolution.* Doubtless he was hampered by the fact that extensive information about Attucks had not yet been discovered, but he was not at a disadvantage to the same extent with regard to Phillis Wheatley. Beginning in 1834, several editions of the *Memoir and Poems of Phillis Wheatley, a Native African and a Slave* had been published in Boston, and copies of it were relatively easily available especially in antislavery circles. The memoir, said its last paragraph, was the work of "a collateral descendant of Mrs. [John] Wheatley," Margaretta Matilda Odell, who since her childhood had been "familiar with the name and fame of Phillis." Since its first appearance this memoir has been the principal authoritative source of biographical sketches of this poet. Whether Brown was familiar with it or not, he wrote quite sketchily and apparently incorrectly about Phillis Wheatley.

One of the distinguished American Negroes about whom Americans were still generally ignorant or misinformed when *The Black Man* was published was Ira Frederick Aldridge

(1807–67), the first great Negro Shakespearean actor. Brown's six-page sketch of the "African Roscius" did not dispel much of the ignorance about him, but it directed attention to him as a pioneer who had succeeded in spite of what seemed to be insurmountable difficulties. A third of the sketch of Aldridge is a review of his performance of Hamlet, which Brown said—apparently with some confusion of details—that he had witnessed while he was in England. A little less than half of the sketch consists of purely biographical details. Most of these Brown quoted almost verbatim from the anonymous and somewhat spurious *Memoir and Theatrical Career of Ira Aldridge, the African Roscius*, a pamphlet of twenty-eight pages, which had been published in London in 1848.[17]

As Brown must have known, nevertheless, a much more reliable source of information about Aldridge's life was already available. This was Dr. James McCune Smith's biographical sketch of the actor which had been published in the *Anglo-African Magazine* for January, 1860, and reprinted on the front page of the *Weekly Anglo-African* for October 5, 1861. Brown was well acquainted with Smith and had read regularly both the periodical and the newspaper. As he must also have known, Smith had been a boyhood friend of Aldridge, had kept in touch with him and his brother through the years, and was familiar with the history of the Aldridge family. It is surprising, therefore, that Brown relied upon the anonymous pamphlet and repeated some of its errors instead of following Smith's sketch.

Brown characterized Frederick Douglass in a sketch of only seven pages. He doubtless considered this comparatively brief sketch sufficient, because in his opinion Douglass was already more widely known than any other Negro then living "except, perhaps, Alexandre Dumas." Whether for the sake of variety or for some more elusive reason, Brown included the sketch of Joseph Jenkins which was originally chapter 28 of his *Sketches*

17. Brown quoted notably from pages 8, 9, 10, and 25 of this pamphlet.

of Places and People Abroad. Probably in deference to Aldridge, he changed his original designation of Jenkins as the "African Roscius" to the "African Talma," with reference to François Joseph Talma, the French tragedian. With the exception of this and one other minor change, he left the sketch unaltered, thus leaving Jenkins still in the shadowland between the real and the imaginary, and leaving the reader wondering whether this sketch belongs to the category of authentic biography.

Singular among the sketches in the book is the story entitled "A Man Without a Name." This is a fictionized account of Brown's own life to the time of his escape from slavery. The title was derived from the instance in which the Youngs peremptorily took the name "William" from him while he was a slave boy and gave him another name which he did not like. Being at least half-fictitious, this story is completely out of place in a series of factual sketches.

The last sketch in the book is that of Sir Edward Jordan of Kingston, Jamaica, a newspaper editor, public official, and statesman. An account of his life had been published on the first and second pages of the *Weekly Anglo-African* for November 24, 1860. Brown was doubtless indebted to that account.

Within a month after the *Liberator* and the *National Anti-Slavery Standard* favorably noticed *The Black Man, Douglass' Monthly* hailed it both as a good argument in support of Brown's two purposes and "as a valuable contribution to the colored literature of the country." Contrariwise, under the date February 22 in her journal, Charlotte L. Forten, then a young schoolteacher and writer, casually referred to the work as "Mr. Brown's silly book."[18] Incidentally Brown had included in the book a flattering sketch of Miss Forten, giving her more pages than he had given to Douglass.

A criticism of the book dated at Boston, January 31, and signed G. L. R. was published on the third page of the *Anglo-*

18. *Douglass' Monthly*, January, 1863, p. 771; [Charlotte L. Forten], *The Journal of Charlotte L. Forten* (New York, 1953), p. 171.

African, for March 7. The *Anglo-African* was the same as the *Weekly Anglo-African* with its title shortened. G. L. R. was probably George L. Ruffin, who was then a Boston barber with a profound interest in reading and writing, and who eventually became a lawyer and also a member of the Massachusetts legislature. G. L. R. confessed himself puzzled as to whether Brown had attempted too much or too little in the book. In his opinion Brown had included so many persons that he did not have space to give sufficient information about the most important ones, had included persons of only local distinction, and on the contrary, had omitted many whom he should have included.

G. L. R.'s criticism was in turn criticized by G. E. Stephens of Philadelphia in a brief article on the front page of the *Anglo-African* for March 28. Stephens suspected that the Boston critic had overlooked the purpose of the book and had been more displeased with the omissions than with the inclusions. Stephens complimented Brown for what he had done "with his limited material" and found the "intrinsic value of the work" in the fact that it publicized many previously unknown Negroes who had achieved remarkable success in spite of handicaps.

Similar in point of view to G. L. R.'s criticism but much more caustic was a review entitled "William Wells Brown's Book," signed by a writer who called himself Amigo, and published on the second and third pages of the *Pacific Appeal* of San Francisco for May 30. "This book," said Amigo, "comes far short of the truth, and is but a poor exhibit of the 'genius' of the black man." Then, after twitting Brown for giving "17 pages to himself and but 7 to Banaker [*sic*]," he dwelt repetitiously on Brown's failure to include in his book better sketches of more and better representative Negroes.

For a long time Brown was constrained to silence with regard to the adverse criticism *The Black Man* received—a silence which must have been considered golden in an era when newspaper controversies were so easily provoked. He did not essay an answer to his critics until July 21. On that date he wrote a letter to the *Anglo-African*, which was published under the heading " 'The Black Man' and Its Critics" in the number of that newspaper for August 8, and which filled three front-page columns. After announcing that the first edition of the book had been sold and that the sceond edition would be off the press "in a few days," he reminded his readers of its purposes and tried to explain why he had made it the kind of book it is. Only after he had considered various plans for the work, he said, had he "resolved to give a short essay on the Negro's antecedents, and a series of still shorter sketches of persons of genius and ability, without regard to past celebrity or notoriety in any manner. I never intended that the book should be considered as a history of our people, or as containing sketches of all our distinguished men, but selected such characters as suited me best to make a book for the *present crisis*."

To Brown "the great blunder" of those who had criticized the book so severely inhered in the fact that they seemed not to understand either its title or its preface. Thus they were misled, he thought, into criticizing "not what was in it, but what was out of it." On the contrary he admitted that if they had read it as thorough scholars and critics, they would have found enough errors in it to justify their giving it "a decent cutting up: for being engaged in travelling," he continued, "while it was going through the press, I did not get a last reading of the proofs, and the stereotyper made mistakes which mortified me exceedingly when the book was printed."

Brown signalized Amigo, whom he identified as William H. Yates, as the worst of the blundering critics. He considered Amigo ignorant not only of the scope of the book but also of what constituted intelligence and greatness. In reply to Amigo's criticism of the want of order in the arrangement of the sketches, he explained only in part convincingly that "sketches of individuals are seldom, if ever, put in alphabetical form; and as for date [*sic*] or merit, the first cannot always be found, and the latter must be decided by the reader." His statement concerning dates was indeed beyond question; but as he must have known, there had long been in print collections of biographical sketches arranged in alphabetical order, and in which relative merit was logically inferable from the amount of space given to the several biographees.

Finally Brown professed himself much less disturbed by the adverse criticism the book had received than pleased by the warm welcome it had been accorded by "the better educated" Negroes as well as by the press "generally throughout the country." To exemplify this welcome, he quoted some of what he called the "cheering words" *Douglass' Monthly* had spoken about the work. Yet being aware that some had found fault with many of the sketches on account of their brevity, he reminded his readers of the difficulty confronting anyone who attempted to write about Negroes, because the facts of Negro history were so generally inaccessible. Hardly in the best of spirits, he opined in a sort of envoy that "Any fool can find fault with a book, but a dozen cannot write one."

Still another comment on the book, one entitled "The Black Man," appeared in the second page of the *Anglo-African* for August 15. This one was signed by a man who called himself "Smith," and who vaguely gave his residence as New Jersey. Admitting that he had kept the book two months before reading it, Smith now adjudged it "the book for the times," as it had been advertised as being, and "undoubtedly deserving of a much wider circulation than it has hitherto received." Apparently he had not read Brown's statement in the *Anglo-African* of a week earlier concerning the selling out of the first edition and the publication of the second—a statement which indicated that the circulation had been at least appreciable. Smith considered the sketch of Joseph Jenkins "equal to the best efforts of either Dickens or Thackeray." Conversely he considered the sketch of Nat Turner "a rather crude compilation of the many interesting facts collected by the industrious author." He wished especially that Brown had discussed the credibility of Turner's confession, "which, however interesting it may be, is, after all, nothing more nor less than a slaveholder's version, or distortion, of a real confession or vindication that was never permitted to reach the ear of the world." With regard to who was included or omitted, he was critical only to the extent of remarking that Brown might have been wise to replace "A Man Without a Name" with a sketch of somebody with a name—for example, Mrs. Mary Ann Shadd Cary.

The second edition of *The Black Man*, revised and enlarged, was off the press at least by August 1. At an antislavery meeting in Abington on that date, Brown sold some copies of it.[19] There seem to have been three simultaneous issues of the second edition of the book, each with a different publisher's imprint. The first of these has the same imprint that the first edition has. The second has the imprint of James Redpath, Boston, and a picture of Fabre Geffrard as a frontispiece. The third issue has a dateless imprint saying that it was "Published for James Symms & Co., Savannah, Ga."

The most important change in this edition was the enlarging of the volume from 288 to 312 pages principally by the addition of four new sketches. The first of these tells about Joseph Carter, who emigrated from Barbados to Philadelphia about 1848, where he succeeded as a cabinetmaker and organ builder. The second tells about James Lawson, a contraband who rendered excellent intelligence service to the Union army in Virginia in 1862–63. The third and fourth sketches, entitled "Captain Callioux [Cailloux]" and "Captain Joseph Howard" respectively, are not biographical sketches. Rather they are a composite account of the heroic attack of the First and Third Louisiana Regiments on Port Hudson in May, 1863. Cailloux and Howard were officers in those regiments, and they figured prominently in the attack. In these two sketches, Brown endeavored to emphasize as well

19. *Liberator,* July 17, 1863, p. 114, August 7, 1863, p. 126; *National Anti-Slavery Standard,* September 5, 1863, p. 3.

as publicize the heroism of Negro soldiers, about whose ability and courage as fighters many were still doubtful.

According to an advertisement in the *Liberator* for November 27, Redpath had recently published a third edition of *The Black Man*. From its description in the advertisement, this seems to have been the same as the second issue of the second edition. When it appeared, the second edition with the joint Hamilton and Wallcut imprint was still being advertised, as it was in the *Liberator* at least until the end of the year. Finally a fourth edition of the work appeared with the date 1865. This one also has Geffrard's picture as a frontispiece but only Wallcut's imprint. Otherwise it is identical with the first issue of the second edition.

Years of Hopes and Fears

On January 1, 1863, an all-day meeting was held in Tremont Temple in Boston to celebrate the issuing of the Emancipation Proclamation. The meeting was sponsored by the local Union Progressive Association. At the opening session Brown read Lincoln's Preliminary Emancipation Proclamation of the preceding September 22 but did not comment on it then or in either of two brief speeches he made later in the meeting.[1] Early on January 2 he left Cambridgeport to keep an engagement to speak that evening at a proclamation celebration in the Bridge Street Methodist Church in Brooklyn, New York. Another of the speakers for that occasion was Theodore Tilton, managing editor of the *Independent* of New York.[2]

1. *Boston Daily Journal*, January 2, 1863; *Boston Evening Transcript*, January 2, 1863; *Anglo-African*, January 10, 1863, p. 2; *Liberator*, January 16, 1863, p. 12.

2. *Anglo-African*, December 27, 1862, p. 3, January 3, 1863, p. 3; *Independent*, January 8, 1863.

Brown remained in metropolitan New York at least a week and probably much longer in its vicinity participating in meetings and giving programs of his own. He had a small part in the "Great Emancipation Demonstration" which was held at Cooper Institute on the evening of January 5, and at which an interracial band's playing of "The Star-Spangled Banner" received "tremendous applause." According to a report in the *New York Daily Tribune* of two days later, "the great hall of the Cooper Union was crowded to its utmost capacity by an assembly of colored people from this city, and all the region about"; and also present were "a large number of the leading merchants, ministers, and lawyers of this city, who were scattered all over the audience, many of them glad to enjoy even a place to stand." The Reverend Henry Highland Garnet, who presided, and the Reverend George B. Cheever made the first and most extensively reported speeches of the evening. It was merely noted that Brown, Lewis Tappan, and a few others spoke.[3]

Before the end of January, Brown was again in Cambridgeport. He was one of the speakers at the Anti-Slavery Subscription Anniversary on the twenty-eighth and at the annual meeting of the Massachusetts Anti-Slavery Society the next day. Both of these meetings were held in the Music Hall in Boston. At the first one, although cognizant that the Emancipation Proclamation did not go as far as was desirable, Brown predicted that its ultimate result would be the complete abolition of slavery, and he expressed the hope that with freedom for the slaves would come equal citizenship for all. One kind of evidence of full citizenship, he asserted, was the right of all physically qualified men to serve in both state and national militias—a right which was still generally denied Negroes.[4]

As Brown might not have known on January 28, two days earlier Edwin M. Stanton, Secretary of War, had authorized

3. *New York Daily Tribune*, January 3, 1863, January 7, 1863, January 10, 1863; *Anglo-African*, January 3, 1863, p. 3.

4. *Liberator*, February 6, 1863, p. 22; *Anglo-African*, February 14, 1863, p. 1.

Governor John A. Andrew of Massachusetts, upon the latter's request, to organize a Negro regiment from that state. After some almost fruitless efforts to organize the regiment, Governor Andrew commissioned George L. Stearns of Medford—upon Stearns's suggestion, according to Frederic May Holland—to supervise the necessary recruiting. Stearns in turn employed several prominent Negroes as recruiting agents. Among these were Brown, Martin R. Delany, Frederick Douglass, the Reverend Henry Highland Garnet, John Mercer Langston, and Charles Lenox Remond. The Negro population of Massachusetts was too small to supply enough enlistees for a regiment; consequently the agents recruited enlistees wherever they could find them. Brown recruited not only in Massachusetts but also in New York, New Jersey, and Pennsylvania. As enlistees were obtained, they were sent to Camp Meigs at Readville, Massachusetts, for training. The group became known as the Fifty-Fourth Regiment of Massachusetts Volunteer Infantry. All of its commissioned officers were white—a fact which soon provoked some disagreement among abolitionists. By the first week in May, thanks to the diligence of the recruiting agents, more than the full complement of men for the regiment had become available. The surplus enlistees became the nucleus of the Fifty-Fifth Regiment of Massachusetts Volunteer Infantry.[5]

The annual New England Anti-Slavery Convention began in the Meionaon in Boston on May 28—the day on which the Fifty-Fourth Regiment sailed from Boston for duty in the Department of the South. At the evening session Brown briefly addressed the convention, rejoicing in the fact that the nation had at last awaked to the necessity of enlisting Negroes as soldiers.

The convention was continued the next day in Tremont

5. Luis F. Emilio, *History of the Fifty-fourth Regiment of Massachusetts Volunteer Infantry, 1863–1865* (Boston, 1891), pp. 2–24; Frederic May Holland, *Frederick Douglass: The Colored Orator*, rev. ed. (New York and London, 1895), p. 297; *Douglass' Monthly*, 5 (April, 1863): 820; William Wells Brown, *The Negro in the American Rebellion* (Boston, 1867), p. 209.

Temple. During that day's afternoon session, there was a discussion as to whether Negro officers were desirable for Negro regiments. Lieutenant-Colonel Billings of the first South Carolina Union Regiment said that "the universal feeling among the soldiers" of that unit was that they did not want Negro officers—that they did not want "a colored man to play the white man over them." Remond spoke of the difficulties he had had in recruiting because of the want of Negro officers. Douglass expressed the hope that such officers would be commissioned on the basis of merit. George T. Downing said that he favored the enlisting of Negroes and whites side by side and the selection of officers of merit "irrespective of color."

Like Remond, Brown testified that he had had difficulties in recruiting because some Negroes who could qualify for military service did not wish to be commanded wholly by white officers. He knew enlistees in the Massachusetts Fifty-Fourth Regiment, he said, who were not inferior to their white officers; and contrary to Billings's observations, he believed in the capacity of Negroes both to command as officers and to obey Negro officers. He considered his belief substantiated by the military success which had been achieved in Haiti under the leadership of Negro officers. Thus he avowed that while he now accepted as a half-loaf the admission of Negro soldiers only into the noncommissioned ranks of the army, he was determined to strive for the other half of the loaf—the commissioning of Negro officers. In spite of the disadvantages Negroes suffered because of race prejudice, he concluded, he would still urge Negroes to enlist in the Union army and would assist them in doing so.

Robert Morris contended that the Massachusetts Fifty-Fourth Regiment should not have been sent to the war zone without some Negro officers. He also explained that because commissions had been withheld from Negroes, he had done nothing and would do nothing to get enlistees for Negro regiments. Speaking frankly as he usually did, Garrison said that he considered Morris's point of view absurd, namely, "that because all that was just was not granted, therefore nothing should be taken." He agreed with Brown that the half-loaf should be accepted and that the struggle for the other half should be continued. He believed, of course, that merit would eventually bring commissions to Negro soldiers.[6]

During the next three months, Brown lectured in various places in Massachusetts and Maine principally on "The War and the Blacks Under Arms" and "The War and the Black Man." Such subjects were especially timely, since the intelligence service rendered by such contrabands as James Lawson, the heroic attack of the First and Third Louisiana Regiments on Port Hudson in May, and the gallantry of the Massachusetts Fifty-Fourth Regiment at Fort Wagner in July had refocused interest on the importance of Negroes in the fight for the Union and freedom.[7]

Meanwhile, from Cambridgeport on August 10, Brown wrote to William Still of Philadelphia a letter which threw considerable light on new developments in his personal interests. He inadvertently dated this letter July 10, but its correct date is ascertained by the following facts: Near its beginning he promised to send Still during the following week a copy of the second edition of *The Black Man*, which was not published until after July 21, the date of the writing of his " 'The Black Man' and Its Critics." Further on in the letter he conjectured that Still "no doubt felt like smiling as you read my article in [the] last 'Anglo' on the 'critics' "—meaning the article just mentioned, which was published in the *Anglo-African* for August 8.

Next there followed the most important part of the letter. "By the by," Brown remarked, "did you know that I have been for many years reading medicine? For the past three years, I have spent all my spare time with doctors and their lectures." While he was in England, he explained, Dr. John Bishop Estlin

6. *Liberator*, June 5, 1863, pp. 90, 91.

7. *Ibid.*, May 29, 1863, p. 87, June 5, 1863, p. 91, July 10, 1863, p. 111, July 17, 1863, p. 115, August 7, 1863, p. 126, August 14, 1863, p. 131; William Wells Brown to Samuel May, Jr., June 21, 1863, Sophia Smith Collection.

gave him some good books on medicine along with "much advice on the profession." He also revealed that for some time he had been giving medical advice and medicine gratis "to all my neighbors, who are green enough to ask it," and that he had recently cured some of his acquaintances of some more or less serious ailments, such as piles and scrofula. "Many of my friends," he said, "want me to adopt the profession, but I study for the love of it"—a love which he had brought out of slavery.[8]

But for some time yet Brown still had antislavery work to do. He had a considerable number of engagements for lectures principally in Massachusetts for the remainder of the year. For some of these lectures his subject was "The Rebellion and the Black Man"—only an old subject slightly reworded. For others it was "A General Emancipation Act."[9]

Early in 1864 Brown, along with several other prominent abolitionists, naively let himself get involved in a subtle maneuver of certain proslavery Democrats to portray both Republicans and abolitionists as advocates of miscegenation, and thereby to help to effect the defeat of Lincoln in the next presidential election.[10] During the last week of December, 1863, Brown and many other abolitionists in Boston and elsewhere received complimentary copies of an anonymous pamphlet of seventy-two pages entitled *Miscegenation: The Theory of the Blending of the Races, Applied to the American White Man and Negro.* It had been printed in New York by Dexter, Hamilton and Company, who listed themselves in its imprint as "General Agents for the Publishers." The date in the imprint is 1864, but the copyright date on the verso of the title page is 1863. The authors of the pamphlet were eventually identified as David Goodman Croly

8. W. Wells Brown to William Still, July [August] 10, 1863, Leon Gardiner Collection on Negro History.

9. *Liberator,* November 20, 1863, p. 187, December 11, 1863, p. 199, December 18, 1863, p. 203.

10. For an account of this maneuver, see Sidney Kaplan, "The Miscegenation Issue in the Election of 1864," *Journal of Negro History,* 34 (July, 1949): 274–343.

and George Wakeman. At the time of its appearance, Croly was managing editor of the antiabolitionist *New York World*, and Wakeman was a reporter for the same newspaper.

Truths, half-truths, traditions, and what appeared to be scholarly theories about races and civilization were so ingeniously blended in the work, that to the unwary it seemed to be not only a sound antislavery argument but also a serious, if impractical, proposal for the solution of the American race problem by means of miscegenation. Enclosed with the complimentary copies of the pamphlet were letters requesting the several abolitionists to send their opinions of it to the "Author of Miscegenation," in care of the publishers' agents. The hope of Croly and Wakeman was to entrap the abolitionists into committing themselves in favor of miscegenation so that their commitments could be used against them and the Republicans in the presidential campaign.

In a speech in Tremont Temple on January 1, 1864, at the celebration of the first anniversary of the Emancipation Proclamation, Brown voiced agreement with the theories set forth in the pamphlet; and soon afterwards he sent the authors a copy of his remarks pertaining to it. He also sent a copy of them to the *Anglo-African*, and they were published under the heading "Wm. Wells Brown on Miscegenation" in the number of that newspaper for February 6.

Most of Brown's remarks consisted of what he had repeatedly said on the authority of Hume and Macaulay concerning the history of the Britons and the Anglo-Saxons. By means of what he added to this, he plunged headlong into Croly and Wakeman's trap. Said he, "The blending of races is requisite to peace, goodfeeling and the moral, mental, and physical development of mankind. It breaks down caste and teaches the brotherhood of man." Then with a somersault in logic, he asserted that because of the prevalence of miscegenation in the South, albeit extralegal, race prejudice was not as great there as it was in the North. He opined that "At the North the negro has been kept at a distance, and the result is, the prejudice which exists in the Northern mind. This rebellion," he concluded, "will extinguish slavery in our land, and the negro is henceforth and forever to be a part of the nation. His blood is to mingle with that of his former oppressor, and the two races blended in one will make a more peaceful, hardy, powerful, and intellectual race, than America has ever seen before."

Two weeks after the publication of his remarks, Brown found himself in a somewhat embarrassing position. The genius of his embarrassment was Samuel Sullivan Cox, a Copperhead member of the United States House of Representatives from Ohio. On February 17 Cox spoke at length in the House against a bill to establish a bureau of freedmen's affairs. Early in his speech he inquired rhetorically as to whether the Republicans would rely upon "the new system, called by the transcendental abolitionists, 'Miscegenation,'" observing that this was "but another name for amalgamation." A few minutes later he exhibited a copy of Croly and Wakeman's pamphlet; and after reading from its title page and table of contents, he said by no means altogether truthfully that "The more philosophical and apostolic of the abolition fraternity have fully decided upon the adoption of this amalgamation platform. I am informed," he continued, "that the doctrines are already indorsed [*sic*] by such lights as Parker Pillsbury, Lucretia Mott, Albert Brisbane, William Wells Brown, Dr. McCune Smith (half and half-miscegen), Angelina Grimke, Theodore D. Weld and wife, and others."[11]

In reply to Croly and Wakeman's letters, all of the persons Cox mentioned in the passage last quoted had commented more or less favorably on the pamphlet, but Brown's was the only comment which had yet been published. Since Cox now frequently read the *Anglo-African*—during his speech he read a passage from the number for January 23—he had probably seen Brown's comment in the number of that newspaper for February 6, if indeed Croly and Wakeman had not already shown him

11. *Congressional Globe,* February 17, 1864, pp. 709, 710.

the originals which they had received from Brown and others. Brown and the other abolitionists who had sent favorable comments had proceeded more faithfully than cautiously and had thus facilitated their own betrayal by their political enemies. Fortunately, however, their embarrassment did not prove insuperable. In spite of the maneuvers of Croly, Wakeman, Cox, and their partisans to make miscegenation an issue in the presidential campaign of 1864, it never became sufficiently important to seriously threaten either abolitionism or the success of the Republican party.

Amid his activities of the last few months of 1863, Brown had found time to write the third version of his novel. This is entitled *Clotelle: A Tale of the Southern States.* It was copyrighted by James Redpath in 1864 and was published by him in Boston early in the same year, probably in February. It was simultaneously published in New York by Dexter, Hamilton and Company, the publishers' agents for *Miscegenation.*

Two advertisements of *Clotelle* appeared on the second page of the *National Anti-Slavery Standard* for February 20—one by Redpath himself and one by J. J. Spelman, a New York bookseller. There was also an advertisement of it in the *Liberator* for March 18 and in subsequent numbers of that newspaper. In all of these advertisements it was listed as number two in Redpath's series of "Books for the Camp Fires." Other works in the series were Louisa May Alcott's *On Picket Duty, and Other Tales,* Honoré de Balzac's *The Vendetta,* and Victor Hugo's *The Battle of Waterloo.* In the advertisement in the *Liberator,* Redpath described the series not only as books for campfires and "Just the books to read to soldiers" but also as "the cheapest books of value published" and "Equaly adapted to *home* fires."

Clotelle is a small octavo volume of 104 pages which was originally bound in green paper covers. It is embellished with five illustrations, the first four being the same four which are found in *Clotel.* The fifth is a reproduction of the frontispiece of Redpath's *The Roving Editor: Or, Talks with Slaves in the*

Southern States, which had been published in New York in 1859. *Clotelle* is a revision not of *Clotel* but of *Miralda*. Leaving the names of all the other characters as they were, Brown changed the name of Miralda to Clotelle but made no important changes in either the character herself or her part in the story. In fact he did not alter either the plots or the setting of *Miralda*.

The revisions consisted almost completely of omissions—some for discernible reasons and some apparently for none. In the first chapter of *Clotelle*, Brown said that Agnes boasted of being "the daughter of an American Senator," and that the father of her two daughters was "a young slaveholder" whom she had served as housekeeper in her younger days. Accordingly Brown omitted the reference to Isabella as "a descendant of Thomas Jefferson." Probably for the sake of brevity and certainly without a serious loss to either thought or style, he omitted all of the verse quotations from the headings of the chapters and most of those which were within them. He not only omitted many passages from the several chapters but also eliminated all of chapter 36, the concluding chapter of *Miralda*, except a one-sentence paragraph. With this he ended chapter 35 and thus ended *Clotelle*.

Having replaced none of the omissions with any noteworthy additions, Brown made *Clotelle* much shorter than either *Clotel* or *Miralda*. He probably shortened the novel to make it comparable in size and price with the other books in Redpath's series. In shortening it as he did, however, he can hardly be said to have made it better than the first two versions.

Brown spent most of January in Boston and its vicinity lecturing and otherwise participating in various meetings. At the first session of the annual meeting of the Massachusetts Anti-Slavery Society in Tremont Temple on the twenty-eighth, he spoke briefly concerning the improvement which had been made in the status of Negroes since the beginning of the war. He observed, nevertheless, that slavery had not been completely abolished—that loyal slaveholders in the border states still held legally and firmly to their slaves, that Kentucky and Tennessee were veritable refuges for loyal slaveholders, and that kidnappers of slaves were still active. Consequently this was no time, he was sure, to abandon antislavery work. On the contrary he was convinced that it must be continued in every feasible way "till slavery is buried beyond all hope of resurrection."[12]

Straightway Brown himself transformed his words into action by continuing to travel and hold antislavery meetings. Between January 29 and May 22 he had engagements for about forty lectures in towns in Massachusetts, Connecticut, Rhode Island, and New Hampshire. His subject for most of these lectures was "A General Emancipation Act" or "Liberty for All." He did most of this lecturing under the auspices of the American Anti-Slavery Society.[13]

At the annual New England Anti-Slavery Convention which was held in Boston on Thursday and Friday, May 26 and 27, Brown attracted considerable attention with two speeches. He hoped, he said in a brief speech during the session Thursday afternoon, that the current interest in the candidates for the Presidency of the United States would not divert attention from the antislavery work that must needs be continued.

> The old work of bringing the right and wrong of slavery before the hearts and consciences of men [he averred] needs to be done now as much as ever. . . . We have heard much debate respecting Mr. Lincoln. I enter but little into it. The colored people of the country rejoice in what Mr. Lincoln has done for them, but they will wish that Gen. Fremont had been in his place. And Gen. Butler (having larger opportunity) has done far more than Fremont. He treated the black men just as he treated other men, and that is what black men want.

12. *Liberator*, January 1, 1864, p. 3, February 5, 1864, p. 23.

13. *Ibid.*, January 22, 1864, p. 15, January 29, 1864, p. 19, February 19, 1864, p. 31, February 26, 1864, p. 35, March 18, 1864, p. 47, April 22, 1864, p. 67, April 29, 1864, p. 71, May 6, 1864, p. 75, May 13, 1864, p. 79, May 20, 1864, pp. 81, 82, 83.

At the session Friday afternoon, Brown again urged continuation of the antislavery crusade lest slavery and its bad influence might survive the war. Said he,

> Slavery has received a severe, it may be a fatal blow. Yet the colored man has everything to fear. Even when Grant's army shall be successful, we, the colored people, will be yet in danger. The advantages we have so far received have come as much through Jeff. Davis as through President Lincoln. The war was begun with the purpose of restoring the nation as it was, and leaving the black man where he was. Now the time has come when you must recognize the black man as on the same footing with the white man. If not, the mission of this war is not ended, and we must have yet more disasters to scourge us into the right way.[14]

As Brown continued his lecturing during the summer, principally in Massachusetts and Maine,[15] circumstances still seemed to justify the fears he had expressed at the convention in Boston in May. For more than a year Negro soldiers had been fighting bravely for the Union, but they had been paid only ten dollars a month, while white soldiers were being paid sixteen. Nor was their pay equalized with that of their white compeers until the middle of the summer of 1864. Almost all of the officers of Negro units were white because the War Department had seen fit to commission only a small number of Negro officers. The medical service provided for Negro units was inferior to that provided for white units. In many instances Negro soldiers were supplied with inferior arms and equipment and were assigned to a disproportionate amount of fatigue duty—some of it for white

14. *Ibid.*, June 3, 1864, pp. 89, 90; *National Anti-Slavery Standard*, June 4, 1864, p. 3.

15. *Liberator*, June 3, 1864, p. 91, June 24, 1864, p. 102, July 15, 1864, p. 115, August 12, 1864, p. 131, August 19, 1864, p. 135, August 26, 1864, p. 139, September 9, 1864, p. 147; *National Anti-Slavery Standard*, August 20, 1864, p. 3.

troops.[16] As a result of an act passed by the Confederate Congress on April 30, 1863, Negro soldiers captured by the Confederates were subject to enslavement or ignominious death. On the following July 30, Lincoln had issued his "Order of Retaliation" decreeing that "for every soldier of the United States killed in violation of the laws of war, a rebel soldier shall be executed; and for every one enslaved by the enemy or sold into slavery, a rebel soldier shall be placed at hard labor on the public works and continued at such labor until the other shall be released and receive the treatment due to a prisoner of war." This order had not been executed, however, after the Fort Pillow massacre of April 12–13, 1864, in which 229 Negro soldiers had been killed or buried alive after the Confederates gained possession of the fort.[17]

On April 8, four days before the Fort Pillow massacre, the Thirteenth Amendment had been passed by the United States Senate by a vote of 38–6, but on June 15 it had been defeated in the House of Representatives by its failure to receive two-thirds of the votes cast. In spite of the heroic part Negro troops had played in the war during the preceding year, uncomplimentary criticism of Negroes as soldiers was still current. Meanwhile antiwar Democrats in the North had begun to talk of a negotiated peace—a peace by which the rebelling states would be permitted to return to the Union with their "peculiar institution."

Reflections on these manifold circumstances prompted Negro leaders in Boston to hold a mass meeting in Twelfth Baptist Church on August 4. Pursuant to a resolution of Congress, this day had been proclaimed by Lincoln on July 7 as "a day of national humiliation and prayer." In accordance with the Presi-

16. George W. Williams, *A History of the Negro Troops in the War of the Rebellion, 1861–1865* (New York, 1888), pp. 145–66, 170–80; Benjamin Quarles, *The Negro in the Civil War* (Boston, 1953), pp. 199–209.

17. *The Collected Works of Abraham Lincoln*, 9 vols., ed. Roy P. Basler (New Brunswick, N. J., 1953–55), 6: 357; Williams, *History of the Negro Troops*, pp. 257–72.

dent's proclamation, the Negroes held "a union prayer and conference meeting" in the church in the morning, but they devoted the afternoon to the mass meeting. The Reverend Leonard A. Grimes presided and limited his remarks to such as were expected of a presiding officer. The meeting was held to bring about "a free interchange of thought on National affairs," but it became an occasion less for the interchange of such thought than for the expression of dissatisfaction with the federal government's treatment of Negroes in general and Negro soldiers in particular.

The first speaker, the Reverend H. H. White, pastor of the Joy Street Church, confessed that Negroes were gloomy and mournful because Negro soldiers had recently been "mown down like grass at Petersburg." Yet being convinced that the Lord was on "'our side" and did not intend for the rebels to prosper, he considered what Lincoln might or might not do relatively inconsequential. He still believed, he declared, that he was right in advising colored men to fight for the Union, and that Negroes should not be discouraged by losses, for God had caused the sacrifice of millions of men in other countries "for the cause of liberty and humanity."

Brown, who was the next speaker, said,

> Mr. White's God is bloodthirsty! I worship a different kind of God. My God is a God of peace and goodwill to men. At first I desired that colored men should go to the war, to convince this God-forsaken nation that black men are as valiant as other men. But our people have been so cheated, robbed, deceived, and outraged everywhere, that I cannot urge them to go. . . . I am almost discouraged. We have an imbecile administration, and the most imbecile management that it is possible to conceive of. If Mr. White's God is managing the affairs of this nation, he is making a miserable failure. I cannot see anything bright, though I believe Liberty and Justice must triumph.

In speeches much longer than Brown's, Drs. J. B. Smith and John S. Rock voiced sentiments similar to his. Robert Morris was the last speaker for the occasion. He reminded the assembly that he had never advised and still did not advise colored men to enlist in the Union army because of the inferior status assigned to Negro soldiers. As he saw matters, Negroes were not likely to get any more by fighting in this war than their forefathers had got by fighting in the American Revolution.[18] Fortunately time proved him to be wrong.

The Boston mass meeting of August 4 was somewhat preparatory for a national convention of colored citizens for which a call was published in the *Liberator* for September 9. The call designated New York City as the place for the convention and October 4 as its date. In the meantime, as was announced in the *Liberator* for September 30, it was decided that the convention would be held not in New York City but in Syracuse. Accordingly it was begun in the Wesleyan Methodist Church in that city on the evening of October 4 and was continued in Wieting Hall there until the seventh.

Brown was one of six delegates from Massachusetts among 145 representing seventeen states and the District of Columbia. At the opening session Frederick Douglass was elected permanent president of the convention, sixteen other delegates were elected vice-presidents, and five others were elected secretaries—all by acclamation. At the first morning session, while the business committee was holding a meeting, Douglass was requested "to entertain" the assembly. He declined to do so and instead introduced Brown, "who addressed the Convention at length," but apparently not impressively enough for any of the secretaries to record anything he said. Anyway the official proceedings of the convention contain no report of this or any other speech he made at any other session.

One product of the convention was the development of plans for the establishment of the National Equal Rights League with John Mercer Langston of Oberlin, Ohio, as its first president.

18. *Collected Works of Lincoln*, 7: 431–32; *Anglo-African*, August 13, 1864, pp. 2, 3.

The general purpose of this organization was indicated by its name. Another product was the succinct and eloquent statement of the fears by which Negroes were still shaken as late as the eve of the presidential election of 1864 with regard to their immediate future in America. This statement, entitled "Address of the Colored National Convention to the People of the United States," fills the last nineteen of the sixty-two pages of the official proceedings of the convention. The principal basis of the Negroes' fears was the possibility of the termination of the war before slavery was completely destroyed and the return of the rebelling states with slavery to the Union, especially if the Democrats won the election.[19]

Brown went to the convention in Syracuse with the intention of spending the following few weeks in central and western New York lecturing on "The Rebellion and the Duty of the Hour."[20] It is not improbable, therefore, that he was one of the delegates who left Syracuse before the convention was adjourned, as George T. Downing noted in a speech during the last session that "so many" of them had done. Central and western New York had long been familiar to Brown. It was the area in which he had begun his career as an antislavery agent twenty-one years earlier, and it was destined to be the area in which he would make his last antislavery lecture tour, for this was his last one.

On the evening of December 5, the recent adoption by Maryland of a constitution which abolished slavery from that state was celebrated with "a grand meeting" in the city hall in Cambridge, Massachusetts. Brown, who had recently returned from his tour of central and western New York, was the principal speaker for the occasion. He delivered what George W. Potter, a Boston correspondent for the *Anglo-African*, de-

19. *Liberator*, September 9, 1864; p. 147, September 30, 1864, p. 159, October 14, 1864, p. 167; *Anglo-African*, October 15, 1864, pp. 1, 2, 3, October 22, 1864, pp. 1, 2; *Proceedings of the National Convention of Colored Men, Held in the City of Syracuse, N. Y., October 4, 5, 6, and 7, 1864* (Boston, 1864).

20. *Liberator*, September 30, 1864, p. 159.

scribed as "an oration of great merit." His speech, which was not new, was mainly an historical sketch of American slavery from 1619 to the Civil War and of the antislavery crusade, together with some rejoicing over the fact that Maryland had recently made itself a free state.[21]

The second anniversary of the Emancipation Proclamation having occurred on Sunday in 1865, it was not generally celebrated until the following Monday. Brown was present at both the Boston celebration of this anniversary and the annual meeting of the Massachusetts Anti-Slavery Society which was held on January 26 and 27, but he had no important part in either.[22] He figured prominently, however, in three meetings which the Negroes of greater Boston held in the middle of February. The House of Representatives having passed the Thirteenth Amendment on January 31, Congress had promptly adopted a joint resolution submitting the amendment to the legislatures of the several states for ratification. The series of meetings were held to commemorate this action of Congress. The first of the series was held in the Joy Street Church on Sunday evening, February 12, Lincoln's birthday. The second meeting was held in Tremont Temple the next evening. Brown was one of its sponsors, and he also presided over it. Especially noteworthy among the speakers were Dr. John S. Rock, Phillips, Garrison, and George Thompson. According to the *Anglo-African* for March 11, at least 2,500 persons were present. If there were, the Negroes must have been greatly outnumbered by the white people in the audience. Said the *Liberator* for February 17, "Although this was intended as a special celebration of the great event by the colored citizens of Boston, strange to say there were scarcely any of them present. . . . Fortunately, a large attendance of their white friends saved the meeting from being a failure."

The third meeting was held in the city hall in Cambridge on the evening of February 16. The Reverend Mr. Rue's singing of

21. *Anglo-African,* December 17, 1864, p. 2.

22. *Ibid.*, January 14, 1865, p. 2; *Liberator,* February 3, 1865, pp. 18, 19.

his original "Sound the Loud Timbrel," together with the audience joining in the chorus and the repetition of "Amen," gave the occasion the tone of a revival meeting for a few minutes. Brown was invited to speak, but instead he deferred to Phillips, who "spoke at some length."[23]

Brown had an engagement "by invitation" to deliver an antislavery lecture in Davis's Hall in Plymouth, Massachusetts, on the evening of March 29, which proved to be within two weeks of the end of the Civil War. His subject for the occasion was "The Rebellion and the Black Man." With this engagement his career as an antislavery lecturer and agent for almost twenty-two years may be said to have ended. With Lee's surrender, which prompted Boston Negroes to hold two jubilee meetings on April 13, the night of slavery with its foul and pestilent congregation of horrors had gone, Brown along with most of his contemporaries believed, and the dawn of freedom had come.[24] It remained to be seen, however, whether the new day would be as glorious as the promise of the morning was.

Brown did not attend the annual meeting of the American Anti-Slavery Society in New York on May 9 and 10. He was doubtless informed soon afterwards, however, about the argument that arose there between Garrison and his adherents on one side and Phillips and his adherents on the other. On the first day of the meeting, Garrison offered a resolution proposing that since the purpose for which it had been founded had been accomplished, the society should be dissolved with the adjournment of this meeting. Contrariwise Phillips immediately moved that since the Thirteenth Amendment had not yet been ratified, and slavery, therefore, still legally existed, "this society calls upon its members for fresh and untiring diligence in finishing the work to which they originally pledged themselves, and putting the

23. *Liberator*, February 17, 1865, p. 27; *National Anti-Slavery Standard*, February 18, 1865, p. 3; *Anglo-African*, March 11, 1865, p. 2.

24. *Liberator*, March 24, 1865, p. 47; *Anglo-African*, April 22, 1865, p. 1.

liberty of the negro beyond peril." After much discussion which was continued on the next day, Garrison's resolution was defeated by a vote of 48–118. Garrison was then renominated for president of the society, but he declined the nomination and Phillips was elected to succeed him.[25]

At the evening session of the New England Anti-Slavery Convention in the Melodeon on May 31, Brown spoke in support of Phillips's point of view. He also argued that Negroes needed suffrage to live safely in the South, and that although slavery had been abolished, Negroes could not prosper there if the old slaveholding class were allowed to resume control of affairs as they had it before the war.[26]

In a speech at the Massachusetts Anti-Slavery Society's celebration of July 4 in Framingham, Brown continued his discussion of these matters. He decried the federal government's policy of putting into office in the former Confederate states those who had been leaders in the rebellion. He observed that either the war had ended too soon or the wrong man was in the presidency, for to him Andrew Johnson was far too sympathetic with the former leaders of the rebellion. He correctly predicted that with those leaders in control in the South, there would be an attempt to establish a new kind of Negro slavery in the region—a slavery resulting from starvation wages and the denial of the right of Negro workers to choose their employers. He admitted that it was now almost impossible for Negroes to gain suffrage in the South, but he was still convinced that the ballot was the only sure means by which they could safeguard their freedom. He accused the federal government of breaking faith

25. William Lloyd Garrison to Mrs. Garrison, May 10, 1865, Anti-Slavery Letters Written by W. L. Garrison; *Liberator*, May 19, 1865, p. 78, May 26, 1865, pp. 81–82, June 2, 1865, pp. 85, 86, 87; [Wendell Phillips Garrison and Francis Jackson Garrison], *William Lloyd Garrison, 1805–1879: The Story of His Life Told by His Children*, 4 vols. (Boston, 1894), 4: 157–61.

26. *National Anti-Slavery Standard*, June 10, 1865, p. 3; *Liberator*, June 16, 1865, p. 94.

with the freedmen by failing to protect them against those who wished to reenslave them. Consequently he warned his fellow abolitionists that they should now be as alert against the pro-slavery forces as they had ever been. In other words he was still taking sides with those who had voted in May not to dissolve the American Anti-Slavery Society. He concluded in a tone half-hopeful and half-defiant that since Negroes had learned to use military arms, any attempts to reestablish slavery in the South would bring about another Saint Domingo, and that if the time came to resist such attempts, he himself would go to the South and join in the good work of resistance.[27]

27. *Liberator*, July 14, 1865, p. 112; *National Anti-Slavery Standard*, July 15, 1865, p. 2.

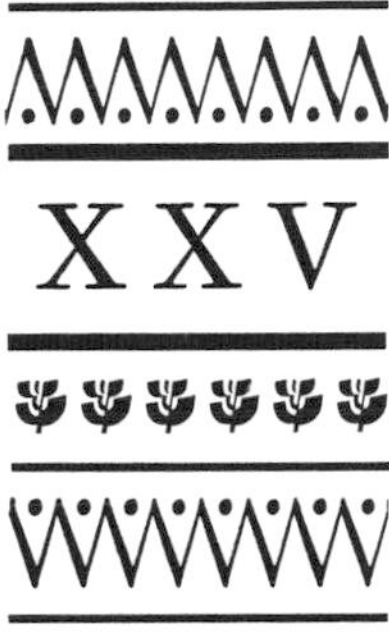

A Doctor Almost in Spite of Himself

IN HIS REPORT PUBLISHED IN THE *Anglo-African* FOR DECEMBER 17, 1864, George W. Potter referred to "Dr. W. W. Brown," identifying him as "the lecturer and author Wm. Wells Brown, Esq., who has turned his attention to a new field of labor." He was referring to the fact that Brown was now concentrating on the practice as well as the study of medicine, as he had been doing for some time. During the preceding summer Mrs. Helen Eliza Garrison, the abolitionist's wife, who had suffered a paralytic stroke in December, 1863, was briefly one of his patients. William Lloyd Garrison, Jr. informed Ellen Wright in a letter he wrote from Boston on August 6, 1864, that

> William Wells Brown has an instrument he imported from Germany, and he goes about curing all sorts of troubles. Headaches he banishes as St. Patrick did the frogs and snakes. This afternoon he has been puncturing Mother. All up and down

her spine the little bunch of needles have been puncturing the skin, and on her helpless arm they have done likewise. Irritation follows . . . and good results also.

But in a letter of September 7, Garrison, Jr. told the same correspondent that "the pricking machine" did not help his mother.[1]

Late in 1864 or early in 1865, Brown began writing "M. D." after his name. He had not received a degree from a medical college; he merely used the familiar abbreviation to identify himself as one now practicing medicine. About this time he opened an office at 34 Winter Street in Boston for the practice of his new profession, but he seems to have kept his office at that address only a short time. By February 2, 1865, he had moved it to 140 Court Street, where he kept it approximately thirteen years. On the date just mentioned, he wrote a letter from this address to William Still of Philadelphia. The main purpose of the letter was to introduce its bearer, Horace J. Gray, Mrs. Brown's brother, who went to Philadelphia apparently to seek his fortune.[2]

The *Liberator* for March 3, 10, and 17 carried a "Medical Notice—The New Cure" in which Brown advertised himself as a "Dermapathic and Practical Physician." The first two printings of the notice contained a paragraph describing "Dermapathy" as "a new treatment of disease." From this paragraph it appears that it was dermapathy which Brown had tried ineffectively on Mrs. Garrison. This paragraph was omitted from the third printing of the notice, probably because it was extravagant if not quackish in its claims for the "new cure"; and afterwards Brown seems not to have advertised himself as a dermapathist.

When Brown wrote his letter of August 10, 1863, to Still, he did not consider himself ready to begin practicing as a full-fledged physician, as he did less than a year and a half later.

1. Garrison, Jr., to Ellen Wright, August 6, 1864, September 7, 1864, Sophia Smith Collection.

2. Brown to Still, February 2, 1865, Leon Gardiner Collection on Negro History.

Presumably, therefore, in the meantime he had not only continued but had also intensified his study of medicine. The fact that Brown had never enrolled in a medical college did not then matter a great deal. "Reading medicine" and studying as a physician's apprentice, as he told Still he had done, were still a popular as well as approved means by which one might prepare himself to practice medicine. And although the nearby Harvard Medical School was looming both large and high on the horizon of medical education, there were still an appreciable number of physicians in Boston who were giving the kind of preceptorial instruction in medicine which Brown said he had had.

When Brown began practicing medicine, there was no state agency in Massachusetts to determine the proficiency of physicians by examination and to grant or refuse to grant them licenses to practice. The Massachusetts Board of Registration in Medicine did not then exist, nor was it organized until 1894, ten years after Brown died. There was the Massachusetts Medical Society, membership in which was possessed of some prestige; but this society had no authority to determine who should be permitted to practice medicine in the state, nor were the majority of the physicians in the state members of it. Brown seems never to have become a member of this society. His failure to do so, however, could hardly have been due to his being a Negro, for long before he began to practice medicine, two Negro physicians of Boston—Dr. John V. De Grasse and Dr. John S. Rock—had been admitted to membership in it. Brown was not listed in Francis H. Brown's *The Medical Register for the State of Massachusetts*, which was published in Boston in 1875, and which contained only the names of members of the Masachusetts Medical Society. But in Samuel W. Butler's *Medical Register and Directory of the United States*, which was published in Philadelphia in 1878, he was listed as an eclectic physician.

Although Brown practiced medicine during his last nineteen years, it is doubtful that he ever succeeded remarkably as a physician. At least the frequent removals of both his residence and his office from one place to another during his last six years do not indicate that he did, for it has always been true that as a rule prosperous people move around less frequently than people who are not prosperous. Perhaps his success as a physician was no greater than it was because he was constantly busy with other things not related to his profession—writing historical works, lecturing, and participating in various reform movements.

The record of the changes in the location of Brown's home and his office during his last nineteen years is found in the Cambridge and Boston directories for 1865–84 and the *Chelsea, Revere and Winthrop Directory for the Year 1884.* Brown kept his home on Webster Avenue in Cambridgeport, where it had been since June, 1860, until 1878. Early in the latter year he moved his home and his office to 7 Decatur Street in the South End of Boston. His reason for moving his office to this location might well have been the fact that the South End was rapidly becoming the center of the Negro population of the city.[3] Two years later he moved his home and office to 28 East Canton Street, still in the South End. After two years at this address, he moved his office to 35 Hanover Street in the East End, and about a year later he moved his home from East Canton Street to 89 Beacon Street in Chelsea. These were his last removals.

From 1868 to 1871 the Boston directories listed Pitts and Brown's clothing store at 24 Brattle Street, identifying William W. Brown of Cambridgeport and Coffin Pitts as its owners. From 1872 to 1874 the directories listed the same store with the same Brown and Mrs. Coffin Pitts as its owners. Unless there was another William W. Brown then residing in Cambridgeport—although the Cambridge directories did not list another one—Brown must have been the business partner referred to in these listings. If he was, here was something else which for six years exacted time that he might have devoted to his profession—

3. John Daniels, *In Freedom's Birthplace: A Study of the Boston Negroes* (Boston and New York, 1914), p. 145.

whether more or less profitably than he spent it is, of course, now unknowable.

At a convention which New England Negroes held in Boston on December 1, 1865, several resolutions were adopted, including one by which it was decided to send a delegate to Washington to represent Negroes to Congress. The convention also voted to raise ten thousand dollars to sustain the delegate in the capital and to finance the work that would be necessitated by his mission there. Brown participated in the convention and also in the efforts to raise the money. But alas the efforts proved futile, and this early, if not the earliest, attempt of Negroes to establish a lobby in Washington failed for want of financial support before anybody knew whether such a lobby would have done any good or not.[4]

Brown was one of the principal speakers at the celebration of the third anniversary of the Emancipation Proclamation in Tremont Temple on January 1, 1866. On that occasion he merely repeated what he had previously said several times concerning the reconstruction of the former Confederate states as it pertained to the freedmen. As the new year advanced, he became preoccupied not only with the practice of medicine but also with things not related to his profession, notably with the promotion of temperance and with the writing of a new book. He also gave enough attention to local affairs to write a letter on July 2 about "The Colored People of Boston" to the *National Anti-Slavery Standard*. Although it fills two-thirds of a column, this letter contains little or nothing either very enlightening or very interesting concerning its subject.[5]

On January 5, 1867, four days after the celebration of the fourth anniversary of the Emancipation Proclamation in Tre-

4. *Boston Daily Advertiser*, December 2, 1865, pp. 1, and 4; *Liberator*, December 8, 1865, p. 194; *National Anti-Slavery Standard*, January 13, 1866, p. 3.

5. *National Anti-Slavery Standard*, January 13, 1866, p. 3, July 14, 1866, p. 3.

mont Temple, Garrison wrote to his son Francis, who was away, noting that he was not present and telling what he had heard about the event. Brown, Douglass, Remond, and George Thompson were among the speakers, but the first two of these were incidentally overshadowed by the last two. "Thompson spoke," said Garrison, "in reply to one of Remond's bitter and railing speeches in a manner that electrified the house." From a report in the *Commonwealth* of Boston for January 5, however, it appears that in his speech, which he delivered at the evening meeting, Remond indulged less in railing than in understandable pessimism. He dwelt upon the disadvantages and inequalities from which Negroes still suffered because of their race and upon "the duties and dangers that still lie before us."[6]

Thompson's speech might have electrified his audience, but it did not put Remond's argument beyond resurrection. Three weeks after the celebration, Brown expressed himself publicly very much as Remond had done. The occasion was the annual meeting of the Massachusetts Anti-Slavery Society in Mercantile Hall on January 25. At the opening session Brown delivered a speech which was summarized on the front page of the *National Anti-Slavery Standard* for February 2 as follows:

> Mr. Wm. Wells Brown said he did not think that the people here understood the position of the colored people of the South. He went into a long argument, showing that their condition was vastly worse than before their emancipation. The negroes had been armed under a promise of freedom, and now that freedom was withheld. He did not believe the action of Congress [in failing to act sooner than it did to safeguard the rights of the freedmen] was intentional, but owing entirely to mismanagement and the contemptible meanness of the President. The only safeguard of the race was in impartial suffrage.

6. Garrison to Francis Garrison, January 5, 1867, Anti-Slavery Letters Written by W. L. Garrison; *Commonwealth,* January 5, 1867, p. 3; *National Anti-Slavery Standard,* January 5, 1867, p. 2, January 12, 1867, p. 2.

Neither Garrison nor Thompson was present, nor did any of those who were there take issue with Brown, as some might well have done with regard to his argument that the condition of Negroes in the South was now worse than it was before emancipation.

Within the next few weeks Brown visited Washington for the first time, as he explained in a letter he wrote from that city on February 18 to the *National Anti-Slavery Standard.* He was favorably impressed by the city in general and especially by the Negro life there, but he was cognizant that the millennium in racial matters had not yet come to the nation's capital or Capitol. In proof of this fact he referred to a recent incident which had became the subject of a considerable amount of local conversation. Said he,

> The upper-ten-dom of the colored population here are much excited over the fact that Mr. A. W. Wingfield, a colored man, who keeps the Senate Restaurant, in the Capitol, where Senators and strangers, visiting that branch, get their refreshments, refused to accomodate [*sic*] John M. Langston, the well-known Ohio lawyer, on account of his color. Mr. Langston, a few days before, had been admitted to the bar of the Supreme Court, and was moving about the Capitol with members of Congress, when this *flunkey* insulted him and disgraced himself.[7]

Brown did not reveal in his letter what business he had in Washington at the time. Most probably, however, he was there with reference to a new responsibility which he had recently assumed as general agent of The Freedmen's National Memorial Monument Association. This was the responsibility of promoting plans for the erection of a freedmen's monument in memory of Abraham Lincoln on the grounds of the Capitol.

The origin and purpose of the organization just mentioned were explained in a printed circular of three pages entitled

7. *National Anti-Slavery Standard,* March 2, 1867, p. 3.

Freedmen's Memorial Monument to Abraham Lincoln. Brown sent a copy of this circular along with a one-page letter he wrote from Canastota, New York, on November 6, 1867, to Gerrit Smith. In his letter he appealed to Smith for a contribution for the erection of the monument. Smith, by the way, did not seem to be greatly inspired by Brown's appeal. In a note at the top of the letter, he said that he had replied on November 9 saying "that I will do a *little*—but not now—"[8]

Having returned home from Washington, Brown was prominent as one of the planners of and participants in a meeting of the Monument Association which was held in Mercantile Hall in Boston on March 11. The purpose of the meeting was to stimulate local interest in the Monument Association—interest which the organization hoped would materialize into contributions. In an article which appeared on the third page of the *National Anti-Slavery Standard* for March 23, a Boston correspondent who signed himself "North" gave a none too enthusiastic account of the meeting. "The attendance was not large," he said, and three of the speakers who had promised to be present were absent. Remond, one of the vice-presidents of the organization, presided and "made a spirited and effective speech." Brown explained the plans of the organization and appealed for contributions from all classes.

Brown's announcement that the monument as designed by Harriet G. Hosmer, a Massachusetts-born sculptress who was then in Rome, would cost $250,000 startled North into criticizing unfavorably the plans of the Monument Association. The idea, he observed, that the freedmen might erect a monument to Lincoln, "since circumstances have caused Mr. Lincoln's name to be more familiar to the mass of the freedmen than Mr. Garrison's," was impressive; but the idea of raising $250,000 "from the pockets of the colored people and their best friends among the whites (two classes very far from rich)," at the time when millions of Negroes in the South were suffering from a want of

8. Brown to Smith, November 6, 1867, Gerrit Smith Miller Collection.

food, clothing, shelter, and employment, was inopportune. For those who had been deprived of so much, provisions for the necessities and comforts of life, for education, and for "the exercise of those rights which give life its value" seemed to him "rightly to take precedence even over a desire to honor one's benefactor by a monument. The monument can wait," he concluded; "the starving cannot wait."

A long letter from a correspondent in Charleston, South Carolina, repeating essentially North's point of view concerning the monument was published on the second page of the *National Anti-Slavery Standard* for May 4. This letter specifically emphasized the plight of the freedmen and their need for education. Also, in agreement with the National Lincoln Monument Association, an altogether different organization,[9] it advocated the erection, not of a monument, but of a freedmen's educational institution as a memorial to Lincoln.

In a short paragraph on the same page, the editor of the newspaper noted that Brown was then busy soliciting funds for the Monument Association and expressed sympathy with "the good impulses which prompt the erection of this monument." Nevertheless he agreed with the Charleston correspondent that an educational institution "for the elevation and culture of the emancipated victims of oppression" would be a better memorial than a monument. Then, as if to mollify his criticism, he quoted a paragraph which had appeared on the fourth page of the *New York Daily Tribune* for April 29, speaking more or less favorably concerning the monument.

As his letter of the following November 6 to Gerrit Smith proves, Brown was still working at that time as the general agent of the Monument Association. It is not probable, however, that he continued much longer as agent or ever collected an appreciable amount of money for the organization. Moreover, if the Monument Association itself remained intact very long, it made

9. *Anglo-African,* September 16, 1865, p. 4.

no remarkable progress toward its goal, nor did it receive any credit when that goal was finally achieved.

A freedmen's monument in memory of Lincoln was eventually erected in 1876, not, however, in accordance with Miss Hosmer's design, but in accordance with a simpler one which had been made in 1866 by Thomas Ball of Boston. It was not erected on the grounds of the Capitol, but in Lincoln Park in eastern Washington. Far from costing $250,000, it cost only $20,000. Of this amount $17,000 had been contributed, mainly upon the solicitations of John Mercer Langston, by freedmen and others who revered the memory of Lincoln. This was paid to Ball for the monument itself. The remaining $3,000 had been appropriated by the federal government to pay for the foundation and pedestal on which the monument rests. When the monument was unveiled on April 14, 1876, the eleventh anniversary of the assassination of Lincoln, none of the officers of the Monument Association except Frederick Douglass had a part in the program. Douglass delivered the oration for the occasion.[10]

A replica of the monument, called "The Emancipation Group," was erected in Park Square in Boston in 1879. The gift of Moses Kimball, it also cost $17,000 "exclusive of the curbing, which was furnished by the city." This monument was unveiled on December 6 of the last-mentioned year, and the program in which it was formerly presented to the city was held in Faneuil Hall on the same day. If Brown attended either the unveiling or the program, he did so only as a spectator. Neither he nor any other officer of the Monument Association had any part in the ceremonies.[11]

Brown attended the annual meeting of the American Anti-Slavery Society in New York on May 7 and 8, 1867, and re-

10. John Mercer Langston, *From the Virginia Plantation to the National Capitol* (Hartford, Conn., 1894), pp. 260–98, 335–36; *New York Daily Tribune*, April 15, 1876, p. 1; *Inaugural Ceremonies of the Freedmen's Memorial Monument to Abraham Lincoln* (Saint Louis, 1876).

11. *Boston Daily Advertiser*, December 6, 1879, p. 1; Moses King, *King's Handbook of Boston*, 7th ed. (Cambridge, Mass., 1885), p. 118.

mained there for the first anniversary meeting of the American Equal Rights Association, which was held in the Church of the Puritans on May 9 and 10. The paramount question before the association was whether it should conduct a joint campaign for woman suffrage and suffrage for Negro men or a separate campaign for each. Some of the advocates of women's rights favored only a joint campaign, for they thought that suffrage should be granted to Negro men only on the condition that it was also granted to women. Others favored separate campaigns, for they feared that a joint campaign would confuse rather than simplify matters. They feared that such a campaign might bolster the opinion that the granting of suffrage to one of these groups should be contingent upon the granting of it to the other—an opinion which they considered untenable.[12]

Brown did not participate in the discussion concerning suffrage. Three weeks later, on May 29, the thirty-seventh annual New England Anti-Slavery Convention was held in the Meionaon in Boston. When at the final session the subject of woman suffrage was brought up, he took the opportunity to say what he had doubtless thought but did not say at the recent equal-rights meeting in New York. He said that although he favored women's rights, he was opposed to a joint campaign for woman suffrage and suffrage for Negro men. He considered the latter too urgent to be made contingent, even by implication, upon anything else. He believed that the liberty of the white men as well as the liberty of the black men of the South and also the security of the nation against future rebellions depended upon the enfranchisement of Negroes, because Negroes would hold the balance of power in the South and could be depended upon to use it for the good of the Union. He voiced again, as he had done at the recent meeting of the American Anti-Slavery Society in New York, his suspicion that former slaveholders were

12. *National Anti-Slavery Standard,* May 18, 1867, p. 3, June 1, 1867, p. 3; *Proceedings of the First Anniversary of the American Equal Rights Association* (New York, 1867), pp. 32–42.

still hoping for the reestablishment of slavery in the South and would do whatever they could to hasten its return. He had recently traveled in Maryland and Virginia, he said, and had talked not only with men in those states but also with men from the deep South, and he had found all with whom he had talked possessed of the belief that without the ballot Negroes would not be safe in the South.

He thought that the American Anti-Slavery Society could do great good, he said, by sending half a dozen agents to the South to talk with Negroes and inform them about their rights. He affirmed himself enough of a Republican to hope for the success of the Republican party. In his opinion, if that party had a mission, it was to save the Negro, especially in the South; and if the party failed in that mission, the Negro would be lost to both himself and the nation.[13] Here, it may be observed, Brown anticipated by several years Douglass's dictum that for Negroes the Republican party was the ship and all else was the sea—a point of view which many Negroes have uncritically and persistently accepted for many years.

The first public notice concerning the new book on which Brown was working especially during the latter half of 1866 appeared on the second page of the *National Anti-Slavery Standard* for October 6 of that year. Therein it was said that the book was to be entitled "The Negro in the Great Rebellion." Before the end of the year Brown copyrighted the work under the title *The Negro in the American Rebellion: His Heroism and His Fidelity* and got the manuscript of it ready for the press. It appeared in the spring of 1867 with the imprint of Lee and Shepard of Boston.

This work is a duodecimo volume of 396 pages. It was dedicated by the author to Wendell Phillips "as a token of admiration and gratitude for his long devotion to the cause of freedom, and his untiring advocacy of the equality of the Negro." In this as in three earlier works, Brown proved himself a pioneer—in this

13. *National Anti-Slavery Standard,* June 8, 1867, p. 1, June 15, 1867, p. 3.

instance a pioneer in the writing of the military history of the American Negro. There had been previous sketches of the part Negroes had played in the American Revolution and the War of 1812, notably those of William C. Nell and George Livermore, but Brown's was at once the first attempt to write a history of the Negro's part in the Civil War and the first attempt to bring together in one work the history of the Negro's part in all three of these wars.

In his preface of one and a half pages, Brown said that he wrote this book because he was "anxious to preserve for future reference an account of the part which the Negro took in suppressing the Slaveholders' Rebellion." But he began the work, he explained, with "a sketch of the condition of the race previous to the commencement of the war" because he thought that such a sketch "would not be uninteresting to the reader." He acknowledged his indebtedness—which was very great—to Livermore's *An Historical Research Respecting the Opinions of the Founders of the Republic on Negroes as Slaves, as Citizens, and as Soldiers* (Boston, 1862) for information concerning the services of Negroes in the American Revolution. Although he did not specifically say so, he was indeed indebted to the same source for information about the services of Negroes in the War of 1812. He acknowledged his indebtedness to newspaper correspondents as well as to "officers and privates of several of the colored regiments" for information about the activities of Negroes in the Civil War.

The first chapter of the book is principally a résumé of the Negro's part in the American Revolution and the War of 1812. More than two-thirds of it is a verbatim compilation of eight passages from Livermore's *Historical Research*. Brown's original writing in this chapter consists of only a few introductory and linking paragraphs. Chapters 2–4 are repetitions, with some additions and some omissions, of three biographical sketches from *The Black Man*—those of Denmark Vesey, Nat Turner, and Madison Washington.

In reference to "the condition of the race" just before the

Civil War, the next three chapters give sketchy accounts respectively of the growth of the slave power after the invention of the cotton gin, John Brown's raid at Harper's Ferry, and the events which culminated in the fall of Fort Sumter. Near the end of chapter 7, Brown commented briefly on the ultimate cause of the war—a subject over which a considerable amount of ink has been subsequently spilled. In a paragraph adapted from the beginning of the sketch of Captain Cailloux in the second edition of *The Black Man*, he said,

> All legitimate revolutions are occasioned by the growth of society beyond the growth of government; and they will be peaceful or violent just in proportion as the people and government shall be wise and virtuous or vicious and ignorant. . . . No government is wise in overlooking, whatever may be the strength of its own traditions, or however glorious its history, that human institutions which have been adapted for a barbarous age or state of society will cease to be adapted for more civilized and intelligent times; and, unless government makes a provision for the gradual expansion ["of its institutions to suit the onward march of society"], nothing can prevent a storm, either of an intellectual or a physical nature. Slavery was always the barbarous institution of America; and the Rebellion was the result of this incongruity between it and freedom.

Briefly and not always accurately, chapters 8–17 recount some of the most significant events of the first two years of the war—events which involved the troublesome question as to whether the war could save both the Union and slavery, and events exemplifying the heroic services of Negroes in the cause of the Union. As examples of such services on sea, Brown recounted in chapter 11 three exploits, two of which occurred near the Atlantic coast in July, 1861. The first of these was the recovery of the schooner *S. J. Waring* by its Negro steward, William Tillman, after it had been captured by the *Jeff Davis*, a Confederate privateer. The second was the liberation of the schooner *Enchantress* through the instrumentality of its Negro steward, Jacob Garrick, after it had also been captured by the *Jeff Davis.* In the heading of the chapter, Brown incorrectly identified Garrick as George Green, but in the few sentences he devoted to the exploit, he did not refer to the steward by name. The third exploit was Robert Smalls' delivery of the *Planter*, a Confederate gunboat, to the Union navy outside the Charleston harbor in May, 1862. Brown had included in *The Black Man* a sketch of Smalls telling much less about the man himself than about what he had done. In *The Negro in the American Rebellion* he altered his account of Smalls but did not improve it.[14]

More than half of *The Negro in the American Rebellion*—chapters 18–40 and 45—deals with events of the last two years of the war. Even more than the preceding parts, this part of the work is discursive and without chronological order—as if Brown recorded the information as it became available to him and without much concern for coherence. There are accounts of the recruiting of Negro regiments in the North, of about a dozen battles in various parts of the South in which Negro soldiers had prominent parts, of Northern opposition to the war, as was evinced by the draft riot in New York City in July, 1863, and of the refusal of the federal government for more than a year to grant Negro soldiers pay equal to that granted to white soldiers. There are also examples of verse, folk songs, and wit and humor, as well as of other things incidental to the war. Chapter 23, on the Battle of Port Hudson (May 27, 1863), is a combination and adaptation of the sketches of Captains Cailloux and Howard from the second edition of *The Black Man*, with the addition of two

14. Accounts of Tillman's exploit were given in the *New York Herald*, July 22, 1861, and in the *New York Daily Tribune* for the same date. An account of Garrick's exploit was given in the *Daily Tribune*, August 1, 1861. Accounts of Smalls' exploit were given in the *New York Commercial Advertiser*, and the *Herald*, May 18, 1862, and in an editorial in the *Daily Tribune*, May 20, 1862. Brown referred generally to several of these accounts.

brief laudatory passages. Brown quoted one of these from the New Orleans correspondence in the *New York Herald* for June 6, 1863, and the other from an editorial in the *New York Daily Tribune* for June 8. Both of these newspapers erroneously referred to the Second Regiment Louisiana Native Guards as participants in the battle, which they were not, instead of to the First Regiment, which did participate in it.[15] Brown corrected the newspapers' error by substituting "First" for "second" in the quotations but did not apprise his readers of his correction.

As if he forgot for a while that he was writing history, Brown took from *The Black Man* the half-fictitious sketch entitled "A Man Without a Name," lengthened it with a sequel, vaguely reentitled it "A Thrilling Incident of the War," and made it chapter 36 in *The Negro in the American Rebellion.* Since this sketch is as much imaginary as factual, it obviously does not belong in this book any more than it belongs in *The Black Man.*

Chapters 41–44 pertain not to the war but to the first year and a half after it—the era of Presidential reconstruction. The first of these chapters is a good but thoroughly uncomplimentary character study of President Andrew Johnson. It is especially remarkable as such, because appearing as soon as it did after Johnson became President, it revealed the qualities of his character which at least contributed to the causes of his impeachment and his ultimate failure as President. The other three chapters tell of the return—all too soon, Brown thought—of the former Confederate leaders to control in the South and of the continuation of the caste system whose foundation was slavery. Chapter 45, which is the last one in the book, is a sketchy account of the formation and services of "the Sixth Regiment United-States colored troops" of Pennsylvania. It was not written by Brown but "was kindly furnished by a gentleman of Philadelphia," from whom Brown received it too late to put it "in its proper place."

Although *The Negro in the American Rebellion* was the first

15. George W. Williams, *A History of the Negro Troops in the War of the Rebellion, 1861–1865* (New York, 1888), p. 221.

book of its kind, the first edition of it seems not to have been reviewed except by the *National Anti-Slavery Standard*, which belatedly and briefly complimented both the book and its author.[16] In an advertisement on an end leaf in the third edition of *My Southern Home*, which was published in 1882, Brown said that almost all of the first edition of *The Negro in the American Rebellion* "was burnt in the great Boston fire, so that but few copies were sold." Presumably he meant the fire of November 9, 1872, which devastated sixty-five acres in the business section of the city[17]—the section in which Lee and Shepard's publishing house was located. The book had been on the market, however, five years before that fire—a sufficient time for an appreciable number of copies to have been sold. In the same advertisement Brown quoted favorable comments on the book from the *National Monitor* of Brooklyn, New York, William Lloyd Garrison, the *New York Daily Tribune*, and the *New York Evening Post*. A "New Edition" of the book—strictly speaking it was only a new printing—had been published in 1880 by A. G. Brown and Company, 28 East Canton Street, Boston. A. G. Brown was Mrs. Annie (Gray) Brown, and the address was that of the Browns' home. Most probably it was this edition which had brought forth all of the comments just referred to except the one made by Garrison, who had died on May 24, 1879. The "New Edition" was posthumously reprinted by A. G. Brown and Company in 1885.

In the spring of 1867, Brown prepared the fourth and final version of his novel for publication. This version, which is a duodecimo volume of 114 pages, is entitled *Clotelle; or, The Colored Heroine. A Tale of the Southern States.* It bears the imprint of Lee and Shepard with the date 1867, and it was off the press by July of that year.

Brown dedicated "this unpretending volume" to his wife, "who, on reading the manuscript," he said, "so much admired

16. *National Anti-Slavery Standard*, September 21, 1867, p. 3.
17. King, *Handbook*, p. 18.

the character of Clotelle as to name our daughter after the heroine." The statement just quoted is at least questionable. Clotelle, the Browns' only daughter, was born nine years after *Clotel* was published and more than a year after *Miralda* was serialized. She was almost two years old when *Clotelle* of 1864 was published and five years old when *Clotelle* of 1867 appeared. There is no character named either Clotel or Clotelle in *Miralda.* The only manuscript version of the novel, therefore, by which Mrs. Brown could have been inspired to name Clotelle after the heroine was the manuscript of *Clotel*—unless Brown kept the manuscript of *Clotelle* of 1864 unpublished for two years, and there is no reason to believe that he did that. Withal, if Mrs. Brown was inspired by the manuscript of *Clotel,* her inspiration came along after the book itself had been published.

With the exception of the prefatory pages and the first paragraph of the first chapter, the first 104 pages of this version are an exact reproduction of *Clotelle* of 1864. The first paragraph is principally a condensation of the first two paragraphs of *Clotelle* of 1864 with the point of view in time changed in accordance with the fact that slavery had been abolished. The four new chapters, 36–39, which lengthened the book by ten pages, constitute a sequel in which Brown carried the story forward through two years after the Civil War.

After the war began, according to this sequel, Jerome and Clotelle Fletcher returned to America "to take their stand with the friends of liberty." They arrived in New Orleans in the spring of 1862, a week after the Union army commanded by Major-General Butler occupied the city and twenty-two years after Clotelle had left there with the wife of her last owner and had escaped with young Devenant to France. While Clotelle devoted herself so wholeheartedly to war relief work that she became known as the "Angel of Mercy," Fletcher enlisted in the First Regiment Louisiana Native Guards, fought in the Battle of Port Hudson, and was killed while he and three fellow soldiers were trying to recover the body of a captain in the Union army.

In October, 1863, Clotelle went to Andersonville, Georgia, to do whatever she could to alleviate the condition of the Union soldiers imprisoned there. With the aid of a trusted Negro servant, she helped ninety-three Union soldiers to escape as a group from Andersonville—an act which necessitated her flight from the locale for her own safety. She returned to New Orleans, where she remained until the end of the war. "In the summer of 1866," said Brown in the last sentence in the novel, "the Poplar Farm [in Mississippi], on which she had once lived as a slave, was confiscated and sold by Government authority, and was purchased by Clotelle, upon which she established a Freedmen's School, and where at this writing—now June, 1867,—resides the 'Angel of Mercy.' "

The *Commonwealth* for July 20 carried a brief complimentary paragraph about the book, noting that it "has many indications of excellence," predicting that "It will interest greatly all who read it," and wishing that "its type were larger and the volume more bulky." The *National Anti-Slavery Standard* for October 5 observed that the story, "although romantic in many of its details, may be accepted as a fair picture of a state of things we trust never again to witness in our country." This newspaper bespoke a wide circulation for the book; but in agreement with the *Commonwealth*, it wished that the volume "might have been printed in larger, clearer type, and thus had the benefit of a more inviting appearance."[18]

In adding the sequel to the story, Brown brought its action up to date and, what is more important, gave it a more realistic and more convincing ending than he had given to any of the preceding versions. Otherwise he did not improve it.

18. *Commonwealth*, July 20, 1867, pp. 1–2; *National Anti-Slavery Standard*, October 5, 1867, p. 3.

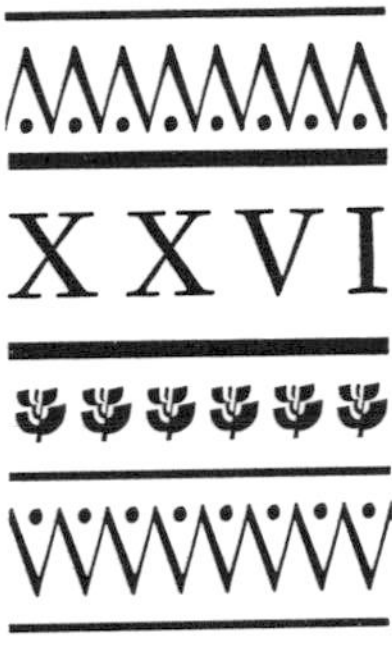

XXVI

New Duties for New Occasions

The abolition of American slavery had reelevated the American slave from an unnatural status as property to his natural status as a human being. As Brown realized, however, something still needed to be done to reinspire American Negroes with the self-respect of which two and a half centuries of bondage had deprived most of them. In order to make them self-respecting and respectable among other people, it was necessary to make them, as well as others, conscious of the Negro's heritage. As his contribution to efforts to do this, Brown continued for some time after the Civil War, as he had done in crusading against slavery, to recount the history of the Negro in speeches as well as in writing.

Brown was the principal speaker at an emancipation celebration in Rand Hall in Troy, New York, on the evening of January 3, 1868. Before an audience which consisted mainly of Negroes, and which filled the hall, he delivered an address on "the heroism and fidelity of the black man during the rebellion," an address composed principally of a recounting of exploits of which he had told in *The Negro in the American Rebellion.* He concluded with an impassioned argument for the enfranchisement of Negroes, his contention being that the ballot was the only means by which Negroes in the South could protect themselves against unregenerate Confederates. His "delivery was unusually free and impressive," said the *Troy Daily Times* of the next day, "and the descriptive portions of the address were so graphically written and so earnestly, vigorously delivered as to awaken at times the wildest enthusiasm."[1] His argument was not new, but it was still timely; for more than a year was yet to pass before the Fifteenth Amendment was submitted by Congress to the several states, and more than two years were to elapse before it was proclaimed a part of the Constitution of the United States.

Late in February Brown went on a lecture tour on which he spent two months in New York and the Middle West. His address in Troy on January 3 had been sufficiently impressive to get him a return engagement in that city during this tour. A notice on the third page of the *Daily Times* for February 29 informed the public that he would lecture on Sunday evening, March 1, in the hall of the Young Men's Association in the same city on "The Origin of the Colored Race." "Mr. Brown is really a finished orator," the notice continued, "a good reasoner, and an entertaining lecturer. He has made elocution a study, and we are quite desirous our citizens should hear him recite some of the eloquent passages, poetry and prose, with which his lectures abound." During the remainder of the tour mentioned above, Brown delivered this lecture several times, and always "it was well received."[2]

1. *Troy* [New York] *Daily Times,* January 4, 1868, p. 3. The *National Anti-Slavery Standard,* January 18, 1868, p. 2, also noted that Brown had lectured at the emancipation celebration in Troy.

2. *Commonwealth,* May 9, 1868, p. 3.

On May 25 Henry C. Wright wrote a letter from Gloucester, Massachusetts, to Garrison. For the nonce Wright's letter is less important than the stationery on which he wrote two of its paragraphs and a postscript. These are on the back and front of a handbill about 4½ in. by 8 in., which Wright thus saved by chance from destruction along with its fellows. The handbill announced that Brown would deliver "his great Historical Lecture on the Origin and Early History of the African Race" in Tremont Temple on Sunday evening, May 10, apparently for the first time in Boston. At the bottom of the handbill were what were purported to be two newspaper comments on the lecture. The first was a quotation from the *New York Evening Post*. The second was an adaptation of a sentence from the article on Brown which had appeared in the *Troy Daily Times* for January 4.[3] This comment originally referred to Brown's lecture of January 3—not to this one.

After an engagement to deliver his "Historical Lecture" in Shiloh Presbyterian Church in New York on May 27,[4] Brown probably had but few or no occasions to deliver it during the following summer, for lyceum lecturing was not generally continued in that season. But during the next fall and winter, he had a considerable number of engagements for his historical lectures as well as other speeches, some of these engagements being far removed from his home.

An emancipation celebration was held in Tremont Temple on January 1, 1869, under the auspices of the National Association for the Organization of Night Schools and the Spread of Temperance Among the Freed People of the South. This organization had been founded by Brown and other leaders on January 1, 1868. Brown both presided and delivered one of the principal addresses at the celebration. Having left Cambridge-

3. Wright to Garrison, May 25, 1868, Anti-Slavery Letters Written to W. L. Garrison and Others; *Commonwealth*, May 2, 1868, p. 3, May 9, 1868, p. 3.

4. *National Anti-Slavery Standard*, May 23, 1868, p. 2.

port a few days later, he spent most of January and February on a lecture tour that took him as far west as Saint Louis. On his visit to that city he saw Enoch Price, his last owner, whom he said he had not seen "for more than thirty years." On the evening of February 16, he delivered in Farwell Hall in Chicago what was described in a report in the *Chicago Tribune* for the next day as "his great historical lecture on 'Hannibal, the Carthagenian Hero.' " According to this report, "There was a very large audience in attendance, a great many being of his own race. Great interest was manifested, and the strictest attention was paid to all that was said. The lecture was a very able one, and Mr. Brown well sustained his reputation as an orator in its delivery."[5]

The American and the Massachusetts Anti-Slavery Societies and the New England Anti-Slavery Convention continued to hold annual meetings for five years after the Civil War; but after 1867 Brown seems to have participated in only one of these meetings, namely, the New England Anti-Slavery Convention which was held in Horticultural Hall in Boston on May 27, 1869. At the afternoon session, Wendell Phillips, who was presiding, offered a resolution proposing that the convention "demand of Congress the immediate enactment of laws that will break up the landed monopolies of the South, and place a homestead within the reach of the humblest of this race [Negroes]." After the enthusiastic applause with which the resolution was received, Brown supported it in a brief speech. He spoke of the disadvantages Negroes suffered and of the necessity for vigilance and constant action for the maintenance of their rights. The resolution was adopted, but needless to say it had little or no influence upon the actions of Congress.[6]

The Fifteenth Amendment, the last of the three Reconstruc-

5. *Boston Daily Advertiser,* January 2, 1869, quoted in *National Anti-Slavery Standard,* January 9, 1869, p. 1; *Chicago Tribune,* February 17, 1869.

6. *National Anti-Slavery Standard,* June 12, 1869, p. 1.

tion amendments, which pertained especially to the freedmen, was officially proclaimed a part of the Constitution on March 30, 1870. The American Anti-Slavery Society now considered accomplished the purpose for which it had been organized thirty-seven years earlier, namely, the abolition of slavery and the securing to Negroes the same civil and political rights as were possessed by other Americans. Accordingly the society held its final meeting in Apollo Hall in New York on April 9 in commemoration of its success. On the preceding day Brown sent a letter to Aaron M. Powell, one of the officers of the society, expressing regrets that he could not attend the meeting and paying a tribute to the leaders of the abolition movement—especially to Garrison and Phillips. His letter along with letters from other prominent abolitionists who did not attend the meeting was published on the front page of the *National Anti-Slavery Standard* for April 16.

After the abolition of slavery, Brown had become more and more engrossed in another reform movement which now seemed urgent to him. This was the cause of temperance, in which he had long been deeply interested, and which was now being promoted by two national secret orders replete with regalia, rituals, and passwords, and with international affiliations. One of these organizations was the Order of the Sons of Temperance, and the other was the Independent Order of Good Templars. Brown became an active member of both of these orders as soon as he was permitted to join them.

The Sons of Temperance, "the pioneer international total abstinence organization of North America," was founded on September 29, 1842.[7] Within twenty years it had grand divisions as well as subordinate divisions in the majority of the states of the United States. For some time the order excluded Negroes from membership. Some of its divisions, however, objected decisively to this policy. In June, 1850, under the leadership of

7. The heading of a letter from E. R. Nickerson of Halifax, Nova Scotia, the most worthy scribe of the order, to me, March 25, 1950.

Charles W. Slack of Boston, the Grand Division of Massachusetts resolved that it would exercise its constitutional right to admit Negroes and would maintain the right of its subordinate divisions to admit all persons "of suitable character, who made application, without regard to *color*!" About a year after the Civil War was ended, the National Division, which included divisions in Canada, abrogated its rule against admitting Negroes to membership, leaving it to the option of the several grand divisions to sponsor integrated or segregated subordinate divisions, as they might deem it expedient to do.[8]

On July 17, 1866, the John Brown Division of the Sons of Temperance was instituted in Boston by the Massachusetts Grand Division. Its first worthy patriarch, its chief officer, was Brown, who had been instrumental in getting it established. Its first chaplain was the Reverend Leonard A. Grimes. This was the second Negro division to be organized in the United States. Why it was organized as such when other subordinate divisions in greater Boston were presumably open to Negroes is a puzzling question, which becomes especially perplexing when it is remembered that Brown, its chief officer, was an avowed opponent of racial segregation.[9]

Before the division was much more than a year old, Mrs. Brown was sufficiently prominent in it to be elected its worthy patriarch for the last quarter of 1867; and during the next ten years at least, as an active member she was second only to Brown himself. In addition to serving again as its worthy patriarch, she was its recording scribe (secretary) for several terms during this period and was occasionally one of its delegates to the annual as well as the quarterly sessions of the grand division.

8. *National Anti-Slavery Standard*, February 28, 1850, p. 159, March 21, 1850, p. 171; *Anti-Slavery Bugle*, July 13, 1850, pp. 174, 175, August 10, 1850, p. 189; *Journal of the Proceedings of the National Division of the Sons of Temperance of North America* (Boston, 1866), p. 41.

9. *Journal of Prooceedings of the Grand Division Sons of Temperance of the State of Massachusetts, 1862–1866* (Boston, 1869), 4: 307, 314, 332.

Brown was initiated into the Massachusetts grand division the day after the John Brown division was instituted. From time to time he not only served as worthy patriarch of the subordinate division and as one of its representatives at the sessions of the grand division but was also a prominent participant in the affairs of the latter. When officers were elected at the grand division's twenty-fifth annual session, which was held in the Meionaon in Boston on October 21, 1868, he was one of eight candidates for the office of grand worthy associate. This was the second highest office in the grand division. To say the least, however, his prospects as a candidate seem to have been dim from the beginning. Of the 293 votes cast, he received only 6, whereas the winner received 187.[10]

Late in the summer of 1870, without diminishing his efforts in the Sons of Temperance, Brown became active in another temperance movement. This one was signalized by a "State Convention for the Promotion of a Prohibitory Political Party in Massachusetts," which was held in Boston on August 17. The convention was adjourned only after it had decided on a platform for the party and had selected a full slate of candidates to run for state offices in the election the following fall.[11]

To the surprise of very few if any, none of the party's candidates were elected. Nevertheless "the friends of prohibition," as they were called by a member of their party, continued for some time their efforts to bring about prohibition by legislation, even though they achieved no success. Early in 1872 several conferences on prohibition were held in Boston, notably one in Wesleyan Hall. Two of the participants in this conference were Brown and Samuel W. Hodges, a prominent member of the Sons of Temperance. The Massachusetts Temperance Commission with headquarters in Boston was organized by this con-

10. *Journal, Sons of Temperance, Massachusetts, 1867–1871* (Boston, 1872), 5: 131.

11. *Boston Daily Advertiser,* August 18, 1870, p. 4; *National Standard* (formerly the *National Anti-Slavery Standard*), August 27, 1870, p. 6.

ference. Brown was made a member of its executive committee, and Hodges its secretary.[12] It is improbable, however, that either Brown or Hodges was ever burdened with duties by the commission, since it seems never to have developed into an active organization.

Under the auspices of the Reform League, a conference "to consider the subject of Caste" was held at Cooper Institute in New York on October 10, 1870. The call for the conference had been signed by Aaron M. Powell. Among those who answered with letters rather than their presence were Brown, Frederick Douglass, and Wendell Phillips. Brown wrote from Boston on October 8, a week after the death of his eight-year-old daughter Clotelle. After regretfully informing Powell that he could not attend the conference, he condemned caste based on color as an "unchristian, unrepublican usage of one portion of the citizens towards another." It was his opinion that "the pulpit and the press" could do a great deal to eradicate it.[13]

The annual meeting of the Massachusetts Grand Division of the Sons of Temperance was held in New Era Hall in Boston on October 19, nine days after the conference at Cooper Institute. At the morning session Brown was nominated for the office of grand worthy patriarch, the highest office in the grand division. Before the session was ended, however, his nomination for this office was withdrawn, and he was nominated instead for the office of grand worthy associate.

The afternoon session, which lasted from two to six-thirty o'clock, was devoted principally to the election of officers—for there was much balloting. All of the seven grand officers except the grand worthy associate were elected on the several first ballots. It took four ballots to elect a grand worthy associate.

12. *Boston Daily Evening Transcript,* January 24, 1872, January 25, 1872; *Boston Daily Advertiser,* January 25, 1872, January 26, 1872; *National Standard,* (then a monthly publication), March, 1872, p. 1, April 1872, p. 5.

13. *National Standard,* October 15, 1870, p. 2.

Brown was finally elected by a small majority. Before the session was adjourned, he was also elected a delegate to the next annual meeting of the National Division, perhaps because he had just been made the second highest officer in the grand division which was to be the host to the next national meeting.[14]

The first annual meeting of the National Division of the Sons of Temperance which Brown attended was held in Lawrence Hall in Boston from Wednesday to Saturday, September 6–9, 1871. He was one of three persons from Massachusetts who were initiated into the National Division at the opening session, "being the first person of his race thus honored." Although he was a newcomer, he participated freely in the proceedings of the meeting. Alonzo D. Moore said in a biographical sketch of him published less than three years later that "his speech in behalf of the admission of the colored delegates from Maryland, will not soon be forgotten by those who were present."[15] The official journal of the proceedings of the meeting does not refer to this speech, but it recorded the fact that the delegates in question were admitted by a vote of 106–27. Brown was one of the speakers at a public meeting the National Division held in the Meionaon on Wednesday evening, and he presided at a public meeting sponsored by the John Brown Division in the Joy Street Church the next evening. At a complimentary banquet given to the order in the Music Hall on Friday evening, he was one of the speakers because of popular demand.[16]

About a week afterwards, pursuant to plans he had announced at the meeting in the Joy Street Church, Brown went to Kentucky to spend a month or two laboring in behalf of the National Association for the Organization of Night Schools and the Spread of Temperance Among the Freed People of the

14. *Journal, Sons of Temperance, Massachusetts, 1867–1871,* (Boston, 1872), 5: 259, 267, 273–74, 275.

15. *Rising Son,* p. 25.

16. *Journal, National Division, Sons of Temperance* (Boston, 1871), vol. 4, no. 4, pp. 5, 11, 12–13, 78, 87, 95–96; *Ibid.* (Boston, 1885), vol. 6, no. 4, p. 22.

South. It was his first trip to his native state since his first owner had taken him away as an infant some fifty years earlier. Alas he was not welcomed everywhere in the state as a boy who had gone away, made good, and returned home might have expected to be. After lecturing in Louisville and places near it, he set out for a meeting which he erroneously thought was to be held in Pleasureville, a village forty-four miles east of Louisville. En route from the village to the meeting, he was captured early in the evening by members of the Ku Klux Klan—whether upon the instigation of Bourbon or bourbon interests is not clear—and held captive in a cottage, whence he was to be taken and lynched early the next morning. But thanks to his ingenuity and his knowledge of medicine, with a hypodermic he put the ailing leader of the mob to sleep; and while the man left to guard him slumbered in drunkenness, he escaped unharmed. He was back home by the middle of October. On the eighteenth of that month, with Mrs. Brown, he attended the twenty-eighth annual session of the Massachusetts Grand Division of the Sons of Temperance, which was held in the Meionaon.[17]

Whether because of Brown's visit or as a result of influences unrelated to it, the long-time organization he had gone to Kentucky to represent did some commendable work in that state as well as elsewhere in the South. In 1872 the organization, of which Brown was perennially president, distributed nearly nine thousand spelling books and a large number of readers and arithmetics among the freedmen. Thus it was reported at the annual meeting of the organization in Boston on January 10, 1873. Writing from Boston to Gerrit Smith on the following October 25, Brown acknowledged anew Smith's previous contributions to the organization and solicited additional help from him, "as we are much in need of spelling books to send to Kentucky." Along with his letter Brown sent a printed folder of three pages five by eight inches. On the front page the officers of the or-

17. *National Standard,* October 7, 1871, p. 5; *Rising Son,* pp. 25–33; *Journal, Sons of Temperance, Massachusetts, 1867–1871* (Boston, 1872), 5: 329, 335.

ganization were listed. On the first of the inner pages, which were filled mainly with statements approving its work, the organization was said to have established 123 schools in the South. Whether Smith responded to Brown's request and how long afterwards the organization continued its work are not known.[18]

From 1872 to 1882 exclusive of 1879, Brown was repeatedly authenticated as a past grand worthy associate from the Massachusetts Grand Division at the annual meetings of the National Division of the Sons of Temperance, but he was absent from as often as he was present at these assemblies.[19] Although at times he was optimistic about the progress of temperance, at other times he had good reasons to feel uncertain about the progress of Christian brotherhood within the Sons of Temperance itself. This fact was emphasized at the annual meeting of the National Division which was held in Providence on July 14–17, 1875. Because Negroes in the South were finding it increasingly difficult to become members of the order, he introduced during the second afternoon of the meeting a resolution intended to forestall racial discrimination in the admission of members. His resolution was essentially the same as a recommendation the most worthy patriarch, Stephen B. Ransom of Jersey City, had made at the annual meeting in Boston in September, 1871, and had repeated at the annual meeting in Chicago in June, 1872. Ransom's recommendation, however, had never been acted upon. Brown's resolution was promptly referred to the committee on constitutions, and when at the following evening session it was brought up for consideration, ten grand divisions voted for it, and thirty-three voted against it, thus overwhelmingly defeating it.[20]

18. *Boston Evening Transcript,* January 13, 1873, p. 1; Brown to Smith, October 25, 1873, Gerrit Smith Miller Collection.

19. *Journal, National Division, Sons of Temperance* (Boston, 1872), vol. 4, no. 5, pp. 4–5, 9–10, 61–62; *Ibid.* (Boston, 1873), vol. 4, no. 6, pp. 5, 11, 66; *Ibid.* (Boston, 1874), vol. 4, no. 7, pp. 5, 63, 74, 78.

20. *Ibid.* (Boston, 1871), vol. 4, no. 4, pp. 26–27; *Ibid.* (Boston, 1872), vol. 4, no. 5, pp. 11–15; *Ibid.* (Boston, 1875), vol. 4, no. 8, pp. 5, 65–66, 72–73, 85.

The last two annual meetings of the national division which Brown attended were those held in Philadelphia on June 14–17, 1876, and in Saratoga Springs on June 23 and 24, 1881. He had no important part in either of these meetings, nor was he present at the final roll call of either. The truth is that after the ideal of Christian brotherhood was so blandly forsaken at the annual meeting in Providence in July, 1875, he became less and less enthusiastic about the National Division. He remained active, however, in the John Brown Division and the Massachusetts Grand Division.[21]

As far as racial matters were concerned, Brown's experience in the Independent Order of Good Templars was not essentially different from what it was in the Sons of Temperance. For a long time after its founding in 1851, the Good Templars admitted no Negroes to membership and avoided the question as to whether it should do so. But the question refused to be ignored out of existence. Instead it arose again and again in one form or another at national as well as state and local meetings of the order. It was eventually considered by the Right Worthy Grand Lodge, the highest assembly in the order, at its general convention which was held in Boston in 1866. On that occasion the order approved of the establishment of Negro lodges but did not consider the question as to whether Negroes should be admitted to membership in white lodges. This question was discussed at considerable length at the annual convention which the order held in Richmond, Indiana, on May 26–28, 1868. At that convention the order decided in effect neither to exclude Negroes as groups or individuals from membership nor yet to encourage them to become members. It merely relegated the question to the state grand lodges and local lodges to decide. Specifically this meant that some lodges in the North might admit Negroes to member-

21. *Ibid.* (Boston, 1876), vol. 5, no. 1, pp. 5, 11, 79, 89–90; *Ibid.* (Lockport, N. Y., 1881), vol. 5, no. 6, pp. 6, 11, 68; *Journal, Sons of Temperance, Massachusetts, 1872–1876* (Boston, 1878), 6: 215, 222, 236, 240, 275, 303, 313, 318, 320, 336, 346.

ship, but that none in the South were likely to do so.[22]

One of the local lodges that admitted Negroes to membership within the next few years was Athena lodge, which had been instituted in Boston in 1859. Brown became a member of this lodge before March 20, 1872, for on that date he was admitted to membership in the Massachusetts grand lodge, and membership in a local lodge was a prerequisite for membership in a grand lodge of a given area. Afterwards he was for some time the deputy of Goddard lodge of Brookline and the county deputy of South Middlesex; and in 1873, under the auspices of the grand lodge, he delivered twenty-one lectures on temperance. Most probably Mrs. Brown joined Athena lodge at the same time that her husband did. Anyway, before the end of 1872 she was elected its secretary—a fact which indicates that she had been a member of it long enough to be reasonably well known among her fellow members.[23]

The question as to what should be the relationship of "the colored population of America" to the order, especially in the South, provoked a considerable amount of discussion at the order's annual convention which was held in Madison, Wisconsin, on May 28–31, 1872, a little more than two months after Brown was made a member of the Massachusetts grand lodge. Brown did not attend the convention, but he doubtless heard about it from some who were present, and most probably, he read about it in the official journal of its proceedings. As a result of the discussion, it was decided that under the auspices of the grand lodges in the South, a separate organization with a different name should be established "among the colored population

22. Independent Order of Good Templars, *Journal of Proceedings of the Right Worthy Grand Lodge of North America, Richmond, Indiana, May 26–28, 1868*, pp. 41–42, 79–83; Lorimer E. Harcus, *I. O. of G. T. A History of the Negro Question, in the Right Worthy Grand Lodge* (Napanee, Ont., 1876), pp. 3–4.

23. *Temperance Album*, December 1, 1872, p. 95, January 1, 1873, p. 111; Mrs. Bertha M. Ashworth, Grand Secretary, Massachusetts Grand Lodge, International Order of Good Templars, to me, December 15, 1947.

of the Southern States."[24] Progress in establishing the separate organization, however, must have been slow, for two years passed before the Right Worthy Grand Lodge was officially informed that such an organization existed.

Meanwhile, on March 11, 1874, there occurred an event which caused Brown to turn his attention for a while from the promotion of temperance and to return in memory to the antebellum antislavery crusade. That event was the death of Charles Sumner in Washington. During the next few weeks memorial programs for Sumner were held in various eastern cities. On Sunday evening, May 17, such a program was held in the Music Hall in Boston. After the usual preliminaries Garrison spoke briefly and then presented Brown, the principal speaker for the occasion.

In a eulogy of Sumner, Brown dwelt upon the late senator's contributions to the cause of freedom and racial equality in America both before and after the Civil War. Said he among other things in concluding his speech,

> The triune powers of liberty, justice, and humanity were invested in Charles Sumner. Webster saved the Union with a million of slaves, but Charles Sumner saved the Union with not a slave in it. Charles Sumner was a statesman, and not a politician. Carthage gave her best honors to Hannibal for his conquest of the first Scipio, England honors the memory of Wellington, but greater praise shall be given to Charles Sumner when the great temple of liberty shall be complete, for he was the chiefest among its builders.

The next morning's *Boston Daily Globe* reported on its second page that Brown's speech "was well written and well delivered, and besides had the merit of brevity."

The first and last annual convention of the Good Templars that Brown attended was held in the Meionaon in Boston on

24. IOGT, *Journal of Proceedings, Madison, Wisconsin, May 28–31, 1872*, pp. 44–45, 48–49, 63–64.

May 26–30, 1874. While he was at the evening session on the second day, he improved some otherwise dull minutes by writing a letter to William Still of Philadelphia. In the second half of the letter, he told briefly about the convention. He informed Still that among "representatives from all the civilized nations," his was "the only colored face here," that "The Negro question comes up tomorrow," and that "Some twenty representatives are here from the South, and many of them look at me in a rather wolfish manner." He concluded his letter when "the prosey [*sic*] speaker who has been occupying the time while I have been writing this" concluded his speech.[25] As Still knew, of course, only those who knew that Brown was supposed to be a Negro would have recognized his as a "colored face." Accordingly his remark about the wolfish glances of the Southern representatives might well have been in a great measure an expression of sensitiveness on his part.

The official report of the sessions of May 28 contains no reference to the Negro question, which Brown had told Still was to be discussed on that day. As Brown must have remembered, however, the Negro question had been incidentally brought up and disposed of on the first day of the convention. At the opening session Right Worthy Grand Templar Samuel D. Hastings of Madison, Wisconsin, had submitted his report. In it, with more than common satisfaction, he had announced that in the several Southern states, Negro lodges were being established under the jurisdiction of white grand lodges. These Negro lodges, he had explained, constituted a temperance organization called the United Order of True Reformers, which had regalia, ritual, etc. different from those of the Good Templars. Thus it appeared that the decision made at the annual convention in Madison two years earlier was at last being put into practice.

Brown needed no especially keen insight to discern an un-

25. IOGT, *Journal of Proceedings, Boston, May 26–30, 1874*, pp. 4–5, 64–65, 69; Brown to Still, May 27, 1874, Leon Gardiner Collection on Negro History.

mistakable sign of the times in this bountiful concession to Colonel James Crow. But if he was not yet disillusioned, he should have been on May 27 when J. J. Hickman of Louisville, the same Kentucky colonel who had been chairman of the committee which had maneuvered the separate organization into existence, was elected the new right worthy grand templar. Brown was naturally displeased with the establishment of the separate order; but since it was already a fait accompli, there was nothing he could do but wait and watch for an opportunity to overthrow Colonel James Crow. Before the convention was adjourned, he and two other delegates gave notice that at the next annual convention they would try to get the order to amend its constitution so that it might establish under its name more than one lodge in the same jurisdiction when differences in race made such advisable.[26]

The next annual convention was held in Bloomington, Illinois, on May 25–28, 1875. Brown was not present, nor was his proposed change in the constitution considered. The place of the annual convention of 1876 was Louisville, Kentucky, the home city of Colonel J. J. Hickman, who was still right worthy grand templar. The time was May 23–27. On the second day of the convention, the Negro question, which had become perennial, was again brought up for settlement. During the next two days there was considerable discussion of the question, with Dr. Oronhyatekha of Napanee, Ontario, taking the lead and contributing profusely to the beclouding of the matter. The discussion was terminated by a vote of 85–58 on a motion of Oronhyatekha's which left the matter where it was at the beginning, which was, in effect, that grand lodges and subordinate lodges had the right to exclude Negroes from membership if they wished to do so.

Immediately after the vote was announced, the representatives from Great Britain and Ireland submitted a decisive resolu-

26. *Boston Daily Globe*, May 27, 1874; IOGT, *Journal of Proceedings, Boston, May 26–30, 1874*, pp. 20–23, 68, 70, 89–90, 111, 112.

tion. In it they first expressed their dissatisfaction with the failure of the assembly to provide "for the practical enforcement, by constitutional provision, of the principle that colour shall not bar those of the African or any other Race from the protection and enjoyment of the full privileges of membership in any jurisdiction of our Order." Second, they announced that "in accordance with the explicit and positive instructions" of the grand lodges they represented, they were withdrawing from their seats in the Right Worthy Grand Lodge, and straightway they withdrew. On the last morning of the convention, these representatives were invited to return to their seats, but they refused to do so or even to receive the committee which had been sent to wait upon them, despite the fact that the right worthy grand templar himself was a member of it.[27] At last the order had been brought to a crisis by the question it had repeatedly failed during twenty-five years to settle right.

After the convention in Louisville, the Good Templars of Great Britain and Ireland organized themselves into the Right Worthy Grand Lodge of the World of the Independent Order of Good Templars, an order separate from the one in America. Within a year after its formation, Brown was commissioned as one of its special American deputies. The new right worthy grand lodge held a convention in Glasgow, Scotland, early in July, 1877. Brown was there as a delegate; and when officers were chosen, he was elected right worthy grand counsellor, the second highest officer in the order.[28]

This was Brown's first time in Great Britain since his sojourn there from 1849 to 1854, and it was destined to be his last trip there. He was in the British Isles from June 20 to August 30. During that time he addressed assemblies in more than thirty cities and towns, many of these being places in which he had

27. IOGT, *Journal of Proceedings, Bloomington, Illinois, May 25–28, 1875*, pp. 63–64, 98; *Ibid., Louisville, Kentucky, May 23–27, 1876*, pp. 79–80, 83–84, 86, 92, 93–94, 134–35.

28. *Good Templars' Watchword* [London], July 11, 1877, p. 1. Herein are a picture and a somewhat inaccurate biographical sketch of Brown.

delivered antislavery lectures more than twenty years earlier.[29]

One of his fellow abolitionists of old with whom Brown renewed acquaintance while he was in Great Britain was Ellen Richardson of Newcastle upon Tyne. Brown spent only a short time in Newcastle; and after returning to America, he failed to keep in touch with Miss Richardson, even if he did not forget her—as he could hardly have done. Five years later, nevertheless, she was still sufficiently thoughtful of him to request Frederick Douglass in a letter to remember her to him. She did not then know where he was or what he was doing, for she had not heard from him in a long time.[30]

In spite of his discouraging experiences with the national temperance organizations in America, Brown continued his temperance work until he died. Under the auspices of the Right Worthy Grand Lodge of the World, he organized grand lodges of Good Templars in Richmond and Norfolk, Virginia, in 1878 and 1879. These were in opposition, of course, to the segregated grand lodges of the American order, and that order noticed them only to condemn them and their organizer. During one season at least, as a means of stimulating local interest in temperance, Brown conducted an essay contest for "the colored youth of the Boston High Schools." The subject for the contest was "The Evils of Intemperance and Their Remedies." The prize for the best essay was ten dollars in gold offered upon Brown's prompting by the Congregational Publishing Society of Boston. The prize was won by Pauline E. Hopkins, who was then only fifteen years of age, and who was inspired by her success in the contest to try to become a writer.[31]

29. Walter Hayler to me, letter and notes concerning Brown, London, August 1, 1949.

30. Ellen Richardson to Frederick Douglass, November 14, 1882, Papers of Frederick Douglass.

31. IOGT, *Journal of Proceedings, New York City, May 25–29, 1880*, pp. 59–60; *Colored American Magazine*, 2 (January, 1901): 218.

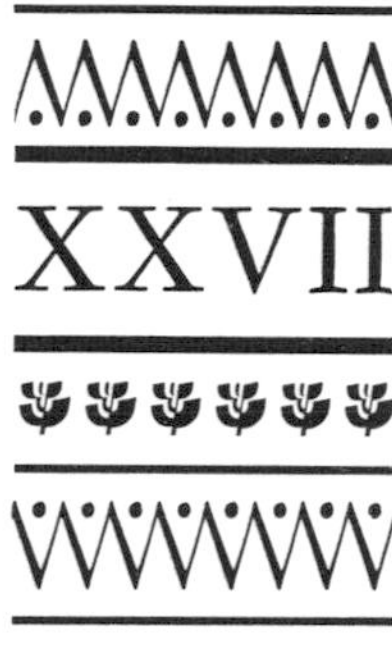

XXVII

Still to Shine in Use

WHILE BROWN WAS BUSIEST WITH THE CAUSE OF TEMPERance, he was also busy writing his fourth and last historical work, which proved to be his longest book. This is *The Rising Son; or, The Antecedents and Advancement of the Colored Race.* Having worked on this book intermittently for some time, he had it almost ready for the press by the middle of the summer of 1873. The history of the completion and publication of it was incidentally recorded in the correspondence between Brown and William Still and that between Mrs. Mary Ann Shadd Cary of Chatham, Ontario, and Still during the last seven months of 1873. None of these letters themselves seem to have been preserved, but letterpress copies of Still's letters to Brown and Mrs. Cary still exist.[1] The copies were made, of course, before the originals were posted.

1. Leon Gardiner Collection on Negro History.

Chapter Twenty-Seven

In a letter of June 14 to Brown, Still referred sympathetically to the fact that Brown had been recently injured upon being thrown from his carriage when his horse ran away. It appears from the same letter that Brown had sought Still's aid in getting biographical sketches of representative Negro men and women for the last chapter in *The Rising Son.* In accordance with Still's request, a Dr. Hines had written a sketch of Fanny M. Jackson, an honor graduate of Oberlin College and then principal of a Negro high school in Philadelphia. Upon seeing the sketch, Miss Jackson had promised to improve it and then forward it to Brown, but she had been so slow in fulfilling her promise that both Brown and Still had begun to doubt that she would keep it. Eventually, however, she sent the sketch to Brown, and he included it in the book. Meanwhile with Brown's approval Still arranged to get a sketch of another woman to replace the sketch of Miss Jackson. In the postscript of a letter he wrote to Mrs. Cary on July 30, he asked her to supply him with information which he might use in writing a sketch of her for Brown's book. He told her that the book was to be published on October 1 by Lee and Shepard of Boston, and he also expressed the hope that he would have "your consent & aid in the matter."

Mrs. Cary was prompt enough with her consent and aid to send Still within a week the information he wanted. In a letter of August 8, Still informed Brown that "if a sketch of Mrs. Cary will now be in time for your book, I have the points necessary to prepare it, and will take great pleasure in doing so without further delay." Brown replied to Still on August 11, thanking him for offering to prepare the sketch and explaining that it would be too late, because "The work is in the hands of the Stereotypers and nearly finished." Thus Still quoted from Brown's letter in a letter of September 9 to Mrs. Cary. "After trotting," Still's quotation from Brown's letter continued, "between two of our best publishers' places for a week or more, at their solicitation, and standing a goodeal [*sic*] of bantering about terms—the little Devil that's in me, got stirred up, and I did everything but Sware [*sic*]." After all of this Brown decided to publish the book himself and to sell it "by subscription only."

About the middle of September, Brown found that after all it was not too late for him to use Mrs. Cary's sketch, and forthwith he notified Still of this fact. Still promptly wrote the sketch and sent it to Brown and presumably also informed Mrs. Cary that he had done so. On October 28 he wrote a letter to Brown in reply to one Brown had written to him on October 24. As Still's letter reveals, Brown had told him that *The Rising Son* had been recently published, and that already there were prospects for the sale in the near future of four hundred copies of it in the South and eight hundred copies in Boston. Still declared himself quite pleased with such prospects, especially during "these hard times." His remark concerning the hard times was an allusion to the panic of 1873, whose bad effects were now nationwide.

In the letter previously mentioned which he wrote to Gerrit Smith on October 25, the day after he wrote to Still, Brown called Smith's attention to "my New Book, 'The Rising Son' which is just out." Along with this letter and the circular concerning the promotion of night schools and temperance in the South, he sent a circular advertising the book. This circular contains the names of eighty-eight biographees. Ten of these were left without sketches in the book, but sketches of three who are not listed were included.

Writing again to Brown on November 7, Still thanked him for a complimentary copy of *The Rising Son* which he had received—"one of your first copies from the press." He was glad to know, he said, that Brown had found the demand for the work greater than the supply, and that he was "doing well with the book at the South."

Within the next few weeks, however, Brown discovered that things pertaining to the book were much less auspicious than they had at first seemed to be. On December 23 Still wrote in reply to a letter of Brown's which he had received on the preceding day, and which was dated December 20. He was glad to hear from Brown, he said, "as I have been often thinking of you in connection with your new enterprise." He then took note of the unfortunate change in the enterprise by quoting a sentence from Brown's letter and adding a brief sympathetic statement: " 'The first edition of the book is gone except about 300 cops [*sic*] with a loss of not less than $200.' I am sorry for the loss." Whether Brown had or had not explained the cause of the loss, Still said nothing specific about it in his letter. It seems from his remarks, withal, that he was inclined to blame the loss not only upon the economic depression then prevailing but also upon a want of interest in the book on the part of those who should have been especially interested in it.

The Rising Son has a picture of Brown as a frontispiece. It was the first of his books to be thus adorned since the publication of *Sketches of Places and People Abroad*. The imprint is that of A. G. Brown and Company, 140 Court Street, Boston, the street address being that of Brown's office at the time. The book was copyrighted by A. G. Brown in 1873, and it appeared late in October of that year, but the earliest date found in its imprint is 1874. The latest date in it is 1885. When the book first appeared, it contained 552 pages, but it was enlarged soon afterwards. Early in 1874 Brown added to the introductory pages a dedicatory poem entitled "Welcome to 'The Rising Son.' " This had been written by Elijah W. Smith, a Boston writer of verse and a printer, who had worked in the office of the *Liberator*. Brown also added a sketch of Smith at the end of the volume, thus finally bringing it up to 555 pages, exclusive of an error in the numbering of the pages in the text itself.

In his preface of less than half a page, Brown explained that he was "compelled to acknowledge the scantiness of materials for a history of the African race," that he had endeavored "to give a faithful account of the people and their customs, without concealing their faults," and that several of the biographical sketches in the last part of the work were "necessarily brief" because of the difficulty of getting information about some of the biographees. Following the table of contents is a "Memoir of the Author," which fills twenty-seven pages. This was written by Alonzo D. Moore, who as a boy in Aurora, New York, had known Brown while he was living in Buffalo and lecturing for the Western New York Anti-Slavery Society.

The text of *The Rising Son* may be divided into five main parts. First, there are eleven chapters dealing with what Brown considered "the antecedents of the colored race" and with African civilization. In these chapters he cited numerous sources of information, some still historically respectable and some better known as imaginative than as historical or scientific works. Not the least ingenious nor the most convincing among the ethnological theories in this part of the book are those which attribute differences in complexion and texture of hair to climate, and variations in physical features to variations in moral and social conditions. Brown did not take credit, of course, for originating these theories. He found them in much of the scientific as well as the travel literature of the first half of the nineteenth century. He was especially indebted for them to Arnold Ludwig von Heeren's *Historical Researches into the Politics, Intercourse, and Trade of the Carthagenians, Ethiopians, and Egyptians* and to James Cowles Prichard's *Researches into the Physical History of Mankind*. Taking these theories more seriously than they deserved to be taken, he had often repeated them in his lecture on the origin and early history of the African race. Had he once thought that they would soon be completely discredited, doubtless he would have made much less of them than he did.

The second part of *The Rising Son* consists of chapters 12–25. This is an historical sketch of Haiti from the introduction of slavery there—more correctly, a chronicle of Haitian rulers from the time of Toussaint L'Ouverture—to the third quarter of the nineteenth century. At least a fifth of this part was not new writing. Brown repeated some of it verbatim from his *St. Domingo* and still more of it, with minor additions and omissions, from the sketches of the several Haitians which he had included in *The Black Man.* In this and the next two parts of *The Rising Son,* he made some changes in what he repeated from his earlier historical works, but in some instances he failed to make simple changes in wording which were necessary to bring his statements up to date.

In the third part of the work, which comprises chapters 26–29, Brown attempted to tell in twenty-two pages about the Negro in Jamaica, South America, Cuba, Puerto Rico, and Santo Domingo. He left this part quite sketchy probably because of a want of information about these places. Most of what he said about Cuba is a literal repetition of the sketch of Placido which he had included in *The Black Man.*

The fourth and largest part of *The Rising Son,* which consists of chapters 30–49, is a cursory history of the Negro in the United States from the introduction of slavery into America early in the seventeenth century to the Reconstruction. Brown wrote only about two-thirds of this part anew. He repeated the remainder from *The Black Man* and *The Negro in the American Rebellion.* Ironically enough, the new writing hardly rivals in interest what he repeated from his previous writing.

The fifth and last part of *The Rising Son* is chapter 50, which is entitled "Representative Men and Women." In its final form this chapter contains eighty-one biographical sketches arranged in no systematic order. Twenty-eight of them are of persons whose lives Brown had previously sketched in *The Black Man.* Brown reproduced several of these sketches verbatim, as he did those of Crispus Attucks and Benjamin Banneker. He added details to some of them to bring them up to date. He shortened many of them by omitting biographical details and quotations from or about the individuals, as he did those, for example, of Phillis Wheatley, Frederick Douglass, Charles L. Reason, John Mercer Langston, and Ira Aldridge. Thus he saved space at the expense of making many of the shortened sketches less informative and less interesting than their originals. He rewrote many of the sketches, improving some, as he did those of James M.

Whitfield, Mrs. Frances Ellen (Watkins) Harper, and William J. Wilson, but without improving others such as those of William C. Nell, William Still, and the Reverend Leonard A. Grimes. He dealt most remarkably with the sketch of Charles Lenox Remond. He reduced it to one-fourth of its original length and concluded it with two uncomplimentary sentences.

Especially noteworthy among the fifty-three new biographees were David Ruggles, Jermain W. Loguen, Harriet Tubman, alias "Moses," and Lewis Hayden. All of these persons had been faithful and daring abolitionists. The first two had died, but the other two were still living. There were also Edmonia Lewis, who was distinguishing herself as a sculptress, and James Madison Bell, who was gaining attention as a poet and lecturer. A considerable number of the fifty-three were preachers and politicians whose future promised to be much greater than their past had been. Brown wrote very brief sketches of most of the fifty-three, or in some instances had others write sketches of them, because he himself did not know much about them.

Together *The Black Man* and *The Rising Son* contain biographical sketches of 110 more or less noteworthy Negroes, most of whom belonged to times long gone. In compiling these sketches, Brown produced a sort of dictionary of Negro biography, in which he gave information about many who, although they did not achieve what is generally considered greatness, did contribute to human welfare, and who might have been forgotten if they had not been thus commemorated.

The *Boston Evening Transcript* for November 7, 1873, said on its sixth page that *The Rising Son* contained "a well-written résumé of the history of the dark hued people of various tribes and lands." The *Congregationalist* for December 11, another Boston publication, observed that the book "has for its subject the progress of the African race out of bondage into liberty and manhood, and is itself a striking illustration of that progress." It was, the *Congregationalist* continued, "the fruit of careful study and reading, and [was] well-written."

Chapter Twenty-Seven

The plan by which Brown attempted in *The Rising Son* to survey the history of the Negro and to exemplify his genius in biographical sketches of distinguished Negroes is somewhat similar to the plan of Henri Grégoire's *De la Littérature des Nègres* (Paris, 1808). A plan more or less like Grégoire's had been partially followed in R. B. Lewis's *Light and Truth*. Brown might have been familiar with Grégoire's book, as he most probably was with Lewis's, but he gave no specific evidence that he was familiar with either. Anyway *The Rising Son* is much more comprehensive than Grégoire's book, and as historical writing it is incomparably superior to Lewis's work. If, therefore, Brown was indebted to Grégoire and Lewis at all, it was only for ideas concerning the basic plan of his book.

It may be readily observed that Brown's historical works are fraught with defects. In all of them there are inaccuracies in details and considerable repetition. None of them evince any study of manuscripts or many official documents on the part of the author. None of them except *The Negro in the American Rebellion* and *The Rising Son* contain footnotes or other specific references of any kind, and many of the references in these works are either vague or inaccurate. Doubtless Brown could and would have removed these defects had he known much about historiography and the methodology of research, but he knew little or nothing about the technicalities of these things, because he had had no opportunity to study them. It is also true that when he was writing history, much of the abracadabra of modern scholarship had not yet been invented, to say nothing of being mysticized into a cult.

Nevertheless Brown must not have been altogether wanting in an intelligent conception of history. He had read some historians—Gibbon, Carlyle, Macaulay, Bancroft, and others—and he must have learned something from some of them. He had also read more or less extensively in the specialized form of history which is biography. In the preface to the third edition of William Roscoe's *The Life and Pontificate of Leo the Tenth* (London, 1827 and later editions), he had found a theory of history with which no fault could have been found even by the high priest of the philosophy of history—Hegel himself. Said Roscoe in this preface,

> History is the record of the experience of mankind in their most important concerns. If it be impossible for human sagacity to estimate the consequences of a falsehood in private life, it is equally impossible to estimate the consequences of a false or partial representation of the events of former times. The conduct of the present is regulated by the experience of the past. The circumstances which have led the way to the prosperity or destruction of states, will lead the way to the prosperity or destruction of states in all future ages. . . .
>
> As in speaking of the natural world, there are some persons who are disposed to attribute its creation to chance, so in speaking of the moral world, there are some who are inclined to refer the events and fluctuations in human affairs to accident, and are satisfied with accounting for them from the common course of things, or the spirit of the times. But as *chance* and *accident*, if they have any meaning whatever, can only mean the operation of causes not hitherto fully investigated, or distinctly understood, so *the spirit of the times* is only another phrase for causes and circumstances which have not hitherto been sufficiently explained. It is the province of the historian to trace and to discover these causes, and it is only in proportion as he accomplishes this object, that his labours are of any utility.

For Brown, as for Roscoe, the value of history consisted primarily not in what it was but in what it did—in the extent to which it influenced the course of human affairs. If human affairs needed reforming, as they did especially in Brown's time and constantly do, then history must help to reform them or be considered a mere pastime.

During his last years, when he might have been expected to take life in a more and more leisurely manner, Brown was still busy with a variety of activities. He was still practicing medicine, doing temperance work, traveling, lecturing, and writing. Like Tennyson's Ulysses he found it dull to pause, to rust unburnished instead of shining in use to the end. Partly in the interest of temperance, partly to satisfy his curiosity about the new South, and partly for pleasure, he took a trip in the winter of 1879–80 to several erstwhile slave states. He went as far south as Huntsville, Alabama, where he spent the Christmas holidays. He spent much of the winter in Tennessee, sojourning in Columbia, Nashville, and Knoxville. He visited Harper's Ferry and also Richmond, Petersburg, and Norfolk. It was his first trip to all of the places just mentioned except the last three.

Brown's last but hardly his best book is *My Southern Home: Or, The South and Its People.* This octavo volume of 261 pages was published early in May, 1880, by A. G. Brown and Company, 28 East Canton Street, Boston. The time of its publication is determined by two facts. The author's preface was dated at Boston in May, and the book was briefly reviewed on the fourth page of the *Boston Sunday Herald* for May 16. Either the book sold rapidly, or the first two editions of it were very small, for the third edition was published in 1882; and it has been said that a fourth edition had been published by 1884.[2] The text is the same in all of the first three editions.

This is the most profusely illustrated of all of Brown's books. In addition to the frontispiece, which is a picture of the author, there are six large textual illustrations. All of these pertain to slavery, and all of them except one had appeared in *Clotel* or *Clotelle* of 1864 and 1867. Although generally complimentary, the review in the *Boston Sunday Herald* was severely critical of the frontispiece. It observed that "The book is illustrated with a coarse wood-cut engraving of the author, which does no justice at all to the handsome features of one of the most able of the anti-slavery orators of the past generation."

The author's preface consists of three sentences. The main

2. Vernon Loggins, *The Negro Author: His Development in America* (New York, 1931), p. 172.

idea in it is his disclaimer of any attempt "to create heroes or heroines, or to appeal to the imagination or the heart"—which means, if it means anything definite, that he was not primarily interested in making this a literary work. Perhaps his explanation was no more than an overstatement whose purpose was to disavow any intentions to do what he feared that he had not done, and thereby to forestall criticism for his failure to do it. Yet if a comparatively recent criticism of the book is valid, Brown achieved more than he implied that he tried to achieve in it; for according to that criticism, this is "his nearest approach to real literature."[3] This judgment is, of course, debatable.

The first three-fifths of *My Southern Home* deals with slave life not only as Brown had experienced it but also as he had heard and read about it; and in writing about it in this book, he necessarily appealed to the imagination as well as the emotions of his readers. He repeated a considerable amount, often verbatim, of what he had said in the several editions of his *Narrative*, the four versions of *Clotel*, *The Escape*, his *Memoir of William Wells Brown*, and also *The Negro in the American Rebellion*. In many instances he identified characters, whether actual or fictitious, by the names he had used for them in those works. He unified this new—or rather, newly organized—history of slave life by making its principal setting a plantation ten miles north of Saint Louis. This he called Poplar Farm and identified Dr. John Gaines as its owner. He had in mind, of course, Dr. John Young and his plantation four miles north of Saint Louis.

In this history of slave life, Brown's technique, although not much of his subject matter, was different from that which he had used when he was an antislavery crusader. As a rule he did not argue now as he had done then; he simply related incidents as interestingly and convincingly as he could—some of them being intentionally humorous—and left his readers to draw their

3. *Ibid.*, p. 171.

own conclusions. He admitted in one passage that some slaves were happy, but he remembered that "It was indeed, a low kind of happiness, existing only where masters were disposed to treat their servants kindly, and where the proverbial lightheartedness of the latter prevailed."[4] Nowhere did he idealize the "peculiar institution," as writers of the school of Joel Chandler Harris and Thomas Nelson Page were already beginning to do apologetically if not defensively.

The last two-fifths of *My Southern Home* is a sketchy and somewhat critical account of the author's trip to the South in the winter of 1879–80. Before he took the trip, Brown was cognizant of the more or less national tendency to confuse equality of citizenship for Negroes with what later came to be called "social equality." He was also aware that the former Confederates, who by various means were rapidly regaining control of their section, were divesting Negroes in the South of the rights of citizenship which the Reconstruction had brought them, and that the federal government was doing less and less to safeguard those rights for them. Thus he was more dismayed than surprised to find wherever he went in the South that by unjust laws and extralegal processes, Negroes were being reduced to a status obviously close to chattel slavery.[5]

Brown was no longer very optimistic about the Negro's future, as he had been early in the 1870's. As he now contemplated the state of affairs in the South, he tried to discover some reasons for it. Already there were in circulation tales concerning Negro domination in the former Confederate states during the Reconstruction. Accepting these tales uncritically, Brown asserted quite erroneously that "All of the Legislatures [of these states] were composed mainly of colored men," and that "The few whites that were there were not only no help to the blacks, but it would have been better for the character of the latter, and for the country at large, if most of them had been in some State

4. William Wells Brown, *My Southern Home: Or, The South and Its People* (Boston, 1880), p. 91.

5. *Ibid.*, pp. 219–29.

prison." The existing state of affairs, he rationalized, had resulted from the natural reactions of the proud, aristocratic erstwhile slaveholders to the misrule of Negroes, carpetbaggers, and scalawags. Nevertheless, without much regard for consistency he paid a high tribute to the Negro politicians whom he had just criticized adversely. Said he, "They reconstructed the State Governments that their masters had destroyed; became Legislators, held State offices, and with all their blunders, surpassed the whites that had preceded them."[6]

Brown did not overlook the faults which so many of the freedmen possessed—shiftlessness, thriftlessness, and intemperance, for example. Nor could he forget that these faults were traceable directly to slavery. Just now, however, he was primarily concerned with the immediate causes of the "moral and social degradation of the colored population of the Southern States." He thought that these causes were poor living conditions and too much emotionalism in religion, together with charlatanry on the part of many who called themselves preachers. He supported his belief with numerous references to incidents he had witnessed or heard about during his recent sojourn in the South.

Still the reformer as well as author, Brown emphasized intraracial cooperation, temperance, education, and literary culture as the means by which Negroes could best improve as individuals and as a group. To discover the importance of literature in the development of a people, he said, one needed only to note the influence of Homer upon the Greeks, Virgil and Horace upon the Romans, Shakespeare and Milton upon the English, and other authors upon their respective nations. Leaving the kind of influence he had in mind unexplained, Brown urged Negroes not to content themselves with the achievements of the colored men and women of the past, but to work in the living present for their advancement.[7]

Negroes, Brown questionably asserted, had never made more than feeble efforts to throw off their chains and thereby to gain

6. *Ibid.*, pp. 180, 182–83.
7. *Ibid.*, p. 242.

the respect of mankind. He admitted that Denmark Vesey's plan for an insurrection in South Carolina "was noble," but he remembered, alas, that Vesey "was betrayed by the race that he was attempting to serve." Speaking somewhat less sympathetically than he had spoken in *The Black Man*, *The Negro in the American Rebellion*, and *The Rising Son*, he now said that "Nat Turner's strike for liberty was the outburst of feelings of an insane man,—made so by slavery." Negro soldiers, he was aware, had fought bravely in many battles of the Civil War; "Yet it would have been far better," he contended, "if they had commenced earlier, or had been under leaders of their own color."[8] Here his criticism amounted to caviling, for as he knew very well, Negroes had entered the war as soon as they were permitted to do so and never had any choice concerning their leaders in it.

During the administration of Rutherford B. Hayes, because Negroes in the South were being deprived of their rights as citizens and were being oppressed anew, they began emigrating in ever increasing numbers from the section. Early in 1879 there was an exodus of Negroes from the Mississippi delta to the north central states, especially to Kansas. This exodus provoked some debate both in and outside the United States Senate as to whether such wholesale emigration was wise or unwise, and many Negro leaders found themselves involved in the debate. Trusting in the efficacy of the Thirteenth, Fourteenth, and Fifteenth Amendments, Frederick Douglass said that "The permanent powers of the Government are all on his [the Negro's] side," and that his rights would "revive, survive and flourish again." Hence Douglass regarded "the present agitation of an African Exodus from the South" as "ill-timed," as "an abandonment of the great and paramount principle of protection to person and property in every State in the Union," and as a movement favored by "neither the laws of politics, labor nor climate."[9]

8. *Ibid.*, pp. 243–44.

9. Frederick Douglass, "The Negro Exodus from the Gulf States," *Journal of Social Science*, 11 (May, 1880): 1–21.

Brown briefly discussed the matter in *My Southern Home.* He considered the South the home of the Negro "by common right," he said; but he insisted that if Negroes could not be protected there as other citizens were, they should go where they would be protected and would have opportunities for advancement. He realized that all of them could not emigrate; but he thought that if large numbers of them did, those who remained in the South would be treated better, because their importance as workers in the section would increase in accordance with the law of supply and demand and would thus increase their bargaining power.[10]

If Douglass's argument was too theoretical—and indeed it was—Brown's amounted to an oversimplification of the situation. It was not simply a matter of faith in political principles nor a question as to whether the federal government could protect Negroes in the South, but a fact that it was not doing so. Yet it was hardly practical for large numbers of them to emigrate without means, in many instances without risking arrest when they attempted to leave the South, and without preparation for the circumstances which might confront them in the places to which they might immigrate. It was to a great extent the proverbial choice between bearing known evils and flying to unknown ones. As to the bargaining power of the Negroes who remained in the South, there was no reason to hope for much from that. Those who were now in control of affairs in the section were doubtless sufficiently influential to forestall the use of such power. But even if they had not been, relatively few if any of them had yet awaked to the necessity of conceding ordinary rights and advantages to Negroes in order to safeguard their own interests and the prosperity of the section. In fact almost a century was to pass—a century characterized by two world wars and the inevitable abolition of regional as well as national isolation—before many of those in control in the section were awaked to this necessity. As neither Douglass nor Brown

10. Brown, *My Southern Home*, pp. 244–46.

lived long enough to discover, there was no quick nor easy ascent from the political and economic avernus into which Negroes in the South were forced after the Reconstruction.

My Southern Home abounds in slave songs and Negro folk songs of the Reconstruction years. Brown had doubtless jotted these songs down upon hearing them from time to time, whether before or during his recent trip to the South. All of them are sufficiently impressive as genuine folk material, but none of them exemplify folk poetry at its very best, although Brown probably considered them the best among the pieces he had collected.

On February 2, 1884, Wendell Phillips, who was one of Brown's ideals, died. On the evening of February 8, two days after Phillips's funeral, a memorial meeting for him was held in Faneuil Hall in Boston. During the meeting, which lasted almost four hours, there were speeches by Brown, Mrs. Julia Ward Howe, and others.[11] This was one of the last public occasions, if not the last one, on which Brown was a speaker. Ere long he found that he himself was "not in the enjoyment of good health," as he had said thirty-seven years earlier in describing Wells Brown, the benefactor who had given him a complete name. Nevertheless he continued many of his customary activities until the last of the following October, when he was confined to his home in Chelsea. After being critically ill for a week, he died there on November 6 at four-thirty o'clock in the afternoon. The immediate cause of his death was a tumor of the bladder.[12]

Reports of Brown's death appeared in at least six Boston newspapers for November 8. There were comparatively long reports on the eighth page of the *Daily Advertiser*, the third page of the *Daily Globe*, and the first page of the *Evening Transcript*. "He was," said the *Daily Globe*, "one of the most

11. *Boston Daily Advertiser*, February 9, 1884.

12. Massachusetts, 43rd Registration, 1884, Deaths, vol. 357, Suffolk-Worcester, p. 363, no. 396, State House, Boston, Massachusetts.

intelligent, earnest and active members of the little band of old-time abolitionists, and commanded the highest respect of all who knew him." The report in the *Evening Transcript* said among other things that "As a prolific writer, commanding a clear intellect and facile pen, he undoubtedly did much useful work." Unfortunately all three of these reports contain errors in biographical details.

The obsequies for Brown were held on Sunday, November 9, a cold but clear and beautiful day.[13] The attending undertaker was George Studley of Boston. A private service was held in the Browns' home in Chelsea at eleven o'clock in the morning. The public funeral was held in the A. M. E. Zion Church on North Russell Street in Boston at noon. The coffin, said the *Boston Herald* for November 10, was "decorated with beautiful floral designs, the gift of the grand lodge of Good Templars, with which body the deceased had stood in close official connection up to the time of his death." The service was conducted by the Reverend J. W. Brown, the pastor of the church, who was assisted by two other pastors of Boston churches. In addition to the eulogy by the pastor, there were speeches by the Reverend Samuel May, Jr., Charles W. Slack, the Reverend James Yeames (a British temperance worker), Lewis Hayden (who had been a pallbearer for both Garrison and Phillips), and others.[14]

After the funeral there was the long drive from the church to the Cambridge Cemetery on the north bank of the Charles River, some distance southwest of Harvard Square. There late in the sunlit afternoon, Brown was interred in range 31, grave number 7. It was the same grave in which Mrs. Harriet Gray, his mother-in-law, had been buried nine years earlier. The location of the grave is given in the records in the office of the

13. Weather report for November 9, *Boston Daily Advertiser*, November 10, 1884.

14. *Boston Daily Globe*, November 10, 1884; *Boston Herald*, November 10, 1884. The *Herald's* report of the funeral together with a picture and an inaccurate biographical sketch of Brown was reprinted in *Good Templar's Watchword* [London], December 1, 1884.

cemetery, but it seems never to have been marked with a stone of any kind.

A man of medium stature, Brown was possessed of a melodious voice, a pleasing personality, and a wholesome sense of humor. From the facts concerning his parentage and the numerous references of his time to his complexion, it appears that he could easily have passed for a white man but deliberately avoided doing so, lest he might have compromised his integrity. For almost three decades before the Civil War, he labored diligently in various ways for the antislavery cause and thereby merited a place of primary importance in the history of abolitionism in America. In the score of years he lived after the war, he worked faithfully for the cause of temperance; and although he thus devoted himself to a waning reform, his service to that reform became an important part of its history. Finally, in conjunction with his activities as a Negro leader, he exercised his genius for writing and thereby left as a legacy especially for Negro authors the stimulation and the challenge of a pioneer in the writing of travel literature, fiction, drama, and history.

Whatever the Browns' reasons for moving to Chelsea were, Mrs. Brown did not remain there very long after her husband died. Early in 1885, *The Rising Son* and *My Southern Home* were again being advertised from 28 East Canton Street, Boston, the address from which the Browns had moved their home to Chelsea.[15] Whether this address was repeated from old advertisements or Mrs. Brown had returned to it is uncertain. If she had, she doubtless remained there only a short time. On January 23, 1885, her sister Henrietta, the wife of Thomas Calvin, a merchant tailor, died after a long illness. At the time, according to the Boston directories for 1884 and 1885, the Calvins' home was at 24 East Canton Street. After her sister's death, Mrs. Brown moved to Calvin's home to keep house for him and his young daughter. By the beginning of 1886, she and the two Calvins were

15. William Wells Brown, *The Negro in the American Rebellion: His Heroism and His Fidelity*, new ed. (Boston, 1885), end-leaf advertisements.

living at 11 East Canton Street, and she and her brother-in-law at least remained at that address until 1900, when they moved to 35 Greenwich Street in Roxbury.

Meanwhile Mrs. Brown continued her temperance work, serving for some time as president of a local branch of the Women's Christian Temperance Union. About noon on September 4, 1902, while she was at home alone, some clothes hanging near the range in her kitchen caught fire. In an attempt to extinguish the fire, she was severely burned. She was taken to the Boston City Hospital, where she died early in the evening. Her funeral was held at noon on September 6 in the same church in which her husband's funeral had been held eighteen years earlier. She was interred in range F, grave number 51, in the Cambridge Cemetery, the same grave in which Mrs. Henrietta Calvin, her sister, had been buried in January, 1885.[16]

16. Pauline E. Hopkins, "Women's Department," *Colored American Magazine*, 1 (June, 1900): 118; Massachusetts, 61st Registration, 1902, Deaths, vol. 531, Suffolk, p. 295, no. 7405, State House, Boston, Massachusetts; *Boston Evening Transcript*, September 5, 1902, September 6, 1902; *Boston Herald*, September 5, 1902, September 6, 1902; records in the office of the Cambridge Cemetery.

BIBLIOGRAPHY

LIBRARIES CONTAINING THE RARE ITEMS LISTED HEREIN ARE designated by abbreviations or in single instances by names following the items. No locations are given, of course, for items which are not rare. Abbreviations are as follows. AAS, American Antiquarian Society. AU, Atlanta University. BA, the Boston Athenaeum. BPL, Boston Public Library. BrM, British Museum. CoU, Columbia University. CU, Cornell University, DU, Duke University. EPL, Edinburgh Public Libraries. HaU, Harvard University. HI, Hampton Institute. HU, Howard University. LC, the Library of Congress. ML, the Mitchell Library, Glasgow, Scotland. NCCD, North Carolina College at Durham. NYHS, New York Historical Society. NYPL, New York Public Library. OC, Oberlin College. SC Schomburg Collection of the New York Public Library. WEF, private library of W. Edward Farrison. WRHS, the Western Reserve Historical Society.

BIBLIOGRAPHY

Manuscripts and Miscellaneous Collections

Adams, A[bigail]. Letters to Thomas Jefferson. June 26, 1787, June 27, 1787, July 6, 1787. LC.

Anti-Slavery—Estlin Papers, 1846–1865. BPL.

Anti-Slavery Letters Written by W. L. Garrison. BPL.

Anti-Slavery Letters Writen to W. L. Garrison and Others. BPL.

Anti-Slavery—Weston Papers. BPL.

Brown, William W. Letter to Hon. John M. Clayton. July 6, 1849. Passport Division, United States, Department of State.

——— Letter to Marius R. Robinson. November 29, 1857. SC.

Bullard, Artemas. "The Impostor Wm. Wells Brown Again." [March, 1851.] Presbyterian Historical Society, Philadelphia.

Gerrit Smith Miller Collection. Syracuse University.

Hathaway, Joseph C. Letter to Thurlow Weed. January 18, 1841. University of Rochester.

Henry P. Slaughter Collection. AU.

Holland, Frederick West. History of the American Peace Cause. 3 vols. in m. 1865. BPL.

Leon Gardiner Collection on Negro History. Historical Society of Pennsylvania.

Papers of Frederick Douglass. Microfilm. LC.

Randall, Henry S. Letter to James Parton. June 1, 1868. HaU.

Sophia Smith Collection. Smith College.

Books and Pamphlets

Adams, Nehemiah. *A South-Side View of Slavery; or Three Months at the South, in 1854.* Boston, 1854.

[Bacon, Thomas.] *Sermons Addressed to Masters and Servants, And Published in the Year 1743* [1749], *By the Rev. Thomas Bacon, Minister of the Protestant Episcopal Church in Maryland. Now Republished with Other Tracts and Dialogues on the Same Subject . . . By the Rev. William Meade.* Winchester, Va. [1813]. DU.

Beard, John R. *The Life of Toussaint L'Ouverture, the Negro Patriot of Hayti.* London, 1853.

[Bibb, Henry.] *Narrative of the Life and Adventures of Henry Bibb, an American Slave, Written by Himself. With an Introduction by Lucius C. Matlock.* New York, 1849. NCCD.

Bowditch, Vincent Y. *Life and Correspondence of Henry Ingersoll Bowditch.* 2 vols. Boston and New York: Houghton Mifflin Co., 1902.

Brawley, Benjamin. *A Social History of the American Negro.* New York. Macmillan Co., 1921.

[Brown, Josephine.] *Biography of an American Bondman, by His Daughter.* Boston, 1856. WEF.

Brown, William Wells. *The American Fugitive in Europe. Sketches of Places and People Abroad.* Boston, Cleveland, and New York, 1855.

——— comp. *The Anti-Slavery Harp: A Collection of Songs for Anti-Slavery Meetings.* Boston, 1848. DU, HaU, OC.

——— *Ibid.* 2d ed. Boston, 1849. NYPL, SC.

——— *Ibid.* Newcastle [Eng.], 1850. CoU.

——— *Ibid.* 3d ed. Boston, 1851. NYPL.

——— *The Black Man, His Antecedents, His Genius, and His Achievements.* New York: Thomas Hamilton, 1863. Boston: R. F. Wallcut, 1863.

——— *Ibid.* 2d ed., rev. and enlarged. New York: Thomas Hamilton, 1863. Boston: R. F. Wallcut, 1863.

——— *Ibid.* [2d ed., rev. and enlarged]. Boston: James Redpath, 1863. SC, WRHS.

——— *Ibid.* [2d ed., rev. and enlarged]. Savannah, Ga.: James M. Symms & Co., n. d. DU.

——— *Ibid.* 4th ed. Boston: R. F. Wallcut, 1865. BPL, LC.

——— *Clotel; or, The President's Daughter: A Narrative of Slave Life in the United States. With a Sketch of the Author's Life.* London, 1853. AU, BPL, CU, DU, HaU, OC, SC, WEF.

——— *Clotelle: A Tale of the Southern States.* Boston and New York, 1864. HaU, SC, WRHS, WEF.

——— *Clotelle; or, The Colored Heroine. A Tale of the Southern States.* Boston, 1867. HU, SC, WEF.

[———] *A Description of William Wells Brown's Original Panoramic Views of the Scenes in the Life of an American Slave, from His Birth in Slavery to His Death or His Escape to His First Home of Freedom on British Soil.* London, [1850]. CU, HU, NYHS, NYPL.

——— *The Escape; or, A Leap for Freedom. A Drama in Five Acts.* Boston, 1858. BPL, CU, HI.

[———] *Illustrated Edition of the Life and Escape of Wm. Wells Brown from American Slavery, Written by Himself.* London, 1851. NYPL.

——— *A Lecture Delivered Before the Female Anti-Slavery Society of Salem, at Lyceum Hall, Nov. 14, 1847.* Reported by Henry M. Parkhurst. Boston, 1847.

[———] *Memoir of William Wells Brown, an American Bondman, Written by Himself.* Boston, 1859. AAS, BA, WEF.

——— *My Southern Home: Or, The South and Its People.* Boston, 1880. BPL, NYHS, SC, WEF.

——— *Ibid.* 3d ed. Boston, 1882. CU, DU, HU, NCCD.

[———] *Narrative of William W. Brown, a Fugitive Slave, Written by Himself.* Boston, 1847.

[———] *Ibid.* 2d ed., enlarged. Boston, 1848. CoU, WEF.

[———] *Ibid.* 4th ed. Boston, 1849. WEF.

[———] *Narrative of William W. Brown, an American Slave, Written by Himself.* London, 1849. SC, WEF.

——— *The Negro in the American Rebellion: His Heroism and His Fidelity.* Boston, 1867.

——— *Ibid.* new ed. Boston, 1880. Brown University.

——— *Ibid.* new ed. Boston, 1885. WEF.

——— *The Rising Son; or, The Antecedents and Advancement of the Colored Race.* Boston, 1873. WRHS.

——— *Ibid.* Boston, 1874. NCCD.

——— *Ibid.*, 10th thousand. Boston, 1874. WEF, WRHS.

——— *Ibid.*, 12th thousand. Boston, 1876. DU.

——— *Ibid.*, 13th thousand. Boston, 1882. NYHS.

——— *Ibid.*, 13th thousand. Boston, 1885. BPL, WEF.

——— *St. Domingo: Its Revolutions and Its Patriots. A Lecture, Delivered before the Metropolitan Athenaeum, London, May 16, and at St. Thomas' Church, Philadelphia, December 20, 1854.* Boston, 1855. BPL, HaU, NYHS, WEF.

——— *Three Years in Europe; or, Places I Have Seen and People I Have Met. With a Memoir of the Author by William Farmer.* London, 1852.

Bryan, William Smith, and Rose Robert. *A History of the Pioneer Families of Missouri.* Saint Louis, 1876. Facsimile by W. W. Elwang, 1935.

Catterall, Helen Tunnicliff, ed., *Judicial Cases Concerning Slavery and the Negro.* 5 vols. Washington: Carnegie Institution, 1926–37.

Child, Lydia Maria. *Fact and Fiction: A Collection of Stories.* New York and Boston, 1847.

[———] *Letters of Lydia Maria Child. With a Biographical Introduction by John G. Whittier and an Appendix by Wendell Phillips.* Boston, 1883.

Clark, George W. *The Liberty Minstrel.* New York, Boston, Albany, and Utica, 1844 *et seq.*

Clarke, James Freeman. *Anti-Slavery Days. A Sketch of the Struggle Which Ended in the Abolition of Slavery in the United States.* New York, 1883.

Coffin, Levi. *Reminiscences.* Cincinnati, 1876.

[Craft, William.] *Running a Thousand Miles for Freedom; or, The Escape of William and Ellen Craft from Slavery.* London, 1860. NCCD.

[Croly, David Goodman, and Wakeman, George.] *Miscegenation: The Theory of the Blending of the Races, Applied to the American White Man and Negro.* New York, 1864. DU.

Curti, Merle Eugene. *The American Peace Crusade 1815–1860.* Durham, N. C.: Duke University Press, 1929.

Daniels, John. *In Freedom's Birthplace: A Study of the Boston Negroes.* Boston and New York: Houghton Mifflin Co., 1914.

[Douglass, Frederick.] *Life and Times of Frederick Douglass, Written by Himself. With an Introduction by Mr. George L. Ruffin.* New rev., ed. Boston, 1895.

———*My Bondage and My Freedom. With an Introduction by Dr. James M'Cune Smith.* New York and Auburn, 1855.

[———] *Narrative of the Life of Frederick Douglass, an American Slave, Written by Himself.* Boston, 1845.

Edwards, Richard, and Hopewell, M. *Edwards's Great West and Her Commercial Metropolis.* St. Louis, 1860.

Emilio, Luis F. *History of the Fifty-fourth Regiment of Massachusetts Volunteer Infantry, 1863–1865.* Boston, 1891.

Foner, Philip S. *The Life and Writings of Frederick Douglass,* 4 vols. New York: International publishers, 1950–55.

[Forten, Charlotte L.] *The Journal of Charlotte L. Forten. With an Introduction and Notes by Ray Allen Billington.* New York: Dryden Press, 1953.

Franklin, John Hope. *The Emancipation Proclamation.* Garden City, N. Y.: Doubleday and Co., 1963.

———*The Militant South 1800–1861.* Cambridge: Harvard University Press, 1956.

———*Reconstruction: After the Civil War.* Chicago: University of Chicago Press, 1961.

Frothingham, Octavius Brooks. *Gerrit Smith: A Biography.* New York, 1878.

[Garrison, Wendell Phillips, and Garrison, Francis Jackson.] *William Lloyd Garrison, 1805–1879: The Story of His Life Told by His Children.* 4 vols. Boston and New York, 1894.

Gephart, William F. *Transportation and Industrial Development in the Middle West.* Columbia University Studies in History, Economics, and Public Law, vol. 34. New York: Columbia University Press, 1909.

Greenwood, Grace. *Poems.* Boston, 1851.

[Griffiths, Julia, ed.] *Autographs for Freedom.* Boston, Cleveland, and London, 1853.

[———] *Autographs for Freedom.* Auburn and Rochester, 1854.

Harcus, Lorimer E. *I. O. of G. T. A History of the Negro Question in the Right Worthy Grand Lodge. Compiled from the Official Records of the R. W. G. Lodge.* Napanee, Ont. 1876. University of Texas.

Harlow, Ralph Volney. *Gerrit Smith: Philanthropist and Reformer.* New York: Henry Holt and Co., 1939.

Heeren, A. H. L. *Historical Researches into the Politics, Intercourse, and Trade of the Carthaginians, Ethiopians, and Egyptians.* Translated from the German [by D. A. Talboys]. 2d ed. London, 1850.

[Henson, Josiah.] *Truth Stranger than Fiction. Father Henson's Story of His Own Life. With an Introduction by Mrs. H. B. Stowe.* Boston and Cleveland, 1858.

[———] *"Uncle Tom's Story of His Life." An Autobiography of the Rev. Josiah Henson.* Edited by John Lobb. London, 1876.

Hinshaw, William Wade. *Encyclopedia of American Quaker Genealogy.* 6 vols. Ann Arbor, Mich.: Edwards Brothers, Inc., 1936–50.

Holland, Frederic May. *Frederick Douglass: The Colored Orator.* Rev. ed. American Reformers Series. New York and London, 1895.

Hutchinson, John Wallace. *Story of the Hutchinsons (Tribe of Jesse).* Compiled and Edited by Charles E. Mann. With an Introduction by Frederick Douglass. 2 vols. Boston, 1896.

Hyde, William, and Conard, Howard L., eds. *Encyclopedia of the History of St. Louis, a Compendium of History and Biography for Ready Reference.* 4 vols. New York, Louisville, and St. Louis, 1899.

Inaugural Ceremonies of the Freedmen's Memorial Monument to Abraham Lincoln, Washington City, April 14, 1876. St. Louis, 1876. Missouri Historical Society.

Influence of Slavery upon the White Population. By a Former Resident of the Slave States. Anti-Slavery Tracts, no. 9. New York, [1855].

Jamieson, Annie Straith. *William King: Friend and Champion of Slaves.* Toronto: Missions of Evangelism, 1925.

[Jefferson, Thomas.] *Thomas Jefferson's Farm Book, with Commentary and Relevant Extracts from Other Writings.* Edited by Edwin Morris Betts. Princeton: Princeton University Press, 1953.

[———] *Thomas Jefferson's Garden Book, 1766–1824, with Relevant Extracts from His Other Writings.* Annotated by Edwin Morris Betts. Philadelphia: American Philosophical Society, 1944.

Johnson, Oliver. *William Lloyd Garrison and His Times; or, Sketches of the Anti-Slavery Movement in America, and of the Man Who Was Its Founder and Moral Leader.* New rev. and enlarged ed. Boston, 1881.

Langston, John Mercer. *From the Virginia Plantation to the National Capitol; or, The First and Only Negro Representative in Congress from the Old Dominion.* Hartford, Conn., 1894.

Lewis, R. B. *Light and Truth; Collected from the Bible and Ancient and Modern History, Containing the Universal History of the Colored and the Indian Race, from the Creation of the World to the Present Time.* Boston, 1844. WEF.

The Liberty Bell, by the Friends of Freedom. 15 vols. Boston, 1839–1858.

[Lincoln, Abraham.] *The Collected Works of Abraham Lincoln.* Edited by Roy P. Basler. 9 vols. New Brunswick, N. J., Rutgers University Press, 1953–55.

Lincoln, Jairus. *Anti-Slavery Melodies: For the Friends of Freedom. Prepared for the Hingham Anti-Slavery Society.* Hingham, Mass., 1843. BPL, DU, LC.

Livermore, George. *An Historical Research Respecting the Opinions of the Founders of the Republic on Negroes as Slaves, as Citizens, and as Soldiers. Read Before the Massachusetts Historical Society, August 14, 1862.* Boston, 1862.

Lloyd, James R. *Lloyd's Steamboat Directory, and Disasters on the Western Waters, Containing the History of the First Application of Steam, as a Motive Power.* Cincinnati, 1856.

Loggins, Vernon. *The Negro Author: His Development in America.* New York: Columbia University Press, 1931.

Marryat, [Frederick]. *A Diary in America, with Remarks on Its Institutions.* 3 vols. London, 1839.

Marshall, Herbert, and Stock, Mildred. *Ira Aldridge: The Negro Tragedian.* New York: The Macmillan Co., 1958.

[Martineau, Harriet.] *Harriet Martineau's Autobiography.* Edited by Maria Weston Chapman. 2 vols. Boston, 1877.

May, Samuel J. *Some Recollections of Our Antislavery Conflict.* Boston, 1869.

Memoir and Theatrical Career of Ira Aldridge, the African Roscius. London, [1848]. University of Pennsylvania.

Mills, James Cooke. *Our Inland Seas, Their Shipping & Commerce for Three Centuries.* Chicago, 1910.

Mitchell, W[illiam] M. *The Under-Ground Railroad.* London, 1860. DU.

Murray, Charles Augustus. *Travels in North America During the Years 1834, 1835, & 1836.* 2 vols. New York, 1839.

Nell, William C. *The Colored Patriots of the American Revolution. With Sketches of Several Distinguished Colored Persons. . . . With an Introduction by Harriet Beecher Stowe.* Boston, 1855.

Nelson, John Herbert. *The Negro Character in American Literature.* Bulletin of the University of Kansas, Humanistic Studies, vol. 4. Lawrence Kan.: Department of Journalism Press, 1926.

[Pierpont, John.] *The Anti-Slavery Poems of John Piermont.* Boston, 1843.

Pierson, Hamilton W. *Jefferson at Monticello. The Private Life of Thomas Jefferson. From Entirely New Materials.* New York, 1862.

Prichard, James Cowles. *Researches into the Physical History of Mankind.* 4th ed. 5 vols. London, 1851.

Quarles, Benjamin. *Frederick Douglass.* Washington: Associated Publishers, 1948.

——— *The Negro in the Civil War.* Boston: Little, Brown and Co., 1953.

Ranck, George W. *History of Lexington, Kentucky: Its Early Annals and Recent Progress.* Cincinnati, 1872.

Randall, Henry S. *The Life of Thomas Jefferson.* 3 vols. New York, 1858.

Redpath, James, *A Guide to Hayti.* Boston, 1861.

———*The Roving Editor: Or, Talks with Slaves in the Southern States.* New York, 1859.

Roscoe, William. *The Life and Pontificate of Leo the Tenth.* 3d ed., corrected. 4 vols. London, 1827.

Scharf, John Thomas. *History of Saint Louis City and County, From the Earliest Periods to the Present Day: Including Bio-*

graphical Sketches of Representative Men. 2 vols. Philadelphia, 1883.

Simmons, William J. *Men of Mark: Eminent, Progressive and Rising. With an Introductory Sketch of the Author by Rev. Henry M. Turner.* Cleveland, 1887.

Smith, H. Perry, ed. *History of the City of Buffalo and Erie County.* 2 vols. Syracuse, 1884.

Special Report of the Bristol and Clifton Ladies' Anti-Slavery Society .... London, 1852. WEF.

Steward, Austin. *Twenty-two Years a Slave and Forty Years a Freeman.* 3d ed. Rochester, 1861.

[Thompson, George.] *Speech of George Thompson, Esq., M. P. Delivered at the Anti-Slavery Meeting, Broadmead, Bristol, September 4th, 1851.* [Bristol, Eng., 1851.]

Trexler, Harrison Anthony. *Slavery in Missouri, 1804–1865.* Johns Hopkins University Studies in Historical and Political Science, series 32, no. 2. Baltimore: Johns Hopkins Press, 1914.

Twelve Years a Slave. Narrative of Solomon Northup, a Citizen of New-York, Kidnapped in Washington City in 1841, and Rescued in 1853. Auburn, Buffalo, and London, 1854.

Wayland, Francis Fry. *Andrew Stevenson: Democrat and Diplomat, 1785–1857.* Philadelphia: University of Pennsylvania Press, 1949.

[Weld, Theodore Dwight.] *American Slavery as It Is: Testimony of a Thousand Witnesses.* New York, 1839.

Williams, George W. *A History of the Negro Troops in the War of the Rebellion, 1861–1865.* New York, 1888.

Wilson, Henry. *History of the Rise and Fall of the Slave Power in America.* 3 vols. Boston, 1872–1877.

Woodson, Carter G., ed. *The Mind of the Negro as Reflected in Letters Written During the Crisis 1800–1860.* Washington: Association for the Study of Negro Life and History, 1926.

Serials. Dates are those for which the several serials were consulted.

American Anti-Slavery Society. *Third Annual Report.* New York, 1836.

——— *Proceedings of the American Anti-Slavery Society, at Its Second Decade, Held in the City of Philadelphia, Dec. 3rd, 4th, and 5th, 1853.* New York, 1854.

——— *Annual Report.* New York, 1855.

——— *Annual Report.* New York, 1856.

——— *Proceedings of the American Anti-Slavery Society, at Its Third Decade, Held in the City of Philadelphia, Dec. 3rd and 4th, 1863.* New York, 1864.

Anglo-African Magazine (New York). 1859 to March, 1860. BPL.

Anti-Slavery Advocate (London). October, 1852 to May, 1863. BPL.

Athenaeum, Journal of Literature, Science, and the Fine Arts (London). 1852, 1854.

Atlantic Monthly. 1861.

British Friend (Glasgow). 1852. Guilford College.

Century Magazine. 1889.

Colored American Magazine (Boston). 1900, 1901. BPL, LC.

Critic, London Literary Journal. 1852.

Eclectic Review (London). 1852.

Glasgow Female Anti-Slavery Society. *Sixth Report.* Glasgow, 1851. ML.

Good Templars' Watchword (London). July 11, 1877, December 1, 1884. BrM.

Independent Order of Good Templars. *Journal of Proceedings of the Right Worthy Grand Lodge of North America.* 1859 to 1871. BPL. 1872 to 1885. New Hampshire State Library.

Literary Gazette and Journal of Belles Lettres, Arts, and Sciences. 1853.

Massachusetts Anti-Slavery Society. *Sixteenth Annual Report.* Boston, 1848. BPL.

——— *Seventeenth Annual Report.* Boston, 1849. BPL.

——— *Eighteenth Annual Report.* Boston, 1850. BPL.

——— *Nineteenth Annual Report.* Boston, 1851. BPL.

——— *Proceedings of the Massachusetts Anti-Slavery Society at the Annual Meetings Held in 1854, 1855, & 1856.* Boston, 1856. BPL.

Minutes of the National Convention of Colored Citizens: Held at Buffalo, on the 15th, 16th, 17th, 18th and 19th of August, 1843. New York, 1843. HU.

Proceedings of the First Anniversary of the American Equal Rights Association. New York, 1867.

Proceedings of the National Convention of Colored Men, Held in the City of Syracuse, N. Y., October 4, 5, 6, and 7, 1864. Boston, 1864. DU.

Proceedings of the National Convention of Colored People, and Their Friends, Held in Troy, N. Y., on the 6th, 7th, 8th and 9th of October, 1847. Troy, 1847. HU.

The Public Good; Devoted to the Advocacy of Great Principles, the Advancement of Useful Institutions, and the Elevation of Man (London). 1851. University of Iowa.

Punch; or, the London Charivari. 1851.

Report of the Proceedings of the Anti-Slavery Conference and Public Meeting, Held at Manchester, on the 1st of August, 1854, in Commemoration of West India Emancipation. London, 1854. HU.

Report of the Proceedings of the Second General Peace Congress, Held in Paris, on the 22nd, 23rd and 24th of August, 1849. London, 1849. Yale University.

Sons of Temperance. *Journal of Proceedings of the Grand Division Sons of Temperance of the State of Massachusetts, 1862–1866.* Boston, 1869. BPL. ——— Ibid., *1867–1871.* Boston, 1872. HaU. ——— Ibid., *1872–1876.* Boston, 1878. Massachusetts State Library.

——— *Journal of the Proceedings of the National Division of the Sons of Temperance of North America.* Boston, 1862 *et seq.* 1862 to 1875. BPL. 1876 to 1885. University of Illinois.

Temperance Album (North Adams and Boston). 1872, 1873. AAS.

Articles in Serials

Coleman, Edward M. "William Wells Brown as an Historian." *Journal of Negro History* 31 (1946): 47–59.

Dunning, E. O. "Private Character of Thomas Jefferson." *New Englander* 19 (1861): 648–73.

Farrison, William Edward. 'Brown's First Drama." *CLA Journal* 2 (1958): 104–10.

——— "A Flight Across Ohio: The Escape of William Wells Brown from Slavery." *Ohio State Archaeological and Historical Quarterly* 61 (1952): 272–82.

——— "The Origin of Brown's Clotel." *Phylon, the Atlanta University Review of Race and Culture* 15 (1954): 347–54.

——— "A Theologian's Missouri Compromise." *Journal of Negro History* 48 (1963): 33–43.

——— "William Wells Brown, America's First Negro Man of Letters." *Phylon, the Atlanta University Review of Race and Culture* 9 (1948): 13–23.

——— "William Wells Brown in Buffalo." *Journal of Negro History* 39 (1954): 298–314.

——— "William Wells Brown, Social Reformer." *Journal of Negro Education* 18 (1949): 29–39.

Hopkins, Pauline. "William Wells Brown." *Colored American Magazine* 2 (1901): 232–36.

"Pauline Hopkins," *Colored American Magazine* 2 (1901): 218–19.

Peabody, Ephraim. "Narratives of Fugitive Slaves." *Christian Examiner and Religious Miscellany* 47 (1849): 61–93.

Temperley, Howard. "The O'Connell-Stevenson Contretemps." *Journal of Negro History*, October, 1962: 217–33.

Newspapers. Dates indicate the numbers of the several newspapers consulted. Where no dates are given, miscellaneous numbers were consulted.

Anti-Slavery Bugle (New Lisbon and later Salem, Ohio). WRHS.

Binghamton [N. Y.] *Daily Republican*, September 3, 1857. Binghamton Public Library.

Boston Daily Advertiser.

Boston Daily Globe.

Boston Evening Transcript.

Boston Herald.
Boston Investigator, July 9, 1851. DU.
Buffalo Commercial Advertiser. Buffalo Historical Society.
Buffalo Daily Gazette. Buffalo Historical Society.
Burlington [Vt.] *Free Press*, July 15, 1856. University of Vermont.
Burritt's Christian Citizen (Worcester, Mass). AAS.
Cleveland Morning Express. WRHS.
Commonwealth: A Journal of Politics, Literature, Art, and News (Boston).
Congregationalist (Boston). LC.
Courant (Edinburgh). EPL.
Daily News (London), September 24, 1852. BrM.
Elyria [Ohio] *Independent Democrat*. WRHS.
Friend of Man (Utica, N. Y.), August 22, 1838. OC.
Herald (Glasgow). ML.
Herald of Progress (New York), December 27, 1862. WRHS.
Independent (New York), January 8, 1863.
Liberator (Boston), 1831–65. 35 vols.
Liberty Herald (Warren, Ohio). WRHS.
National Anti-Slavery Standard (New York). BPL, LC.
Newark [N. J.] *Daily Mercury*, January 19, 1849. Newark Public Library.
New Lisbon [Ohio] *Aurora*. WRHS.
New Orleans Bee (L'Abeille). DU.
New York Daily Tribune.
New York Evening Post.
New York Herald.
Owego [N. Y.] *Times*, September 10, 1857. Tioga County Historical Society, Owego.
Pacific Appeal (San Francisco), May 30, 1863. University of California, Berkeley.
Paterson [N. J.] *Daily Guardian*. Free Library of Paterson.
Philadelphia Daily Evening Bulletin.
Pine and Palm (Boston and New York). BPL, LC.
Poughkeepsie [N. Y.] *Daily Eagle*. Adriance Memorial Library, Poughkeepsie.
Scotsman (Edinburgh). EPL.

Times (Hereford, Eng.), December 17, 1853. Hereford *Times* Office.

Trenton [N. J.] *Daily State Gazette and Republican.* New Jersey State Library.

Troy [N. Y.] *Daily Times.* Troy Public Library.

Vergennes [Vt.] *Citizen,* July 11, 1856. BA.

Vermont Christian Messenger (Montpelier), October 19, 1855. Vermont State Library.

Washington [D. C.] *Evening Star.*

Weekly Anglo-African, later *Anglo-African* (New York), 1860–61 (incomplete), AAS; 1861–62 (incomplete), LC; 1861–65 (incomplete), HaU.

Worcester [Mass.] *Daily Spy.* Wisconsin State Historical Society.

Yates County [N. Y.] *Chronicle* (Penn Yan, N. Y.). Penn Yan Printing Company.

INDEX

Adams, Rev. Nehemiah, *A South-Side View of Slavery*, 254, 277, 361
"Address" to the Prince of Wales, 322
African Civilization Society: defense of, 310; opposition to, 309, 312
Aldridge, Ira Frederick, 370–71
Allen, Rev. William (Northhampton, Mass.), speech at Versailles, 152
American Anti-Slavery Society, 85–87, 422; final meeting, 423
American Colonization Society: opposition to, 141, 142, 143, 289, 309; plea for, 289
American Equal Rights Association, 409
American Slavery as It Is, 47
Anthony, Susan B., 288, 290, 291, 293
Anti-Slavery Advocate (London), founded, 202
"Appeal to the White Citizens of the State [Massachusetts]," 329

Bacon, Edmund (Thomas Jefferson's overseer), 211–12
Bancroft, George, 316
Banneker, Benjamin, 368–69
Beard, Rev. John R., *The Life of Toussaint L'Ouverture*, used by Brown, 256–57, 370
Bell, James Madison (Negro poet and lecturer), 443
Beman, Rev. Amos G. (New Haven, Conn.), 76, 77

Benton, Thomas H., Fourth of July oration of, 22
"Blind Slave Boy, The," 32–33
Boone, Daniel, 4
Bowditch, William I., 241, 244
Brooks, Preston Smith, 281, 287
Brown, Annie Elizabeth (née Gray, Brown's second wife), 297, 309, 415, 424, 454; death, 455; marriage, 314
Brown, Clarissa (William Wells and Elizabeth Brown's daughter): birth, 66–67; in school in France, 197; schoolmistress, 245; trip to England, 192–93
Brown, Clotelle (William Wells and Annie Elizabeth Brown's daughter), 416; birth, 362; death, 363
Brown, Elizabeth (née Schooner, Brown's first wife): death, 170-71; letter to *New York Daily Tribune*, 169; marriage, 62; separation from Brown, 107–8
Brown, Josephine (William Wells and Elizabeth Brown's daughter), 270–71, 272, 273; *Biography of an American Bondman*, 7, 272; birth, 73; in school in France, 197; schoolmistress, 245; trips to England, 192–93, 275
Brown, Wells, 55–59, 452
Brown, William Wells, 11, 30, 46–47, 241, 322, 393, 395, 403, 408, 419; on Rev. Nehemiah Adams, 254–55, 261; African Civilization Society, opposed to, 309, 312; American Anti-Slavery Society, agent for, 106, 251, 265, 275, 287, 288, anniversary speech, 1860, 315–16, first meeting attended, 85, opposes dissolution, 397–98; on American Bible Society, 117; antislavery lecturing begun, 81–83; "Appeal to the White Citizens of the State [Massachusetts]," opposed to, 329–30; assistant to Dr. John Young, 24; attempt to escape, 36–37; birth, 6–9; Buffalo, antislavery work in, 70–72; on Robert Burns, 237; Canada, on Negro life in, 349–50, trips to, 75, 341–48; on Thomas Carlyle, 189–90; the Civil War, on cause of, 412; on Henry Clay, 89; clothing store, co-owner of, 402; on Hartley Coleridge, 185; committeeman, National Convention of Colored Citizens, 1843, 76; complexion, 14–15, 235, 259; conflicts, with Liberty party, 101, 104–5, with Charles Lenox Remond, 111, 310; considered South unable to maintain slavery, 292; controversies, with Mrs. Elizabeth Brown, 168–70, with Rev. Artemas Bullard, 168, with Frederick Douglass, 262–64, with Henry Highland Garnet, 78–80, 310–11, with Rev. John Scoble, 166, 201; Convention of Colored Citizens, 1859, presides at, 308–10; criticized by Martin R. Delany, 345, in "Who Made Thee a Prince and Judge?" 345; Crystal Palace, visits to, 187–90; death, funeral, and burial, 452–54; on Martin R. Delany, 344–45; disunion speeches, 86–87, 267, 292; doubt of his being a fugitive slave, 119, 121; Dublin, Ireland, visit to, 146–47; earliest extant manuscript of, 84;

education of, 22, 61, 198–99, 203; emancipation, on its benefit to Northern factory workers, 364, 366; emigration of Negroes from United States, opposed to, 309, 312, 364; employed on steamboats, 19, 22–23, 40–41, 61, 62; employed by James Walker, 28–32; England, first speech in, 155; escape in Cincinnati, 51–52; farewell program for (Boston), 141–42; favors slaves' right to win freedom by revolution, 286–87; on Millard Fillmore, 248; first child (William Wells and Elizabeth Brown's), 63; first lecture trips, 82; first marriage, 62; first published writing, 78–80; first speeches in Boston, 109–10; five years abroad, summary of, 244; freedmen, on difficulties of, 397, 422, 448; his freedom, negotiations for, 237–42; on free labor versus slave labor, 122; Fugitive Slave Law, speeches against, 178–79, 180; general agent, Western New York Anti-Slavery Society, 97; Geneva suffrage convention, 1845, leader in, 96–97; grant of land from Gerrit Smith, 98–99, 115, 204; Great Britain, trips to, 145–46, 435–36; guest at Tocqueville's soiree, 151; Haitian immigration, inconsistency about, 336, promotion of, 334–35, 337, 341, 350, 352, 353–54; half slave and half free nation, argument against, 268; Harwich riot, beaten at, 130; history, conception of, 444–45; on Thomas Hood, 242–43; on the inconsistency of American slavery and democracy, 218, 259; journalistic work, 199–201; Ku Klux Klan in Kentucky, captured by, 427–28; last antislavery lectures, 394, 396; last night in slavery, 49; lectures (especially notable), on John Brown's raid on Harper's Ferry, 312–13, before the Female Anti-Slavery Society of Salem, 117–18, "Historical Lecture on the Origin and Early History of the African Race," 421, before the New York Anti-Slavery Society, 258–60; in reply to William Lowndes Yancy's lecture on Negro inferiority, 320–22; in Saint Thomas' Episcopal Church (Philadelphia), 255; lecture trips (extensive), to Middle West, 420, 421–22, to New York, 284, 288–90, to Ohio, 88–91, 265–67, 284, 288, 290–94, to Scotland, 179–82, to Vermont, 271, 281–82, 318–19; lecturing opposed by preachers and others, 88, 96, 104, 271, 318–19; on Abraham Lincoln, 389–90; Lincoln memorial monument, agent for, 405–7; on Lincoln's message to Congress, 359; London, first speech in, 157–58, residence in, 154; manual labor school, idea for, 181; marital trouble, in Buffalo, 91, 92, 93, in Farmington, N.Y., 107–8, in Boston, 127–28, 131–32, in London, 168–70; Harriet Martineau, visit with, 183–85; Massachusetts Anti-Slavery Society, agent for, 107, 111, 268, 275,

287; medicine, practice of, 399, 400, 401–2, study of, 383–84, 401; Melrose Abbey, visits to, 182; miscegenation, in favor of, 385–86, 387; Missouri, removal to, 10; Monroe, Mich., winter in, 63–66; James Montgomery (poet), visit with, 165; name changed to Sandford, 13; at Negroes' meeting on "National affairs," 1864, "I am almost discouraged," 392; Negroes' prowar resolutions, opposed to, 332–33; Negro exodus from the South, in favor of, 451; Negro inferiority, denial of, 320–21, 363, 367–68; for Negro suffrage, 409–10; New Orleans, trips to, 34, 46; open letter to Rev. William Allen, 152–53; opinion of slaveholders' religion, 26–28; optimistic about abolitionism, 274; panoramic views exhibited, 173, 176; parentage, 3; passport, 140–41; Peace Congress, 1849, delegate to, 139–40, 142, 143, speech at, 149–51; Elizabeth Pease, visit with, 164; Philadelphia, visits to, 128, 134, 246, 247; his place in history, 454; on Alexander Pope, 202–3; Poughkeepsie, N.Y., lyceum lectures in, 357–59; on John Randolph (antislavery impostor), 269–70; reasons for going to Europe in 1849, 140; Republican party the ship, all else the sea, 410; residences, in Boston, 109, 402, in Buffalo, 69–70, in Cambridgeport, 317, 402, in Chelsea, 402, in Cleveland, 60–67, in Farmington, N.Y., 93–94, 107–8; returns to America, 1854, 245–46; rides as railway freight, 88–89; Marius R. Robinson, difficulty with, 293–94; Saint Louis, removal to, 17–18; second marriage, 8, 314; sold to Samuel Willi, 38; sold to Enoch Price, 42; the South, trip to, 446; Charles Sumner, eulogy on, 432; a target for eggs etc., 83, 95; temperance work, 72–73, with Good Templars, 430–36, with Sons of Temperance, 423–25, 426–27, 429–30, with state temperance organizations, 425–26; travels in continental Europe, 199; Underground Railroad, conductor on, 67, 74–75; Washington, D.C., visit to, 405; Booker T. Washington, forerunner of, 309; welcome meetings for, 249–51; West Indies, visit to, 74, 336, 352; on "What ought to be done with the Traitors and the Slaves," 358, 359, 361–62; white relatives in Kentucky, 6, 316; Whittington Club (London), guest of, 160, honorary member of, 172

—Works: *The American Fugitive in Europe*, see *Sketches of Places and People Abroad;* "The American Slave Trade," 119; *The Anti-Slavery Harp*, 32, 122–26, 138–39, 164–65; "An Appeal to the People of Great Britain and the World," 195; *The Black Man*, 4, 366–72, 376–77, criticism of, 372–76; " 'The Black Man' and Its Critics," 373–75; "Celebrated Colored Americans," 338–40; *Clotel; or, The President's*

Daughter, 24, 215–28, criticism of, 228–31; *Clotelle; or, The Colored Heroine*, 415–17; *Clotelle: A Tale of the Southern States*, 387–88; "The Colored People of Canada," 342, a pioneering study in regionalism, 350; "Colored People of the Empire State," 353; *A Description of William Wells Brown's Original Panoramic Views*, 174–76; *The Escape; or, A Leap for Freedom*, 24, 283, 296, 297–301, 303–4; *Experience; or, How to Give a Northern Man a Backbone*, 277–78, synopsis of, 279–80; "Fling out the Anti-Slavery Flag," 125; "Lament of the Fugitive Slave," 40, 138; *A Lecture Delivered Before the Female Anti-Slavery Society of Salem*, 118–19; letter to London *Times*, 191; letter "to His Master," 160–61; "Life at the South," 314, 315, 358; "A Man without a Name," 372, 376, 414; *Memoir of William Wells Brown*, 7, 313; *Miralda; or, The Beautiful Quadroon*, 323–28; *My Southern Home*, 415, 446–52, 454; *Narrative of William W. Brown*, 3, first edition, 112–15, second edition, 121, third edition, 133–34, fourth edition, 138, British editions, 155–57; *The Negro in the American Rebellion*, 410–15, 420; "Opposition to Emigration," 334–36; *The Rising Son*, 82, 437–44, 454; *St. Domingo: Its Revolutions and its Patriots*, 255–58, 370; *Sketches of Places and People Abroad*, 252–53, criticism of, 253–54; "The Slave's a Man for A' That," 139; *Three Years in Europe*, 203–6, criticism of, 207–9; "A True Story of Slave Life," 210–11, 217; "Visit of a Fugitive Slave to the Grave of Wilberforce," 171–72

Brown, William Wells, Jr. (William Wells and Annie Elizabeth Brown's son), 329

Buchanan, James (President), 259, 330

Bullard, Rev. Artemas (Saint Louis), 168

Burleigh, Charles C., 86, 295

Buxton Settlement, 345–47; opposition to Negro teacher, 346–47

Cailloux, Captain (Union army), 376, 413

Cary, Mrs. Mary Ann Shadd (Chatham, Ont.), 376, 437, 438, 439; opposed to Haitian immigration, 350–51

Catron, John (United States Supreme Court), 315, 361

Chapman, Mrs. Maria Weston (editor, The *Liberty Bell*), 84, 119; at Peace Congress, 1849, 148, 149–50, 153

Child, Mrs. Lydia Maria, 228; open letter to Mrs. J. C. Mason, 313–14; "The Quadroons," 175, 224; "The Stars and Stripes," 301–03

Chinn, Thomas Withers (Louisiana slaveholder), 148–49

Clay, Henry, 89, 200, 226

Clayton, John M. (U.S. Secretary of State), 140, 153

Cobden, Richard (British statesman), 148, 152

Colburn, John (Saint Louis), 19–20
Colman, Mrs. Lucy Newhall, 291, 293
Colonization of Negroes, opposition to, 360
Constitution of the United States, fugitive slave law in, 85
Convention of Colored Citizens, 1859, 308–10
Cook, Grove (Dr. John Young's overseer), 10
Cox, Samuel Sullivan (congressman from Ohio), accuses abolitionists of favoring miscegenation, 386
Craft, William and Ellen: escape from slavery, 134–35; flight to England, 179; lecture trips with Brown, 136–37, 179–88; removal to Boston, 136
Croly, David Goodman, 384–85, 386

Dawn Institute (Ontario), 347
Disunion convention, Cleveland, 1857, 291–92
Disunion, doctrine of, 85–86
Douglas, Stephen A., 361
Douglass, Frederick, 248, 371, 393, 408, 410, 436; "Bibles for the Slaves," 117n; Buffalo, visit to, 75–76; controversy with Brown, 262–64; "The Heroic Slave," 340; Liberty party, opposed to, 77–78; *Narrative* quoted, 7; Negro exodus from the South, opposed to, 450; political abolitionism, in defense of, 267–68
Downing, George T., 309, 311–12, 330, 394
Draft riot in New York City, 413
Drake, Mrs. F. H., 115

Elgin Settlement, 345–47
Elizabeth (Brown's mother), 3, 4, 5; her children, 9; sold to Isaac Mansfield, 20; sold by Isaac Mansfield, 39–40; whipped by Grove Cook, 10
Elizabeth (Brown's sister), 9, 20, 35
Emancipation necessary for Union victory, 331, 364
Emancipation Proclamation, 365, 379
Estlin, Dr. John Bishop (Bristol, England), 167, 185, 186, 187, 197, 214, 216, 383–84; death, 281; defends Brown, 166
Estlin, Mary Anne (Dr. Estlin's daughter), 167, 172, 213

Farmer, William (British journalist), 8, 157, 187, 194, 209
Forten, Charlotte L., 249, 251–52, 270–71, 372
Foster, Stephen S., 86; in Harwich riot, 129, 130; pessimistic about abolitionism, 273
Frank (slave fortune-teller, Saint Louis), 45–46
Freeland, Major (Saint Louis), 18–19
Fugitive Slave Law, 1850, 177

Garnet, Henry Highland, 76, 116, 310–11, 380; *An Address to the Slaves of the United States of America*, 77; favors Liberty party, 77–78
Garrett, James (Buffalo), 91, 92, 93
Garrick, Jacob, hero of schooner *Enchantress*, 412–13
Garrison, Mrs. Helen Eliza (wife of William Lloyd Garrison), 286, 399–400

Garrison, William Lloyd, 74, 216, 248, 250, 251, 382–83, 395, 415, 423; disunion resolution of, 86; honored in Newburyport, 133; "I Am an Abolitionist," 123; opposed to emigration of Negroes, 337, 338; optimistic about abolitionism, 273–74, 286; presentation program for, 141; proposes dissolution of American Anti-Slavery Society, 396–97
Garrison, William Lloyd, Jr., 283, 296, 399–400
Gay, Sidney Howard (editor, *National Anti-Slavery Standard*), 88, 91, 137, 149
Goodell, William (Utica, N. Y.), 105, 125
Greek Slave, The (by Hiram Powers), 187–88
Greely, Joseph (Enoch Price's agent), 239, 240, 241
Greenwood, Grace, 227
Griffiths, Julia (editor, *Autographs for Freedom*), 172n, 340
Grimes, Rev. Leonard A. (Boston), 314, 352, 424

Haitian immigration: opposed, 337, 351–52, 355–56; promoted by James Redpath, 333, 348, 351
Hamilton, Thomas (publisher, New York City), 323, 367
Harper, Mrs. Frances Ellen (née Watkins), 287–88, 443
Harwich (Mass.) riot, 129–31
Haskell, Friend (Dr. John Young's overseer), 17, 23
Hathaway, Joseph C. (Farmington, N.Y.), 81, 86, 107, 110, 111, 112; writes preface for Brown's *Narrative*, 114
Hayden, Lewis (Boston), 443, 453
Heeren, Arnold Ludwig von, *Historical Researches*, 441
Helper, Hinton R., *The Impending Crisis*, 122, 320
Henson, Josiah (Uncle Tom of *Uncle Tom's Cabin*), 181, 191, 304, 347
Higgins, George (Brown's father), 5
Higginson, Thomas Wentworth, 133, 338–39, 369
Hopkins, Pauline, 436
Hore, Rev. Edward (Ramsgate, England), 238, 239
Howard, Capt. Joseph (Union army), 376, 413
Hudson, E. D., 99, 105, 106
Hugo, Victor, 147, 148, 387
Hutchinson Singers, 125

"Jefferson's Daughter," 125–26
Jefferson, Thomas, 125, 211–12, 217, 218–19, 220, 226, 388
Jenkins, Joseph, 253, 371–72, 375
Johnson, Andrew (President), 397, 414
Johnson, Oliver, 106, 259, 286
Jordan, Sir Edward (Kingston, Jamaica), 372

Kidnapping of free Negroes: of Solomon Northup, 86; of a boy in Georgetown, Ohio, 90–91
King, Rev. William (Buxton Settlement), 345–46
Ku Klux Klan captures Brown, 427–28

Langston, John Mercer, 393, 405, 408
Lawson, James (Union intelligencer) 376, 383

Lee, Simon (Brown's grandfather), 3–4
Lewis, Edmonia (sculptress), 443
Liberty party convention, Buffalo, 1841, 78
Lincoln, Abraham, 384, 391, 405, 406, 407; favors colonization of Negroes, 359–60, 368; freedmen's monument to, 408; on recruiting Negroes for military service, 365
Livermore, George, *An Historical Research*, 411
Loguen, Rev. Jermain W., 443
Loggins, Vernon, 230
Loring, Ellis Gray, 86
Lounsbury, Rev. Thomas, "seven sermons against abolitionism," 96
L'Ouverture, Toussaint. *See* Toussaint L'Ouverture
Lovejoy, Elijah P., employs Brown, 20–22

Marryat, Captain Frederick, 175
Martin, Rev. John Sella, 309, 310, 320; supports Negroes' prowar resolutions, 333
Massachusetts Anti-Slavery Society, 422
Massachusetts Fifty-fourth Regiment, 381
Mathews, Rev. Edward S., 194, 195, 252–53
Mawson, John (Newcastle upon Tyne), 165, 166, 216; Brown's host, 163
May, Samuel, Jr., 106, 215, 216, 267–68, 269
May, Rev. Samuel J. (Syracuse, N.Y.), 248
Miller, Salome, 222
Miscegenation: The Theory of the Blending of the Races, 384–85
Mitchell, Rev. William M. (Underground Railroad conductor), 53–54
Moore, William (Dr. John Young's nephew), 13
Morris, Robert (Boston), 120, 142, 331, 332, 382, 392–93
Mott, Mrs. Lucretia, 280, 386

National Association for the Organization of Night Schools and the Spread of Temperance, 421, 427
National Convention of Colored Citizens: of 1843, 76–78; of 1864, 393–94
National Convention of Colored People, 1847, 116–17
National Equal Rights League, 393–94
Nat Turner, 226, 338–39, 369, 375–76, 411, 450
Negroes' meeting on "National affairs," 1864, 392–93
Negroes' prowar meeting, 1861, 331–33
Negro life in Ontario towns: in Chatham, 344–45; in London, 343–44; in Saint Catharines, 342–43; in Windsor, 348
Negro lobby in Washington planned, 403
Negro recruiters for military service, 381, 382
Negro soldiers unfairly treated, 390–91, 413
Nell, William C., 3, 116, 240, 248, 249, 288, 370, 411; presentation speech to Garrison, 141
Nelson, John Herbert, 229–30
"No Union with Slaveholders," 85, 86, 87

Page, Daniel D. (Saint Louis), 26–27, 168
Passports not granted to "persons of color." *See* John M. Clayton
Paton, Andrew (Glasgow), 176, 179
Peace Congress: of 1849, 147–49; of 1850, 173
Pease, Elizabeth (Darlington, England), 139, 143, 146, 164, 264–65
Peck, Rev. John (Rochester), opposes the doctrine of natural rights, 97
Pennington, Rev. James W. C., delegate to Peace Congress of 1849, 147
Phillips, Wendell, 86, 250, 257, 258, 410, 423; death, 452; opposes dissolution of American Anti-Slavery Society 396–97
Pierpont, John (antislavery poet), 126
Pillsbury, Parker, 110, 241, 386; in Harwich riot, 129, 130
Pitts and Brown's clothing store (Boston), 402
Powell, Aaron M., 288, 290, 291 293, 423
Powers, Hiram, 187–88
Price, Enoch (Brown's last owner, Saint Louis), 42–43, 240, 266, 422; on Brown's age 8; letters, to Rev. Edward Hore, 238–39, to Edmund Quincy, 120, 238
Prichard, James Cowles, *Researches into the Physical History of Mankind*, 441
Purvis, Robert, 106, 211, 312

Quincy, Edmund, 86, 106; criticism of Brown's *Narrative*, 112–14

Redpath, James, 333, 348, 351, 376, 377; begins publishing the *Pine and Palm*, 334; *A Guide to Hayti*, 370; *The Roving Editor*, 387–88
Reform League (New York), 426
Remond, Charles Lenox, 76, 77, 84, 104, 111, 248, 293, 310, 404, 443; host to Brown, 249, 251
Richardson, Ellen (Newcastle upon Tyne), 240, 241, 436
Robinson, Marius R. (Salem, Ohio), 293–94
Rock, Dr. John S. (Boston), 392, 395, 401
Roscoe, William, *The Life and Pontificate of Leo the Tenth*, 444–45
Ruggles, David, 132, 443

Scoble, Rev. John, 347; defames Brown, 166, 201
Seward, William H., 96–97
Slack, Charles W. (Boston), 423–24, 453
Slave marriages, 44
Smalls, Robert, hero of the gunboat *Planter*, 413
Smeal, William (Glasgow), 176, 179
Smith, Gerrit, 366, 406; grants of land to Negroes, 98, 204
Smith, Dr. James McCune (New York), 86, 371, 386
Smith, Rev. John B., 308, 310
Smith, Rev. Thomas Paul, farewell speech to Brown, 141
Spear, Rev. Charles, 164; trip to England, 192–93
Stanton, Edwin M., authorizes organization of Negro regiment, 380–81

Still, William (Philadelphia), 128, 383, 400, 433, 437, 438; writes sketch of Mrs. Mary Ann Shadd Cary, 439
Stowe, Calvin Ellis (Harriet Beecher Stowe's husband), 213
Sumner, A. M. (Cincinnati), 76, 77
Sumner, Charles, 258, 281, 287, 317; death, 432

Thome James A. *See* Weld, Theodore Dwight
Thompson, George (London), 197, 331, 395, 404; Brown's first meeting with, 154; criticism of *Three Years in Europe*, 207; goes to America, 178; returns to England, 1851, 193
Tillman, William, hero of schooner *S. J. Waring*, 412
Toombs, Robert Augustus, 274, 362
Toussaint L'Ouverture, 255, 256, 441; compared with Napoleon and George Washington, 257–58
Trexler, Harrison Anthony, *Slavery in Missouri*, 27
Tubman, Harriet, 443

Vesey, Denmark, 369–70, 411, 450
"Virginian Slave, The," 187–88

Wakeman, George, 385, 386
Walker, James (slave trader), 7, 23, 40–41, 219; employs Brown, 28–32, 33–34
Wallcut, Robert F., 142, 272, 367, 377
Ward, Samuel Ringgold, 213, 241
Washington, Madison, 339–40, 369, 411
Webb, Richard D. (Dublin, Ireland), 146, 147, 187
Webster, Daniel, 110, 178, 200, 432
Weld, Theodore Dwight, 386; *American Slavery as It is*, 47
West Indian emancipation celebration, 1851, 193–96
Weston, Anne, 197
Weston, Caroline, 112
Weston, Deborah, comment on Brown, 111
Wheatley, Phillis, 370
White artisans, refusal to work with Negro artisans, 343–44
Whitfield, James M. (Buffalo), 442–43
Whittier, John Greenleaf, 123, 216
Willi, Samuel (Brown's second owner, Saint Louis), 38, 40, 42
Wilson, Henry, denounces Preston Smith Brooks's assault on Charles Sumner, 287
Wright, Ellen, 305, 399
Wright, Henry C., 305, 421
Wright, Martha Coffin, 280, 284–85

Yancey, William Lowndes, 319–20
Young, Dr. John (Brown's first owner), 4, 5–6, 35, 37, 447; religion of, 24–26